NATIVE CALIFORNIANS

A Theoretical Retrospective

by

Lowell J. Bean and Thomas C. Blackburn

BALLENA PRESS
P.O. Box 711
Ramona, California 92065
1976

Reprinted by permission of The Journal of California Anthropology: —
    Ecology and Adaptive Response among the Tolowa Indians of
        Northwestern California by R. A. Gould.
    The Pomo Kin Group and the Political Unit in Aboriginal California by
        Peter H. Kunkel.
    Power and Its Applications in Native California by Lowell J. Bean.

Reprinted by permission of The Indian Historian: —
    Chumash Inter-Village Economic Exchange by Chester King.

Reprinted by permission of The Regents of the University of California: —
    Social Organization and Status Differentiation Among the Nomlaki
        by Walter Goldschmidt.
    Yokuts-Mono Chiefs and Shamans by Anna H. Gayton.
    Religion and Its Role Among the Luiseño by Raymond White.

Printed in the United States of America.
Second printing: 1976

Contents

Introduction

The number of books of readings on various anthropological topics has grown at such an alarming rate in recent years that we feel slightly defensive at contributing to what might be regarded by some as pedagogic overkill — especially when our chosen topic is already represented by a reader that has enjoyed considerable success over the years, and which is currently available in a new edition (Heizer and Whipple, *The California Indians*). Yet like most books intended essentially for classroom use, the collection of readings presented here represents our response to what we feel to be a deficit in the materials readily available to either students or teachers wishing to acquire more insight into the complex dynamics of aboriginal life in California, as well as an attempt to present some of the general parameters of the new theoretical orientation or perspective that seems to us to be so clearly emerging from the work of contemporary Californianists.

California has been referred to as a land of contrast and paradox, a characterization that is as apt anthropologically as it is sociologically or geographically. Perhaps no area of the world of similar size has been more thoroughly investigated or described by anthropologists (many of whom began distinguished scholarly careers by conducting ethnographic field studies of specific California societies), with the result that the data base available for the testing of hypotheses is virtually unprecedented. Yet curiously enough, the development of theory has tended to fall far behind the accumulation of ethnographic information in recent decades, and the serious student who attempts to place the ethnographic data within a modern anthropological context is liable to be overwhelmed by the sheer mass of virtually undigested material available to him — much of it collected at a time when description was an end in itself, and theory differed considerably from what it is today. The literature on the native peoples of California is voluminous and potentially invaluable, even if its value to the discipline of anthropology as a whole has remained scarcely realized — but it is a body of data that until quite recently has remained strangely unaffected by the external ebb and flow of academic fashions and theoretical perspectives, and somehow irrelevant to the greater questions capturing the interest and commitment of the anthropological fraternity.

Fortunately, however, sweeping changes are occurring which promise to make California once again an area of more than passing interest to both the student and the professional. An increasing number of younger anthropologists are rediscovering the State, and there is a growing awareness within the profession that few areas of the world offer greater opportunities for the study of a wide range of ecological and cultural processes. Consequently, there has been a dramatic increase in the number of papers appearing in recent years that reflect a commitment to the development of theory applicable to a wider arena than California itself, or which provide significant re-interpretations or syntheses of older data that greatly alter previously accepted views on aboriginal life. We have included as many of these recent contributions as possible in the present anthology.

That a renaissance of sorts is occurring in the study of California Indians is evident — the reasons for the renewal of interest, however, are complex and less readily apparent. Certainly the existence of a tremendous descriptive data base, practically unparalleled ecological, cultural and linguistic diversity, and a long prehistoric and historic cultural sequence are contributing factors, though they do not in themselves constitute a necessary and sufficient cause for the change in perspective that is taking place. That has its roots in several different developments, some of them indigenous to California and others external to it, which seem to have evolved along convergent lines.

One of the most influential of these developments has involved what is usually referred to as cultural ecology. An interest in the general topic of man-land relationships, is, of course, of respectable antiquity within the State (cf. Barrett, 1908 or Gayton, 1946), and elsewhere classic studies such as Kroeber's "Cultural and Natural Areas of Native North America" (1939) or Steward's "Basin-Plateau Aboriginal Sociopolitical Groups" (1938) were at least partially inspired by California data. But this interest received considerable impetus within the State during the 1950s as a result of the involvement of a number of local anthropologists in the Land Settlement Claims Case, which focused specific attention upon the

environmental adaptation and territoriality of indigenous populations, and made available hard data on population sizes, resource
bases and demography that could be utilized in the testing of a
variety of new hypotheses. Two papers by Beals and Hester (1956,
1958), Baumhoff's ''Ecological Determinants of Aboriginal
Populations'' (1963), and Kunkel's ''Yokuts and Pomo Political
Organization: A Comparative Analysis'' (1962), are examples of the
ecologically oriented research stemming either directly or indirectly
from the Land Settlement Claims Case. White's *Luiseño Social
Organization* (1963) and Bean's *Mukat's People* (1972) are more
contemporaneous examples of this particular theoretical focus.

A second major factor underlying the renewed interest in
California has involved the reappearance of evolutionary
perspectives within the discipline of anthropology itself. As cultural
evolutionism has gained increasing respectability through the work
of such scholars as White, Steward, Service and Sahlins, more and
more attention has come to be focused upon the simpler levels of
sociocultural integration (and especially upon hunting and
gathering peoples) where significant evolutionary processes and
causative factors should be more readily isolable. This has resulted
in an increased data base, more sophisticated comparative studies,
and a heightened awareness of the exceptional nature of California
hunters and gatherers. The data presented in such books as *Man
the Hunter*, for example, have served to underline the fact that
most California societies bear a more striking resemblance to
Melanesian chiefdoms than they do to Australian or African bands
— a fact that has justifiably called into question some of the
standard cliches and overly simplistic generalizations regarding
hunters and gatherers that have been anthropological dogma for so
long. Thus a growing number of Californianists have begun to
realize that they control data of considerable value for the
generation or testing of hypotheses of marked relevance to
anthropology as a whole — and have begun to utilize that data.

Still another major development promoting the renaissance in
California studies involves changes in archaeological theory and the
appearance of what is often referred to as the 'new archaeology'.
The paradigm that seems to be emerging in archaeology now is
based upon a synthesis of cultural ecology, cultural evolutionism
and general systems theory, and an increasing number of California
archaeologists are being influenced by it. Since at one time many

archaeologists in California conducted both archaeological and ethnographic research at various stages of their careers, archaeology within the State has always been closely allied with ethnology as a matter of course — but one notable consequence of the new paradigm has been the development of what might be called ethnoarchaeology, in which the archaeologist conducts research on contemporary peoples in order to obtain insights or test hypotheses concerning the operation of prehistoric cultural systems. As a consequence, much of the impetus in California studies in recent years has come from archaeologists rather than ethnologists, a trend that needs to be at least partially reversed if the early promise of the work done so far is to be fully realized.

A final development that has had some impact in recent years entails actual additions to the data base itself, particularly in the form of archival materials such as the unpublished and previously inaccessible ethnographic field notes of men like John P. Harrington and C. Hart Merriam. Harrington's notes alone may virtually double our knowledge of aboriginal California when they have been fully explored — they certainly constitute an almost unparalleled resource whose potential remains scarcely realized by most Californianists. However, this situation is rapidly changing. The Harrington notes are presently being catalogued, and the appearance of new works utilizing material drawn from them (such as Blackburn's,forthcoming *December's Child*) should generate considerable scholarly interest in this incredibly rich source of information. The Merriam collection has now been catalogued, and Robert Heizer has edited and published major portions of this important body of data. Valory recently completed a catalogue of the anthropological archives housed at the Bancroft Library, while a general guide to archival materials relating to Native Californians prepared by Lowell Bean and Sylvia Vane will soon be available from Ballena Press.

In addition to the archival sources just discussed, some ethnographers have continued to explore the field for new data, often with surprising success — their information often constitutes much more than a simple addition of new facts to old, perhaps by allowing a synthesis of previously unrelated data which may in turn lead to the formation of new hypotheses and insights. Workers such as White, Shipek, Handelman, Gould and Bean (among others) have demonstrated that an amazing quantity of data on aboriginal life is still obtainable, some two hundred years after massive acculturation first began to affect the State's native peoples.

As indicated above, the new perspective on aboriginal California that is emerging has its roots in a number of complex and partially interrelated factors, some of the more significant of which would certainly include an emphasis on cultural ecology, a concern for the development of broadscale hypotheses regarding evolutionary processes and causative variables, an interest in the application of systems models, and an involvement with the testing of archaeologically derived hypotheses against data from contemporary societies. Most of the papers included in this anthology reflect one or more of these concerns to a considerable extent. But the new perspective can perhaps best be characterized as involving a fresh appreciation for the very real complexities of aboriginal cultures in the State, with considerable stress placed upon the integration and systemic nature of those cultures. Thus most of the studies that have appeared in recent years have suggested in one way or another that earlier analyses overlooked important integrative functions, significant economic, social or political processes, or evidence of unusual complexity in various spheres of social behavior that might reasonably have been interpreted as indicative of surprising levels of cultural development on the part of the California Indians. A consensus of opinion is developing, especially among younger scholars, that the data on the native peoples of the State are in need of serious reexamination in terms of modern perspectives, and that the anthropological fraternity has been just as guilty (albeit more subtly) of perpetuating denigrating myths about indigenous Americans as any other segment of Anglo-American society.

In assembling this volume, we have perforce deliberately excluded papers concerned primarily with archaeology, linguistics or physical anthropology, or with the complex period subsequent to contact with European cultural traditions. In thus focusing on the "ethnographic present," we do not want to give the impression that we feel any lack of concern for other topics — indeed, we hope to follow the present anthology with a second devoted entirely to the historic period and the varied responses of the Native Californians to the often traumatic events which so drastically altered their original way of life. But limitations of space and funding, combined with the large number of possible selections we might have included in this volume, have mitigated against the kind of truly eclectic but overly voluminous work that might reasonably be considered a fair representation of the extensive literature concerned with California's native peoples. Students who wish to pursue topics not dealt with in the present work will find Bean and King's *ʔAntap: California Indian Political and Economic Organization* useful, while the *Journal of California Anthropology* is rapidly becoming the major forum for the discussion of new and innovative research on every facet of native life — past, present and future. In addition, the California volume of the forthcoming *Handbook of North American Indians* will provide excellent summaries of the information compiled to date on evey ethnic group in the state, and will constitute a handy reference guide for students and scholars alike.

The papers which have been included in this anthology have been selected with a number of different objectives in mind, some of which have occasionally conflicted with one another. Consequently, the decision to include or exclude a particular study was sometimes difficult to make, and it is quite likely that our final choice will, in many cases, fail to satisfy the knowledgeable reader. Certainly a number of worthy contributions to the literature on California Indians have had to be excluded for one reason or another, but it is our sincere hope that those articles which have been selected will more than compensate. Obviously, a primary objective of any reader such as this must be to touch upon all major facets of the subject matter dealt with, both topically and geographically — to provide the student, in other words, with some grasp of the richness and variability of material, social and ideological life in Native California. But more importantly, we wish to show some of the variety of ways in which contemporary anthropologists have approached the analysis of indigenous societies, and highlight what seem to us significant perspectives that have contributed new dimensions to our understanding of aboriginal life. Thus, each paper in this anthology is more than simply a presentation of data, however useful — it is also an attempt by an anthropologist to deal meaningfully with the flux of events in cultures that collectively represent a resource of exceptional value to the understanding of human behavior in all times and places.

-The Editors

BEAN AND LAWTON — SOME EXPLANATIONS FOR THE RISE OF CULTURAL COMPLEXITY IN NATIVE CALIFORNIA WITH COMMENTS ON PROTO-AGRICULTURE AND AGRICULTURE

In an article written initially as an introduction to Lewis' suggestion (1973) that fire was used as a significant economic device, Bean and Lawton discuss the complexities of hunting and gathering techniques in Native California and describe the ecological and social significance of the methodologies employed by native peoples in manipulating their environment in order to achieve maximally efficient levels of energy extraction. The authors argue, in fact, that agricultural techniques were known to California's native populations, and that agriculture of the type commonly associated with the Greater Southwest was probably practiced by groups (e.g. Diegueño, Cahuilla, Kamia) in regions where ecological conditions were favorable and where it provided a viable, competitive alternative to the sophisticated, well established economic institutions found in other parts of the state.

GOULD — ECOLOGY AND ADAPTIVE RESPONSE AMONG THE TOLOWA INDIANS OF NORTHWESTERN CALIFORNIA

The native peoples of northwestern California have long been noted for their emphasis on individualism and wealth-questing as primary bases for social interaction. In a detailed study of the ecological adaptation of the Tolowa to their rich and varied environment, Gould demonstrates that such behavior is a natural consequence of a situation in which an optimizing strategy of resource exploitation becomes not only possible but logical, and aggrandizement functions to support and maintain the traditional subsistence procurement system. This valuable case study of a society employing an optimizing strategy (in sharp contrast to the satisficing strategy universally reported for hunters and gatherers in the past) serves as a useful illustration of the growing emphasis in anthropology on ecological interpretations of ethnographic information, as well as an excellent example of the potentialities inherent in California data for the development and testing of hypotheses of wide theoretical relevance. The student is encouraged to read Gould's other fine paper (1966b) on Tolowa wealth-questing in conjunction with the present article.

GAYTON — CULTURE-ENVIRONMENT INTEGRATION: EXTERNAL REFERENCES IN YOKUTS LIFE

Gayton, in a pioneer exploration of the complex interaction that takes place between a culture and its environment, provides us with an example of the way in which one of California's more complex cultural systems integrated major ecological, material, social, ritual and ideational factors, and suggests that the environment can act as a stabilizing element or ideational brake against forces which might encourage culture change. She demonstrates that the seasonal-subsistence round, the ritual round, social structure and cosmological concepts all served to provide a balanced guide to daily behavior for the members of Yokuts society. Her article also reflects the emerging interest in ecological, psychological and cognitive anthropology that was beginning to develop in the early 1940s. The reader is encouraged to read Gayton's superb ethnographic accounts of Yokuts culture (1945, 1948), which are fine examples of thorough reporting and solid cultural reconstruction.

BEAN — SOCIAL ORGANIZATION IN NATIVE CALIFORNIA

In the following article Bean attempts to provide a general schemata for social organization in Native California that differs considerably from those advanced by earlier writers. It is based upon an extensive review of most of the relevant ethnographic literature, and is supported by recent archaeological interpretations (Bean and King, 1974). Some of the more significant features of native social organization noted by Bean include international relationships, trade alliances, confederations, and developing nations. Bean also stresses the significance of hierarchical social interaction, both within and between groups, for the proper understanding of culture in Native California. In "Some Explanations for the Rise of Cultural Complexity in Native California with Comments on Proto-Agriculture and Agriculture," Bean and Lawton attempted to explain the development of such elaborate systems among hunters and gatherers. In later papers in this volume, Blackburn and Bean discuss the philosophical and cognitive foundations that support these kinds of social structures.

Thus a consensus is emerging that hunters and gatherers, by extraordinary manipulative technologies and sophisticated social and economic institutions, may often achieve surprisingly high levels of sociocultural development.

GOLDSCHMIDT — SOCIAL ORGANIZATION AND STATUS DIFFERENTIATION AMONG THE NOMLAKI

In a classic functional analysis, Goldschmidt provides a model of Nomlaki society that nicely demonstrates the way in which concepts of wealth and prestige, in combination with a secret society and craft specialization, helped to integrate otherwise weakly organized kinship groups into a cohesive system. Like the papers by Gayton, Blackburn and King which follow later in this volume, Goldschmidt's article illustrates and underlines a number of the general points raised by Bean in the previous selection, and emphasizes once again both the ubiquity and importance of nonegalitarian social systems in Native California. The interested student is encouraged to read McKern's classic paper on Patwin functional families (1922), in which the rigid control of economic specialization by an elite was first clearly formulated.

GAYTON — YOKUTS-MONO CHIEFS AND SHAMANS

The following article by Gayton is another classic study in California anthropology. Gayton was one of the first scholars to recognize the close integration of religious and political institutions among Native Californians, pointing out that the Yokuts shaman — as in most societies — plays a significant political role in addition to his more commonly recognized medico-religious role, and thus has a prominent position within the power structure of the society. She also clearly details the ambivalence felt by Native Californians toward their people of power. The shaman was respected and heeded because he had the power to do either good deeds or evil. But his control was not omnipotent — he could lose his position, or even his life — if he did not perform in a completely professional manner. Gayton also demonstrates how mythology, political and economic institutions, and shamanism articulated as parts of a well balanced system of cultural life. Due to the considerable length of the original version, the present paper has been extensively edited and shortened — the interested student is encouraged to read this paper in its complete, unedited form.

BLACKBURN — CEREMONIAL INTEGRATION AND SOCIAL INTERACTION IN ABORIGINAL CALIFORNIA

The following paper provides a further examination of some of the complex social institutions that enabled Native Californians to achieve high levels of energy extraction from varied and often unpredictably fluctuating environments. Building on Bean's (1972) suggestion that ritual congregations were ecologically significant throughout southern California, Blackburn utilizes both historic and ethnographic data to demonstrate the considerable importance of the ritual system to the ecological, material, economic, social, political and ideational life of the people. The differences that are revealed between northern and southern California exchange systems may have a number of significant ramifications as far as other contrasts between the two areas are concerned.

LUOMALA — FLEXIBILITY IN SIB AFFILIATION AMONG THE DIEGUEÑO

In the following article, Luomala has described the social organization of the Diegueño (Tipai-Ipai) in a new and innovative way. Her article nicely demonstrates the complexities of lineage-based societies among the Yuman speakers, and significantly reminds us of what happens to deviant individuals in these ordinarily rigid and highly structured groups. She also demonstrates that the Diegueño (like their distant linguistic relatives the Pomo) maintained a very flexible attitude toward their world, unlike other lineage-based societies to the north. Luomala, in collaboration with another colleague, has also written one of the finer papers on the psychological anthropology of Native

Californians (Toffelmier and Luomala, 1936), a paper which, in conjunction with the articles by Devereux and Aginsky presented later in this volume, provides significant insights into the cognitive world of the native peoples.

KUNKEL — THE POMO KIN GROUP AND THE POLITICAL UNIT IN ABORIGINAL CALIFORNIA

Kunkel's paper presents a new and reasonable model of social organization among a major segment of Native Californians. He suggests that there were two primary structural principles by which people organized themselves for social interaction: lineality and bilaterality. Lineality was emphasized in Southern California (as among the Diegueño just described by Luomala), while bilaterality characterized much of Northern California. Kunkel thus provides a set of variables which appear to be functionally related to many other facets of Native California life — e.g. social status systems, the nature and degree of complexity of formal religious associations, world view, and the like. We anticipate that Kunkel's paper will stimulate new research as other scholars test his ideas against differing bodies of data. In conjunction with this article, students are encouraged to read such classic works on social organization as Gifford (1926a), Kroeber (1954), and Goldschmidt (1948).

KING — CHUMASH INTER-VILLAGE ECONOMIC EXCHANGE

King, by combining data from such varied sources as historic documents, archaeological excavations, and ethnographic archives, convincingly argues that the Chumash Indians of southern California had a complex, thoroughly monetized economic system. The Chumash (like the Nomlaki described in an earlier paper by Goldschmidt) were thoroghly imbued with a concern for wealth, and their interest in the acquisition of property, development of trade, and specialization of labor underscore the fact that these were basic themes throughout Native California, rather than characteristics found in isolated areas only (as some earlier scholars have suggested). King's paper (like Blackburn's earlier article) is a good example of the potentialities inherent in an eclectic approach to old data utilizing contemporary models.

AGINSKY — THE SOCIO-PSYCHOLOGICAL SIGNIFICANCE OF DEATH AMONG THE POMO INDIANS

Aginsky, the author of the following article, is among those who have contributed most significantly to our understanding of native cultures and their response to European contact. Here he explains the Pomo attitude toward death, suicide and disease, and explores the effects of culturally induced anxiety. The topic of magical disease and death is now better understood by anthropologists, with Walter Cannon and others describing the psychosomatic processes by which culturally induced stress can actually kill or cause illness. This phenomenon, discussed here in relationship to the Pomo, was present throughout Native California. Its universality explains in part the sophistication and success of psychiatric healing as a technique among native peoples.

DEVEREUX — MOHAVE SOUL CONCEPTS

Devereux, who has written extensively on many facets of Mohave culture, here describes in detail one part of the rich psychological and philosophical structures that contrasted so strikingly with the seeming poverty of Mohave material life. Soul "behavior" was integrally connected with knowledge, life and death, with each kind of soul functioning in a different context. Devereux nicely demonstrates the sophistication and subtlety of Mohave thought, a characteristic noted by every student of this fascinating and paradoxical culture. The Mohave were undergoing rapid cultural change at the time of European contact, and were in the process of achieving a level of sociocultural integration comparable to that of a nation-state.

GARTH — EMPHASIS ON INDUSTRIOUSNESS AMONG THE ATSUGEWI

The Atsugewi of northeastern California (presently included as part of the Pit River Indians) continue to hold cultural values akin to those described by Garth in the following article. While culturally similar to the peoples of northwestern California in their concern for rank, private property, and the acquisition of wealth, the Atsugewi (perhaps from ecological necessity) seem to temper this emphasis by the addition of "generosity" or a sharing reciprocity to their ideational inventory. It should also be noted that although they live in a rather sparse environment (in comparison with other Native Californians), they still have a rather complex system of social ranking, and are as clearly nonegalitarian as their neighbors to the west or southwest.

WHITE — RELIGION AND ITS ROLE AMONG THE LUISEÑO

In an elegantly written selection (reminiscent of some of the recent work of Carlos Casteneda), a philosopher-anthropologist interprets the Luiseño "theory of knowledge," and demonstrates the systematic way in which a philosophy may act to conserve the old while serving as a catalyst for new ideas within a culture over time. The concept of a hierarchically arranged universe, and a deep concern for a system of thought which rationally explains all phenomena, are still pervasive among the Luiseño in terms of day-by-day decision making on the reservations mentioned — Rincon and Pauma — although in rather subtle ways. Students interested in other examples of the application of philosophical paradigms to the study of Native California cultures should see Lee (1938, 1944, 1951) Halpern (1955), Goldschmidt (1951), Bean (1972), or Blackburn (1975). This selection is part of a longer chapter on Luiseño religion; students are encouraged to read the unedited version, as well as White's 1957 paper on "The Luiseño 'theory of knowledge'."

HANDELMAN — THE DEVELOPMENT OF A WASHO SHAMAN

Handelman, in the following article on a contemporary Washo shaman, describes the manner in which men of knowledge viewed themselves in the context of their individual cultures, and the way in which they maintained an eclectic attitude toward "power" sources. Handelman is a good example of a modern ethnographer who has continued to discover important new data in what was previously regarded as a depleted, if not exhausted, area of research. In a later article (1972) he shows how the shaman, so often reported in a negative manner in ethnographic accounts and viewed with considerable ambivalence by the other members of his society (as in the paper by Gayton presented earlier in this volume), actually saw himself as a professional person bound by a strict moral code.

BEAN — POWER AND ITS APPLICATIONS IN NATIVE CALIFORNIA

In order to understand how people behave, it is necessary to understand the basic assumptions they make about the universe in which they live. In the following paper, Bean provides some generalizations about the cosmological assumptions implicit within the sacred poetic literature of most Native Californians, and discusses their relationship to the concept of power. Although many variations occurred from group to group, of course, and each assumption was not present in every part of California, the philosophical model developed by Bean clarifies many aspects of native cognitive life and sheds light on a number of specific ethnographic puzzles. Blackburn's *December's Child* (1975) applies a similar paradigm to a particular society, that of the Chumash, while White's paper (presented earlier in this volumne) illustrates many of the same points.

Some Explanations for the Rise of Cultural Complexity in Native California with Comments on Proto-Agriculture and Agriculture

by Lowell John Bean and Harry Lawton

Current anthropological interest in hunter-gatherer ecology and research findings on hunters and gatherers in marginal-subsistence environments of Australia, South Africa, and the Great Basin of the United States have brought renewed attention to the California Indians. Anthropologists are finally coming to a realization that cultural development in California was extraordinarily rich and complex despite what would appear to have been the limitations of the native economic system.

Henry Lewis's paper on burning patterns in northern California represents an extremely important new contribution to our knowledge of California's hunting and gathering economy. Lewis has employed a systems approach to present the first geographically broad and ecologically oriented demonstration of a primary means of environmental manipulation used by northern California Indian groups to increase plant and animal resources. In fact, it seems probable in view of Lewis's findings that burning was the most significant environmental manipulation employed by California Indians. A new understanding of the role of native burning, coupled with our knowledge of other aspects of hunting and gathering in California, makes it now possible we believe to provide a more adequate explanation than previously presented for the failure of agriculture to spread across the state prior to European contact.

Until the twentieth century, the problem of why agriculture did not become established in California was never really dealt with except in terms of aboriginal lassitude or deficient intelligence. Any survey of historical accounts by Spanish missionaries and explorers reveals for the most part an abysmal lack of curiosity about the culture of California Indians. As Harrington (1934: 1) pointed out, nothing worthy of being called an ethnological treatise survived the Spanish occupation of California except Father Geronimo Boscana's *Chinigchinich*, written in 1832, late in the mission period. The primitive state of the native economy was characterized for Father Boscana (Harrington 1934: 55) by the fact that ". . . in no part of the province was to be found aught but the common, spontaneous productions of earth." If agriculture was a hallmark of civilization to the Spanish, so it was with the later nineteenth century American historians, products of an agrarian society, who viewed farming as the evolutionary goal of human civilization. The romantic myth of the mission fathers tutoring culturally retrograde Indians in crop-growing achieved such popularity in this period that the native cultures of California had little appeal for scholars. Even to Bancroft (1883: I, 324), it was axiomatic that along the shores of the Pacific man had "sunk almost to the darkness of the brute."

Despite views of some early anthropologists to the contrary (Barrows 1900; Gifford 1931), pioneer researchers in California generally accepted the historical dogma that the westward extension of southwestern agriculture halted among the Yuman peoples of the Colorado River. Any data suggesting agricultural knowledge existed among some California groups was attributed to being the result of mission influence. Hooper (1920: 328) for example, first noted the presence of characteristic plants of southwestern agriculture in Cahuilla myth, but left unexplored Kroeber's (1908: 41) assertion that the Cahuilla were not farmers. Only recently have anthropologists begun to investigate the extent to which crop-growing may have penetrated California and why it was not extensive.

In another recent paper, Henry T. Lewis (1972: 217) pointed out one of the main barriers to a more profound understanding of the cultures of native California and the means by which these predominantly hunting and gathering peoples exploited their environment:

> Ecologically, we must ignore the evolutionary assumptions that the development of agriculture was somehow natural and desirable. Instead of viewing agriculture as an imminent goal of human evolution, we should rather ask the question: Why should hunters and

gatherers become agriculturists? While this suggestion may be at variance with our most cherished ideas of "progress" and "human development," we can more effectively pose ecologically pertinent questions if we are not overburdened by a mass of unexamined folk assumptions which cannot be tested.

Lewis has suggested such ecosystem analyses as his own may assist anthropologists in posing new questions as to the role which men, using certain technological strategies, played in a given system of environmental relationships. Indeed, his paper is rich in suggestive material deserving study by anthropologists. We shall concern ourselves, however, with the light which his paper may throw on the problem of why agriculture failed to spread in California. First, we will briefly review the literature concerned with this problem. Then, we will summarize some additional data compiled by Lewis and ourselves indicating that burning was also a significant form of environmental manipulation among Indians in the southern part of California. Although Aschmann (1959) presented evidence that fires set by Indians in southern California were a factor in the persistence of the wild landscape, he provided no data from Spanish sources showing the practice was aboriginal and little data on burning among specific Indian groups. Finally, we shall discuss Heizer's thesis that California was in a Preformative stage that can be termed "semi-agricultural" at the time of the Spanish conquest, and seek to apply this idea in terms of Lewis's findings.

THE PROBLEM OF ABORIGINAL
AGRICULTURE IN CALIFORNIA

Although his hypothesis in recent years has been credited to others, H. J. Spinden (1917) appears to have been the first to suggest that the acorn economy of California prevented dispersal of agriculture westward from the Colorado River, where it was practiced in the pre-hispanic era. In discussing those intermediate types of environment most favorable to agriculture but where it failed to become established, Spinden (1917: 270), wrote:

> The abundant harvests of wild acorns in California, of
> wokas in southern Oregon, of wappato along the

Columbia, of camas and kous in the pleasant uplands of Idaho, and of wild rice in the lake regions of Minnesota and southern Canada were effectual barriers against the intervention or spread of agriculture among the tribes inhabiting these regions.

While Spinden's views on the origin and distribution of agriculture in the Americas were immensely influential in their time, his hypothesis concerning California remained almost forgotten until it was revived independently by other researchers in the 1950's.

As early as 1908, A. L. Kroeber explained the presence of a gourd rattle obtained from the Desert Cahuilla as a trade item from the Colorado River. Kroeber (1908: 62) asserted: "If the Cahuilla of aboriginal times used such rattles they must have obtained them by trade, as they did not practice agriculture or raise gourds." Two decades later, Kroeber formulated the first major hypothesis to receive any considerable attention for the lack of agriculture in California. His hypothesis was primarily cultural, and considerably more sophisticated than the cultural explanations of earlier historians. Kroeber (1925: 41) wrote as follows:

Agriculture had touched only the periphery of the state, the Colorado River bottom, although the seed-using and fairly sedentary habits of virtually all the other tribes would have made possible the taking over of the art with relatively little change of mode of life. Evidently, planting is a more fundamental innovation to people used to depending on nature than it seems to those who have once acquired the habit. Moreover, in most of California, the food supply, largely through its variety, was reasonably adequate, in spite of a rather heavy population — probably not far from one person to the square mile on the average. In most parts of the State there was little mention of famine.

Six years later, admittedly influenced by the views of his colleague, Carl Sauer, the cultural geographer, Kroeber abandoned his cultural explanation for an environmental one, which he set forth in his book *Cultural and Natural Areas of Native North*

America. Although first written in 1931, this work was not published until eight years later, but presumably represented Kroeber's final evaluation of the problem. At the same time, it must be noted that Kroeber was always open to new ideas, and he is known to have entertained other explanations in his classrooms. Heizer (1958: 25) recalled Kroeber discussing the possibility that the efficient acorn economy was a chief barrier to agriculture as early as 1935 in his classrooms.

Kroeber's (1939: 211) environmental hypothesis asserted that native agriculture failed to develop in California, "because of its dry summer, for which so far as maize was concerned no amount of winter precipitation could compensate." This same argument was presented first in print by Sauer (1936: 295) as follows:

> Lack of contact with agricultural peoples can hardly account for the absence of agriculture on the Pacific Coast of the United States. The Indians of southern California were in communication with agricultural peoples along the Colorado. It is not likely that California Indians refrained from experimenting with the crops grown on the Colorado River. The resistance to the westward diffusion of agriculture was probably environmental rather than cultural. The crops which were available had little prospect of success in winter-rain lands. Maize and squash especially were ruled out by the rain regime, but the conditions also are predominantly unfavorable for beans. The Pacific Coast of the United States as a land of Mediterranean climate, had to wait on the introduction of crops from the European Mediterranean.

Although Heizer (1958: 25) has stated that since 1946 he has accepted the concept that the acorn economy of California constituted the chief obstacle to acceptance of agriculture, the environmental position advanced by Kroeber and Sauer has dominated much of the literature on the subject for the past two decades. Driver (1961: 55) summed up the climatic-environmental position in his textbook, *Indians of North America,* where he noted that rainfall west of the Colorado River averages only a few inches annually, and that where there is sufficient quantity of rainfall "it comes at the wrong season for maize." More recently, Underhill (1965: 252) wrote:

West of the Colorado the Desert continues with plenty of
seed grasses and berries and with small game; but there is
no summer rain for corn growing . . . Among these
southern California Shoshoneans, there were no planters
in ancient days and no planting ceremonies.

While it is true that there is a very direct relationship between
rainfall and yield of maize and that the so-called "corn belt" of the
United States appears to possess the best combination of
temperature, rain, sunshine, soil, and topography for high-yield
production, few anthropological writers on the subject have really
understood the matter fully in agricultural terms. Most frequently
they have confused the pertinent issue of amount and spacing of
rainfall with the idea of a "wrong" rainfall regime for corn in
California. However, there is no need to engage in a long technical
discussion of optimum conditions for corn-growing since the
historical record indicates this problem is beside the point.

Forbes (1963: 1) first attacked the notion that a summer
rainfall regime was essential to corn-growing in California. In spite
of dry summers, he pointed out that California's subsistence was
largely based upon maize from 1769 until the 1850's, and California
Indians were principal growers of those crops. Actually, despite
repeated statements in anthropological literature that California
has never been a notably corn-producing state, corn production
reached its peak in 1890 when more than two million bushels were
harvested in the state (Hardy 1929: 221). Nevertheless, Forbes
neglected to consider whether corn-growing became possible only
with introduction of irrigation by the Spanish. Concerning this
problem, a wealth of data indicates California agriculture in the
post-contact period was not always irrigation dependent.

A few examples will suffice: Lt. E. O. Ord (1848: 123) reported
Indians in the San Dieguito Valley near San Diego gathering from
twenty to forth *fanegas* of maize on unirrigated lands. Hayes
(1929: 92) noted in 1853 that an American settlement near Los
Angeles "raised every species of vegetable and corn, without
irrigation, such is the humidity of the soil." Indian Superintendent
Thomas J. Henley reported in 1854 that corn yeilds that year were
far below average on Tejon Reservation because crops were not
irrigated and a drought had occurred (Caughey 1953: 138). Brockett
(1882: 592) stated that corn planted in April and May in California

matured without rain in areas where soil mositure was abundant. Finally, although a summer rain regime may be desirable for high yeilds of corn, it should be noted that the Spanish explorer Lt. José Estudillo (Bean and Mason 1962: 36) observed Cahuilla Indians near Thermal on the Colorado Desert planting corn, pumpkins, melons, and watermelons in the month of December, 1824.

In recent years, various researchers have pointed out flaws in the environmental argument (Weatherwas 1954; Jennings 1956; Heizer 1958; Meighan 1959; Forbes 1963; Bean 1968; and Lawton and Bean 1968). Jennings (1956) suggested that the dry southern California desert played a role in impeding the advance of agriculture from the Colorado River to the coast, but felt climate could not be accepted as the sole explanation. One major cultural reason he offered for the failure of agriculture to become established among coastal Californians was the specialization to a marine environment which these people had adopted. The cultural efficiency attained by Indian groups along the coast in exploiting the sea, he hypothesized, permitted them a reasonably abundant living. Meighan (1959) pointed out that the Archaic stage was not necessarily inferior in subsistence techniques to simple agricultural communities. Where the environment is favorable, as it was in all of California except the desert regions, Meighan suggested, the people may work out such an efficient ecological adaptation that they are actually better off than developmental agricultural peoples. He viewed the fact that California supported the greatest density population in the United States without agriculture as of the greatest significance to discussion of this problem.[1] Walton Bean (1968) also emphasized the general abundancy of a natural food supply in California, hypothesizing that agriculture failed to spread into California because the native population was in a "Malthusian equilibrium."

Only a few researchers have challenged the prevailing view of anthropologists that California Indians were non-agricultural by arguing that pre-contact agriculture may have actually existed in certain parts of California (Barrows 1900; Gifford 1931; Treganza 1946; Bean and Mason 1962; Forbes 1963; Lawton 1968; Lawton

---

1. Current conservative estimates for California's aboriginal population place it at 250,000 persons (Heizer and Whipple 1971: 66). Villages of 1,000 or more persons have been estimated for some California groups (Kunkel 1962).

and Bean 1968; Shipek 1971; Bean 1972; Bean and Saubel 1972; and Wilke and Fain 1972). Although Patch (1951) reported on the presence of irrigation ditches in east central California, which he believed might be aboriginal, he did not concern himself with whether crops were grown or the ditches employed solely to carry water to stands of native plants. Presumably, Patch assumed that the irrigation ditches of Eureka Valley were used in the same manner as ditches constructed by the Owens Valley Paiutes to irrigate natural plots (Steward 1929).[2]

The earliest of these arguments for aboriginal agriculture in California was presented by David Prescott Barrows (1900), who was the first anthropologist to work with the Cahuilla. Unfortunately, Barrows so fully accepted his own premise that agriculture was aboriginal that he failed to solicit data on the question at a time when it might have been solved ethnographically. Barrows (1900: 71) summarized his position as follows:

> It is easier to imagine that knowledge of agriculture with seed of corn, squash, and bean came to them (the Cahuilla) long ago across the desert, than that they learned of these things only in this century.

Gifford (1931) reported that the Kamia of the New River and Jacumba areas were planters, but Castetter and Bell (1951: 36) found his data inconclusive, since it covered only the historic period. Treganza (1946) argued the feasibility of agriculture among the Kamia and Southern Diegueño, although he noted his archaelogical evidence was based on caches of crop seeds from the Jacumba area stored in the historic era. Bean and Mason (1962: 36, 104) urged consideration of pre-contact agriculture

---

2. The possibility that the Owens Valley irrigation ditches were aboriginal, as Steward (1929) originally believed, was subsequently weakened with the discovery that these Indians could have learned ditch irrigation from Anglo settlers moving into the area in the 1850's. Recently, however, the authors have found a new source (Guinn 1917) tending to support Steward's initial opinion that the ditches were aboriginal. As early as 1859, an expedition under Lt. Col. Edward F. Beale of Fort Tejon discovered extensive irrigation ditches, miles in length, being used by Owens Valley Paiute to irrigate grass seeds and tuberous roots (Guinn 1917). Proto-agriculture in Owens Valley thus deserves renewed investigation.

among the Cahuilla, observing the Romero expedition of 1823-24 found Indians planting crops near present-day Thermal.

Forbes (1963) presented an area-by-area sequence of historical data relating to agriculture among Indians west and northwest of the Colorado River. The data presented on native agriculture, even for the Cahuilla, were only semi-persuasive in arguing a case for aboriginal agriculture in California. Forbes, however, did present highly convincing data for pre-contact agriculture in northern Baja. His work had the virtue of being a pioneer study suggestive of the merits of applying an ethnohistorical approach to the problem.

Lawton (1968) surveyed myths of both missionized and non-missionized California Indian groups for agricultural motifs or elements (such as mention of crop plants). He found no crop plants mentioned in more than 200 myths of missionized coastal groups and some of the non-missionized northern California groups. Agricultural motifs or elements were present in the myths of the non-missionized Cahuilla, Kamia and Southern Diegueño. All three groups also had corn or crop origin myths. Lawton also noted that native words for corn, beans, and watermelon were present among the Cahuilla. Although the same held true for the Southern Diegueno and Kamia, their languages are Yuman and therefore crop words are Yuman-derived. Crop words among coastal missionized groups were all of Spanish derivation in word lists from the historic period.[3]

Lawton and Bean (1968) reported the presence of proto-agricultural techniques among the Cahuilla and argued the agricultural technology of the Cahuilla in the early post-contact period conformed more closely to that of the native Colorado River Agricultural Complex than to that of the Spanish missions. They suggested agriculture diffused in the pre-hispanic period to a number of Indian groups in desert areas west of the Colorado River, forming what they termed the Western Frontier Agricultural Complex. In subsequent unpublished research, they have concluded this complex was mostly confined to certain ecological

---

3. Corn may have occasionally reached the coast through trade in the pre-contact period. The Cabrillo log reported the Chumash as being familiar with maize in 1542, which they said was grown three days journey into the interior (Bolton 1967: 26). The word *Oep* was recorded as the Chumash word for maize but it appears in no subsequent vocabulary lists.

niches of the Colorado Desert capable of supporting agriculture, both in northern Baja California and California. Among groups they believe engaged in limited agriculture, mostly of the "kitchen garden" type, are the Cahuilla, Kamia, Southern Diegueño, Chemehuevi, certain Paiute groups, and possibly the Serrano, Paipai, and Kiliwa. (Note: many researchers now prefer the native word Kamia for all Diegueño.)

Shipek (1971) presented ethnographic data on wild plant cultivation and environmental manipulation among the Diegueño and Luiseño and some historical data on agriculture. Wilke and Fain (1972) reported discovery of a cultivated gourd in a rock shelter near Cahuilla fields known to have been farmed in the 1850's. Wilke is engaged in seeking archaelogical evidence for aboriginal agriculture on the Colorado Desert.

In summary, the case for aboriginal agriculture in northern Baja California appears established, although how widespread it was remains unknown. Corn, beans, pumpkins, and watermelons were being grown in 1788 by *gentiles* near Mission San Vincente (about 135 miles south of San Diego) with seeds obtained from Colorado River Indians (Forbes 1963: 8-9).[4] Mission diffusion is unlikely, since crop-growing was not yet established at this mission. For California, during the past year Lawton, Bean, and Wilke have turned up several sources (Heintzelman 1857; LeConte 1855; and Veatch 1858) indicating farming was practices as early as the first decade of the nineteenth century by Indians along the New River and at Alamo Mocho, who principally carried out flood-water farming. Crop-growing was not well established at Mission San Diego until 1777, and the first successful crops were grown at Mission San Gabriel in 1773. Thus, unless new ethnohistorical evidence to the contrary can be found, there remains only a gap of a quarter century or more in which it would have been possible for agriculture to diffuse from the missions to non-missionized Indian

---

4. On April 13, 1785, Second Lt. José Velásquez, four days out of San Diego and probably about 20 to 40 miles south of Jacumba in northern Baja, climbed a hill to survey the desert plain. He noted smoke at the base of the mountains, and was told by his Indian guide that this was a rancheria where wheat was planted. (See C-A 3, Bancroft Library, p. 195; we are grateful to William Mason for calling this report to our attention.) Wheat, a European introduction, reached the Colorado River about three-quarters of a century before the Spanish conquest in California.

groups of California on the Colorado Desert. This quarter century should be weighed in considering the problem against hundreds of years in which agriculture had the opportunity to spread from the Colorado River tribes to the New River. Nevertheless, despite the increasingly strong circumstantial case for agriculture in the California portion of the Colorado Desert, the problem is unlikely to be resolved without archaeological proof. Current research on aboriginal agriculture in the desert interior, however, does not challenge the general view that agriculture was neither adaptive nor necessary for an attractive existence for most California Indian groups. It does suggest that the desert was no barrier to diffusion of agriculture from the Colorado River to coastal areas.[5] Probably the less extensive food resources of the desert were a stimulus to adoption of agriculture. The San Bernardino and San Jacinto mountain ranges appear to have been the boundaries of the farthest westward extension of native agriculture.

PATTERNS OF BURNING IN SOUTHERN CALIFORNIA

Downs (1966) summarized data demonstrating that environmental manipulation played a significant role in the subsistenced of Great Basin hunting and gathering groups, and discussed the much abused concept of "incipience" as it relates to a period before fully developed agriculture appears in a culture. Reviewing Downs' findings, Riddell (1966: 256) suggested a closer look at California groups might reveal more evidence of environmental manipulation than previously suspected and show that aboriginal subsistence patterns were more complex than usually imagined. A review of ethnohistoric and ethnographic sources conducted by the authors over the past two years on southern California Indian groups

---

5. Cabrillo's log indicates that the coastal Indians were familiar with corn, which may have occasionally reached the coast through trade. Two intriguing references to maize occur in the diaries of members of the Portolá expedition. Father Crespi reported that north of Pismo an Indian brought the Spaniards liberal quantities of "pinole, atole, and some very good tamales which seemed to be made of corn" (Bolton 1927: 271). Miguel Costansó also noted that the tamales "appeared to have been made of corn" (Costansó 1911: 145). That both men, accustomed to Indian foods, were impelled to record similar comments suggests the problem was discussed with some perplexity by the Spanish around their evening campfire.

supports Riddell's assertion. In this essay, however, we shall confine ourselves chiefly to providing examples of burning from the literature which indicate Lewis's findings for northern California also are applicable to the southern part of the state.

Lewis contends that burning by northern California groups was a means of enhancing both plant and animal resources. Aschmann (1959) was first to suggest in detail that native burning in southern California had such an influence. "The wild landscapes are products of plants and animals adjusting to reasonably stable physical environments and each other," Aschmann (1959: 34) observed. At the same time, he argued, deliberate extensive burning by the native population had been a continuing feature of those environments, not only for hunting, but to maintain desirable plant associations (Aschmann 1959: 48):

> Above all, the Indians would burn the landscape to promote the growth of desired grasses and herbs in the following season. Modern authorities are still uncertain of the long-range effects of repeated burning in specific situations. Did it cause the degradation of a complex chapparral to the less useful chamise or coastal sage association or did it expand the oak-grassland parks? Most likely shifts in both directions occurred in different climatic and ecologic situations. In any event, the wild landscape the European explorers found was a product of millenia of such disturbances.

Aschmann concluded that disturbances such as burning produced an extremely favorable environment in southern California for plants which invested much of their vital energy in storing concentrated food in their reproductive parts. Such plants made it possible to maintain a rich flora and were crucial factors in the human population density of southern California, one of the most concentrated districts in the continent north of Central Mexico (Aschmann 1959: 56).

Evidence burning was practiced for various purposes prior to the establishment of the Spanish missions can be found in a number of sources contemporary with European contact. The earliest mention of fire being used by Indians in southern California is in the log of the Cabrillo expedition, which reported "many smokes" were seen in early October along the San Diego coast northward (Bolton 1967: 24, 33). These fires may have been only signalling activity or hearth fires, but they were so ubiquitous around the mainland of San Diego that the Spaniards give the name of Bay of Los Fumos (Bay of Smokes) to San Diego Bay.

In 1602, Vizcaino reported that between Coronado Islands and San Diego the Indians "made so many columns of smoke on he mainland that at night it looked like a procession and in the daytime the sky was overcast" (Bolton 1967: 80). On that same voyage, Father Ascensión also commented on the numerous smoke columns from the mainland, which he attributed to efforts by Indians to signal the Spanish offshore (Bolton 1967: 116). Johnston (1962: 87-88) argued that such spectacular blazes would not be a product of ordinary domestic activities. She suggested that the fires were beacons to guide Indian fishermen in from the sea at night, although she provided no firm evidence for nighttime maritime activity among the coastal groups.

The extensiveness of the blazes, however, and the fact that they seemed so impressive both by day and night far out at sea suggests they may not have been simple signal fires. Both Cabrillo and Vizcaino sailed up the coast in September-October. Some of the blazes may have been natural, since these periods coincide with the peak of the southern California brushfire season. At the same time, however, burning during this period when all grass seeds had already been harvested would conform to Lewis's findings of a summer and late fall burning pattern in northern California.

Significantly, evidence that southern California Indians practiced burning as a means of environmental manipulation is supplied in the 1792 journal of the naturalist José Longinos Martínez (Simpson 1938). Longinos Martínez makes it clear that the practice was widespread from the middle of Baja California at Fronteras (Mission San Borja) upward into Alta California (Simpson 1938: 51):

> In all of New California from Fronteras northward the gentiles have the custom of burning the brush, for two purposes; one, for hunting rabbits and hares (because they burn the brush for hunting); second, so that with the first light rain or dew the shoots will come up which they call *pelillo* (little hair) and upon which they feed like cattle

when the weather does not permit them to seek other food.

During the Portola expedition march of 1769-1770 from San Diego to San Francisco, Father Crespi repeatedly observed burned-over grasslands. His first report of burning was south of San Onofre, where the expedition "crossed some mesas covered with dry grass, in parts burned by the heathen for the purpose of hunting hares and rabbits" (Bolton 1927:132). Seven other examples of burned grassland were also reported by Crespi (Bolton 1927: 143, 197, 199, 201, 214, 222, 225). Near Chualar, Crespi stated that a valley was "short of pasture on account of fires set by heathen" (Bolton 1927: 201). On Soquel Creek, he reported that good pasture was found "although it has just been burned by the heathen who do not permit themselves to be seen" (Bolton 1927: 214). The fires may well have been a product of rabbit hunting, but it should be noted that Crespi at no time actually witnessed a rabbit drive in progress. In all likelihood, he was extrapolating the purpose from practices observed among Indians elsewhere. The time of the burnings reported were from July to October.

One entry in Crespi's journal merits close attention. On the fourth day of the Portolá march, north of Carlsbad in the valley where Mission San Luis Rey was later founded, Crespi (Bolton 1927: 129) reported that the expedition "descended to a large and beautiful valley, so green that it seemed to us that it had been planted." Crespi was an attentive traveler, who routinely made detailed comments on the abundance of native grasses and intermixed plant cover. Significantly, two Indian villages lay at opposite extremities of the valley plain. Agricultural specialists to whom we showed this passage suggested that the effect described would most likely be produced if the natives of the village had burned the adjacent plain. Such burning would have encouraged growth of annual grasses at the expense of perennial plants and given an appearance of cultivation.

Father Serra noted a similar valley in his march up the Baja peninsula. Two weeks journey south of San Diego in June of 1796, Serra (Tibesar 1955: I, 101) reported entering a valley "more than a league in width, and in parts so green that, if I did not know in what country I was, I would have taken it, without any hesitation, for land under cultivation.'' Here again signs of Indian occupance were found, although the natives had fled.

Among the Yuman Indians of the Colorado River agricultural plots were cleared prior to planting by burning (Castetter and Bell 1951: 140). Despite Longinos Martínez's early observation that burning to encourage wild plant production was widespread, however, only a few examples of this practice can be found in anthropological and other modern literature on southern California Indians. This probably reflects the extreme disruption of the native economic system which occurred in the south as compared with the greater stability in the post-contact period of many of the northern California groups covered in Lewis's essay.

Bean (1972: 47) reported that grasses were periodically fired by the Cahuilla to improve production. Chia was also fired by the Cahuilla (Bean and Saubel 1972: 115). Drucker (1937: 9) reported chia was burned for plant improvement by the Cupeño, Mountain Cahuilla, Northern Diegueño, and Southern Diegueño. Katherine Luomala (personal communication) reports that grasslands were fired by the Diegueño to improve seed yields. Shipek (1971: 10, 11) said coastal Diegueño informants reported their ancestors burned to encourage grasses and flowering annuals, which provided supplementary foods as well as browse to keep deer, antelope, and rabbit populations at a high level. Basket grass, she reported, was burned every three years to maintain quality. Ground was also kept clear beneath oaks and pines by burning. Lee (1937: 48) wrote that burning of basket grass by the Southern Diegueño encouraged taller plants with thicker stalks. Lee (1937: 52-53) also stated hillsides were fired to encourage growth of desirable food plants. Shipek (1971: 11) reported that diaries of San Diego settlers and local newspaper accounts indicated Indians of the area were still burning extensively as late as 1870. According to Shipek (personal communication) these latter sources indicate most burning took place in the late summer through late fall.

Evans (1873: 208), traveling through the Coachella Valley in 1863, reported that the Cahuilla were burning their mesquite groves and smoke columns could be seen throughout the valley. He was told that burning destroyed mistletoe which afflicted the mesquite. Informants have told us that burning also encouraged new growth in mesquite and thinned stands. Native palm stands of *Washingtonia filifera* were regularly fired by Cahuilla shamans to kill pests and diseases causing damage to trees and decreased crops (Patencio 1943: 69). This technique was rediscovered in the 1930's by the U.S. Department of Agriculture as an effective means of killing parlatoria date scale and red spider mites in palm oases (Stickney, Barnes, and Simmons 1950: 8). Vogl (1968: 86) stated such burning of native palm kills off outer vascular bundles, making more of the limited water supply in an oases available for palm reproduction or for a larger palm population. It may also expose enriched, moist mineral soils beneath fronds and other heavy litter, favoring new palm growth and germination.

Data obtained by anthropologists from informants on the use of fire in hunting in southern California is much less detailed than information on the northern part of the state. No information has been recorded for some of the coastal mission groups, whose populations were already decimated by disease early in the mission period. However, there is sufficient data to suggest use of fire in hunting was probably widespread in southern California. A cursory survey of the literature provides the following examples.

Harrington (1943: 6) recorded use of fire in rabbit drives by the Fernandeño and in driving antelopes into enclosures by the Emigdiano Chumash and Kitanemuk Serrano. Sparkman (1980: 198) reported firing of wood rat nests and use of fire to drive squirrels from burrows among the Luiseño. Drucker (1937: 7) listed communal animal drives (game not stated) with fire among the Mountain Cahuilla, Southern Diegueño, Chemehuevi, and Yuman Indians. Hooper (1920: 368) recorded a Desert Cahuilla myth in which rabbits were driven from brush by fire. Bean (1972: 65) reported fire was generally used among the Cahuilla to flush game. Castetter and Bell (1951: 217) noted that the Cocopa and Mohave fired tule areas to flush rabbits, and the Cocopa set fire to rats' nests. The Yumans built circles of brush fire to concentrate prey, especially rabbits (Castetter and Bell 1951: 214-15). Brush along river sloughs was fired by the Kamia in rabbit hunts (Gifford 1931: 26). Spier (1923: 337) reported that the Southern Diegueño used fire to drive rabbits from brush.

Among more northerly groups in the southern part of the state not covered in Lewis's paper on burning, Steward (1933: 253, 254; 1934: 434; 1934: 39, 184) listed rabbit drives with fire by the Mono Lake Paiute, use of fire in deer drives of the Owens Valley Paiute, and use of fire in communal antelope and rabbit drives by the Ash Valley Paiute.

THE PREFORMATIVE STAGE IN CALIFORNIA

Heizer (1958: 23) urged that the nature of the economy and density and stability of population achieved in late prehistoric times in Central California and western southern California was such that these areas should be classified as Preformative in the historical-development classification of archaeological cultures developed by Willey and Phillips (1955). The Preformative Stage, which follows the Archaic, is signalized by the introduction of agriculture, which is dependent upon marked population increase and large stable villages. Heizer defined Preformative as "semi-agricultural" and argued that this status had been achieved in California through an abundant and assured food supply primarily provided by the acorn.

In attempting to verify Heizer's contention that gathering in California was fully equivalent to the manner of life of other aboriginal peoples who practices primitive forms of farming, Ziegler (1968) employed the term "quasi-agricultural" as descriptive of the acorn-salmon economies of north-central California. He concluded that these quasi-agricultural economies were reasonably equivalent to proto- or semi-agricultural societies elsewhere. Such economies allowed manifestations of leisure time and diversity of labor not only in "non-vital" occupations, but also in an apparent over-elaboration of assignments even in "vital" professions (Ziegler 1968: 64).

Quasi-agriculture seems to us an appropriate term to apply to the acorn-salmon industry, but not to the over-all pattern of native economies in California. Here, for reasons we shall indicate in our discussion later, Heizer's term "semi-agricultural" seems most satisfactory for an all-encompassing term for the native California economy. California's native economy, we suggest, should be viewed holistically rather than by tribelet or cultural region to be seen in broad ecological perspective. To distinguish some regions as "semi-agricultural" only on the basis of greater food abundance or superior gathering management is to fail to recognize that quasi-agricultural or semi-agricultural processes overlap into every cultural region in California. Indeed, California's native economy was far more complex in terms of energy extraction processes than can be apprehended by a primary focus upon such features as the acorn-salmon industries with the assumption that all other hunting and collecting activities were supplementary.

Without challenging the idea that the acorn economy, where wild oak were harvested like horticultural tree crops, was indeed a ''quasi-agricultural'' gathering activity, we should like to emphasize that it was not the only feature of native plant gathering which suggests that California was in a pre-agricultural stage. Lewis's paper, as we shall see, provides new insight into another possibly equally important aspect of the hunting and gathering economy.

Even for the marginal-subsistence environment of the Great Basin, Downs (1966: 41) demonstrated that variations on the primary hunting and gathering theme and environmental manipulations had considerable significance. They were probably even a more significant part of gathering activities in California, because there was a far greater range of plant resources to be exploited, requiring a continuum of plant knowledge which had to be applied in the context of a rich variety of specific plant associations. Without denying the importance of the acorn as a primary staple, we question the over-emphasis on the acorn economy in the literature, which has tended to make researchers neglect other features of the gathering pattern deserving scrutiny. The ''quasi-agricultural'' pattern postulated by Ziegler for the acorn harvest also may be said to be applicable to methods of harvesting mesquite, pine-nut, and agave. In addition, one also finds present among some California groups — possibly most of them if sufficient information were available — evidence for both incipient agriculture and proto-agricultural manipulations. In support of the latter statement, we shall briefly summarize some of the available data on proto-agriculture in California.

Wild tobacco was planted and grown by the Diegueño (Luomala unpublished), Cahuilla (Bean and Saubel 1972: 92), Wintu, Maidu, Miwok, Yokuts, Panamint, Hupa, Yurok, and Karuk (Kroeber 1941: 14-15). No evidence for tobacco planting exists among most of the missionized coastal groups, which led Kroeber (1941:14) to hypothesize that tobacco planting was confined to a long, irregular area stretching southeastward from the Oregon coast to south-central California. The recent addition of the Cahuilla and Diegueño as tobacco planters, however, suggests that a preference for Spanish tobacco grown at the missions may have resulted in abandonment of native plantings, if they existed, and a subsequent lack of ethnographic knowledge of the practice by most missionized southern California groups.[6]

The Diegueño sometimes planted seeds from wild plants or transplanted wild plants to areas where they could be better tended (Luomala unpublished). According to Luomala's informants knowledge of the care of wild plants was handed down from generation to generation. Among plants they recalled as being transplanted were the wild onion (*kamashuk*) and tuberous roots called *mishwi* and *ptokolp*. Shipek (1971: 10) reported her Diegueño and Luiseño informants "knew exactly which of the native plants could be propagated by cuttings, which could be transplanted, and which could not." Cuero (1968: 32), a Diegueno woman, reported her people always cleared a small spot near their dwelling to plant "some of the greens and seeds and roots that they liked, just the things that grow wild." The Cahuilla replanted smaller corms of the wild hyacinth to ensure crops the following year (Bean and Saubel 1972: 47) and various other tubers (Lawton and Bean 1968: 23). J. P. Harrington (field notes, 1925) recorded a Cahuilla myth on the planting of agave. Cahuilla medicine men cultivated their own special plots of medicinal herbs and tobacco (Lawton and Bean 1968: 23). Patencio (1943: 91-95, 99-102) stated native palms were planted at some of the desert oases by Cahuilla.

Semicultivation of several wild seed plants, a practice that was aboriginal and first observed by Alarcón in 1540, is reported for the Mohave, Yuma, Cocopa, and Maricopa among the Colorado River Indians, who were also agricultural (Castetter and Bell 1951: 167-168). Among such plants cultivated were panic grass, foxtail millet, crowfoot grass, and curly dock. Planting of sunflower seed may also have been aboriginal with the Mohave (Castetter and Bell 1951: 196). Steward (1933) reported that the Owens Valley Paiute increased the natural yield of several species of wild plants by irrigation (see note 2). Patch (1951) reported the possibility of

6. Father Junipero Serra set aside a section of the garden at Mission Carmel in 1774 for tobacco planting (Tibesar 1957: 11, 147). Serra's decision to plant tobacco at the missions was prompted by the fact that from San Diego to Monterey the natives invariably begged him for Spanish tobacco.

aboriginal irrigation, presumably of wild plants, for the Eureka Valley.

The proximity of the Great Basin to California also makes it worth noting that fifteen of nineteen groups covered by Steward (1941:281) and seven of fourteen groups reported by Stewart (1941: 376) burned vegetation to encourage growth of wild plants. In addition, Steward (1941: 281) reported that seven of his nineteen groups engaged in collective sowing of wild seeds, most frequently lamb's quarters. Sowing occurred after burning.

The Cahuilla regularly pruned mesquite by breaking and cutting branches to improve growth patterns and provide easier access to beans in their mesquite groves (Patencio 1943: 59). In the historic period, the Cahuilla are known to have conducted an irrigation ditch to mesquite stands near Thermal and flooded them. Irrigation of mesquite traces back as early as the 1850's (Wilke and Lawton unpublished). McMillan (1956: 29) reported that Lily Baker, a Maidu informant, stated her people cleaned around elderberry bushes and removed dead portions for better growth of this natural food. Some tendance may have occurred with the wild grape among California Indians. Father Crespi (Bolton 1927: 4) reported in 1769 that the plain near the port of San Diego was dotted with wild grapevines "which look as if they had been planted . . ." Again, in the valley where Mission San Luis Rey was later founded, Crespi (Bolton 1927: 131) reported that in the vicinity of two native villages there were many wild grapes and "one sees some spots that resemble vineyards." Fallowing was a regular practice among the Cahuilla with certain plants not gathered in some years "to let the ground have more seeds for another year" (Patencio 1943: 69). Similar practices are reported for the Diegueño and Luiseño (Shipek personal communication). Pedro Fages reported fires were set at the foot of the *teczuma* plant, a flower he described as similar to the rose of Castile, to make the buttons eject an oily seed (Priestly 1937: 79).

The proto-agricultural activities summarized here for California groups testify to considerable sophistication in knowledge about practices needed to improve harvests for specific plants and plants in general. We are still in need of a full inventory of proto-agricultural practices throughout California, but this cursory review indicated that incipient agriculture existed among some California groups.

THE IMPLICATIONS OF LEWIS'S PAPER
ON NATIVE BURNING

In projecting ethnographic reports onto models of ecosystem relations, Lewis has demonstrated that fire was a major factor in a system of aboriginal environmental relationships and functioned in a number of ways to increase both animal and plant resources in California. His paper opens up many avenues deserving investigation, but we shall concentrate on problems raised specifically by his discussion of burning of the Woodlands-Grass environments. The ideas offered here should be considered primarily as hypotheses deserving of more intensive research.

Lewis has shown that burning of the woodlands grassbelts increased grasses and forbs and would have improved browse for deer, antelope, and other game. The extraordinary abundance of game in California, particularly in woodlands-grass areas of the coastal valleys, is testified to by all of the Spanish explorers of the contact period. La Pérouse (1968: I, 441) during his 1785-88 voyage, expressed his astonishment at the wealth of game, saying "No country is more abundant in fish and game of every sort." Partridges alone in the grassland plains, he noted, were found in covies of three or four hundred. Father Serra, who commented repeatedly on the plentifulness of game, was struck by the lack of timidity of rabbits in grassland valleys, "which frisk playfully and plentifully around" (Tibesar 1955: 107). Other comments on the abundance of deer, antelope, elk, rabbit, and other game by Spanish writers may be found in Smith and Teggart (1909: 19, 259), Costansó (1910: 67), Tibesar (1955: 87), Bolton (1967: 74-75, 80), Priestley (1937: 12, 35, 60, 77), Bolton (1911: 149, 153), Bolton (1927: 34, 127), not to mention many other sources.

Burning the woodlands grassbelt, particularly in areas near villages, would have concentrated game in specific locations for ready accessibility in hunting, since browse in burned-over areas would have been richer. Thus, we suggest burning may have constituted a form of game management or incipient herding. Data on hunting technology of California Indian groups is sparse in most ethnographies and chiefly concerned with describing weapons and other tools employed. Few researchers have investigated hunting concepts, including the extent to which taboos may have served to abet game management. McMillan (1956: 29) did report an example of the Maidu cutting grass during the fall months and piling it near water so that waterfowl would concentrate near this food supply during winter.

Dimbleby (1967: 81-82) suggested that the opening up of woodlands to grasses, through some form of human activity such as herding, provided a shock stimulus for grasses to gain a foothold, subsequently resulting in man's exploitation of cereal grains through agriculture. Hunting drives by California Indians over many generations could well have provided such a shock stimulus in the Woodlands-Grass belt, leading to an eventual ecological understanding that fire was also a tool for increasing grass seed plants and should be regularly employed in the California environment. Although Burcham (1959), Clar (1959), and Heady (1972), as Lewis points out, are skeptical that the California Indians had sufficient numbers and technological skills to have any significant impact on the environment, such an impact need not have been massively widespread to have substantially improved the subsistence level of native populations in the coastal valleys. The primary effect of burning would be to greatly increase both plant and animal resources near villages, where hunting and gathering could be better organized and more efficiently concentrated over a smaller area, thus resulting in increased leisure for other pursuits.

One of Lewis's most stimulating ideas concerning native burning appears in another paper (Lewis 1972: 213). When California shrublands are burned in late autumn, he notes, the seasonal pattern of succession begins with grasses (which sprout earlier and more readily because of the nutrients provided and the clearing of surface cover), followed by legumes and other forbs through winter, spring, and early summer. The pattern of succession lasts several years, until individual species of grass become rare and absent, succeeded by other taxonomic groups until a chapparral stage is reached. With reburning, this succession is repeated. In view of these facts, Lewis suggests:

> . . . By taking advantage of the internal dynamics of the secondary succession induced by fire man would without any introduction of seed on his part, create a series of successions of resources essentially no different (except that cultivation, planting, and weeding would not take place) from the harvesting pattern of some swidden

farmers who exploit successive but often different crops
following a first-year burn.

The analogy with swidden farming strikes us as particularly
apt. We would like to hypothesize, however, that the plant
succession was probably of less interest to California Indians than
the first stage of that succession — the native grasses. Almost
nothing is known about the native grasses of California at the time
of contact. The European wild grasses rapidly invaded California
ranges after Spanish contact and gained the dominant foothold. By
the middle of the nineteenth century, wild oats, wild mustards, wild
radishes, and other Mediterranean cover had spread over most of
the California rangeland. Native grasses may still be found, but as
Anderson (1956: 763) observed it takes a well-informed botanist
going over the vegetation item by item to show how small a
percentage of the range is made up of California indigenous plants.

Regular burning by the Indians of the coastal valleys may have
exercised a selective influence on the genotypic strains of native
grasses. Literature from Spanish sources indicates that some of the
wild grains were impressive even to Europeans. The Cabrillo log
(Bolton 1967:30) speaks of a seed "the size of maize" which was
white and used in making tamales by the natives. Vizcaino (Bolton
1967: 85) reported the Californians had a "grain like the *gofio* of
the Canary Islands." Father Garcés stated that the San Jacinto
plain was thickly grown with grasses, one species of which bore a
seed much like rye. Garcés (Bolton 1930: II, 346) added: "I have no
doubt this is the grain which the Gileños call wheat, for they told me
that near the sea there was wheat which they harvested without
planting it . . ." Coastal Diegueño insist that the white seeds of a
grain which is no longer part of the native flora was harvested by
their ancestors and even up into the early twentieth century (Shipek
1971: 18). They described this grain as larger than the native
grasses, but only about half as large as wheat. Grass seeds in
archaelogical sites in California are rarely given close scrutiny
beyond a routine botanical identification. More intensive study
might determine if there were grains with the unusual
characteristics mentioned in Spanish accounts.

The Spanish literature of the contact period is full of
extravagant praise for the verdant grass meadowlands of the
coastal valleys, where population concentration was heaviest.

Frequently, references are made to Indians harvesting their "fields" near villages. There is considerable testimony to the effect that these "fields" had circumscribed boundaries and were considered property by the Indians.[7] Father Jayme (Geiger 1970: 39-40) in a letter of October 17, 1772 complained that the Spanish soldiers had turned their animals into the "fields" of the Indians at a village near Mission San Diego and "they ate up their crops (*semillas*)." Three other villages about a league or so from the mission, he reported, had made similar periodic complaints. Clearly, these "fields" were richer than other pasturage, leading to disputes between the Spanish and Indians.

Spanish accounts also make frequent mention of harvesting activities by the natives, but fail to describe these operations in specific detail. Other seedbeating is mentioned, but rarely in the context of any specific plant being gathered. In 1790, Captain James Colnett reported seeing the Indians near Bodega Bay using seedbeaters to gather "grass or wild wheat seed" (Howay, 1940). The anthropological literature customarily assumes seedbeaters were used throughout the state on grasses as well as plants.

Drucker (1939: 9) reported that almost all of his southern California informants said grass was gathered with a seedbeater. One third of these informants, however, also said grass was cut. What we do not know is whether some grass species, possibly taller ones, were cut in southern California, whereas the seedbeater may have been employed with others.

The most intriguing reference to harvesting wild plants by California Indians in the Spanish literature appears in an official 1772 report on the establishment of Mission San Diego. Father Francisco Palóu (Pourade 1969: II, 17) states in this report:

---

7. In 1943, Heizer and Beardsley (1943) first described seven fired clay human figurines found in California. Since then other figurines, making a total of 28 and two hollow body effigies, have been described from central California to northern San Diego County (Heizer and Beardsley 1943; Heizer and Pendergast 1955; True 1957; Wallace 1957; Davis 1959; and Hedges 1973). The figurines are believed to have been used in ceremonial or ritual contexts, although the exact nature of their functions remains undetermined (Hedges 1973). Elsewhere in the southwest, effigies have been known to be placed in the fields by some agricultural groups to protect crops. True (1957) noted that association of figurines and increase rites in many agricultural societies has

> The savages subsist on seeds of the *zacate* (wild grass)
> which they harvest in the season. From these they make
> sheaves as is the custom to do with wheat . . .

Bundling of grain into sheaves has always been considered an innovation introduced by the missions. Yet here we find the Diegueno harvesting grass in sheaves at the close of the aboriginal period. How extensive this harvesting method may have been and whether it was employed by other coastal groups we don't know. The implications of such a technique are highly significant, however. Although we have found no other reference to sheaving in the Spanish literature for California, Shimkin and Reed (1970: 173-174) assumed that sheaving was aboriginal with the Shoshoneans of the Carson River Basin, Nevada.

Sheaving of grasses by the Diegueño, however, does suggest that they probably also engaged in sowing and that these grasses may have been "semi-domesticated" or on the way to becoming semi-domesticated when the Spanish arrived in California. Harvesting methods have a direct influence on the strain of a species if the process is repeated over a number of generations. If the method of harvesting demands that the inflorescence remain intact, then only seeds which do not disperse themselves readily will be collected (Helbaek 1960; Wilke, Bettinger, King, and O'Connell 1972: 205). As a result, collected seeds can be expected to have a high frequency of genes responsible for sturdy, non-shattering inflorescences and a concommitant low frequency of genes responsible for a fragile, easily shattered inflorescence

---

been well documented, but that lacking direct archaeological evidence or ethnological information the use of figurines in increase rites locally was unlikely. True (1957: 296) added: "However, ownership of hunting grounds, oak groves, and other seed sources by individuals, families, and village complexes, suggests a grove management situation that was conceivably not far removed from early agricultural economies in other areas. Ceremonies to increase the acorn crop are said to have been performed in the old days." We should like to call attention to a historical reference which suggests effigies were used in California to protect wild plant crops. In his description of the Chumash, Pedro Fages (Priestly 1937: 32-33) wrote: "They are idolators like the rest. Their idols are placed near the village, with some here and there about the fields, to protect, they say, the seeds and crops. These idols are nothing but sticks, or stone figurines painted with colors and surmounted with plumage. . ."

(Zohary 1969: 60). When harvested seed is planted and the process repeated over a number of generations, a relatively pure strain of species ultimately results. On the other hand, if the method of harvesting utilizes the natural ability of the plant to disperse seeds, such as occurs in seedbeating when seeds are simply knocked from plants, then harvested seeds have gene dispersal frequencies comparable to the vast majority of wild plants (Wilke, Bettinger, King, and O'Connell 1972: 205).

Unless sowing were carried out by the Diegueño, sheaving alone would have tended to remove superior strains of grass from the fields eventually, since seed dispersal would have been predominantly from the inferior plants missed during cutting. We therefore should like to hypothesize that the Diegueño in all probability engaged in sowing of native grasses. Burning, sheaving, and sowing would have been selective factors resulting in superior and possibly even semi-domesticated strains of grasses among the Diegueño.[8] The only mention of sowing in the literature for southern California is among the Diegueño. Shipek (1971:17) reported that elderly Diegueño informants told her that wild grass in aboriginal times was cultivated first by burning the land and then by broadcasting seed. While scholars generally have reservations concerning statements made by informants about aboriginal times, Palóu's account would appear to provide reinforcements for the practice of sowing.

How important were the native grasses in the California Indian diet? Anthropological emphasis has usually been on the acorn as the primary staple for much of California. As Kroeber (1971: 297) pointed out, however, the oak is absent from many areas and did not grow in the higher mountains, in the desert, and on most of the immediate coast. Food resources were bountiful, however, with hundreds of available foods to fall back upon. A review of the

---

8. Michael Kearney (personal communication) suggests burning and harvesting practices of California Indians may have resulted in semi-domesticated grasses less able to resist the invasion into California of wild European species. After 1769, when the coastal Indians had been rounded up by the missions, normal native practices related to burning and harvesting of native grasses would have been disrupted. Spanish cattle over the next fifty years probably weakened stands of native grass, creating numerous ecological niches for invasion by Mediterranean grasses well adapted to grazing. This may explain the rapidity with which European grasses took over.

Spanish literature indicates to us that grass seeds were an extremely significant staple. Both Palou (Pourade 1969: II, 17) and Longinos Martínez (Simpson 1938: 51) stressed grasses as a significant element in the coastal diet. During the march of the Portolá expedition of 1772, acorns and pine-nuts were occasionally given to the Spanish by the Indians of the coastal valleys, but *pinole* and *atole* made from the native grasses were available in large surplus and brought forth and given to the Spanish in large trays and baskets at almost every village (i.e., Bolton 1927: 44-45).

THE RISE OF CULTURAL COMPLEXITY IN CALIFORNIA

Lewis's paper on native burning has forced us to reevaluate the food-subsistence patterns of California Indians, particularly the significant role of grasses in their economy. This reevaluation has led us to the conclusion that no single factor, neither the acorn complex nor marine technology, were primary in militating against the spread of agriculture in California. We conclude that Heizer was correct in hypothesizing that California was in a "semi-agricultural" stage at Spanish contact. This can be seen reflected in the existence of proto-agricultural techniques, in the quasi-agricultural patterns of harvesting acorn, yucca, mesquite, and pine-nuts, and in the application of burning to enhancing plant and animal resources. In short, agriculture was an unnecessary alternative for the California Indian because of an efficient, interlocking series of energy extraction processes, some of which were semi-agricultural.

Until Lewis's paper, the significance of the burning process in the large inventory of techniques of environmental manipulation used by California Indians was not demonstrated and considered by most authorities to be conjectural at best. Lewis has shown that burning was an important part of the rich technological inventory of energy extraction processes and tools used by California Indians, which included invention of leaching for acorn and buckeye, grinding implements for hard seeds, canoes for acquiring marine mammals and fish, complex fishing and trapping gear, granaries fo storing large supplies of food, hermetically sealed containers, artificial water-utilization methods such as digging wells and building reservoirs on the desert, and a variety of proto-agricultural techniques.

The technological processes and complex social organizations of California's hunters and gatherers were integrated with value systems which encouraged increased productivity and the acquisition of surpluses. The abundance of plant and animal resources and the development of storage techniques and other truly skilled applications of human ingenuity allowed these people to develop beyond the normal parameters of hunting and gathering, particularly in the sociological, philosophical, and religious realms. The social structures of native communities, autonomous corporate groups called tribelets by Kroeber, were characterized by extra tribal alliances and political confederations sometimes achieving the level of nationhood. Within communities, populations were administered by very powerful hereditary chiefs and a bureaucratic elite whose principal function appear to have been control and management of production and distribution (Strong 1929; White 1963; Bean 1972; King 1974). Between groups, intra-group adaptive mechanisms existed which included such institutions as ritual and kinship reciprocity and the trade fairs which encouraged and routinized controlled production and redistribution of foodstuffs and manufactured goods. In many instances, native groups had reached the level of an incipient class system, which recognized hereditary ruling elites, bureaucrats and artisans, ordinary persons, poor or lower classes, and sometimes slave or outlaw groups. Elites intermarried with elites among other groups, speaking and behaving in ways that affirmed and maintained their status (Bean 1974).

There is considerable evidence now that after the Europeans arrived and imposed their status concepts and economic system upon native California, traditional social hierarchies were generally obscured from view, weakened, or destroyed. Chester King (1974) has suggested that Spanish colonization resulted in (1) imposition of the new dominant hierarchy headed by a Spanish king; (2) a reduction in the importance of local native hierarchies with a loss in the significance of food storage and other facilities controlled by these hierarchies; and (3) introduction of new agricultural and pastoral technologies with a reduction in native population from disease which made possible opportunities for attaining wealth and power on the part of those of low birth. This view is counter to Gifford (1934) and others who have argued that the extraordinary cross-tribelet leadership roles in the nineteenth century of such leaders as Juan Antonio and Antonio Garra were a product of European contact. Instead, ethnographic reconstructions now indicate these historic roles were more consistent with native traditions and that the Spanish built on the foundation of the aboriginal hierarchies by appointing "generals" among Indian groups who were also traditional leaders of local political units.

Within the aboriginal social-religious institutions, which had probably been established for several thousand years, smoothly articulated intergroup relationships were regulated by ritual institutions of ritual congregations and secret societies or cults, confirming and demonstrating who had economic and political privileges, always supported in a ritual and cosmological referent of some sort. These institutions were responsible for distributing energy within the various subsystems, so that temporal or spatially related inequities in food and other economic goods could both be alleviated or maintained, depending on the particular needs of a corporate group. Such institutions provided a buffer against extremes in energy potential among different groups, which sometimes were a cause of conflict or wars. They also significantly increased the productive capacity of any single group beyond that permitted by environmental and technological limitations.

Alliances and trade fairs also increased the energy input for any single group. Trade routes appear to have reached the logical parameters of natural barriers and ecological needs. For example, in southern California, where there were few barriers to intercultural communications, trade alliances associated with military commitments extended from the west coast across the state into Arizona. Several such alliances provided routinized trade routes allowing a considerable exchange of goods across several ecological zones and directed that flow along ecological lines rather than cultural or linguistic ones. Agricultural products also must have occasionally passed along these trade routes in addition to shell beads, obsidian, and other goods, and undoubtedly knowledge of agricultural practices along the Colorado River. The abundance of California's food resources and highly developed techniques of energy extraction, however, made it unnecessary to adapt an agricultural mode, except in some of the marginally productive desert areas.

The style of cultures represented in California now appear to provide the model sought by cultural evolutionists who pursue knowledge about the upper limits of sociocultural integration possible without an agricultural base. California stands out as perhaps exemplary of many hunting and gathering regions which were later occupied or transformed by agricultural systems. Frequently, anthropologists have concluded that hunting and gathering peoples were forced into marginal environments by people adopting agriculture or that those hunters and gatherers who achieved maximal socio-political development proceeded to adopt agriculture and thus have been lost for analytical purposes. A reexamination of California from a fresh viewpoint — the idea that hunting and gathering societies there may have been analogous to many primitive agriculture societies elsewhere — should provide new perspectives on ideas suggested by cultural evolutionists and ecologists. It should help in answering many questions about the upper or maximal levels of sociocultural integration that hunting and gathering groups can achieve. From such knowledge will come a better understanding of the complex processes by which man thrusts forward toward the logical potential of his environmental and technological growth.

Ecology and Adaptive Response Among the Tolowa Indians of Northwestern California

by R. A. Gould

There is currently a strong trend in the anthropology of California Indians to gather new data and reexamine earlier findings in the light of problems raised by worldwide studies of hunter-gatherer ecology and archaeological explanation. A growing literature addresses the subject of traditional and contact-period Indian adaptations within both pristine and altered ecosystems throughout California. Building upon this, there is also a growing interest in the implications of such adaptations for increased size and stability of settlements, development of class and status hierarchies, the roles of trade, warfare, and ritual as mechanisms for reallocation of resources, and other social elaborations. The rationale for this revitalized interest in California Indian anthropology has centered on a developing awareness that many if not most ancient hunter-gatherers lived in well-favored, temperate environments comparable to those of California, and that it was in settings like these that major evolutionary developments relevant to agriculture took place (Bean and King, 1974: 6).

Thus we cannot do as Sahlins (1972: 8) and some others suggest and simply dismiss or exclude relatively affluent hunter-gatherers like the Northwest Coast and many California Indians as "special cases" that are somehow unrepresentative of hunter-gatherer ecology and economy. Instead, we must look for processes of adaptation that differentiate hunter-gatherers, and in this regard it is especially useful to examine and compare the extremes of the hunter-gatherer spectrum. What ecological relationships can account for essential differences in social and economic organization among societies as different as, for example, the Kalahari Bushmen and Australian desert Aborigines as opposed to the Northwest Coast and northwestern California Indians? Rather than review the whole range of differences, this paper will focus on one key aspect of this process of differentiation: the contrast between what I shall term here *sharing* vs. *aggrandizive* systems of resource allocation.

Most ethnographic and historic hunter-gatherers possess social mechanisms, usually based upon kinship, that enable them to share food and other key resources and the access to these resources with other members of the same society. Arguments like Sahlin's about the essential "affluence" of hunter-gatherer life (Sahlins, 1968: 85-89; 1972: 1-39) notwithstanding, most hunter-gatherers must find ways to overcome uncertainties in availability of resources. Most often this is done by means of widely ramified kinship networks that allow people who are experiencing scarcities to share food and in some cases even to take up residence with their better-favored relatives. Systems like this tend to be egalitarian, since an individual sees his long-term security and that of his immediate family as depending upon the maintenance of kin obligations by means of gift-giving. He thus is eager to "give away" any food or other goods that exceed his immediate needs, since he knows he can expect return "gifts" at some later time when he has real need. Under these conditions, the personal accumulation of surpluses is actively discouraged. Security rests in the development and maintenance of the widest possible network of kin with whom one may share food and access to resources in times of need.

Such a sharing system can be contrasted with aggrandizive systems that encourage individuals or individual families to accumulate and store surpluses as security against shortages. This could be called the "money in the bank" approach to security, and it is uncharacteristic of hunter-gatherers generally. In this case, instead of generosity we find thrift, which is to say, both systems call for a calculation of returns at a later date, but they do so in different ways. Neither system is altruistic. Aggrandizive systems may be associated with incipient or developed status or class hierarchies, since such accumulations are generally unequal and become more or less concentrated in the hands of certain individuals or families. We do not normally associate such aggrandizive behavior with hunters and gatherers, since the literature (Service, 1966; Lee and DeVore, 1968; Coon, 1971;

Bicchieri, 1972) has emphasized the importance of sharing behavior in most if not all hunter-gather societies.

The Tolowa Indians of northwestern California are of special interest because they were one of the very few hunting and gathering societies we know of that operated on a purely aggrandizive basis. This paper will show how the Tolowa adapted to the ecological requirements of the northwestern California region and will try to begin at least to answer the question: What ecological relationships are necessary to account for the rise of an aggrandizive and ultimately status-differentiated social system? This paper assumes at the outset that a simple abundance of natural resources is not, in itself, sufficient to account for this development, although it is one part of the answer. Moreover, there may well be other avenues to status differentiation, even among hunter-gathers, than simply aggrandizive behavior. Recent studies by Bean (1972), for example, show how individuals among the Cahuilla may have acquired status as managers in the business of redistributing resources. But the Tolowa present us with an extreme case of aggrandizive behavior to an extent unmatched by any other known hunter-gatherers and by few other societies as well, giving us the opportunity to examine this particular mode of adaptation.

THE "FITNESS" OF ABORIGINAL CALIFORNIA ADAPTATIONS

A cautionary note is being sounded by Heizer (1974) about the dangers of accepting published and archival data on traditional California Indian culture at face value, because a long time has elapsed since much of this information was first collected and since it has also been a long time since any California Indians lived off the land in a traditional manner. Much of this data is erroneous, and the judgement needed to assess its accuracy today is not always well informed (Heizer, 1974: 29). There is no easy answer to these general criticisms, but certainly there are safeguards that present-day students of California Indians can use that go beyond such obvious measures as checks for internal consistency and historical and archaeological verification. Since much of the renewed interest in California Indians centers on problems of an ecological nature, perhaps we can borrow a page from the ecologist's notebook and apply a general principle which has seen wide use in the field of biological ecology. This is the idea of *fitness*, which can be defined as, ". . . the general level of the health of the total ecosystem," (Clapham, 1973: 229). This term cannot be adequately quantified, but it subsumes relationships between ecological variables that can be measured, albeit sometimes in a gross form, and that can serve as guides to the general fitness or health of the ecosystem under examination. For example, we can observe and measure limiting factors in an ecosystem — that is, ". . . any condition that approaches or exceeds the limit of tolerance for the organism or group in question" (Odum, 1975: 108). Limiting factors exist for human as well as natural ecosystems, and we can be sure that any human situation that violates these limits will be maladaptive and will either fail or else require radical adjustments before it will regain its fitness.

It follows then that any reconstruction of aboriginal California Indian cultural systems can be tested against its fitness with respect to the environmental requirements that could be viewed as possible limiting factors. Such a test requires a high order of environmental reconstruction. Perhaps we can return at this point to Heizer's criticism that there has been a "loss of adequate evaluation of earlier reports" by the new generation of California archaeologists and ethnohistorians, who lack the assurance offered by firsthand knowledge of traditional California Indian culture (1974: 30). Since such firsthand knowledge of California Indians is no longer possible, a new basis for informed judgement is needed. I suggest that expanded and rigorous application of the ecological idea of fitness, beginning with an examination of possible limiting factors vis-a-vis cultural variables in the reconstructed system, will provide a basis for judgement at least as well informed as the ethnographic background acquired through firsthand knowledge of traditional California Indians. This approach, of course, goes considerably beyond California studies and can be applied to any part of the world where cultural reconstructions are being attempted.

To apply the concept of fitness in a different way, some cultural reconstructions will "fit" the requirements of their total ecosystems better than others, and a very poor fit suggests a poor reconstruction. Of course, one cannot always assume that all aspects of human behavior in a cultural system conform optimally to the ecological requirements in which that system operates. But extreme cases, in which limiting factors are apparently violated, thus threatening the health of the cultural system, should be examined with skepticism and perhaps even held in abeyance until new evidence permits one to see a closer "fit". This proposition can be stated as a "Principle of Negative Determinism", which argues that certain key ecological requirements must be met by every cultural system. Failure to meet these basic requirements will lead to failure or change in the cultural system. The ecological requirements in question do not necessarily determine the specific characteristics of the cultural response (so much for that hoary old straw man, environmental determinism!), but they do limit the options open to people in any given habitat and they do mean that prolonged lack of cultural conformity to these requirements will not occur.

This test has its complexities. It is possible for more than one kind of cultural adaptation to operate successfully within a single area. The literature abounds with examples like the Pygmy hunters and Bantu-speaking farmers of the Congo Forest, and the Athabaskan-speaking hunter-gatherers and Pueblo cultivators of the American Southwest, whose widely differing adaptive responses within the same region are of long standing. Each culture was fully aware of the other in its area and interacted with it regularly, yet each retained its own basic mode of subsistence. Hunters and gatherers do not automatically become farmers simply because a) their country is suitable for farming, and b) they know about farming. The point is that each of these cultures occupied its own ecological niche within the area, and any attempt to reconstruct one of these cultures adequately must also recognize the specific characteristics of the niche it occupied. While a given habitat may contain several potential niches exploitable by alternative kinds of economic or social action, there is no reason to expect that all potential niches in a habitat will be occupied. This seems to have been especially the case in aboriginal California, where areas suitable for cultivation were not cultivated, despite cases where the basic knowledge of agriculture was available. Thus the Principle of Negative Determinism must always be applied relative to a particular ecological niche, which in turn requires that one be willing to make certain assumptions about the culture and especially its level of technology. But given these assumptions, this principle is workable and can be applied to cultural reconstructions as a test of their possible validity.

THE NORTHWESTERN CALIFORNIA ECOSYSTEM

TOPOGRAPHY AND CLIMATE

This is a region of rugged topography and heavy annual rainfall. The coastline alternates between stretches of sandy beach and rocky headlands, and offshore there are numerous rocks and islets. There is a narrow coastal plain composed of Pleistocene-and Pliocene-age deposits of sand, and a short distance inland one encounters low but steep hills which increase in height as they merge with the foothills of the Siskiyou Range about 20-25 miles inland, ultimately reaching heights up to 7000 feet. These hills are cut by the North, South, and Middle Forks of the Smith River and their tributaries, forming deep gorges in some places. Except for the coastal plain and a number of small flats along the bottoms of these gorges there is little level ground anywhere in this region.

Along the coast annual rainfall averages up to 100 inches, with annual averages of up to 120 inches recorded for some areas slightly inland like Gasquet Flat. This rainfall is augmented the year-round by frequent and heavy coastal fogs that completely cover the coastal plain and ocean-facing gorges. Rains are strictly seasonal, with about 80% of recorded falls occurring in the period from early October through late March each year. Despite this heavy annual rainfall, the area occupied by the Tolowa Indians was served by a river (the Smith River) of modest size when compared with the Klamath and Trinity Rivers nearby. Temperatures are mild but cool during most of the year, with strong and cold northwesterly winds prevailing along the coast during the summer months. Snow rarely occurs on the coastal plain or in the nearby gorges but is common during winter at elevations above 2000 feet.

VEGETATION

Much of the coastal plain is subject to the effects of wind-borne salt spray from the ocean and is thus treeless and covered only by assorted grasses and low shrubs. At various distances inland, beyond the reach of salt spray, there is a belt of low spruce and pine, and on the Smith River coastal plain there was a dense stand of redwood, now destroyed by logging. The redwood belt extends inland 8 to 12 miles, wherever the coastal fog can penetrate and wherever there is protection from the coastal winds. The redwood forest itself was an important basic resource for the Tolowa for houseplanks and canoes, and the forest also contained ferns used in making baskets and was frequented by game animals like deer and elk, but on the whole it was a poor area for food resources. Still further inland, where the hills attain heights of over 2000 feet, one finds large areas dominated by Douglas fir forests extending in some cases continuously from the tops of the hills to the edges of the river. On scattered flats along the east edge of the redwood belt and in the gorges in the Douglas fir area there are grassy, parklike openings containing small oak groves. Just inland, too, from the redwood belt there is an isolated but distinct area of chaparral vegetation covering mainly the steep hills along the drainage of the North Fork of the Smith River. This is a mixed chaparral containing various species of manzanita and madrone along with open stands of ponderosa pine, and it sometimes can be seen to merge with south-facing slopes containing tanbark oak and madrone on mountains which are otherwise densely covered with Douglas fir.

Mention should also be made of the vegetation associated with the marine and riverine components of the ecosystem. Along the lower course of the Smith River, where it emerges onto the coastal plain, and also along the margins of Lake Earl, Lake Talawa, and Dead Lake one finds swales containing tule and camas lilies. Camas, though not abundant in this area, was eaten by the Indians, and tule rushes were used for fashioning mats. These marshy areas also sheltered various ducks and geese, though these, too, were of secondary importance compared to other food resources in the area. Along the coast, especially in various rocky inlets, large amounts of seaweed accumulate. The Tolowa collected this seaweed, dried it, and ate it as a condiment. It also served as moisture-absorbent packing material in storage baskets, especially when storing food.

TOLOWA RESOURCE PROCUREMENT SYSTEMS

As the foregoing description should suggest, the Tolowa

Indians lived in a relatively small area (about 650-700 square miles altogether) composed of rugged terrain and complex microhabitats of varying richness in terms human food potential. Despite the fact that logging, mining, and other historic activities have done much to alter some of these microhabitats, this region has a remarkably detailed literature covering indigenous food resources and their ecological associations. Sources like Smith (1929), Rostlund (1952), Greengo (1952), Hewes (1942), Kroeber and Barrett (1960), Schaeffer (1958), Hedgepeth (1962), Wolf (1945), and Baumhoff (1963) provide useful accounts of different basic resources, and Lewis (1973) has recently offered data bearing on possible modifications to the ecosystem by the Indians through their use of fire.

From all of this detail it is possible to develop a picture of the ecological requirements for successful hunter-gatherer adaptations in this area. In order to clarify these relationships, I shall use a modified version of Flannery's "Procurement Systems" (1968) approach in my analysis. That is, I shall examine the universe of edible resources in this region from the point of view of how human beings must organize their movements, technology, and social groups in order to collect them effectively. Various classes of resources may be grouped according to their commonalities with regard to how they are obtained by a human population. These commonalities will provide a basis for observing the nature of interactions between aspects of human behavior and particular ecological variables, leading finally to a view of the total cultural system operating aboriginally in this area.

To start off, I shall distinguish between Major or Staple Food Procurement Systems and Minor or Supplemental Food Procurement Systems. A staple I define here as any food that constitutes at least 30% of the total diet by weight at the time it is collected. Ideally such staple foods should be identified through direct observation and weighing at the time of collection, but, as this is plainly impossible with California Indians, we must be content with estimates based on data available on the various resources together with existing reconstructions of the traditional subsistence economy. The Major or Staple Food Procurement Systems identified here are so overwhelming in their natural abundance (as measured by recent studies) and were so emphatically stated by informants and historic sources to be of importance that I feel reasonably well assured in designating them as staples, even without first-hand quantified observations. Supplemental foods never attained the quantitative importance of staples, but one should not overlook their possible importance with respect to varying the diet and at times perhaps even providing much needed nutritional elements.

MAJOR PROCUREMENT SYSTEMS

Procurement System No. 1 — Large Sea Mammals

One species dominated this procurement system, the Steller sea lion, *Eumetopias jubata*, primarily because the larger islets off this particular part of the Pacific coast are among the largest summer rookeries for this gregarious species. Steller bulls can weight as much as 2000 lb., although the females are smaller. The smaller California sea lion, *Zalophus californianus*, also occurs on this coast during the summer and was hunted, but this species does not breed there and was less common than the Steller. Other pinnipeds that were hunted include sea otter, *Enhydra lutris;* Northern fur seal, *Callorhinus ursinus;* and harbor seal, *Phoca vitulina*. Whales were not actively hunted but were consumed whenever found stranded on the beaches.

Sea mammal hunting required perhaps the most complex technology and highest level of group organization of any activity in Tolowa culture. Sea lions were hunted from large redwood dugout canoes up to around 40 feet in length (Powers, 1877: 69; Gould, 1968). These canoes could be handled in the unprotected seas off the northwest California coast and were used for hunting on the rookeries that were farthest out to sea — Northwest and Southwest Seal Rocks, approximately 6½ miles offshore. The preferred method for killing sea lions was to land on the rookeries and club the animals to death, although animals in the water were often harpooned. The Tolowa and their coastal neighbors used sophisticated composite harpoons for this task as well as for hunting other swimming sea mammals. Late each summer there was a first sea lion hunt, akin to the pattern of the first salmon ceremony and other "first fruits" ceremonies seen elsewhere on the north Pacific coast (Gunther, 1926), involving ritual prohibitions and restrictions on individual hunting until the "season" was offically opened. Each of the Tolowa coastal villages had one of the large canoes, and sea lion hunts in these canoes were carried out under the leadership of a single individual (Hewes, in Kroeber and Barrett, 1960: 118; Gould, 1968: 27). The annual first sea lion hunt represented an even higher degree of unification, in that all of the participating canoes from the different villages travelled together to the rookeries before the actual hunt commenced (Gould, 1968; 26-28). Once the killing of the animals began, however, the men in each canoe hunted on their own, and each boat independently brought its catch back to its own village. No doubt many sea lions were taken by individual hunters or small groups of men on the rookeries that lay close inshore. For this all that was needed was the small (about 15 feet-long) river dugout canoe together with clubs and harpoons. But serious offshore sea lion hunting required a level of technology and group interaction well in excess of most Tolowa activities.

Sea lions were valued for their meat and oil, and the amounts of both after a successful hunt were prodigious. A single large canoe could be counted on to bring in at least 1200 lbs. of edible sea lion meat after a single offshore hunt. This figure is based upon statements by informants that a single large canoe could handle one Steller bull or up to four Steller females at one time. Figures given by White (1953: 398) indicate that Steller bulls average 1600 lbs. live weight, with about 70% of this, or 1300 lbs. consisting of edible meat. Steller females average 450 lbs. live weight, of which 70%, or 315 lbs., is edible meat. The animals are reliable in their regular appearance in large numbers at the rookeries every year, making this an exceptional resource, and the Tolowa had access to more extensive rookeries than their coastal neighbors; although the coast Yurok, too, were known for their effectiveness at sea lion hunting, especially at Redding Rock (Kroeber and Barrett, 1960: 117).

Procurement System No. 2 — Marine Shellfish

The principal bivalve collected by the Tolowa was the sea mussel, *Mytilus californianus*. This species is abundantly available along rocky shores at the mid-tide zone where there is strong surf action to sweep in nutrients. This species was favored for its abundance, the relatively large size and amount of edible muscle and other tissue of the individual bivalves, and its generally good flavor (Greengo, 1952: 65). Mussels are available in large numbers the year round, but during the late summer months they may ingest the marine dinoflagellate, *Gonyaulax catenella*, which, while it does no harm to the mussels, can cause severe and even fatal poisoning to people who eat infected shellfish. The Tolowa were aware of the risk of mussel poisoning, but informant testimony indicates that people sometimes became ill and died from eating poisoned mussels despite a general awareness of these dangers.

Nutritional tables cited by Greengo (1952: 83) provide a rough but useful estimate of food value for sea mussels based on figures derived from the closely related *Mytilus edulis* of the east coast of North America. According to these figures, 100 grams of cooked mussel meat can provide 18.2 grams of protein, or about one-half the adult daily requirement. So the daily protein needs of an active adult man could be met by eating only 50 sea mussels, and, in addition, mussels are rich in vitamins B_1, B_2, and C. Cooking was generally done by placing the mussels directly in the fire and allowing them to cook in the shell, although mussels and other shellfish were often sun- or fire-dried too.

Sea mussels were collected on an individual basis, usually by women. Collection was easy and rapid and was limited only by unusually heavy surf. Fifty mussels, the amount posited for an adult person's daily protein needs, could have been collected by a single woman in about ½ hour under optimal conditions, with the only strenuous work being the business of carrying large burden-baskets full of shellfish back to the village. Many other species of shellfish were collected, too, including the common littleneck, *Protothaca staminea*; rock scallop, *Hinnites multrugosa*; northern razor clam, *Siliqua patula*; Washington clam, *Saxidomus sp.*; giant chiton, *Cryptochiton stelleri;* short-spine sea urchin, *Strongilo sintrodus;* and various large barnacles. Like mussels, these could all be collected efficently by individuals, although many of the clams are found on the sandy beaches and required more effort to locate and transport than did mussels and other shellfish that tend to be concentrated on the rocky parts of the shoreline.

Procurement System No. 3 — Acorns

Although relatively poor in acorn-bearing oak trees compared to other parts of California, northwestern California contains three species of oak that bear well and provided a staple food for the aboriginal Tolowa. These three species are: valley oak, *Quercus lobata*; canyon oak, *Q. chrysolepus*; and tanbark oak, *Lithocarpus densiflora*, and it is the last-named species that is most abundant in the part of northwestern California inhabited by the Tolowa. These trees occur in groves mainly on small, grass covered flats in places alongside the Smith River and its branches and in some small clearings along the east side of the redwood belt, and they occur dispersed as well along the slopes of various canyons. These dispersed trees were little used by the Tolowa, since they occur on slopes too steep for easy movement or collection, but groves situation on the flats were heavily exploited. Farther inland one finds large oak groves covering portions of the open, grassy bald areas on the tops of many hills and low mountains, but these areas lay beyond the normal foraging range of the Tolowa and were exploited by other groups. Few of the best oak groves from former times remain intact today, owing to commercial stripping of bark from the tanbark oak and because of roadbuilding and residential development on these precious parcels of level land.

The oaks drop their acorns in late fall, and one must collect them fairly fast, since leaving acorns on the ground for long renders them susceptible to infestation by weevils. Tanbark oak acorns are thick-shelled, however, and thus less susceptible to spoilage after falling than other species (Wolf, 1945: 51). Acorn-collecting was a group activity, though not in the more formal or organized manner of ocean hunting of sealions. Families would congregate at the oak groves and harvest the acorns, but the actual collection and later transport and processing of the acorns into edible form was performed on an individual or family basis. Families had to leave the coast at this time, although the distances they travelled were not great. The oak grove farthest inland that was regularly used by the Tolowa occurred near the present location of Gasquet Flat, about 15 miles from the sea. Women with burden-baskets full of acorns would move constantly back and forth between the oak groves and their home villages on the coast during this period, and they processed and stored the acorns in these coastal villages. Before leaving an oak grove after the annual acorn collection, families set fire to the grass over the entire flat. Tolowa informants claim that this was done to reduce underbrush and keep the grass from growing too high so that it would be easy to see and pick up the fallen acorns during the next year's harvest, a practice similar to that reported for the Kacha Pomo of Redwood Valley (Kniffen,

1939: 378).

As is well known throughout the literature on California Indians, acorns require processing before being rendered edible. The Tolowa, like other California groups, pounded and leached the acorn meat until it was free of tannic acid. To accomplish this they used ground stone pestles and large flat rocks as mortar-bases with basketry hoppers to contain the acorn meat as it was being pounded. This technology, while elaborate, was easily operated within the context of the Tolowa family group (i.e. a man's wives and children). At this point it may be useful to distinguist a technology of this nature, which I term *appliances*, from those involving a wider social context, which can be called *facilities*, (not to be confused with an earlier and quite different definition by Binford, 1968: 272). Here I define an appliance as any artifact that must be left more or less permanently at the place where it is used and which is used by a mimimal social group performing the task in question. A facility, by contrast, is an artifact that is built, used, and in some cases, maintained, by a task group larger than the minimal social group. The Tolowa ocean-going canoe and its accoutrements may be regarded as a type of facility, in the same way as, for example, the Kepel fish weir of the Yurok (Waterman and Kroeber, 1938). In the context of this paper, the concepts of appliances and facility refer specifically to food-collecting and food-processing implements, although these definitions need not be restricted to subsistence in other contexts. Tolowa acorn pestles and mortar-bases were appliances in the strictest sense of the definitions offered here.

Estimates by Wolf (1945: 51, 63) indicate that, when dried, 100 lb. of whole *Lithocarpus densiflora* acorns will yield 69 lb. of food material; 2.93% protein, 12.08% fat, 20.14% fibre, and 54.43% carbohydrates, with the remaining 10.42% consisting of water, and ash. In terms of total nutrients, tanbark oak acorns are less impressive than other species of oak, owing mainly to the unusually high percentage of fibre contained in the thick shell, but they are still to be regarded as significant in an area where so much of the rest of the diet was rich in fats and proteins and, at the same time, somewhat short in carbohydrates. California acorns as a whole are high in calories, estimated at 2,265 calories per pound (Baumhoff, 1963: 163).

Wolf (1945: 31-33, 51) estimates that the production of acorns by tanbark oak trees was about equivalent to that of the Kellogg oak (*Q. kelloggii*), a tree whose productivity is slightly less than the 20 acorns per square foot of collecting ground per season or 160 lb. per tree each season noted for the blue or Douglas oak (*Q. douglasii*). In two surviving groves of tanbark oak, one at Pappas Flat on the Middle Fork of the Smith River and the other near Big Flat, on the South Fork of the Smith River, I counted mature oak trees in excess of 200 at each grove, while at a smaller flat near Indian Bar on the South Fork of the Smith River I noted approximately 70 mature trees. These observations, made in 1972, must be viewed as minimum estimates, since all three of these areas were at least partially logged in historic times. Still, if we take a conservative estimate of 125 lb. of acorns per tree (slightly below the productivity of Douglas and Kellogg oak) and apply it to these three remnant groves, (minimum number, 470 trees) we arrive at a figure of 58,750 lb. or 29.4 tons of acorn per season, of which about 28,788 lb. or 14.4 tons would have consisted of usable food materials when dried. Incomplete through they are, these estimates should indicate the enormous magnitude of the Tolowa acorn harvest under good conditions, especially since informants have pointed out the locations of five additional flats that formerly contained much larger oak groves than the few that I observed in 1972.

Procurement System No. 4 — Anadromus Fish
Baumhoff (1963: 180) correctly indicates the river fisheries resources of the Tolowa as ''secondary'' in comparison to the much larger fisheries along the Klamath River, but he also notes that the Smith River is frequented by all of the major anadromus species of fish in this region, including salmon that run both in fall and spring. Of overwhelming importance in this regard were King salmon (*Oncorhynchus tschawytscha*) and Coho salmon (*O. kisutch*). These fish often ran in large numbers on the Smith River and were taken by the Tolowa with spears, net-traps, and various kinds of weirs (Kroeber and Barrett, 1960). Most of these devices were built and used by small groups of closely related individuals, mainly individual families, but Drucker describes a communal fish weir at a spot called munsontun about 5 miles upstream from the mouth of the Smith River:

''Communal weir . . . built at summer low water on riffle

at munsontun and/or militcuntun (latter site probably older). Owner gathered, prepared materials; called kin and friends to put in. Anyone who helped given fish. V-shaped row of alder stakes, supported by slanting braces on downstream side, supported panels of hazel wickerwork. Point of V was downstream. 2. center stakes driven first, to accompanienment of formula; if easily set, weir was successful. Basketry "trap" a rectangular wicker mat doubled, end and part of side sewn together to make wide-mouthed closed cylinder, placed in apex of weir. Men went upstream, heated rocks in fire, with formulas, from canoes threw rocks in deep holes, shouted, splashed, to drive fish into weir . . . Weir left to be swept away by high water." (Drucker, 1937: 232).

While this device did not compare in magnitude with either the Tolowa ocean-going canoes for sea lion hunting or the Kepel fish weir of the Yurok, it can certainly be rated as a facility according to the definitions provided earlier. Present informants are uncertain in their recollections of this device, and the social organization surrounding its construction and use remains vague.

Salmon meat is rich in calories, averaging around 1000 calories per pound (Rostlund, 1952: 4). Like other freshwater fish, salmon are rich in a wide array of vitamins (A, D, B_1, B_2, and even some C in the roe), protein (about 15-20% in edible portions), and fat (although this last-mentioned nutritional component is highly variable according to season, feeding grounds, and other factors) but are generally lacking in carbohydrates. Rostlund (1952: 5-6) concludes: "The table of calories shows that the high-calorie fishes are the very ones that characterize first-class fishing regions such as the Atlantic and Pacific anadromus areas . . .", and the Smith River, despite its small size, lay in the heart of one such first-class fishing region.

Other anadromus fish besides salmon were taken. Steelhead (*Salmo gairdnerii*), candlefish (*Thaleichthys pacificus*), and Western sea lamprey (*Entosphenus tridentaus*) were caught regularly, though never in quantities approaching those of salmon. Hewes (in Kroeber and Barrett, 1960: 25-26) described an unusual technique for catching lamprey employed by the Tolowa using a gaffing chute in shallow water with a white pebble floor. This was a night-fishing technique, and informants have shown me the place where it was used, on a shallow riffles at the confluence of the Middle and South Forks of the Smith River (where these white pebbles occur naturally). This technique, like most other fishing methods of the Tolowa, required the efforts of only a few individuals and could be carried out by members of a single family. With the possible exception of the salmon weir at munsontun, Tolowa riverine fishing did not require the need for large groups of families to reside together at special camps near the place where the fish were taken.

Procurement System No. 5 — Waterfowl

Various species of ducks, geese, rails, and murres were caught by the Tolowa, but cormorants (*Phalacrocorax sp.*) were of by far the greatest importance in the total diet. Cormorants were captured at their nests on the series of rocks and sea stacks not far offshore from Point St. George, Pyramid Point, Battery Point, and several other localities, during a brief period in mid-summer when the nestlings are unable to fly and could be taken easily (Howard, 1929: 378-383; Gould, 1966a: 84-85). No dietary figures are available for cormorants, but there is no doubt that this was a staple food during the time it was collected. The Indians went out to the cormorant nesting areas in small river canoes, either individually or in family groups, and used clubs to take the immature birds. Aside from the element of timing, no special techniques or organization were required to make efficient use of this resource.

Procurement System No. 6 — Surf Fish

Abundant runs of smelt (*Spirinchus starksi* and *Allosmerus attenuatus*) appear on the beaches of northwestern California in late summer, although the size of these runs is known to vary considerably from year to year. The fish were easily taken by individuals using the traditional V-shaped dip net in the surf, and efficient technique that has been widely adopted and used by whites living in the area today. There is nothing about the use of these nets that requires any organized effort above the level of the individual fisherman, but the catch can be so massive that transporting it may be difficult. Observations made in 1965 and again in 1972, both years when the smelt runs were large, indicated

that a single man can net as much as 200 lb. of fish in less than
½-hour, although, of course, some time must be spent beforehand
in locating the best runs along the beach. Many Tolowa and other
Indians in the area today continue to live along the beaches during
August and early September in order to catch smelt, which are still
much sought after. Today the Indians use small trucks or 4-wheel
drive vehicles to transport the heavy tubs of fish to the camp, but in
former times this was done by women using burden baskets. Fish
that are not eaten fresh are spread out on driftwood logs to dry in
the sun while women and children living at the camp shoo away
seagulls. Final drying is done on the sand, and the fish are covered
at night to keep off the fog. This part of the operation takes several
days, depending upon the amount of sun, and involves constant
attention but little laborious effort. Thus to exploit smelt efficiently
in aboriginal times, as today, it is necessary to have people camped
in reasonably large numbers nearby, although no organized group
effort is needed to collect or process the fish.

Sea perch, particularly the redtail surfperch (*Holconotus
rhodoterus*), were cuaught aboriginally off the beaches by
individual fishermen, and this practice continues today among both
Indians and whites, especially in the summer. Sometimes the total
catch of fish may be large — the largest I have seen weighed 75 lb.
and was taken in about 4 hours by one fisherman — but this was
and still is a secondary activity compared to smelting.

MINOR POCUREMENT SYSTEMS

Various land mammals, edible berries and plants, and ocean
fish were frequently obtained by the Tolowa, although none in
amounts that could approach those of the items designated here as
staples. Deer and elk were hunted in the interior, and Lewis
(1973: 49-56) has pointed to the possible importance of burning by
Indians of this region as a means of enhancing the game resource.
However, deer and elk are solitary game and cannot be hunted *en
masse*. Stalking and pit-snares were used by individual Tolowa
hunters to good effect, but total amounts of meat taken in this way
cannot have been great compared to even the least productive of
the staple food procurement systems.

Ocean fishing, like the hunting of land mammals, was often
done by individuals and may also have been a pastime during

organized sea lion hunts, but the total catch was probably not overwhelming. Various sharks, hake, halibut, rockfishes, lingcod, sculpins, and other kinds of fish were caught, some from boats when the sea was calm and some directly from the rocky parts of the shoreline. Finally, the edible bulbs of camas lilies, salal berries, salmon berries, huckleberries, and other edible plants were collected by women during the summer months, to supplement and add flavor to the overall diet.

In terms of both staple and supplemental resource procurement, the Tolowa seem to have collected just about every kind of edible food that was available to them — with a few exceptions. Informants were emphatic about not eating bear, raccoon, skunk or porcupine owing to a taboo based on the idea that the forelimbs of these animals looked like human hands and that thus there was something vaguely cannibalistic about eating them. Drucker's observations (1937: 232) indicate similar restrictions, although his list of tabooed foods is longer and included, in addition, dog, coyote, cougar, sea gulls, and all birds of prey, along with oddments like land bird eggs, snakes, frogs, dove and octopus. None of these species had the potential of being a staple food resource. However it is interesting to note that faunal remains recovered from the proto-historic Tolowa levels excavated at the Point St. George Site included black bear, raccoon, coyote, and probably sea gulls as well (Gould, 1966a: 81-84). This evidence suggests that perhaps these food restrictions were limited in some way and that at least some of these supposedly tabooed species were consumed by the aboriginal inhabitants of this region.

TOLOWA SUBSISTENCE STRATEGY

SEASONALITY

The seasonal occurrences of the major staple foods are summarized in Fig. 1. In consulting this Figure, one must remember that the exact periods of availability always varied somewhat from year to year, though not greatly. Marine shellfish were available all year, but the poisonous period, especially for mussels, would, in some years, have eliminated this resource during the period indicated. The wavy line for anadromus fish is intended to show that some salmon were available the year round at sea and particularly at the mouth and lower reaches of the Smith River. The fall and spring salmon runs are indicated in the Figure as solid blocks, but data about the time of the steelhead run was uncertain, so it has not been shown. Western sea lamprey ran up the Smith River in July and August but are not shown either, since their numbers did not approach those of the salmon. Only cormorants are indicated under Waterfowl, and only smelt are shown under Surf Fish, since these were the principal species taken in each case.

In terms of timing, Fig. 1 shows that staple foods of one kind or another were available to the Tolowa continuously throughout the year. Peak periods for harvesting occurred during mid-June to mid-September (sea lions, cormorants, and smelt) and early September to early November (acorns, salmon), with the latter peak representing the only period during the year when interior resources predominated over coastal ones. Note, too, that for over six months of the year more than one staple was available in harvestable quantities. In some cases this was true for natural species that occur close together, like acorns and salmon (i.e. oak flats invariably lay close to salmon-bearing streams), but there were occasions during some years when scheduling of resource collection became a problem. This was especially true in late August - early September when a particularly fine smelt run might continue into the beginning of the acorn harvest. These two resources occur far enough apart geographically for it to be impossible for both to be harvested simultaneously. But scheduling problems of this kind were the exception rather than the rule, which for at least half the year was *simultaneous harvesting whenever possible.*

STORAGE AND SCARCITY

The "lean" period of the year tended, as was true in most of California, to be early Spring, as Baumhoff (1963: 161) notes, before the start of the Spring salmon run. However, "lean" in this case does not mean famine. Informants have always agreed that there was never any famine in this area, although we know that: 1) for 4-5 months of the year only a single staple, shellfish, was

Figure 1

MAJOR (STAPLE) TOLOWA INDIAN
PROCUREMENT SYSTEMS

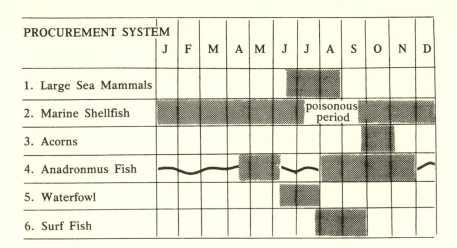

PROCUREMENT SYSTEM	J	F	M	A	M	J	J	A	S	O	N	D
1. Large Sea Mammals							▓	▓				
2. Marine Shellfish	▓	▓	▓	▓	▓		poisonous period		▓	▓	▓	▓
3. Acorns									▓			
4. Anadronmus Fish	~	~	~	▓	▓	~	~	▓	▓	▓	▓	~
5. Waterfowl						▓	▓					
6. Surf Fish								▓	▓			

1. Large Sea Mammals (mainly Steller Sea Lion, *Eumetopias jubata*; also some whales; sea otter, *Enhydra lutris*; California sea lion, *Zalophus californianus*; Northern fur seal, *Callorhinus ursinus*; and harbor seal, *Phoca vitulina*).

2. Marine Shellfish (mainly California sea mussel, *Mytilus californianus*; also common littleneck, *Protothaca staminea*; northern razor clam, *Siliqua patula*; rock scallop, *Hinnites multrugosa*; Washington clam, *Saxidomus sp.*; giant chiton, Cryptochiton stelleri; short-spine sea urchin, *Strongilo sintrodus*; etc.).

3. Acorns (mainly tanbark oak, *Lithocarpus densiflora*; also valley oak, *Quercus lobata*; canyon oak, *Quercus chrysolepus*).

4. Anadromus Fish (mainly King salmon, *Oncorhynchus tschawytscha*, and Coho salmon, *O. kisutch*; also steelhead, *Salmo gairdnerii*; western sea lamprey, *Entosphenus tridentatus*; candlefish, *Thaleichthys pacificus*).

5. Waterfowl (mainly cormorant, *Phalacrocorax sp.*; also various ducks, geese, rails, and murres).

6. Surf Fish (mainly smelt, *Spirinchus starksi* and *Allosmerus attenuatus*; also redtail surfperch, *Holconotus rhodoterus*).

available in significant quantities, and 2) amounts of particular staples might vary greatly from one year to the next, something that was especially true of acorns, salmon, and smelt. The diversity of resources plus their general abundance ensured that a natural crop failure of a staple like, for example, acorns, would not undermine the economy to the extent of becoming a limiting factor. Shortages of a particular food resource may have led to temporary nutritional imbalances, but the caloric needs of the population were easily met at all times. One important way of overcoming shortages is storage, and the Tolowa possessed a well developed technology for preparing and storing food. Shellfish, fish, and sea lion meat were all sun dried and/or smoked in large quantities in addition to being eaten fresh. Dried meat and fish were kept in large storage baskets within the dwelling houses on the coast, as were acorns. Periodically, in sunny weather, acorns were taken out of their baskets by the women and laid on mats to dry, thus preventing or at least retarding damage from fungus and insects. Informants agreed that the amounts of food thus stored were prodigious, filling many large baskets that stood atop the parapet that lined the housepit in each dwelling house.

Under these conditions, shortages, when they occurred, took place only in context of individual families rather than throughout the society at large. That is, there could be shortages of food without famine. Such shortages were not commonplace but occurred often enough for informants to recall them (see especially Gould, 1966b: 77-78, for examples). According to the informants, these shortages resulted more from improvidence by the families concerned that they did from any actual shortage in the environment. Each family harvested most of its own staple foods and prepared these for storage by its own efforts. Only the hunting of large sea mammals (Procurement System No. 1) and the possible use of the munsontun fish weir for catching salmon (Procurement System No. 4) required families, or at least the adult males in these families, to unite their efforts, however temporarily, in food-getting activities. Similarly, there was no sharing of food between families following a natural harvest except in the case of sea lions and stranded whales, both of which are creatures too large for any one family to handle effectively or to consume on its own. This view of Tolowa subsistence agrees with the earlier observation that:

"By subsistence economy is meant the exploitation of the
plentiful natural resources available to any industrious
individual. Although there were privately owned fishing
sites, ordinarily these were used freely by any person
within the village group . . . Individuals who had been lazy
or inefficient in gathering food . . . were forced to buy it
(i.e. with prestige goods like dentalia shell beads,
red-headed woodpecker scalps, and obsidian blades)'' (Du
Bois, 1936: 50),

although it is apparently contradicted by the further observation by
Du Bois that:

". . . they (the Tolowa and Tututni) are not accustomed to
translate the value of dried salmon or a basket into
dentalia and then make exchanges whose dentalia
equivalents are of equal value. In the realm of subsistence
economy the Tolowa-Tututni were on a barter basis
without translation into another medium'' (Du Bois,
1936: 50).

Perhaps the best way to reconcile these apparently contradictory
statements is to point out that there really was no "subsistence
economy" among the Tolowa above the level of the individual
family — that is a man, his wives, children, and close adherents.
Except for the general division of shares of sea lion and whale meat
there were no sharing or barter-based exchanges of food, although
sometimes improvident families or individuals experienced
shortages and were forced to "buy" food with their prestige goods.

SEASONAL MOVEMENT AND RESOURCE TENURE

Only Procurement System No. 3, Acorns, required any
wholesale movement of people away from the coast, and this was
only for a few weeks during late fall. As mentioned earlier,
productive oak flats were situated only a short distance from the
coast, generally between 5 and 15 miles inland, so traveling
distances were never great even between the most widely
separated staple resources. In consequence, the Tolowa followed a
seasonally regular but narrowly circumscribed pattern of movement
between harvesting areas. In late summer, usually August, families

moved from the large coastal villages onto the beaches to camp for several weeks while the smelt were running. Then they moved inland to various oak flats where they could collect acorns and, at the same time, fish during the fall salmon run. At the end of the acorn harvest these families would make their way individually back to the coastal villages where they remained for the remaining 9-10 months of the year.

These seasonal movements were not organized, wholesale movements of village populations. A wealthy headman generally took the initiative in such a move, but it was up to each family to move on its own. Moreover, families did not move to the beaches or the oak flats as village entities. Villages broke up in late summer and were reconstituted in the late fall upon return from the oak flats. Finally, movements away from the villages did not mean total abandonment of the villages, since women constantly traveled back and forth between the collecting areas and the villages carrying basketloads of fish and acorns to place in storage.

The seasonal pattern of village unity and dispersal is reflected in traditional concepts of land and resource tenure. Tracts of shoreline were claimed by particular villages. These tracts were well defined, and the boundaries between them were defended, especially in cases where whales became stranded on the beaches. With one exception, every Tolowa village claimed tracts of shoreline that included both rocky headlands and sandy beach, thus ensuring that each village had access to the staple resources available in each of these microenvironments. The single exception was the village of ʔectsuuled, situated on a neck of land between Lake Earl and Lake Talawa, only a short distance from the ocean. In this case the lakes themselves may have furnished resources in a localized concentration sufficient to offset this village's lack of a rocky foreshore, but the argument remains speculative and is not intended to explain away this exception to the general pattern. Individuals and individual families, however, claimed ownership of particular oak groves or even specific trees as well as fishing and eeling places along the streams, and it was to these places that they moved in the late fall. There was no clear correlation between villages and interior collecting areas, and there were no bounded and defended village tracts in the interior. Individuals or families wishing to use interior resources not their own had to seek permission from the owners, and, although informants say this permission was granted, they also stressed that it was not granted automatically. Unfortunately our knowledge of the rules governing such permission remains vague, although there were disputes (and subsequent indemnities) arising from ambiguities of ownership or failure to obtain permission.

POPULATION AND SETTLEMENT PATTERN

Estimates of the pre-White contact population of the Tolowa vary widely, ranging from an extreme low by Cook (1943: 4) of 450 individuals to extreme highs by Cook (1956: 101) and Baumhoff (1963: 231) of 2,400 individuals. Kroeber (1925: 883) estimated the pre-contact Tolowa population at 1000. By 1910 a U.S. Government census of northwestern California and southwestern Oregon revealed that only 383 Tututni and 121 Tolowa Indians remained in this region (Curtis, 1907-1930: 96), and it has never been possible in post-contact times to make accurate estimates of the aboriginal population of this area by means of direct enumeration. The estimate of 450 individuals at the time of contact is certainly too low, and considering the extent of proto-historic and historic village sites in the area, the estimate of 1000 also seems too low. In terms of the somewhat subjective grounds of abundant natural resources of this region and wide extent of archaeological and historic remains, the highest estimates appear to be the best offered so far. If one accepts such high aboriginal estimates one must also accept the idea that epidemic diseases like measles and cholera introduced by White contact had a devastating impact on these populations, leading in a few years to populations reduced to a few hundred. Although it cannot be quantified in any way, informant testimony strongly supports this idea of a population catastrophe due to introduced diseases.

Baumhoff (1963: 188) has suggested that the aboriginal population of the Yurok and other Klamath River groups was well below the potential carrying capacity of this region, at least with repermanent structures, despite the fact that most villagers left the coast for about two months each year. These villages occupied a coastal strip that represented only a small fraction of the total area used by the Tolowa — perhaps 35 square miles out of a total of 700. Thus if one computes an average population density of 3.43 people per square mile, one must also remember that for about 9-10 months every year the actual population density was probably more like 68.6 people per square mile, thanks mainly to the richness of marine resources to which this narrow coastal strip provided access. Except for occasional forays by individuals or families to hunt and fish, and the fall acorn and salmon harvest, most of the Tolowa hinterland remained unused and unoccupied most of the time.

THE NATURE OF TOLOWA SUBSISTENCE

The Tolowa and their coastal neighbors present an example of a "resource optimizing" subsistence system. It was a system that aimed at deriving the highest possible level of harvesting productivity without consideration of potential risk. The particular seasonal patterns of movement and residence adopted by the Tolowa, together with occasional efforts to unite above the level of the individual family in the pursuit of particular resources (sea lions and salmon) were all part of a subsistence strategy, whether conscious or unconscious, that sought to collect all harvestable resources at their time and place of maximum availability, and to a very large extent it was successful. There was little occasion for the Tolowa to be concerned with the problem of scheduling, that is, they rarely had to choose among harvesting two or more resources that appeared simultaneously in widely separated niches. Yet, at the same time, their basic staples were varied, and reliable, and furnished a reasonable balanced diet. Few other examples in the literature on hunter-gatherers offer such a picture of total affluence in subsistence with, at the same time, a minimum risk. No shortages in any single resource or resource procurement system can be pointed to as a limiting factor in either the short or long run of Tolowa economic life.

Under such optimal conditions one might expect that the aboriginal population was expanding, and indeed it may have been. Archaeological evidence in the form of increases in the number and size of sites, suggests that the Indian cultures of this coastal region experienced a phenomenal growth in population during the last 2000 years. Human settlement at the Gunther Island site (Hum-67) on Humboldt Bay was well established by 1050 years ago (Heizer, 1964: 132) and a radiocarbon date of 310 B.C. predates the period

of intensive, proto-historic Tolowa settlement at DNo-11, the Point
St. George Site (Gould, 1972). These two dates suggest that this
major expansion of population began sometime between 1000 and
2000 years ago. Additional radio-carbon dates from the Tsurai Site
(Hum-169) at Trinidad Bay, Patrick's Point (Hum-118) and two sites
further north along the Oregon coast (Ti-1 and Cs-23) range
between 500 and 150 years ago and serve to document the further
growth and spread of human population along the northwest
California — southwest Oregon coast during the last 1000 years.
There is no way of knowing at this time how much of this growth
was due to natural increase and how much was due to migration,
but there is a good possibility that the trajectory of this growth was
continuing up to the initial historic period. However, we lack vital
statistics, so any attempt to model population growth against
resources in this area would be purely speculative. One thing seems
clear, however, and it is that whether or not the population was still
expanding at the time of White contact, it had not yet reached a
critical level that placed strain upon the economy.

The foregoing discussion of Tolowa subsistence is intended as
a corrective to the tendency in the literature for anthropologists
(and here I include myself) to focus their past attentions upon the
more conspicious elements of northwestern California Indian social
behavior — especially wealth-questing. But, more importantly, it is
also intended as a basis for a reanalysis of these social activities. To
what extent should wealth-questing and concomitant social
activities among the Tolowa be regarded as adaptive behavior in
the context of the total northwestern California coastal ecosystem?

WEALTH-QUESTING AS AN AGGRANDIZIVE MECHANISM

Because of the balanced, abundant, and varied nature of their
wild staple resources, the Tolowa did not experience famine. As
mentioned earlier, shortages of food did occur, but were felt only at
the level of the individual and his immediate family. Since each
family was able, largely through its own unaided efforts, to collect,
prepare, and store its own staple and supplemental food resources,
there was no compelling need for sharing networks between
families. Before we can begin to explain the presence of an
aggrandizive system of resource procurement and use, we must
first understand why a sharing system was not necessary. In the

case of the Tolowa, it was not simply that they lived in an environment rich in natural resources but that their natural resources became available at times and places where they could be harvested economically by individuals and individual families. Aside from sea lions and some salmon, no other food procurement systems required a cooperative effort above the level of the individual family to harvest, prepare, or store staple foods. Indeed, one could argue that individual families, because of their greater flexibility, were more responsive to fluctuations in the availability of certain resources and could move quickly and easily to take advantage of them. Large cooperative groups would, in all probability, have been unwieldy and without advantage. The basis for economic success in the sphere of subsistence among the Tolowa rested almost entirely upon the efforts of individuals and individual families, and these efforts were as well or better rewarded than would have been the efforts of larger, cooperative foraging and hunting groups. The partial adoption of this latter operation in the case of ocean sea lion hunting and perhaps some salmon fishing shows that the Tolowa were ready to use cooperative techniques when it was obviously to their advantage, but that otherwise such techniques were avoided.

On the other hand, personal and family aggrandizement of food resources by means of efficient collection, preparation, and storage worked well and adequately met the needs of all but the most improvident or unlucky. Women were the primary producers in Tolowa society. Although men performed physically intense activities like sea lion and land mammal hunting and carried out most of the tasks related to salmon fishing (especially the constructions of weirs), canoe building, and house construction, it was the women who collected the bulk of the acorn harvest and who did most of the shellfish collecting. Women collected drift timber off the beaches for firewood. While men actually netted smelt in the surf, it was the women who carried the catch back to camp and took charge of drying the smelt for storage. Similarly, women prepared acorns and all other foods for storage and consumption. Thus the amount of food a family could accumulate and store was directly dependent upon the number of women in the household. A man with several hardworking wives and daughters could store up large reserves and not only could he use these as security against possible scarcities, but he could also commission "feasts" when he wished to recruit people to construct a large canoe or house. In a sense this was a form of redistribution of food, but this redistribution did not extend to people who were in need of food due to shortages. Instead, all food was distributed with the clear expectation of immediate repayment, either in labor (as with canoe-building) or in prestige goods (as when a improvident family ran short of food). In those rare cases when a family short of food could not pay for it, it was given grudgingly as a form of charity;

> "If they (people short of food) were too poor to pay for it, they were given food by others but they were looked down upon. 'Anybody could do what he liked with them." (Du Bois, 1936: 50).

Thus a man with several industrious wives and daughters could, in time, expect his household to accumulate larger reserves of food than families with fewer active women.

Women were "working capital" in the fullest sense. As stressed elsewhere (Gould, 1966b), women were a source of bridewealth that consisted of specific prestige goods — redheaded woodpecker scalps, dentalium, and obsidian blades, to mention the more commonly circulated items. Direct exchange of prestige goods for food occurred but was uncommon. More important was indirect exchange through the purchase of women as primary producers by means of prestige goods. A man purchased a wife in the hope that she would work hard to maintain his family's domestic food supply, but he also bought rights to the bridewealth any daughters she might bear would eventually attract. Direct patrilineal inheritance, indemnities, trade, gambling, and other schemes were also important avenues to wealth in so-called prestige goods, although views have differed concerning the relative importance of these approaches to wealth and the manner of their manipulation. Du Bois (1936) distinguished between "prestige" and "subsistence" economies within Tolowa society. The prestige economy was based on transactions involving the special goods mentioned above, while subsistence was on a barter basis, with no exchanges between the two economies. Thus, Du Bois concluded, the prestige goods acquired and manipulated by the Tolowa were not all-purpose currency, to be subdivided and exchanged for goods of any kind. Drucker (1937: 241) accepted Du Bois' basic distinction between prestige and subsistence goods but nevertheless argued that prestige goods were true money. He pointed out on the one hand that kin-based exchanges of food could not be called a special economy, and on the other hand that prestige goods could be used by the Tolowa bo buy everything that was for sale and therefore were true money. Du Bois (1936: 55-56) emphasized the importance of manipulation and haggling on the part of Tolowa men to achieve wealth, Drucker (1937: 242) stressed the role of direct, patrilineal inheritance as the principal means of becoming a wealthy man. In my analysis (1966b) I have accepted Du Bois' emphasis on manipulation as an avenue to wealth, but I have stressed the importance of bride-purchase as a specific form of manipulation that tends to break down her sharp distinction between prestige and subsistence economies.

The eventual result of all these manipulations plus direct inheritance was that wealth goods as well as food became concentrated in particular households — those of wealthy men or miixašxe — and one such wealthy man usually appeared as paramount within each village. These men were not formal chiefs, and they lacked authority in most matters. But they acted as intermediaries in marriage negotiations and indemnity settlements, and they were in a position to initiate projects like canoe- and house-building and the annual first sea lion hunt. Given the optimizing nature of traditional Tolowa subsistence procurement systems, the presence of a non-authoritarian leader in each village who could take the initiative in the few subsistence activities that required cooperative organization and who could marshall resources to construct the facilities necessary for these activities can be regarded as highly adaptive. The institution of a "wealthy man" in each village provided a higher degree of ecological fitness for Tolowa society than would a purely egalitarian system, since without some form of leadership the opportunities to harvest sea lions and salmon would have been severely limited.

Of course ecology cannot "explain" all the particular manipulations and attendant symbolism of wealth-questing among coastal northwestern California Indians. What this paper has tried to show is that the essentially aggrandizive nature of wealth-questing is interrelated in a consistent manner with the optimizing subsistence behavior of these people. Indeed, this paper has gone further and shown that at least some aspects of wealth-questing, particularly the brideprice and the institution of the wealthy man, arise from and in turn support traditional Tolowa subsistence procurement systems. In this sense, wealth-questing, as an expanded form of a wider type of behavior I have termed "aggrandizive" can be regarded as adaptive for hunter-gatherers living within the northwestern California coastal ecosystem. By contrast, sharing and redistributive behavior with regard to subsistence resources are more adaptive within ecosystems that contain a greater element of risk, where risk-minimizing rather than optimization is important. Placed as they are near the pole of greatest affluence and least risk within the whole spectrum of known ethnographic and historic hunter-gatherer adaptations, the Tolowa case points the way to a hypothesis that should be tested whenever possible: *Among hunter-gatherer societies aggrandizive behavior increases with respect to the total economy in direct proportion to the opportunity for optimal harvesting with minimal risk by individual family or household groups.*

Culture-Environment Integration: External References in Yokuts Life

by Anna H. Gayton

One of the aspects of culture dynamics which has received particular attention in recent years is that of integration. Pattern, complex, configuration, integrating factor, and theme have been used as labels for those culture elements which seem to cling together about some core of thought or action. When such constellations interpenetrate various aspects of a total culture they are regarded as integrators — cohesive forces binding parts, if not wholes, of a culture together. The function of the "theme" as a dynamic factor has recently been set forth by Dr. M.E. Opler with some pertinent examples of active patterns in Chiricahua Apache life (Opler, 1945). I interpret his construct of "theme" to be essentially the more familiar "culture pattern," in the ideational realm, with the factor of emotional surcharge taken into account as the active ingredient. Unlike some anthropological concepts, his has the virtue of being grounded in specific ethnographic realities.

An earlier paper by Dr. Du Bois demonstrated both cohesive and disruptive action in Tututni culture deriving from the weatlh concept, and still earlier, the three-way forces of mythology, chieftanship, and shamanism maintaining social balance in Yokuts life were described by the present writer (DuBois, 1936; Gayton, 1930). The most intellectualized account of cultural integration is that for the Hopi by Dr. Thompson in which no mechanism of integration is shown save an all-pervading logic of the mind (Thompson, 1945).

In the abstract we have to assume that some of these basic cultural currents work for or against each other; others, and perhaps the bulk of culture elements, may be neutral. When Opler completes his thematic analysis of Apache culture, presumably the counter-balance of the driving parts within the structure will be revealed (cf. Opler, 1946). Meanwhile, the integrations described in the papers mentioned above deal exclusively with immaterial culture — political organization, economics, social or religious or aesthetic values — without relation to externals, especially so broad an external as environment. Environment, when considered as relevant to culture, is usually limited to its place in the subsistence or material aspects — the phase of native life known as exploitation of environment which has been described with increasing frequence in recent years in ethno-biological studies. Thus, the thematic factors of social life on the one hand and the environmental factors of material culture on the other have been left as disparate parts which move in the total culture without any direct conjunctive action.[1]

In at least one culture, that of the Yokuts and Western Mono of the San Joaquin valley foothills, there is an intimate relation between important immaterial phases of the culture and the environmental setting. This will be described, and in so doing the function of the environment as a culture stabilizer, possibly even as an active integrator, will become evident.

There is nothing essentially new in this viewpoint. The relation of culture to environment in the determination of culture areas was given a broad treatment by Dr. Wissler, whose conclusions have been succiently reëxpressed by Dr. Kroeber in his own more recent extensive survey of culture areas, ecology, and culture climaxes in North America. Thus:

> We can accept Wissler's findings on the relation of culture areas to environment. He concludes that environment does not produce a culture, but stablizes it. Because at many points the culture must be adapted to the environment, the latter tends to hold it fast. Cultures therefore incline to change slowly once they have fitted themselves to a setting, and to enter new environment

---

1. That something similar to themes exist in material culture is evident when techniques are considered with their aesthetic goals and standards of craftsmanship. For example, Dr. O'Neale's study of Yurok and Karok basketry is replete with the ideational overtones of the craft (1932). If integration is a verity as a cultural process it should be demonstrable in material as well as immaterial forms of culture.

with more difficulty than to spread over the whole of the natural area in which their form was worked out. If they do enter a new type of territory, they are subject to changes. Once fitted to an environment, they are likely to alter radically only through some factor profoundly affecting subsistence, such as the introduction of agriculture (Kroeber, 1939: 6).

Wissler made an early attempt to fix the psychological factor in the relationship of environment to culture, and while matters such as instinct, mental level, and schools of anthropology in vogue at the time somewhat obscure the main issue of his treatise, his "reaction point of view" may still be examined profitably.

By reaction we mean the conception that external things and relations impress the mind so as to be at least the occasion for return action . . . The problem for us is, however, Do such stimuli or impressions determine or modify culture? (Wissler, 1911).

Nor did Dr. Boas omit the environmental factor when he said,

The explanation of the activity of the mind of man . . . requires the discussion of two distinct problems. The first bears upon the question of unity or diversity of organization of the mind, while the second bears upon the diversity produced by the variety of contents of the mind as formed in the various social and *geographical* environments (Boas, 1916: 103).

Without emphasizing the subsistence link which already has been the chief concern of culture-environment studies, the paper in hand will demonstrate how large a part of one culture was enmeshed with its natural surroundings. Environment herein is meant to include any or all externals of the culture and the people (culture-bearers), though, naturally, culture itself and even physiology are recognized as environment to the individual. For our present purpose the Yokuts and neighboring Western Mono of the Sierra Nevada foothills may be considered culturally one in spite of linguistic and other habitual differences. Emphasis will be on foothill rather than valley Yokuts, the Wukchumni in particular as exemplifying the norm of the cultural features described.[2]

II

The seasonal round of the year had three phases in native terms which fitted with the San Joaquin valley climate: Winter (tomo'kšiu) began about November and lasted through February; Spring (tisa'miu) was roughly March through May; and Summer (haiya'di) was from June through October.[3] These were: a cold rainy season when plant life was in a productive lull and habitation was settled; next a season of warmth with stream, river, and lake floods, and stirring plant growth culminating in the massive blooming of field flowers and foothill shrubs; and then the long hot dry season of harvest seeds bringing a constant drift to temporary camps which ended with the gathering and storing of the staple acorn crop.[4]

The ceremonial round of Yokuts culture was closely fitted to the seasonal cycle of plant and animal activity. There was no winter ceremony unless possibly the oho'wiš, an indoor curing ceremony and shamanistic display involving fish and water animals.[5] This was a time for evening instruction by the telling of myths and by the forcing of boys and girls 10 to 15 years of age to rise in the night and bathe in chilly waters. Austere men concerned about their supernatural power and spiritual vigor would do the same. Indoor occupations flourished, although men hunted daily unless the weather were excessively wet and cold. Houses were patched against winds and soaking rains. Acorns were brought from main storage bins to individual store houses, thence to the dwelling to be shelled as needed. Men and women gathered in houses at dusk to

---

2. The letter Y after a tribal name denotes Yokuts, WM, Western Mono. All ethnographic material unless otherwise noted is from Gayton, 1948.

3. A fourth season, Fall (wusa'o), was mentioned only upon inquiry, if at all, by my Central Foothill informants, and I believe it to be a modern interpolation. The Northern Foothill people clearly recognized a fall season, as indicated by my own and Dr. Driver's informants (1937: 150).

4. Twelve "moons" were counted and named by both Yokuts and Western Mono, but no ethnographer has the complete record.

5. Described by both Kroeber and myself, not fully understood by either in description, meaning, or extent; not listed by Driver (1925: 507; 1937).

drink the lime and tobacco emetic, then retired home to dream and secure supernatural benefits. By mid-December prospective datura-drinkers began to refrain from meat-eating. Shamans danced to prevent general sickness or to predict the next summer's seed crops.

In late February or early March came the first public ceremony, the drinking of tañai (Datura meteloides) by youths and others seeking special knowledge: dream help, second sight, or a view of their future life. This was never held later in the year because the plants were "too strong." The spectacle was attended by people of the local and adjacent communities. For the participants, the critical period was the twelve days prior to the drinking, in which a semi-fast was maintained, and the twelve following days during which meat was still tabu; at the conclusion of which time, as with all Yokuts festivities, a feast was given and meat eaten.

Soon after this (late March, April, and early May) the lavish, colorful blooming of wildflowers engaged Yokuts attention. Crowns of flowers, constructed like the shaman's feather crown, were worn by young and old of both sexes; armloads of flowers were plucked and danced to with special songs. Pleasure came from their beauty, their fragrance, and their indication of a plentiful seed harvest to follow. Winter rainbows forecast plentiful seed crops, for they were seen as four bands of color (magenta, blue, yellow, orange) of four flowers whose seeds were prized.[6]

In April, when rattlesnakes were rousing from hibernation, came the very important Rattlesnake Ritual, sponsored by the shamans controlling the creatures, and participated in by all persons as a preventative from injury by rattlers during the summer months. This ritual, which included a snake-handling display and concluded with a feast, was attended by both local and extra-community persons.

On the lower Kings River, the Choinimmi (Y) and probably other tribes within the area of the spring salmon run (about May) held a simple river-side ritual at their principal fishing sites. The

6. Play with flowers, so incompatible with conventional notions about Indians, was widespread in the West. Without especially seeking them the following references come to hand for Miwok, Maidu, Paviotso, Klackamas, and Taos: Barrett & Gifford, 1933: 222-3; Powers, 1877: 325; Lowie, 1924: 306-7; Jacobs, 1936: 12; Parsons, 1940: 121.

local chief ate the first salmon speared, after cooking it and praying
to Salmon for a plentiful supply. Then others partook of a salmon
feast, and the season, so to say, was officially open. (Some foods
were "moiety-owned," e.g., blackberries and mushrooms north of
Kings River; the possessing moiety collected but could not partake
until they had feasted the other moiety with the food.)

Disruption of village life came in late spring or early summer
— from May onward, depending upon the condition of the seed
harvest. Chiefs directed the general exodus in a minor way,
publicly stating that now was the time to go, and families departed
for their habitual summer camps. At these, men caught fish and
small game which they dried for winter use, and, as the women
collected loads of seeds, transported the heavy burdens back to the
village storage bins. There were no special ceremonies for this
season of dispersed households; instead local and more
spontaneous entertainment took place: there is record of shamans
dancing at summer camps; there were pleasure dances in which
both sexes participated; children played late in the long evenings;
and stories (myth-instruction) were tabu. Camp locations varied
with the change of crops — toward the valley, into the hills — but
all in all the moves probably encompassed not more than a twenty
mile span, on the average, for anyone.

There is some evidence that early fall was a season of general
sickness for people in the San Joaquin valley, especially for those in
the swampy region near the lake. The evidence is tenuous; whether
the illness was due to stagnant, contaminated or alkaline water, to
heat stroke, to an increase in tularemia as the result of greater
handling of rabbits and ground squirrels, it is impossible to say. [7]

September saw a return to the villages: winter storage
preparations were made, and with view to the complete
reëstablishment of normal community life plans were started for
the great event of the year, the Annual Mourning Ceremony
(luni´ša). To this end much material — foodstuffs in abundance,
treasures of baskets, feather ornaments, money — had been
prepared or saved. Preparatory loans already had been floated to be
returned at high interest at he time of the festivity, usually late
October. Necessary supplies of deer meat were obtained by special

7. A comparable summer sickness of waterfowl in this area is on record
(Grinnell, Bryant, and Storer, 1918: 17).

hunters at the very time of the event. Guests came by the hundreds. Obviously such large-scale entertainment could be managed only at the season of most plentiful food supplies.

Thus October saw the greatest of the year's festivities, the six-day ceremony of special rites, one for each day, climaxing in the all night mourning and distribution of wealth, followed by the ritual cleansing, and ending with a feast, game playing and dancing, the acquisiton of foods, gifts, and exchanged treasures. These affairs might be held in two or three Yokuts-Mono tribes during this period (roughly late September to early November), and the same persons attend them, at home as hosts, elsewhere as reciprocal ritual participants, or as visitors.

November brought the final seasonal ceremony, the Bear Dance (nŏhŏ'ó ká maič), which marked the first use of the new acorn crop by all persons of the Bear lineages — sometimes for other people as well.[8] This brief but exciting performance ended with a feast of acorns prepared and served by Bear people to their guests, after which they themselves partook. The dance was timed to follow the final harvesting of acorns and coincided with the time when bears betook themselves to winter hibernation.

Thus ended the ceremonial year, with mourners released from their restrictions, with storehouses filled, with houses repaired, and with long evenings ahead in which to tell the prehistory of the Yokuts world.[9] Six public ceremonies dependent upon or motivated by environmental changes had engaged the community's attention, interest, and support during the year: Datura Drinking, Flower Festival,[10] Rattlesnake Ritual, Salmon Rite, Annual Mourning Ceremony, and Bear Dance. There were no other important community festivities; that is, all whole-community or whole-tribal ceremonies were determined by the seasonal calendar. While other events of interest occurred and were witnessed as spectacles by those who carred to be there, those of greatest public importance all had basic environmental associations.

Trade relations of material importance to Yokuts and Western

---

8. Lineage attributes and functions have been described in Gayton, 1945.

9. The adventures of the pre-human animals, not, be it noted, the history of the tribal unit, of humans, or of distinguished individuals, or of "gods."

10. Flower Festival is my label for convenience; public interest and reaction to the floral season was general and was patterned, but not welded into a named ceremonial form.

Mono were regulated by environmental conditions. Thus, during
the spring when high water filled the sloughs connecting lower
Kings River and the north end of Tulare Lake, large parties of
Yokuts, e.g., Choinimni, traveled by balsa from the foothills to the
lake area to fish, trade, and doubtless intermarry.[11] Cultural
affinity between Northern Foothill Yokuts and Lake Yokuts
probably in part is due to this large scale social intercourse made
possible at the season of high water.

Trade relations between Eastern Mono (Owens Valley Paiute),
east of the Sierra Nevada, and their linguistic relatives and
neighbors of the Yokuts, the Western Mono, were limited to a few
summer weeks when known mountain passes were open to foot
travel. The trans-Sierra visitors, not welcome in Yokuts villages,
rarely ventured alone beyond the Western Mono groups. However,
occasionally a woman coming over with a trading party remained
there for the winter: once caught on the west side of the mountains
she had to remain till the following season. Sometimes she had a
child with her, bore a Yokuts child, or was pregnant by the
following summer.[12] The diffusion of the triangular winnowing tray
and hooded cradle of Eastern Mono type amongst Yokuts women
may have been abetted by this circumstance as much as by
impersonal trade with the neighboring Western Mono.

In the southwestern section of the San Joaquin valley trade
with the coastal people, e.g., Chumash, may have been temporarily
halted by severe weather in the Tejon country (the intervening
mountainous region), but not sufficiently to enforce long residence
on incoming tradesmen.

Thus two types of environmental factor, topographic access or
hindrance, and "weather permitting" or hindering, affected the
economic relation of the foothill Yokuts with their neighbors. Easy
access does not necessarily mean exchanges of goods or other
cultural items, but barriers do retard them. On the other hand,
differing environments mean different products, and had Eastern
Mono products been identical with Yokuts (yet equally inaccessible)
the impetus to exchange would have been wanting. The
topographic barrier was surmounted, but the weather barrier could

11. A unique account of such a trip is given in Latta (1929: 29-31).
12. Always they eventually returned home to Owens Valley, I was told;
none appear in Yokuts genealogies.

not be, and it presumably served to maintain the strangeness and hostility between Eastern Mono and Yokuts, which only was assuaged temporarily and periodically by the presence of the mutually acculturated intermediaries, the Western Mono.

As suggested by the adjustments of trading periods to the seasonal environment, the physiographic setting was a factor in other tribal relationships and directional emphases. The plain or floor of the San Joaquin valley is abruptly ended on the eastern side by the rising wall of the Sierra Nevada; there is no slow progression. Of the foothills, the most meagre are treeless cones planted at the edge of the valley floor; behind them are higher, larger, interlocking cones blending into sharply massed mountains above which stand snow-capped peaks. This topographic antithesis was reflected in non-material culture of the Yokuts. A directional distinction of eastward, upstream, mountainward (no'tu) versus westward, downstream, plainsward (to'xil; da'tu) gave names to the moieties (where they occurred): Nutuwich, Tokelyuwich; it regulated spatial arrangements at large ceremonies; wars and competitions in myths were attributed to uplanders and lowlanders; and in cosmogonic beliefs eastward beyond the mountains is the mysterious "home" of the supernatural animals, while westward beyond the ocean is the "home" of the dead, a place of feasting and merriment.

Other directions of the conventional six were also important.[13] North (hosi'm) and south (homo't) were constantly used as general designations for other Yokuts people, individuals or groups, when the tribal name was not known, i.e., "northerner" (hoso'mo), "southerner" (humti'nin). East and west (nutu'wič; tokelyu'wič) were rarely used for directional labels for tribes, not because they were moiety names (which the Central Foothill Yokuts lacked entirely) but because the east-west span of the valley is short, and close knowledge of neighbors by tribal name ran along the east to west flow of the streams. Comparably, the intervening watersheds discouraged north-south travel. In general, westerner (to'kya) was a term for any people living far west or southwest of the Yokuts (e.g., Salinan, Chumash), while collectively unknown eastern groups were called mountaineers (do'mtui). The north and south

13. Usually named in order: S,W,N,E,U,D. (No color symbolism was associated with direction.).

dimensions of the valley are greater, and tribal contacts in the floor
of the valley were so aligned along the water flow between Kern,
Buena Vista, Tulare Lakes, and the lower San Joaquin River.

Of the two other directions, up (ti´pin; sky, above) and down
(ati´l), the latter had no special significance beyond myth reference
to an underground gambler whose home might be reached via a
badger or gopher hole.14 Upward, "aboveness," was of great
religious significance, the embodiment of sacredness and
supernatural power. Veneration was manifest in many ways,
especially in a religious-motivated looking upwards, looking at the
stars and sun with prayerful phrases on the lips, basking in the sun,
getting magic "airshot" from the sun during shamanistic contests.
Supernatural power was called ti´pni; it was the essence of all
"aboveness" and the power derived therefrom, though the term
might be applied to anything weird, holy, or peculiarly
hyperphysical.

To the earth itself (di´nit) there was no special attitude, nor to
the plants growing on it save the narcotics tobacco (so´´og) and
Datura (ta´ñia). For example, for all the essential uses earth was
excavated without special concern — house, sweathouse, or grave
pits, for pottery, colored earths for paint. Similarly ordinary stones
were taken for implements, motars and pestles, though previously
shaped stones such as the "charmstones" of weather shaman,
were regarded with awe, as ti´pni.

On the other hand, water (i´dik), especially that of springs, was
venerated: "water is immortal because it is everywhere; it is living
all the time." Springs were addressed prayerfully, sacred eagle
down was scattered near them, and a little water was sprinkled on
oneself with a request for long life. Other expressions of this
attitude are found in early morning bathing (more than a mere
cleansing act), and in myths, wherein submersion or application of
water was the standard method of magical resuscitation.

The stars were not ignored; on the contrary, the Morning Star
especially was of great importance: people should be up in time to
see it, greet it with a prayerful request for "a good world" and
longevity. The Pleiades gave luck to gamblers; other stars were
dangerous lures to men. Eclipses of moon or sun were hailed with

14. There was no concept of stratified worlds, or of previous and
successive worlds.

shouts of discouragement, and excessive thunder was admonished to cease. In short, even heavenly bodies were part of the immediate, reachable environment.

Aspects of time, of the place of animals and of man in the world were embodied in Yokuts verbal narratives (mythology). The grand chronology was divided into two major parts — a remote past or prehuman era, and recent times or human era — an ancient "then" and an immediate "now." The prehuman era was that of a world created and occupied by birds and animals of superanimal and superhuman powers. To Eagle, with his bird and animal assistants and companions, was attributed the building of the world, the institution of certain cultural, social, and physical features of man and his way of life. This prehistoric period, described in a fairly full but not elaborately detailed stock of stories, came to an end with the creation of mankind by Eagle and the subsequent transformation of these bird-and-animal people into their present known forms. All this happened beyond the memory of man, but the past continued into the present in the immediate ubiquity of the animals themselves. Beliefs about them were being constantly reinforced by daily happenings in the circumjacent wilds.

The "earth-diver" creation myth was singularly appropriate for the San Joaquin valley people: in aboriginal times the valley bottom was filled with water and as far as the eye could see stretched tule beds thriving along the innumerable sloughs and swampy shores. At least once in the memory of each generation the seasonal flood increased to enormous, alarming proportions. Entirely congruous then, was the belief that once the world was all water and that Eagle, in his omniscience, asked Duck to dive and bring up a speck of sand from which to make a solid earth. Then Falcon and Crow, each flying north on parallel routes, dropped earth to form the pair of mountain ranges, Coast on the west, Sierra Nevada on the east. Coyote stole the sun to provide light, and Jack Rabbit stole fire which Bat had discovered. Falcon and Crow got Tobacco, which gave itself to them; Deer gave himself as food; Cougar hunted him, though Coyote spoiled easy success; Bear made a sweathouse and showed other animals how this should be done; all animals save the carnivores drank *Datura* ceremonially. Eagle wanted immortality, but Coyote argued against it, thereby losing his son, Blue Lizard. Falcon was a hero; his wife Duck, when stolen by Condor was sought by Crow and Bottle-Fly. When Eagle finally created man, Lizard offered his hand as a model. Then Eagle felt the animals should leave and he gave each his choice of habitat and of future service to human beings, as (beside those named above) Skunk and Owl would help shamans, Quail would help women in childbirth, and so on. Then they all "fley off" eastward where today they still exist and know how mankind treats their counterparts on earth. During the animal or prehistoric era the social system was like that of today: Eagle the chief, Dove his messenger, Coyote a clown, Magpie an advisor, and so on.

To sum up, Yokuts verbal narratives embodying world history pictured a prototype of the world as they themselves knew it: man and animals changed places, so to say. And, if Yokuts imagination projected backwards the social system of their present, it no less brought forward and attributed to living animals the power they had in the past. Hence, the Yokuts view of the animal world was of more than a subsistence potential. Animals were a power potential as well. It is notable that mythic interest and importance was spread among several species of birds and animals; a few were important but there was no single hero or trickster who usurped the spotlight.

This rather tedious recital leads to a most characteristic circumstance of Yokuts and Western Mono culture: that men and animals are peers. The animals were here first; today all dwell together, and while men may exploit these creatures for food and power they may not do so without due regard for their reactive and capricious qualities. It is difficult to convey the subtleties of Yokuts-Mono attitudes, their own position relative to other living beings in the world, without resorting to anecdote. As an example, then:

> Palaha, who was a fine hunter, told of an experience. He set up a rude platform in an oak tree where he intended to hide just before dawn to drop acorns down as a bear lure, than shoot the animal as it fed. He went out as planned — it was barely light. As he came under the tree something hit him on the head; acorns were falling from the platform. Looking up, he saw a small bear standing on the framework and nuzzling at the hoard of bait which rolled off the sides. This Palaha thought excessively funny: that their positions should be reversed, and that the bear was

doing to him what he had intended doing to the bear. But beyond this was the sense that the bear thought it funny too, that somehow it was intentional on the animal's part to indulge in a humorous trick.

So often has this intangible appeared when Yokuts or Western Mono speak of the activities of birds and animals that it is clearly an unconscious or unvoiced attitude of equivalence as living creatures in one small world.

The most potent and personal association between the Yokuts-Mono and their faunal contemporaries was manifest in the combination of social and religious systems which provided an animal symbol of patrilineal source to every person. This creature was no less a source of supernatural power than others of the animal world which might be approached for aid if superhuman enablement were desired. A specific relation between tutelary and protégé (po´ša and poša´m, respectively) existed both for the totemic (patrilineally inherited) animal and for the randomly sought individual animal patron. There was probably no person in Yokuts and Western Mono society who did not have what we may call a social symphysis with some animal, at least in incipient form, and in most cases moderately strengthened by reverential observances such as abstinence from its flesh (compulsory for a totemite), propitiation by prayer and eagle-down offerings, dream contact, and possession of a sacred symbolic talisman. In most highly developed form for shamanistic or power quests, these behaviors became a personal preoccupation essential to the maintenance of a beneficent attitude on the part of the animal tutelary.

The reverence for Eagle, Falcon, Cougar, Bear, Coyote (and lesser creatures in lesser ways) was actualized in ceremonies performed over their carcasses by persons of those lineages they symbolized, and witnessed by the usual audience of interested and, in part, participating villagers. The hunters of deer had to observe care in handling their kill. The underlying motive of these acts was that animals who were not "treated right" on this earth, at death reported to their prehistoric counterparts in their eastern home., and the offended creatures would no longer give their support (as either a subsistence or a power source) to the transgressor.

Although in theory it was the primordial animal in its vague eastern home which motivated its living counterpart, it was the latter with which the people were concerned. The reverential relation was a direct one, and in turn it was from the actual animal that help came. Many anecdotes from Yokuts and Mono describe how the tutelary suddenly appeared in a moment of need, though the mechanism of help, beyond a mere appearance, is left undefined — presumably it was "power" (ti´pni) that forced success.

The personal-and-animal association was formalized socially in professional shamanism and politically in the official capacities of chief, messenger, and dance manager — cultural elaborations which have been described elsewhere. And the informal culture of Yokuts and Western Mono abounded in minor, casual usages and references to faunal life.

For the sake of rounding out the picture and not emphasizing exclusively the aspect of culture with which we are concerned, a brief note should be made of Yokuts rituals which were not related explicitly to the extra-personal world. Brief is sufficient, for there was only one set of rituals, that for "life crises," which were not engaged with or dependent upon some seasonal condition in nature. These were the naming of an infant, the mother's cleansing rite, girl's puberty (bethrothal) rite,[15] and the private mourning ceremony. With the exception of the naming ceremony all were ritual cleansing ceremonies following the standard pattern of ritual laving, gift exchange or ritual payment, and feasting. In a sense, the great Annual Mourning Ceremony combined two ritual series for Yokuts and Western Mono: basically it was an exaggerated form of the private or family mourning ceremony, but because of its size and consequent dependence upon adequate food supply it necessarily occurred in a season of abundance. Thus the seasonal, public, or community ceremonial series, and the non-timed, private, or familial series were combined in the Annual Mourning Ceremony. Both series had a feature in common: they were concerned with initial occurrences of certain events, those in nature of yearly repetition, and those of the individual life which, once acknowledged, were usually allowed to pass unnoticed at later recurrences. The formal purification of the person by washing, in

15. A formal marriage by gift exchange might occur after the betrothal at first menses, but the two rites were not clearly separated by Yokuts and Western Mono; either or both might be made, but the second was not emphasized and seldom followed the first.

the private rituals, is indicative of the different psychological character of that series.

III

The dependence of subsistence and material culture (food, medicine, shelter, weapons, raiment, utensils, ornaments) upon environment is basic and of tremendous importance in all cultures so primitive that no extraneous supply of these things are available to relieve the people, as individuals or communities, from direct concern with their immediate natural resources. From the outset, we have taken this for granted as the fundamental culture-environment relationship from which, for Yokuts and Western Mono like almost all other North American Indians, there was no escape. But for these people the cultural concern with natural surroundings was not limited to utilitarian vlue.

Yokuts and Western Mono ceremonies were engaged with environmental features of annual recurrence, and cosmic cultural history, religious beliefs, official status, and family relationship symbols were associated with their faunal co-habitants.

This is a culture-environment form of integration of more than a merely mechanical sort: features of the environment which are not essential to basic subsistence are caught up into the ceremonial, social, and religious superstructure. Does this mean that a culture which carries more environmental references is less subject to change — is more stable — than one which has less? The general question cannot be answered with our data, but so far as the culture here used in demonstration of the problem is concerned, it would seem reasonable to assume that Yokuts-Mono culture, because of the form its interest in externals took, was held to its pattern by environmental stimuli.

With the exception of terrain (though perhaps in a locale subject to flood even this need not be expected), "environment" is not a static thing — with a thousand complexities it lives and moves in constant impingement upon simple dwellers on the earth. Much of that life and movement is regular and repetitive: the weather, floral, and faunal changes on a broad seasonal scale, and lightness and darkness, sun, moon, and stars, temperatures, animal and floral behaviors were on schedule in the narrow diurnal round.

The reiterative factor would seem to be an impressive one in the maintenance of cultural activity which has once been linked to it: the right time comes for a complex of behaviors — a ceremony — and that time is an ephemeral thing which the culture must meet in a series of events of immutable order. The natural schedule cannot be changed, and the ceremonies are performed — if they are to be performed at all — at the convenience of the environment, not the convenience of the people, so to say.

External reminders of cultural forms were met at any turn in the trail, on every hand, day in and day out, where animal creatures roamed or flew. They were living symbols of themselves in the religious and political systems of Yokuts-Mono culture, and as inescapable in their roles of superhuman contributors to the mode of Yokuts life as were any utilitarian plants or trees which provided materials for foods and tools. Inasmuch as the environmentally attuned parts of Yokuts-Mono culture were nuclear or thematic the natural features in which they had their basis may be said to have some dynamic force as cultural integrators in the functional sense (Opler, 1945).

However, I am too uncertain as to how integration (as a cultural process) may work in actuality to wish to propose that cultural changes away from these forms could not occur. For example, the symbol might become more important than the actuality, e.g., the weazel's skin, the shaman's sacred talisman imbued with supernatural power, might usurp the shaman's concern with the beast itself in real life and in his dreams. Shifts in emphasis are unpredictable and entirely possible even while forms still are mechanically adjusted to external features. The mere fact that a thing — say Eagle — has one hundred connotations in Yokuts culture against one of Goldfinch does not preclude loss of Eagle's role in that culture, although the greater entrenchment is in his favor.[16]

I do not want to evade the psychological aspects of cultural integration for it seems to me that no full discussion of it as a

---

16. A somewhat amusing aside here: the appearance of metal money with Eagle thereon was in perfect conformity with aboriginal Yokuts thought. Eagle, as the symbol of the chiefly lineage and as the dream-helper for acquisition of wealth, was manifestly not only the rightful but the inevitable imprint for the invading White culture's coinage — as informants frequently and proudly pointed out.

dynamic or functional process can do so profitably; yet this phase of integration is too complex to be entered into here and is really tangential to our focal interest — environment in culture. Hence only a few points will be mentioned.

First, the reiterative mechanism of seasonal environment may set up a conditioned response in the individual reared in a seasonal ceremonial routine. We are accustomed to consider "conditioning" in small neural units, or as specific behavioral components, yet, in so small and simple a society as Yokuts or Western Mono village the larger rhythms of social life must impress the infant from birth onward with increasing clarity and firmness. Just as the gross culture configurations are being absorbed, so must be the culture-environment configurations, and the environment's own configurations. By the time a youth has reached the verge of adulthood, the annual cycle of cultural events moving with the environmental cycle of weather, floral and faunal changes, has been repeated fifteen times. By this time too, the symbolic meaning of certain animals for his individual person — as primordial activators of his way of life, as tabu foods or as legal kill, as patrilineal totem, as source of supernatural powers — have been established, and he bears a personal relation to various animals, manifest in respectful actions. These actions constantly evoked by the immediate presence of these creatures in his daily, common living as a Yokuts.

Dreams of animals were essential as a source of supernatural powers and came both unsought and sought to these people. No depth psychology is needed to understand the composition of their mental imagery, which had these things, and almost only these things, to draw on, in fact could not escape nor exclude them from constant sight. It has seemed probable to me, though I have no absolute evidence, that a considerable part of the Yokuts' occupation of thinking about ("day dreaming" about) animals, perhaps preferred ones if certain specific powers were desired, constituted as normal a mental activity as, say, reading in our own culture. In a sense, it was a pastime concerned with something not necessarily present, with standardized mental symbols and imagery but in no sense psychopathic unless (in either case) carried beyond the average behavioral norm. For Yokuts, any one who wanted to could have some minor supernatural powers, as convenient and useful; extremists became professional shamans.

There is some suggestion in my materials and experience with Yokuts and Western Mono persons, that considerable emotion and anxiety surrounded the dream-helper animal once a constant relationship had been established between tutelary and protégé. Emotional pleasure, pride, and satisfaction ("security" perhaps) in the tutelary's benevolence, and anxiety over loss of this benevolence through either offense to the animal or of loss of the power to a malicious shaman, was exhibited time and again. Of this I am sure: that the sense of intimacy between a person and "his" actual animals in the environment was deep and real. Thus, for example: "Rattlesnake is my posǎ; if he'd bitten any other horse it would have killed him sure — but it didn't kill *mine*";[17] "Eagle was mad at me; that's why my baby was sick" (excessive milk curds diagnosed as Eagles faeces in an infant's mouth). This association, between an individual and an animal, routed through the religious or social system, is the personalized aspect of the more general human-animal equation appearing in broader terms in the culture (as exemplified in the earlier anecdote).

In a culture with both material and intangible concern for features of its natural surroundings it seems difficult to dismiss environment as "of rather minor importance in personality formation" (Linton, 1945: 11). Even though, "between the natural environment and the individual there is always interposed a human environment (culture) which is vastly more significant" (Linton, 1945: 11), the role of external environment in the human environment (culture) can be of major importance and therefore, through the cultural mechanism, be of deep psychological significance. It is possible that a basic element of the mental state known as nostalgia, or the state of intense uneasiness in strange surroundings, is the year by year, life long conditioning of an individual to a specific topographic configuration, flora, and fauna (Opler, 1938: 12,33). The subtle interplay of locale or geographic form and personal psychology have been disclosed in a recent study of Yurok childhood orientation (Erikson, 1943).

The intense immediacy of native environment in all its

---

17. The ill-logic (in our thinking) that a "benevolent" rattlesnake should have bitten the man's horse *at all*, is completely submerged in the prideful satisfaction that the horse did not die, was merely temporarily ill and recovered.

aspects is a condition not too easily realized by the academic field investigator from our own denaturalized civilization, especially when the people under study already have lost their aboriginal setting — as have most of our North American Indians. The natural condition might be succinctly stated as: the less culture, the more environment. The anthropologist is hyper-conscious of the cultural mechanism as the selective or distorting lens through which the native views his environment. But for the native the lens does not exist; he deals directly with the externals which impinge upon him. Environments are seen and modulated in terms of the reacting culture, but the impact of externals is there and cannot be expunged from a plenary consideration of the factors affecting integration (or the lack of it) in a total culture.

So extreme have been the controversial views on the determination or non-determination of culture by environment that we have eschewed the problem where the more flexible or intangible portions of culture are concerned, leaving Wissler's query on the effect of external stimuli on the mind of man still unanswered.[18] Since few would doubt that primitive cultures are adjusted to their local environments, it would seem well to move toward an analytic examination of the specific kind and degree of articulation we may find in a variety of cultures, or of divergences in basically identical cultures in a similar environment (e.g., Maidu, Miwok, Western Mono, Yokuts, along the central segment of the Sierra Nevada foothills). Culture as a spatial and temporal continuum should present new formulations of integration as analytic attention moves from culture to culture geographically and historically, and the environmental ingredient at each phase may offer some clues as to the relative persistence of the nuclear patterns.

---

18. Kroeber's previously cited *Cultural and Natural Areas of Native North America* deals with cultures in gross and as categorized by our "culture area" systematization; emphasis is on terrain, ecology, population, economic surplus, and culture climax.

Social Organization in Native California

by Lowell J. Bean

INTRODUCTION

The nature of social organization in Native California has been the subject of research by anthropologists for nearly 70 years. As research has continued through these several decades, a picture of increasing complexity has emerged as one scholar after another has added seminal concepts which provide the necessary understanding for more complex forms. The earlier view that California Indians were rather simple folk has been replaced by a realization that they were peculiarly complex hunters-and-gatherers whose social systems were similar to those of peoples with presumably greater technological advantages: e.g., horticulturalists and some agriculturalists. The data presented in this paper suggest that this development of social mechanisms has allowed for a maximal use of resources across ecological and political boundaries.

THE BASIC SOCIAL UNITS

Perhaps the most important contribution to our understanding of political California was the discovery by Gifford that the lineage was the principal political and corporate unit in much of California (1926). He suggested that the lineage was the universal political unit, and where it was lacking, lineage disintegration had occurred — a position no longer subscribed to by Californianists. Kroeber approached the problem of social organization differently. In his earliest writings he noted that the nature of political life in California was sufficiently different from other areas of North

America that a special explanatory model was necessary (Kroeber 1954). He conceptualized the "tribelet" as the basic land-owning group, pointing out that the "so-called tribes" in California were usually non-political ethnic nationalities. He noted that variations from this common pattern occurred on the Colorado River and in the northwestern part of the state. He suggested that the tribelet (or village community) was the equivalent of the tribe among some other American Indians, since it was usually the largest group over which any one person, leader or chief had recognized authority, and was the largest group which was autonomous, self-governing and independent. He suggested that an able chief might be known, respected and listened to among neighboring tribelets, but his actual following was limited to his own tribe, and strictly so. He said:

> In any strict sense, the word "tribe" denotes a group of people that act together, feel themselves to be a unit, and are sovereign in a defined territory. Now, in California, these traits attached to the Masut Pomo, once again to the Elem Pomo, to the Yokaia Pomo, and to the 30 other Pomo tribelets. They did not attach to the Pomo as a whole, because the Pomo as a whole did not act or govern themselves, or hold land as a unit. In other words, there was strictly no such tribal entity as "the Pomo"; there were 34 Pomo miniature tribes (Kroeber 1954: 38).

Kroeber defined the non-political ethnic nationality as a cultural unit — a group of people sharing a language, culture and history, and, to some degree, philosophical concepts. Kroeber compared the California non-political ethnic nationality to European socio-cultural conditions:

> A hundred years ago the Germans were indubitably a nationality with common language, general customs, ideas, and a sense of being related, but were not yet a Nation in the sense of having a unified political government or supreme State. They were a nationality comprising many regional variants, such as Prussians, Bavarians, Saxons, Hessians, Wesphalians, and others. It is these regional groups, and their particularistic

governments, that might in some measure be said to correspond to the Masut, Elem, Yokaia, and other tribelets whose aggregate composed the Pomo nationality (Kroeber 1954: 39).

Kroeber suggested that there were probably over 500 tribelets, and conservatively estimated that they ranged between 100 and 500 persons per group. The higher figure of 1000 persons now seems more reasonable, and the estimated number of tribelets may be reduced as more encompassing social structures are recognized. Among the Cahuilla, for example, 50 or more lineages were organized in approximately 12 sibs or tribelets. The recognition of political confederations further alters the total number of these autonomous groups.

Tribelets were composed of varying types of family groups and household groups comprised of parents, children, collateral, lineal or affinal relatives and sometimes non-relatives. Kroeber suggested that the average family size was 7 or 8 — with a range of 5 or 10 people per family (Kroeber 1954). However, tribelets varied in structural form. In south-central and central California they were usually composed of patrilineages which were the basic corporate groups within a tribelet and occasionally the tribelet itself. Often several lineages were linked into clans, or a tribelet was composed of persons from several unrelated lineages, one of which was dominant (e.g., Diegueño). Descent in these groups was traced over 3-5 generations. Women married out shortly after puberty, but usually maintained rights in their natal lineage. Adult women in the tribelets were consequently from various other lineage groups, since lineage exogamy was the rule.

The population density of pre-contact California groups varied according to ecological conditions; the least advantageous environments required more territory for smaller numbers of people. Population density of tribelets probably ranged from 0.5 per square mile to as high as 10 (Yokuts-Chumash) or more persons per square mile. Tribelet territories ranged from 50 square miles (Miwok) to as much as 6000 square miles. Figure 2, taken from Kunkel (1962), indicates variations for central California which are probably modal. S.F. Cook's latest calculation for the total population of the state is 300,000 persons.

The traditional ethnographic model postulates that each group expanded to the greatest extent that the requirement for cohesiveness permitted, thus lowering subsistence competition and conflict. A more modern model attributes the equilibrium between resources and population to a complex system of socio-economic checks and balances (e.g., ritual reciprocity, exogamy and trade feasts).

There was usually a central town which served as a political, ritual and economic center, and several subordinate smaller settlements. Council meetings and legal or legislative debates were held at the principal village, and large caches of food, goods and treasures were maintained there. The settlements were variously occupied permanently or seasonally; often each had a chief, usually the head of a lineage or extended family or, where kinship was less important, a wealthy man (e.g., northwest California). The basis of political authority varied from ranked inherited chieftainships within a tribelet to situations where one or more wealthy and powerful men were titular co-chiefs.

The two major variations in the California pattern noted by Kroeber were on the Colorado River and in northwest California, where various groups centered around the lower Klamath River (Tolowa, Hupa, Chilula, Wiyot, Karok, and Yurok) shared a cultural tradition which suggests alliances to the northwest coast, and forms of social organization which had not developed the socio-political rigidity and complexity of central and southern California. In northwestern California political organization was characterized by extreme fractionalism (Kroeber 1954: 43); the tribelet was a loosely connected set of separate settlements, and people clustered in a town or village which did not have the sense of cohesiveness and continuity of other areas. Individualism or atomism was the rule. Status, prestige, honor, and renown deriving from the possession (usually inherited) of property, was their style. Each man strove for himself and his family (within certain class boundaries), and not the community as a whole. Competition rather than cooperation was emphasized as an ideal, although certain ritual safeguards against flagrant individualism were imposed by the religious and legal system. These characteristics are not in themselves unique to northwestern California, but they stand out because of the relative lack of sociological and ritual modifiers which other groups used to take the raw edges off competition, individual achievement and capitalistic effort.

It has been said that two forms of organizational style were used in California tribelets. The lineage principle was the principal device in the area south of San Francisco (and perhaps in the Sacramento Delta), with some exceptions (e.g., Tübatulabal and Kawaiisu, and perhaps the Chumash). Kunkel has argued (1974) that northern California tribelets were generally composed of ambilocal residential corporate kin groups, and that villages were composed of multi-kin groups rather than modified lineages which have been disturbed by historical process, as Gifford supposed, or incipient clans as argued by Goldschmidt (1948). In central California each village had one or more chiefs, each the head of a kin group composed generally of ambilaterally related people, sometimes, as with the Pomo, with a matrilineal and matrilocal bias.

Another pattern existed in the Sacramento Valley where villages consisted of one or more extended residence groups with patrilocal tendencies. People were linked patrilaterally, and chiefly succession and inheritance of property tended to be patrilineal (note the contrast with the Pomo) and associated with Omaha kinship terminology. However, there were no corporate unilineal groups such as were common in southern California.

In the northwestern part of the state the Hupa, Yurok, Karok, Tolowa, and Wiyot also favored patrilocal residence. There settlements consisted of one or more residential kin groups led by a wealthy man, his extended family, and various collateral kin and hangers-on (Kunkel 1974). The exact patterns of social organization in north-coastal and northeastern California are unclear or the data conflicting. The general northern California pattern, however, appears to differ significantly from that of southern and south-central California. There the unilineal principle provides the focus for clearly defined and rigid corporate groups, rather than loosely organized tribelets based upon ambilateral extended-family forms (which result in highly flexible, fluid corporate groups based upon residence rather than on kinship per se).

Examples of political confederations have been suggested for the Chumash (one author has suggested they were "national states"; L. King 1969) Pomo, Miwok, Patwin, Shasta, Gabrielino, Diegueño, and Salinan. Thus, we see a thrusting upwards in socio-political integration in recent times, and probably not, as Gifford argues, as a product of European influences. Other levels of organizational structure superceded these confederations. Trade, ritual and military alliances are noted all over the state, and correlate rather neatly with ecological parameters. In northern and central California stable trade and military alliances seem to have involved at least three tribelets, often members of different ethnic nationalities, whose ecological potential was mutually useful (e.g., ocean, river, foothill and mountain peoples allied for mutual exchange and protection). These alliance structures appear to have been determined by ecological factors, extending to the logical, naturally imposed limits within an area. Thus in northern and north-central California the distances are small — from the coast, inland to mountain ranges. There another interlocking alliance picks up and moves further east. In southern California alliances extended across deserts and mountains through passes from the Pacific Coast into Arizona and New Mexico. At least three alliance bands crossed this broad area together. These linked the Diegueño with the Yuma, the Gabrielino with the Cahuilla, Halchidoma, and Coco-Maricopa groups, and the Chumash with the Yokuts and Mohave (Forbes 1965: 80). There are indications also of north-south alliances on the coast: Gabrielino, Chumash, and Salinan, and the Miwok to the Southwestern Pomo.

Between the level of political confederations and alliance levels, which sometimes were coterminous, there were ritual congregations associated with the jimsonweed cult which linked each southern California tribelet with other tribelets and ethnic nationalities (Bean 1972). It is suggested that the Kuksu and World Renewal rituals did likewise for central and northern California groups (Kroeber and Gifford 1949).

THE INTERFACE CENTERS

Cross-tribelet interfacing appears to have commonly involved peoples within a radius of 50-75 miles in ritual or trade feast contexts, which sometimes brought several hundred to several thousand people together. Cult centers, such as those described by Kroeber for the World Renewal system (where a few centers or towns held the World Renewal rituals for a large area), are a case in point. Another is recorded among the Yokuts where Estudillo observed upwards of three thousand people at a single ritual mourning ceremony. Similar centers are described for the Chumash (Point Mugu), Gabrielino (Povongna), and Diegueño (Pamo). Communities of this sort hosted trade fairs, mourning ceremonies, or whatever, and simultaneously served as nodes or centers for intense socio-political and economic interaction. The economic equilibrium maintained through this network involved as many as a dozen or more villages or tribelets, two or more nationalities, and several ecological zones (e.g., coast, foothill, riverine-mountain). These partners in social interaction, along with the well-developed money systems in Native California, were the most important social devices for exploiting economic resources in the area, since they expanded the amount and diversity of energy potential of every tribelet to include part of the resources of most of their neighbors.

MOIETY ORGANIZATION

Gifford was one of the first scholars to appreciate the presence and sociological significance of the moiety concept in native California. In 1918 he noted the presence of totemic moieties in south-central and southern California and in Arizona from north to south. They are found among the Miwok, Mono, Central Yokuts, Salinan, Kitanemuk (?), Serrano, Cahuilla, Cupeño and Luiseño. According to Strong (1929), it is possible that the Gabrielino were the point of origin for the concept. Among these groups moiety exogamy was associated with ritual reciprocity, and consequently moieties served to define potential marriage alliances as well as religious, economic, and sometimes military alliances. These, accompanied by rules which forbade marriage within five generations, created very extensive social networks between neighboring groups, since marital partners were necessarily sought from a wide sociological and ecological base.

Totemic associations often involve taboo or privilege relationships to animals or birds which signal social relationships associated with ritual and economic privileges or responsibilities. Yokuts examples are rather clearly documented by Gayton (1930); here totems were held to be off-limits for exploitation by the people symbolized by them. Thus a person holding these totemic statuses was responsible for the proper care and keeping of the totem animals on earth. This was done among the Yokuts by their being obliged to redeem the totem animal, from any person killing or capturing one of them, by paying a price and subsequently providing the proper burial or disposition of the body. This sytem maintained the man-land-animal balance in nature so that totemic guardians would continue to cooperate with man on earth. It further acted as a means of economic redistribution, since individuals controlled valuable totems (eagle feathers, for example, were extremely valuable economically) and since an ambitious or lucky hunter could thus bring an extra economic advantage to his hunting endeavors.

There are indications that among some Yokuts, Gabrielino, Kitanemuk, Chumash and Juaneño there was a pseudo-moiety structure like that found among central California groups (Strong 1929). In central California and among some southern California groups pseudo-moieties functioned in social and ritual activities, but they did not control economic exchange as they did in south-central and southern California. The Pomo and their neighbors possessed these pseudo-moieties, since they were not based on descent per se, but they did sometimes regulate what part of a village a person lived in and his place in the ceremonial house. The populations of these villages were usually divided into two divisions — e.g., east-west, north-south, up river-down river. Apparently an individual could choose the side he wanted to join, often the side of his mother's brother. This arrangement was consistent with the kind of flexibility found in marriage residence, kinship and inheritance of any important position.

MARRIAGE

Marriage was a closely regulated institution in native California. Young girls were usually married shortly after puberty to young men not much older than themselves. Great differences in age between spouses was rare, but it could happen — especially if the husband was a wealthy or powerful man.

As with most institutions in California, wealth and kinship were fused. The wealthy people of high rank usually married their children into comparable families. The extreme example of this situation occurred in northwest California where the "personal worth" of an individual was measured in terms of "bride price." Valory puts it this way:

A child's identity and status depended primarily on that of his parents', of the nature of their union (whether an expensive brideprice), and the status of their parents. Children born of High, in a sense, had a head-start, although Yurok society may lend the appearance of being basically "democratic" in that any man might, by stint, establish himself and his house in the aristocracy. A bastard (ka mu ks) was socially defined as one whose parents had not had an established union by virtue of brideprice, and he was abused and ridiculed throughout his life in High circles, and not permitted to enter the all-important society of male sweathouse culture (1970).

The northwest examples should not be seen as exceptions so much as extreme examples of patterns found throughout the state. Among most peoples birth determined social rank, and women were used in a complex system of economic and political strategies for the long range benefit of their own families or lineages. The rank of lineages and other factors in addition to wealth influenced an individual's personal worth more than brideprice per se. Throughout the state generation rules determined the boundaries of spouse selection. Close relatives were not suitable for marriage (except possibly the mother's brother's daughter among the Miwok). Marriage was discouraged to any relative related within 3 to 5 generations, the specific number of generations depending upon the particular group. In the southern half of the state, where lineage systems and moieties were principal articulators of social relationships, individuals could not marry within their lineages, clans or moieties, nor within the given number of generations prescribed by a generation rule. Consequently, the average tribelet was virtually without potential spouses for their own members, who thus necessarily married into neighboring tribelets and established affinal relationships across group boundaries. Exchanges of economic goods and the ritual participation which articulated economic and political life were usually ordered by kinship obligations. In war and peace, marriages influenced who would be attacked, the relative intensity of combat, and the like.

Most men had only one wife (but might divorce and remarry several times during their lifetimes); however, polygyny was generally accepted throughout California and there are rare scattered references to polyandry (Gifford 1922). Generally it was considered proper for a chief to have more than one wife simultaneously, a reflection of the economic and political needs of his office.

Shamans also commonly had more than one wife; this indicated their possession of sufficient wealth to support more than one, and a willingness of families to ally with them. As with chiefs, it also served to mark their greater social prestige as men of power.

DIVORCE

Since marriage was a matter of concern to families, individual interests were often subordinated to group needs, and divorce, which would disturb the economic and political alliances set up by marriages, was discouraged. There are frequent examples of the difficulties of personal adjustment, especially for the bride, with frequent running away and subsequent forced returns until absolute incompatibility was established. Divorce, however, was possible.

A man divorced a woman with greater ease than vice versa, usually because of sterility, laziness or sexual infidelity. Cruelty on the part of the husband or his family was the principal reason for a woman leaving her husband. An expectation that a wife would eventually be protected from an unfavorable marriage by her own kin served as a safety mechanism for the wife, since a woman usually retained some basic rights within her own kin group.

Sororal polygyny was commonly practiced. Where multiple wives were permitted, a man often married two sisters, an arrangement the wives preferred to the alternative of sharing household responsibilities with someone not related to them. This condition is frequently reflected in kinship terminology, where the mother's sister is thought of as a surrogate mother and sometimes called by the same term. A similar reflection occurs often in the terms used by a husband to his wife's sister.

Alliances and proper child care were also encouraged through the practice of levirate and sororate rules. The custom of marrying the sister of a deceased wife protected the inter-family relationship and presumably promoted a positive continuity in child rearing. It was rarely, however, an absolute rule, the woman in this case having more of a voice in the matter than in an initial marriage. The success of a previous marriage alliance was no doubt a determining factor.

In the opposite case, the wife married the brother or close kin of the deceased husband. This was probably the more common and comfortable form, since it did not require the socialization of new personnel, and it more easily protected the inter-family alliance structure and child rearing aspects of the marriage. Marriage was not only an economic mechanism, it had political and class-maintaining functions as well. In all tribes there were frequent instances of marriage with other ethnic units (e.g., Shasta with Modoc, Luiseño with Diegueño). A Gabrielino case in point revealed one village (Tungva) had intermarriages with 13 other villages, three of which were in other language groups — Chumash, Yokuts, and Kitanemuk (Forbes 1966).

CLASSES

The ethnographic literature of California documents the frequent incidence of class distinctions, expressed in behavior and in native terms for such statuses as "wealthy person," "commoner," "poor person," "drifter" or the like. It appears that a tripartite system existed in most groups (sometimes a 4-part system) characterized by elites or nobility, commoners, the poor, and sometimes slaves or vagabonds (see Figure 1).

These classes or ranked positions were stabilized by the fact that upper-class people (chiefly families) tended to inherit rank and capital resources. They controlled distribution systems through control of political and ritual privileges and/or the control of capital resources and surplus. They maintained special knowledge (a great tradition) and often spoke a special refined language which set them apart from others. They tended to marry among themselves, and their rank was also justified in cosmological postulates and normative terms.

These were not completely closed class systems; mechanisms for some social mobility were available. Individuals could increase their social rank by manipulating economic affairs, the classic but not unique example being in the northern part of the state (Yurok, Tolowa). Shamanic roles, although they tended to be controlled

Figure 1

— INTERNATIONAL ELITES —

	1	1	1	1	1	
Elites	2	2	2	2	2	Elites
25% of	3	3	3	3	3	25% of
popu-	4	4	4	4	4	pop-
lation	5	5	5	5	5	ulation
	6	6	6	6	6	
	7	7	7	7	7	
	8	8	8	8	8	
	9	9	9	9	9	
	Tribelet 1	Tribelet 2	Tribelet 3	Tribelet 4	Tribelet 5	

(1) Nobility — Chiefs, their immediate family; unilaterally or bilaterally determined; often titled people.

(2) Bureaucrats — Chiefs' assistants, messengers, managers, callers; often hereditary status.

(3) Religious Specialists — Cult members, shamans, diviners, curers, ritual managers, officials and performers.

(4) Specialists — Extraordinary craftsmen who earn praise for their contribution in society in all acceptable categories; e.g., bow-makers, basket-makers (usually women), potters, exceptional hunters. These are often candidates for bureaucratic roles.

often members of chief's extended family

THE ABOVE CATEGORIES PROVIDE CHANNELS FOR SOCIAL MOBILITY FROM LOWER SOCIAL CLASSES. THE TALENTED, SKILLED OR POLITICALLY ADEPT ARE BROUGHT INTO MANAGEMENT IN CATEGORIES 2, 3 and 4.

(5) The rank and file — Men and women without formal rank or special skills which set them apart from the rest of the community.

(6) Poor-Indigent — Widows, orphans, lame or ill people who do not contribute significantly to the economic system and who have no other mitigating talent or quality which elevates them in rank.

(7) There is generally a stigma attached to families who are poor without socially acceptable cause. Included here, although somewhat lower in rank, are partial stigmatites of various types; e.g., bastards, bums, lazy ones, beggars.

(8) The socially disconnected or full stigmatites; these are people who are unacceptable to social groups; they have no secure place in the social scheme of things; e.g., vagabonds or "outlaws."

(9) Transvestites do not seem to fall easily into any of the above categories. It would appear they come from any rank.

through inheritance or secret societies, were theoretically open to any person with special talent, or the ambition and willingness to assume the arduous responsibilities of the role. If they were approved by the elites, they could become wealthy and enter actively into ritual and political institutions which controlled society.

The class distinctions were tied to family traditions as a rule. McKern's (1922) description of functional families among the Patwin was an early recognition of what now appears to be a patterned process; i.e., craft, political and religious specializations were often family- or lineage-linked and ranked.

Several authors have clearly indicated that subordinate classes were also firmly linked to lineages or families (e.g., Yurok, Cahuilla, Atsugewi, Diegueño, Chumash, and Yokuts). It is clear that members of different kinship groups had differential access to status positions, and nonegalitarian behavior was generally more often the case than not. It is now evident that in most tribes a rigid and authoritarian social structure prevailed, and that differences in rank were usually inherited.

CHIEFS

Chiefs were economic administrators, managing the production, distribution and exchange of goods. They were usually subordinate to no other authority, although they were variously influenced by councils, secret-society officials, shamans and other officials and wealthy men. Since his primary function was to control the collection, distribution and exchange of food stores, money and valuables for the benefit of the group, the chief needed ties with other corporate groups, since every group was in danger of occasional food stress in the absence of economic exchange arrangements with other corporate groups. Intermarriage, ritual alliances, and gift-giving between chiefs, and other reciprocal acts symbolized the sealed agreements which corporate administrators maintained with one another.

Chieftainship or headmanship was generally hereditary; it was consistently correlated with wealth. If a man were not conspicuously wealthy before he assumed office, he was after holding the office, having become the economic administrator of the tribelet. A candidate for the chieftainship, however legitimate by hereditary standards, was replaced (usually by a brother or another son of the previous chief) if he was clearly unsuitable in temperament and talent, or unwilling to serve.

The chief lived in relative luxury in comparison with other men; his house and household were conspicuously large, his clothing extravagant, and his possession of signs of office such as regalia and shell bead money, food stores, and treasure goods greater than others. He was usually released from ordinary labor (the Atsugewi were an exception), and was supported by the community, inasmuch as his many functions required freedom from ordinary routines.

He was a man of prestige, feared and respected. He usually married several women (often from different tribelets), daughters of other chiefly or wealthy families, and thus provided himself and his children with kin among the elite of other communities. Occasionally the role of the chief extended throughout a confederation of tribelets. The groups in this confederation might (as among the Shasta) or might not constitute the entire membership of an ethnic nationality.

In post-contact times many chiefs used their traditional role to bring together larger numbers of people. They were recognized by European authorities, and were able to carry on negotiations with Europeans so that a more successful accommodation was accomplished, since they could negotiate from a greater power base.

SHAMANS

The religious functions of the shaman will be discussed at greater length in a subsequent paper on cults and world view. It is sufficient to say here that they were the principal religious functionaries throughout the state. They frequently assumed priestly status, and the role was often carried simultaneously with others. Shamans specialized in various activities, and a man might be both a chief and shaman, engaging in various types of curing or sucking, divination, or control of particular guardian spirits. Shamans were integral to the political, economic and legal institutions. Nowhere were they separate from these institutional frames. Gayton's classic discussion of the role of shaman, which describes the close integration of chiefs and shamans in political and economic institutions, applies generally to the entire state (Gayton 1930).

Shamans ranked second only to chiefs in authority and prestige, but they were more often criticized than political leaders. It was generally assumed that they were both malevolent and good, although some argue that this is a matter of differing philosophies or conceptions of the role between professionals and laymen. Shamans were paid for their services. Their roles tended to be inherited and maintained in family lines, although inheritance was not as rigidly determined as that of chiefs.

COUNCIL AND MANAGERS

The chief was assisted by a managerial or administrative class that was usually associated with the ritual or cult systems, since it was through ritual that many economic and political affairs were articulated in native California; thus in addition to the obvious administrators such as assistant chief and messenger, there were honorific positions such as dancer or singer.

These bureaucrats usually composed the council of "elders" who provided advice and consent to chiefs. These councils existed at each level of socio-political organization. Above the tribelet level, tribelet chiefs formed councils. At the tribelet level, councils were composed of subchiefs within the group (e.g., lineage leaders, extended family chiefs, and others, depending on the individual social structure of each group). At the lineage level the chief, his assistant, and other officials comprised the council. Since age as well as rules of succession was usually a basic criterion for bureaucratic roles, councils tended to be composed of elders (men over 40 seems to have been normal). They were also frequently close relatives of the chief, since while bureaucratic positions were not necessarily inherited positions, they did tend to be passed along in family lines, especially the chiefly family. Thus a chief often had considerable administrative experience before he assumed his position, since he usually had an official position prior to his becoming chief.

In council, consensus was considered an ideal; it appears that decision-making was accomplished for the most part, however, in an informal manner, so that consensus could be overtly realized without public conflict. The shaman was often used in these meetings to "bless" the gathering, divine a propitious occasion for the meeting, and perhaps bring supernatural knowledge and opinion into the process.

On occasion, when conflict was still unresolved, expert or higher opinion was brought to bear on the group by calling in higher-level chiefs (e.g., at a village council, the tribelet chief or a chief of another tribelet).

Chiefs' assistants (subchiefs, boy chiefs) were found in all groups. Their principal duties were to communicate to the people from the chief and vice versa. They sat in council meetings, thus acting in a judicial capacity, served as substitutes in the absence of a chief, and often succeeded him in office. They also often acted as master of ceremonies at ritual events, and took care of protocol when visitors came to the village.

Since chiefs required information from the community and from the outside, the assistant or sub-chief often acted as a messenger or reporter to the chief. In more complex societies this was a separate role and a chief's messenger was appointed by the chief because of his ability to talk and his "powers of observation." Beals (1933) describes "Native gossip columnists" among the Nisenan who traveled to other villages at night and reported their activities to the chief the next day. Traveling singers and traders also gathered socio-political data which they reported to their chiefs. These various officials were found in all California societies in either permanent, fulltime positions or temporary positions. Among the Yokuts the office was restricted to a particular lineage and had a totemic symbol. For the Patwin, several chiefs' assistants are listed.

Several bureaucratic or managerial roles were commonly found either separately or in combination among other groups; these include clowns, dance managers and other ritualists, peacemakers, and war chiefs. The "clown" or jester made fun of the chief, acted disrespectfully, and sometimes pointed out the chief's foibles to the public. His burlesqueing role served to emphasize the usual respect which was due the chief. This role was often inherited, and often incorporated into another such as that of chief's assistant.

Since ritual was so pervasive in California, the role of ritual manager was indeed important. In some groups it was clearly separated from that of chief, while in others the chief or his immediate assistant was the principal manager of these affairs. Where secret societies and sacred roles were less clearly integrated (as among some Pomo groups) or where secular powers were present, it was a role separated from political office.

War chief and peacemaker (negotiator) were usually temporary offices; a skilled warrior would be selected as war chief by the council or the chief. Chiefs rarely assumed this role, nor did they usually engage in combat; they were expected to seek peace, but a peacemaking role was sometimes formalized into a ranked position.

SPECIALISTS AND OTHER PROFESSIONALS

Professionalism or occupational specialization, outside of the activities described above, created status differentiation and provided economic advantages for many. Although most people could manage most mundane tasks, there were those who, because of ability or training or birth, specialized in and sometimes monopolized an activity or craft which brought them prestige and wealth.

The degree of specialization varied from one tribe to another in direct proportion to ecological advantages and population density. Specialists occurred in all groups (e.g., trading, basket-making and clam-shell disk manufacture), but in some it was more casually developed or more dependent on ability or personal choice than training and inheritance. In the more complex societies "craft guilds" were established, which controlled an industry. In central and southern California, entrance into a guild was by purchase. In the Chumash case, upon the death of a guild member the right to produce the craft apparently reverted to the guild and was resold to a new member (L. King 1969).

More moderate controls have been described for the Patwin, Nomlaki and Pomo (McKern 1922; Goldschmidt 1951; Loeb 1926), in which "functional families" controlled an activity and a spiritual guardian. One or at best a few members practiced the specialization. In other groups the craft tended to be inherited from parent to child, but it could be sold to another person.

Craft techniques were often kept secret; Beals suggests that

Nisenan craftsmen practiced in the privacy of their homes late at night so they would not be observed. Some craftsmen exchanged their products for other goods and were often completely relieved from other subsistence activities, as in the case of the Clear Lake Pomo money-maker (Gifford 1922: 386), though often they simply acquired a more prestigious and economically advantageous position in the society by expanding their income base.

In the northwest area rich men had slaves to do their manual labor for them, so they could spend their energy making luxury items to reinforce their wealth (Willoughby 1963).

Women were less involved in specialization activities than men — though basket-making, mid-wifing, herbalism and shamanism (especially among the northwestern groups) were important female activities in California.

In central and (apparently) coastal southern California, specialists stood as a class between the nobles (chiefly families) and commoners, protected by religious institutions or proscriptions attached to their crafts in the form of guardian spirits or membership in a secret society. They were somewhat analogous to medieval burghers — the first townsmen, since it appears that they clustered somewhat in larger towns (which tended to be trade centers) where their crafts would have more ready markets. In central California, where community residence was more flexible than in other areas (e.g., southern California, where there were lineage-based corporate residence groups), it is likely that urban clustering was more possible. The ability to select residence may have been an important stimulus to the development of urban tendencies.

COMMONERS

The category of "commoner" or ordinary person included those without rank, people who were not conspicuously important either in terms of inherited rank, wealth, talent or position. They were primarily visible in contrast to their superiors, who are described so frequently, and their inferiors, who are described infrequently but in negative terms. The impression one receives of this "silent majority" is that they were a ruled class, highly intimidated by their social superiors who controled spiritual, economic and religious institutions which the ordinary people were expected to support by donation (taxes), gifts and various fees imposed by specialists and managers. It was more than simply a matter of supporting a few administrators; it appears that with a few exceptions they supported a class of elites.

The ordinary person was frozen into an almost feudal situation in his land of birth, since there was little opportunity for geographic mobility and little escape from the restriction and control of his own local group. At best he could migrate through a kinship tie to another village where relatives would support his social placement, or become a vagabond or wanderer who might be allowed to reincorporate into a new fixed group.

Commoners were generally reluctant to travel; they were provincial in thought, tied mainly into local social networks, although there were some itinerant entertainer-traders and the like that came from these ranks. They were exceptional, since commoners usually did not have the protection of high status or numerous kinfolk of rank in other communities. People traveling were only welcome and safe so far as the prestige of their village and its chiefs extended, and the status of their own kin or formal trading partners, who resided in foreign areas and who protected them, was also crucial. Thus people of high rank were the specialists in cross-cultural interaction.

Commoners had a set of traditions and values somewhat different from their "betters." Their knowledge was of the ordinary rituals, the "folkloric" (little traditions) rather than the esoteric aspects (great traditions) of their culture. They shared a dependence on the people of power, provided them with deference and recognized their right to rule by tradition, divine right (supernatural power implied by rank) and shared philosophies which pictured them as sometimes beneficial and fair and occasionally malevolent and exploitive.

LOWER CLASSES

The presence of lower classes has been generally unrecognized except in the literature on northwest California, where Kroeber and others detailed very precisely the dynamics of social mobility. Katherine Luomala, however, has described people who may very well have been typical in much of the state — the vagabonds, "an aggregate of non-conforming individuals who congregated seasonally without organization identification" (Luomala 1963). They were people who sometimes infiltrated stable lineages as social "poseurs." They were allowed fictive membership if they were useful to the group. Luomala found that there was a generational continuity of these "morally loose" people, who behaviorally were also associated with irresponsibility, theft and the like. One irregularity in descent continued through subsequent generations so that a chain of disregard by legitimate sib members developed   and   a   class-like   situation   prevailed (Luomala 1963: 296-8).

The presence of this sort of social situation in much of the state (e.g., Atsugewi, Tolowa, Nomlaki) suggests that this "class" accounts for many of the peculiarities and conflicts which occur in the literature about social organization. It explains what happens to deviant individuals — surely they were not *all* socialized into the system as "proper" people, or accepted despite their "deviancy" through mechanisms such as institutionalized transvestism, slavery or severe legal sanctions.

SLAVERY

In northern and southern California certain tribes institution-alized slavery in a manner reminiscent of the northwest coast culture area. The Karok, Hupa, Klamath, Modoc and perhaps the Wappo kept slaves. The Mohave and Yuma on the Colorado River also kept slaves, and perhaps occasionally the Kamia (Murdock 1967). Slaves were usually taken from other ethnic groups. The Atsugewi were a favorite target for capture by the Modoc and the Chemehuevi by the Mohave. They were taken usually in raids; the Shasta acquired Atsugewi slaves through the Modoc. While slavery was generally not a hereditary status, sons of slaves tended to have lower status than children of ordinary or wealthy people. Oftentimes slaves were eventually returned as part of a negotiation between groups in conflict, and escape was apparently common.

SPECIAL SOCIAL ROLES: SPECIAL FRIENDS, TRADING PARTNERS AND OTHER FICTIVE KIN

In those societies where the family, extended family or lineage was the primary means of articulating social relationships, and where trust was rarely extended beyond these units, the role of trading partner, special friend, or a fictive kin relationship was a very important device by which persons could extend their social, psychological, economic and political networks to larger areas.

These roles are most clearly described for the Pomo and other central California groups, but they were also important in other California groups (e.g., among the Cahuilla, a special friend was called by the same term used for a fellow moiety member). Among the Pomo the special friend was a ritually established relationship cemented by the exchange of a valuable gift — usually a feather basket — and the relationship was considered to be quite a special one, involving a sociologically primary relationship.

The trading partner relationship was found throughout the state, sometimes reinforced by intermarriage. The relationship assumed a high level of trust and reciprocity; often the partners operated in a relationship where, at least formally, the service of liaison to one another superceded a profit motivation. Thus the advantages of the non-profit, reciprocal economic relationships generally found within the extended family or lineage in native California are extended to a foreign group.

SUMMARY

The population density, extensive social scale and societal complexity that developed in California were not just a consequence of efficient technology (e.g., proto-agricultural techniques) and a fortunate environment (e.g., acorns, salmon) which provided an extraordinary amount of energy potential; they were also a consequence of specific social institutions which served to increase productive resources and redistributed energy in such a way that the resultant sociocultural complexity was truly analogous to that customarily found in horticultural and agricultural societies. These social institutions were as follows:

(1) An extension of economic and political alliances by

marriage rules (3-5 generations) and/or moiety exogamy meant that all corporate groups (tribelets) had affinal relationships in several other groups with differing economic potentials.

(2) Ritual obligations and kinship obligations required that whenever a group held a ritual, they would necessarily invite ritualists and relatives from other corporate groups. Obligatory gifting and fee payments occurred in these contexts and they were opportunities for formal trading relationships to develop.

(3) It was publicly acknowledged that certain persons had administrative rights to the production and distribution of goods (e.g., sanctioned through membership in secret societies, or involving the roles of chief, shaman, craft specialist, and the like).

(4) Formal or informal trade feasts were set up between groups living in different ecologic areas, so that goods from the mutually advantageous but politically separate areas were exchanged for those of others.

(5) A banking procedure was implicit in all of these situations, in that subsistence goods could be transformed into treasure goods, money, or craft goods.

Figure 2: Comparative Figures on Yokuts and Pomo Populations
[After Kunkel 1962]

A. Comparative Distribution of Yokuts and Pomo Tribelet
Populations — Maximum and Minimum Estimates

| | *Yokuts Tribelets* | | | | *Pomo Tribelets* | | | |
| | *Maximum* | | *Minimum* | | *Maximum* | | *Minimum* | |
Tribelet Populations	*No.*	*%*	*No.*	*%*	*No.*	*%*	*No.*	*%*
4000 plus	1	2.7	0	0.0	0	0.0	0	0.0
3000-3999	0	0.0	0	0.0	0	0.0	0	0.0
2000-2999	1	2.7	0	0.0	1	3.8	0	0.0
1000-1999	8	21.6	2	5.4	9	34.6	2	7.7
900- 999	0	0.0	0	0.0	3	11.5	2	7.7
800- 899	3	8.1	1	2.7	0	0.0	0	0.0
700- 799	1	2.7	2	5.4	0	0.0	0	0.0
600- 699	19	51.4	0	0.0	0	0.0	2	7.7
500- 599	2	5.4	3	8.1	2	7.7	3	11.5
400- 499	0	0.0	5	13.5	3	11.5	1	3.8
300- 399	1	2.7	6	16.2	5	19.2	7	26.8
200- 299	1	2.7	15	40.5	2	7.7	6	23.1
100- 199	0	0.0	3	8.1	1	3.8	2	7.7
0- 99	0	0.0	0	0.0	0	3.8	1	99.9

B. Comparative Distribution of Yokuts and Pomo Principal-Village
Populations — Maximum and Minimum Estimates

| | *Yokuts Villages* | | | | *Pomo Villages* | | | |
| | *Maximum* | | *Minimum* | | *Maximum* | | *Minimum* | |
Village Populations	*No.*	*%*	*No.*	*%*	*No.*	*%*	*No.*	*%*
1000 plus	6	16.2	1	2.7	3	11.5	1	3.8
900-999	1	2.7	0	0.0	2	7.7	0	0.0
800-899	0	0.0	0	0.0	0	0.0	0	0.0
700-799	1	2.7	2	5.4	0	0.0	0	0.0
600-699	3	8.6	1	2.7	1	3.8	2	7.7
500-599	1	2.7	1	2.7	2	7.7	1	3.8
400-499	2	5.4	0	0.0	3	11.5	1	3.8
300-399	4	10.8	4	10.8	4	15.4	5	19.2
200-299	7	18.9	12	32.4	6	23.1	5	19.2
100-199	12	32.4	8	21.6	5	19.2	10	38.5
0- 99	0	0.0	8	21.6	0	0.0	1	3.8

Figure 3: California Kinship Systems [After Murdock 1949, and others]

Kin Type	Location	Comments
Eskimo	Chimariko, Wiyot, Yana, Atsugewi	Nuclear family functionally dominant social group; bilateral descent + extension of incest taboos; low population density + associational flexibility. Monogamy predominant; frequent presence of kindreds & demes.
Hawaiian	Hupa, Karok, Modoc, Yurok, Klamath, Sinkyone, Coast Yuki, Nisenan, SW Pomo, Washo, Kawaiisu, Foothill Yokuts, Monache, Tubatulabal, Panamint, E. Mono, Mohave, Chemehuevi	Bilateral kinship reckoning; lack of exogamous kin groups; limited polygyny; bilocal extended families; generation terms for nieces & nephews; bilateral extension of incest taboos; often bilateral demes. Murdock suggests most California kinship systems were originally Hawaiian.
Yuman	Wintu	Tendency toward bifurcate merging developing unilocal residence before appearance of unilineal descent + with weakly developed lineage concept among some Wintu. Transitional state, according to Murdock; probably Dakota system formerly. Wintu — indicates evolution of types from Hawaiian, to Yuman, perhaps to Dakota and finally some to Omaha.
Dakota	Luiseño, Cahuilla, Cupeño, Yuma, Serrano, Kiliwa, Maidu, Tolowa, Shasta, Diegueño, Kamia	Murdock correlates patrilineal social organization with Iroquois cousin terminology. Polygyny; patrilocal family; exogamous lineages (sometimes moieties). Lineage usually basic corporate group. Organized in clans (Cahuilla, Cupeño), sibs (Diegueño), moieties (Cahuilla, Serrano, Cupeño). Exogamy with lineages, clans, or moiety. Sororal polygyny common. Levirate and sororate present. Bifurcate collateral; bifurcate merging for aunts & nieces.

Kin Type	Location	Comments
Omaha	Nomlaki, Patwin, E. Pomo, N. Pomo, Miwok, Wintun, Valley Yokuts, Lake Yokuts	Patrilineal descent; perhaps matrilateral cross-cousin marriage among Miwok & others. Overriding of generations + refinement of kinship group as production + distribution unit. Indicative of patrilineality; most highly developed form. Murdock feels passed through a Dakota stage. Baumhoff suggests this type correlates with the high population density of the Sacramento River area. Its presence with Lake and Valley Yokuts supports this hypothesis.
Crow	S. Pomo, Wappo	Lineality overwhelms generation criteria.

Social Organization and Status Differentiation Among the Nomlaki

by Walter Goldschmidt

Nomalaki society was organized on two major axes: the geographic-familistic and the wealth-status system. In Nomlaki society the system of wealth, the geographically patterned groupings, the use of kinship, and the political organization were all inextricably woven, so that a discussion of the social system must take all these institutional mechanisms into account. This chapter, therefore, will discuss the village, the clanlike family grouping, the secret association, and the system of wealth and status.

A general preview of this social system will act as a guide through the details that follow. The society was divided geographically into a series of autonomous villages, each presided over by a headman whose position was semihereditary and whose powers were limited. The village was also basically a family group within which all were patrilineally related except the women who married into the family. These family-village groups were called *olkapna*.

Cutting across this system of localized groupings was a recognized social class differential. Fundamentally, the status distinction was based on wealth, since the economy of the Nomlaki included a monetary system and a number of material items that were privately owned by persons of prestige. In turn, this development of wealth and prestige was associated with a rather intensive specialization of crafts and professions, although certain basic economic tasks appear to have been the province of all. A secret society, with an initiatory ordeal designed to produce a coma or trance, was the institutional mechanism that supported and sanctioned both the system of wealth status and the specialization into crafts and professions. Through this initiation the individual became a recognized member of the elite and at the same time could acquire through a dream experience the right to engage in a specific craft or profession. The association of this elite acted as a mechanism for unifying the otherwise atomistic village-family system.

The description of any social system partakes of the nature of a construct. Individuals act toward certain ends; the system as such is not recognized by the members. In the present ethnography this construct was pieced together from fragmentary information. It should be repeated here that the Nomlaki social system became defunct in the third quarter of the nineteenth century. Much of the detail has been lost even to the memory of the oldest informants, none of whom knew Nomlaki culture before it was affected by whites. I believe, however, that in its major outlines the description is accurate, and I have indicated points on which doubt still remains. As a check upon this construct I have included many quotations from informants, so that the reader can examine critically the basis upon which the synthesis rests.

THE LOCAL GROUP

The people we call Nomlaki were not a united tribe. There were no institutional mechanisms for effecting tribal unity, although a vague sense of tribal identity prevailed. The Nomlaki were divided into numerous (but unnumbered) local groups. Each of these local groups centered in a village or *kêwêl*; it held a certain amount of land in common and generally had a second area of land in the mountains of the Coast Range.

The *kêwêl* consisted of a chief's house (*êlkêl*) surrounded by a group of individual family houses. A diagrammatic sketch of such a village is shown in figure 1. The chief's house was the focal point of the village. The individual family houses faced toward it. In the chief's house were centered the group activities: gambling, smoking, storytelling, and the important "sweating dances." The chief's house had something of a sacred character. Children and women were especially admonished to comport themselves with restraint when they entered it. In front of the *êlkêl* was an open area that acted as the village square, where ceremonial and secular gatherings took place.

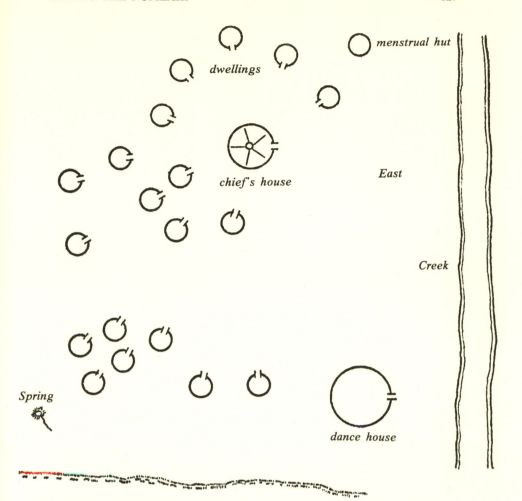

dwellings

menstrual hut

chief's house

East

Creek

Spring

dance house

Draw

Fig. 1. Diagram of a Nomlaki village. The small houses were grouped about the larger chief's house, which they faced. The chief's house faced the stream, into which the men plunged after certain sweating ceremonials. Later houses were built toward the spring, which was the source of water. The large house was a postwhite addition, away from the remainder of the village. The menstrual hut was at the opposite end of the village from the water supply.

The diagram was prepared by Jones. It does not represent a particular village, but shows characteristic relationships.

In a three-quarter circle about the chief's house were gathered the brush shelters or *latcikêl*, popularly called wickiups. A single family of man, wife, and minor children lived in each of these shelters. In rare cases of polygamy the second wife apparently shared common quarters. The circle had no significance, and if the village grew, houses would be placed beyond, usually toward the source of water. The menstrual hut was built on the opposite side of the village from the water source, in an "out-of-the-way place" where it would be "out of danger." In historic times the large, multipost dance house was placed off to one side, usually at some distance.

There were anywhere from five to fifty family houses in a single village, with a population of from twenty-five to more than two hundred persons. An average of a hundred persons in a village seems a conservative estimate. Villages were frequently within calling distance of one another.[1]

THE KIN GROUP

The village comprised, in a sense, a single kin group. These kin groups were named, patrilineal, exogamous social units, the members of which considered themselves blood relatives whether or not the ties of kinship could be directly ascertained. These groups were called *olkapna*. The men and unmarried women of each village were members of the same olkapna, so that the social unit had a primary economic function. When, as was occasionally reported, the same olkapna name occurred in two separate villages or when otherwise unrelated persons claimed the same olkapna name, they considered themselves to be of the same group; the men "called one another brother," and intermarriage was forbidden. The olkapna must therefore be considered clans.[2]

Each olkapna was named. Table 1 shows the names of the nineteen known to informants, as well as an indication (where

1. Kroeber has estimated the aboriginal population of the Wintun as between twenty-five and forty-five persons for each hundred square kilometers. Since he places them marginal to the area of higher density, they probably fall at the upper level of this range (Kroeber, 1939: 154).
2. I have elsewhere discussed the relationship of the olkapna to similar familistic groupings in central California and the importance of this situation to the theory of clan development (Goldschmidt, 1948). While the formal requirements for clan organization are filled by the Nomlaki olkapna, the

possible) of the meaning, the approximate location, and the affiliation of one or more persons for each. In the names no pattern is discernible. Some are clearly place names (e.g., *sênkênti*, in which *kênti* is a locative meaning "down under"); others have reference to people (e.g., *dolitewa* and *Nomleak*'). However, most of them cannot be translated at all. Informants refer to these names occasionally as surnames, which indicates their analogy to our own family names and refers to the patrilineal character of affiliation.

The olkapna were patrilineal. Genealogical data could not be obtained, but wherever reference was made to inheritance or affiliation, it was referred to as patrilineal. Inheritance of personal property was not important, since most possessions were destroyed or buried with the dead. But inheritance of affiliation and attitudes of kinship followed patrilineal lines. According to informants, the mother's relatives were "not considered important." Affinal relatives were likewise secondary to consanguine ones. For instance, it was the family of a deceased person who made the decisions about his burial; the spouse did not participate in plans for this important rite.

The exogamic character of the olkapna is clearly established. An informant said, "No sunsunu would ever marry another sunsunu." The following statement is indicative of attitudes toward olkapna exogamy.

(Jones:) Once there was a family (olkapna) that did not associate with other families but lived to itself in a small fertile valley. They would only marry their own people, and when one or two did drift out they would go right back. The women never went out, and no outsiders ever visited them. They stayed apart — isolated, I suppose — because they were ashamed of the way they lived, and finally the whites scattered them.

They were not particularly poor. If a man saw one of them, he would talk to him but would only speak of them

---

implications of clan organization were certainly not fully realized. The absence of any ceremonial sanctions or of great emotional content suggests how incompletely the olkapna fulfilled the potential role of clan organization. Because of this marginality and in accord with sound practice, I shall employ the native term rather than the word "clan" in reference to these groups.

TABLE 1
OLKAPNA GROUPS AMONG THE NOMLAKI

Name	Location	Members
1. *pôxmalê* (to make fire)	Elder Creek, north of Paskenta, Lance Ranch	Ellen James, Andrew Freeman, Bill Freeman
2. *tcekôn* (*tcek*, strings)	Ull Place, northwest of Paskenta	Dominic, Dominic's grandfather, Nettie Hastings, Alice Joe
3. *kellebî* (*kel*, house)	Mountain House, west of Paskenta	Jones's mother, Maggie Hoksy, Joe Freeman
4. *tcistawa*	near Paskenta	Dick Raglin's mother, Andy Freeman's maternal grandmother
5. *nômpômha*	Lopom, near Paskenta	Molly Freeman, Anne Raglin
6. *sunsunu* (*sunu*, bird's nest)	Newville, *kolaiêl*	Lee Kirk, Burrows' brothers
7. *appak*	Elder Creek, north of Paskenta	Jordan's mother
8. *luiko* (sore eyes?)	original Paskenta	
9. *yaitowa*	near Paskenta	Andy Freeman's maternal grandfather
10. *sênkênti* (down under the "rabbit stick")	near Newville	Bill Finnell
11. *dôkôki*	one near Lowrey, another at Tehama	
12. *dolitewa* (north people?)	near Newville	
13. *ta·ponas*	Burrows' place, Dry Creek ("not our people" — Jones)	
14. *holotcitci*		
15. *p'ana*		
16. *nomleak‘* (western language, cf. Nomlaki)		
17. *tcô·k* (young oak tree)		(Jones: "Katalmen rancheria of *Noimôk* tribe, also a few in our tribe.")
18. pôhwai		
19. soyê’	near Paskenta	George Freeman

as animals or coyotes when he got back home. The women never married out. Some captain must have taught them that "devil way." D's mother was one of that tribe — that's why he is the way he is. (D had an unsavory reputation with the other tribe members.)

The unity of the olkapna was demonstrated by Jones in another context. A River Wintun woman took care of him at one time, saying, "Your mother and I are sisters through names. Any child of any *kellebî* (olkapna) are my relations — you are almost a son of mine." This suggests that the bond was equally matrilineal (as does the kinship identity of a sister's child with children when a woman is speaking), but it must be recalled that Jones had no paternal relatives among the Nomlaki.

KINSHIP REGULATIONS

The olkapna was central in a general system for the regulation of interpersonal relationships through bonds of kinship. As is generally true, related persons had certain mutual rights and obligations that ordered behavior.

Some generalizations can be made about the function of the relationship system in the ordering of interpersonal behavior. Although a distinction was made between father and his brothers, wife and her sisters, husband and his brothers, the children of these relatives were not distinguished. A stepparent was called by the term of parent's sibling. These facts are in accord with the levirate and sororate usages found among the Nomlaki. Thus the father's brother could become the father (but was called uncle or stepfather), and his children could become siblings, as they were already identified.

Some features of the system supported the integrity of the olkapna organization. Chief among these features was the identification of parallel cousins and siblings. The olkapna ties were strengthened also by the fact that a man identified his brother's children with his own; a woman identified her sister's children with her own. It was not, however, a system perfectly aligned with a clanlike organization, for group identities and differences were not regularly demonstrated.

Of eight principles on which kinship was based (Kroeber,

1909: 77ff.; Lowie, 1934), the following were important: sex of relative, consanguine *versus* affinal relationship, generation differentiation, lineal *versus* collateral relatives, cross *versus* parallel relatives, differentiation of age within generation, and sex of speaker. Age of connecting relative was not brought into the picture.

Kinship regulated behavior in many situations. Details of obligation and duties are discussed elsewhere, but a few may be mentioned here. Co-wives might or might not be sisters, but "if a man has two wives they claim sisters even though they might not be." Both the sororate and levirate were reported. In this connection, a man and his sister-in-law had license to "talk rough with one another" and to indulge in vulgar horseplay. On the other hand, a man was expected to avoid any association with his mother-in-law and to behave with extreme decorum with his father-in-law and discuss only matters of importance. A woman avoided her father-in-law, but she spent a great deal of time with her mother-in-law, who acted as her "protector."

CHIEFTAINSHIP

Nature and Function. — Over each village was a captain, *tcabatu*, who had usually succeeded his father but who owed his power as much to his personality as to inheritance. The captain was a leader, not a ruler. His first duty was to advise, admonish, and direct his followers. Thus each day he arose at dawn, climbed on the roof of his *êlkêl*, and planned the day. He would start his harangue to the people with moralistic clichés: "Do right, don't get into trouble, help your neighbor," accompanying his words with great, sweeping gestures. Then he would call persons or groups by name and give duties to each. Thus he might have some men investigate the source of a specific grass and report on their finds; he might have youths gather wood, women make porridge. If a dance or social gathering was to be held, he would give each person his duty for that event. The harangue, which had begun with moral admonition, might end: "If you have to strike an enemy, that's different. You have to protect yourself."

This function of the chief was probably his most important one, and being a "good talker" was a prime requisite for the office. He could, however, hire a man to do the talking, especially in connection with important social functions. This was expensive, since the talker (*tc êwê*) received good pay for his services. A prospective chief often went into the woods to practice talking — behavior showing a commendable attitude in the youth.

Small villages were often close together, and a single captain might be over a group of them. This suggests that the chief was not simply the olkapna elder. The chief's influence might occasionally extend over a larger territory than his own particular domain. Jones said that Dominic's grandfather, who was head of *tcekôn* family, which owned a fertile section of land on Elder Creek, was sought out by people from as far away as Newville for his advice in disputes. His less popular son did not have this influence; perhaps the introduction of whites altered the circumstances.

The second major function of the chieftain was that of arbiter. As a rule, disputants endeavored to arrive at an agreement between themselves. But if such an agreement could not be reached, the chief might be called in to arbitrate. More detail on legal disputes appears below.

The chief was also expected to make decisions on matters affecting his village. Thus, if a group of men wanted to build a dance house, they would bring their plan to their chief, who would render a presumably final decision. Any person of importance might leave the village in protest against some action by the chief, but that was his only recourse beyond his powers of persuasion.

Finally, the captain played an economic role. He was, under prewhite conditions, a rich man — perhaps the richest in the village, but not necessarily so. He kept on hand a supply of perishable necessities of life for use when visitors came to trade. It was his duty to be always in a position to trade. Thus a war might be ended by an agreement to barter goods, and it was apparently necessary for the prestige of the group to make a good showing in these postwar negotiations. Furthermore, any family falling short of food replenished its stock from the chief's larder.

Such loans from the headman's supply were either paid for with beads, rope, or some other item of fairly standard value, or later returned in kind. Acorns were, however, kept in a common granary to be drawn upon by each family. They were not the property of the headman, but it was his duty to see that no person took more than his reasonable share.

The role of the chief as an economic stabilizer was reflected in a similar pattern in connection with feasts. The rabbits killed for a ceremonial occasion were placed in a common pile and redistributed by the chief to the family heads according to their individual needs. Each family would roast and pound their rabbits, making patties of the pounded meat. A youth was sent around with a basket to collect one of the patties from each family head for the chief, who thus had a supply of meat for any latecomers or for children who became hungry later in the evening.

Succession of inheritance to the chieftainship was from father to son, though a brother might inherit before the son. A cousin or grandson might succeed in the absence of closer relatives. If there were no one to take the place, the old men of the group would meet to appoint a successor. A chieftain father would train his son from boyhood for his position, especially in the art of oratory. People would give presents to the prospective chief "so that he knows his place." He would also be under close scrutiny by the people, because if a man was felt to be unworthy, the rules of succession could be overridden by the demand of the men of the village, who apparently made some kind of formal acceptance of the successor.

Aside from the social prestige of the office itself, the chief gained status through his wealth. One reason for his advantageous economic status was that he was in a position to trade with outside persons was well as with villagers. Furthermore, he apparently used the supplies brought in by other people for his trading activities. The chieftain also enjoyed an immunity from the more menial tasks, such as ropemaking and hunting, and lived from the produce of his fellows' labors, just as he enhanced his wealth by using their goods as capital in trading. Also because of his position he was able to marry rich wives — usually several of them — which in turn improved his economic position. He was, in fact, expected to marry a rich man's daughter, any other match being frowned upon. Such marriages were often contracted by the girl's parents while the bride was still a child, perhaps at about the time the chief inherited his position. This girl would receive special attention in keeping with her future position.

Female chiefs. — Occasional women chiefs were reported among neighbors of the Nomlaki. One informant mentioned an elected female chief who was the male chief's wife, but his statement is unclear. Women of high status enjoyed some distinctions, as in the case of the future chief's bride-to-be.

> (Jones:) Charms are men's property. Only the daughter of
> a big man is counted as a man and must be considered for
> any important business. A woman may become a chief. No
> common woman could keep a charm, but a "queen sort of
> a woman" could take such property.

Modern chiefs. — Of all the captains in the memory of the
informants, the grandfather of Kroeber's informant Dominic
(Kroeber, 1932:355) was the most vivid. Dominic, with whom Jones
had lived as a boy, evidently painted this ancestor as an important
man, but he did not accord his father such a rank. These men
belonged to the *tcekôn* olkapna, which owned fertile lands in the
region near the present Lowrey, California. Dominic's grandfather
was pictured not only as a peaceable man and a good talker (lesser
captains came from distant villages for his advice) but also as one
willing to fight when necessary. His great virtues, as described by
Jones, were his ability to talk, his generosity, and his kindness.
Dominic, although considered a chieftain, was said to have been a
poor talker and seems to have been unpopular.

The postwhite chieftain of Paskenta who looms largest in
native memory was Captain Jim, *sayê*. "He handled the whole
outfit. He went from one village to another to see how the people
were getting along. The people took care of him. Captain Jim was of
the *tcistawa* olkapna." Since Captain Jim's death there have been a
number of Nomlaki who were selected to act as chief, but none of
them had any real influence or authority.

The "peacemaker." — A separate functionary in the political
structure was the "peacemaker," an office that might be filled by
the chieftain or by a separate person. He was "right next to the
captain, a man who doesn't have to work or hunt but only has to
entertain visitors; just naturally a good talker, he says things in
such a way that it just seems the right thing to do."

This persuasive personality appeared at the scene of battle,
either between combatants in a blood feud or at a war, and
attempted to induce the disputants to come to an amicable
agreement. More specific data as to his function appear below in
the war stories.

Summary. — At this point it may be advisable to summarize the social structure as far as it has been examined. The area was divided into autochthonous villages or village groups. The population was divided into several clanlike extended families called olkapna. The village comprised a single extended family as well as the married-in women, the temporarily married-in men, the persons who for some reason adopted the village as their home — that is, there was a loose correspondence between village and olkapna. The villages or village groups were led by a chieftain. This leader's power was a result of his personality, his ability to talk, and his wealth; it was derived by hereditary right with the approval of the important men of the tribe; it was limited by the necessity of conforming to a considerable degree to the will of these men.

THE HUTA GROUP

The initiatory body. — In order to understand the political system of the Nomlaki it is necessary to examine the organization known as the Huta society and the social status of the initiates. However, very little is known either of the exact functions of the group or of the formal organization of this body as a secret society.

Jones and Andrew Freeman were the only informants who could be persuaded to give information about the Huta. Neither of them had ever been members of this group. Other informants considered it unimportant, their reasons being unclear. Thus Molly Freeman said: *"Huh'ti* is just a sweat. It doesn't make doctors or any such thing." Jordan analyzed it thus: "Huta was a contest to see who could stand the most heat. They dance around the fire in the sweat house. After they have stayed in there as long as they can, they run out and jump into the creek." These statements may be given little consideration in view of the data I was able to extract from the accounts given by both Jones and Freeman.

The initiation ceremony took place in the semisubterranean sweat house. The candidates underwent a series of food taboos during the day before the night's ceremony in order to avoid "smothering" from the heat of the fire. Manzanita was the preferred firewood because of the intense heat it provided. The naked initiates danced around the fire to the accompaniment of singers, the split-stick rattle, and a drummer who performed on the log drum. The songs were sung in what Jones called "Indian

Latin," the meaning being unintelligible to those not already initiated. The dancing continued until the candidates became exhausted. When they fell they were dragged away from the fire and left prone on the floor of the sweat house. During this period of coma, dreaming might take place. Water might be thrown on the comatose dancers. Then, at three or four in the morning the revived initiates left the sweat house and plunged into the near-by creek. Neither food nor water was taken until the feast that followed, probably about daybreak. At that time acorn mush and other foods were consumed and nonalcoholic "wine" made from crushed manzanita berries was drunk. Then the initiates described whatever dreams they had had. These dreams were interpreted and instruction was given by the older members of the society.

Freeman said definitely that this ceremony took place in the spring, but both he and Jones also referred to its being held upon the construction of a new sweat house. How long the actual ceremony lasted is uncertain. The dancing certainly took place at night within a twelve-hour period, but Freeman indicated that the instruction of the candidates might last for as much as four or five days.

Powers described what was undoubtedly this ceremony when he said:

> They have nothing that can be considered a religious ceremony, unless it is one of their fanatical dances in the assembly chamber, wherein they act in an extraordinary manner, running around naked, leaping and whooping like demons in the execrable smudge and heat, and stench, until they are reeking with perspiration, when they clamber up the center pole and run and plunge neck and heels into the river. Sometimes they fall into a swoon, like the plantation negros in a revival when they are affected with "the power," and lie unconscious for two or three days. I cannot believe this is any religious frenzy . . . (Powers, 1877: 241).

Women were rigidly excluded from all the proceedings, and it is clear that there was no public announcement of what was to take place. The officials for the ceremony seem to have been a dance leader (*dauheimê*), a wood gatherer, and two attendants (workmen, *tcînit*) who lifted the exhausted initiates away from the fire. Neither of the informants knew on what basis the candidates were selected except that they were young men of between sixteen and thirty. The number chosen was given variously as four or five, or fifteen to twenty. Jones says that the candidates were tested and tempted in order to determine whether they were properly secretive and could be relied upon to keep the secrets of the society.

Boys unable to stand the heat of the fire or the other tests were excluded. Those who passed the ordeal of prolonged dancing and the heat of the fire may be subdivided into two classes. Those who dreamed might become seers (*tlahit*). They were expected to sing upon recovering from the coma into which they had fallen. It may be mentioned, however, that both informants specifically said that the shaman's power was not acquired in this way. Nondreamers were apparently instructed in various crafts or techniques, becoming specialists.

Members of this secret organization called each other brother and were expected to help each other. The closeness of the bonds within the organization is witnessed by the fact that members who divulged a part of the esoteric knowledge of the group would be sought out and killed, one reference indicating that hired assassins from among the Shasta were employed for this purpose.

Trading between individuals who had passed the Huta ordeal seems to have been a recognized and possibly an important aspect of the society. Jones indicated this in particular. This feature of the functional aspect of the group in addition to the emphasis on reciprocal help between members indicates quite clearly that the organization was something over and above the village and olkapna affiliation. Reference was also made to the fact that a deceased member was mourned in a ceremony held in the sweat house by fellow members of the society, after which the body was returned to the relatives for the regular Nomlaki mourning and burial ceremonies.

The above outline of the nature, the organization, and the function of this group is necessarily incomplete. Nevertheless, the Huta initiates, though not a named body, were a formal organization of males possessed of esoteric knowledge that led to the control of certain crafts or to other special positions within the society. Some of the principal points on which data are lacking have to do with the special prerequisites for membership, the relation between the organization and the tribal captain, and more particularly on the precise nature and extent of the control exercised by this group in various crafts and professions. It is quite certain that the Huta organization had a large measure of control over the wealth as well as over the political power of Nomlaki society. Some aspects of the nature of this control are discussed later in the sections on trade and specialization. The society appears to have included the artisans in certain leading professions and to have maintained trading relationships; common men did not ordinarily enter into large-scale trading activities.

Relationship of the Huta to the Kuksu system. — The Huta initiation of the Nomlaki was undoubtedly part of the religious-cult system of central California. This has been the subject of several specific studies (Kroeber, 1925, 1923, 1932; Loeb, 1932, 1933). In Kroeber's early work he anticipated the presence of an element of the Kuksu system among the Wintun.

> For the Central Wintun information is doubtful. The Colusa Patwin declares that the characteristic Kuksu forms, such as the Hesi ceremony and Moki impersonator, were not known beyond uppermost Stony Creek . . . Beyond, on Grindstone and the middle course of Stony Creek, and about Paskenta only ''common'' dances were made, the southerners declare (Kroeber, 1925 369).

On his map of ''Ritual Cults of California,'' Kroeber credits the Wintun with possession of the complex, largely because of their wedgelike location between tribes known to possess it (Kroeber, 1925: pl. 74). He recognized that if the cult was practiced by the Wintuns, it lacked some of its outstanding dramatic features in their hands.

In his later review of the data, Kroeber notes the absence of Hesi, Moki, and Kuksu, and excludes the Central Wintun (now generally called Wintun) from the area possessing the system (Kroeber, 1932: 358, 393). Loeb, influenced by Kroeber, did not make investigations in Wintun territory.

There are indications that the Nomlaki version of the secret society was not related to specific Kuksu or Hesi societies of the Patwin, but rather to a more obscure part of the system, the Wai-saltu society. The following is excerpted from Kroeber's

statement on this part of the Patwin religious system, with italics
supplied.

> The wai-saltu or north spirits perform the ceremony called
> waiyapai, *north dance*. This is separate both from the
> group of dances associated with the hesi and from the
> kuksu ritual. It appears to have an initiation of its own,
> though what seems to be such was not so designated by
> informants; at any rate *only those who belong can
> participate, or even be present at part of the ceremony*.
> The wai-saltu therefore evidently formed a separate
> organization. This is in some respects the counterpart of
> the Pomo kuhma or hahluigak and Yuki hulk'ilal, the old
> native ghost society as distinct from the modern
> revivalistic ghost dance. One Patwin informant stated that
> the wai-saltu acted like ghosts, and their get-up, cry, and
> actions appear to bear out the same idea. But the ghost
> concept is not so clear in the Patwin mind as it is in the
> mind of the Pomo and Yuki, who consistently speak of the
> performers as representing ghosts or "devils," that is,
> spirits of deceased human beings. The Patwin do however
> look upon the ceremony as powerful and dangerous as
> compared with the hesi. The wai-saltu performers are
> supposed to go actually insane; the Pomo-Yuki ghosts are
> merely strange and terrifyingly queer. In both cases the
> performers are numerous, simply costumed, and
> undifferentiated.
>
> Not all the Patwin practiced the wai-saltu . . . For the
> Cortina hill Patwin, a wai-saltu ceremony is reported . . .
> *References to the north recur throughout the
> wai-saltu*, just as the kuksu is associated with the south . .
> *Some Patwin informants restrict the wai-saltu
> ceremony to men*, but one explicitly mentions women
> participants or members. Children are not taken in; the
> initiates are adult.
>
> The ceremony lasts three elapsed or four counted
> days. The performers are completely blackened with
> charcoal, which disguises them, and wear little or nothing
> but a feather headdress and perhaps a tule shirt or clout.
> Their shout is rendered as a prolonged ha or o-o-o or

ho-ho-ho-ho.

On the last afternoon they sweat intensely, bleed at the mouth or nose, become demented, run out and off, and sometimes fall into swamps where they lie helpless and drown, to be ritualistically brought to life later, in the dance house. Each performer is followed by relatives, who watch and "herd" him and try finally to drive him back to the dance house for ritual doctoring to restore him to sanity. The performance is evidently the initiation into wai-saltu membership . . .

The older members seem not to go crazy, but presumably direct the people who guard the wandering novices. The head master or director, the tantu, lies still in the dance house, reciting and perhaps partly enacting a formula which relates to the travels of the spirit wai-saltu and is probably the esoteric myth explanatory of the rite (Kroeber, 1932: 315-7).

The above suggests that the Wai-saltu had the following in common with the Huta initiation: the association with the north; the apparent limitations to adult males; the limitation of participants to actual members; the process of sweating; the induced comatose state with the implications of death and rebirth; and the general association with the wealth complex (among the Patwin in the form of purchase of this privilege). Finally, we may note the term waiyapai, translated as "north dance" to yapaitu, (spirit) among the Nomlaki.

Therefore, the Huta may be placed in the sacred-society system of which the Kuksu cult is a part. The implications are that it represented an earlier, simpler stratum of the system and that the elaborations practiced in the south were never adopted by the Nomlaki. At the same time the Huta represented a northern outpost of the ritual form. There is no evidence of this cult among the Wintu, whose culture has been described in detail, the Yana, Achomawi, or Atsugewi. The extension of the pattern to include the Central Wintun alters the distribution in such a way as to include nearly all the people holding river-bottom lands in north-central California, and limits it to areas of relative low altitude. Whether this association has any special significance is not readily apparent.

The Nomlaki data suggest a close association between the

secret-society initiation and the central California wealth complex. This complex may be formulated: initiation — social status — wealth — money — trade; that is, the initiation ceremony marked off those with high social standing, persons who acquired wealth, handled money, and engaged in trade in wealth objects. It was suggested earlier that the wealth pattern was derived from the south, whence, incidentally, the raw money came. It seems likely that the Huta initiation spread northward from some southern center in connection with this money economy and wealth status. It seems likely that the pattern of accumulated wealth might have been limited to the richer and more densely populated valley and foothill lands.

STATUS AND PRIVILEGE

The Huta initiation marked off an elite from the body of ordinary people among the Nomlaki. This distinction into two separate social classes based upon initiation into the secret society pervaded all aspects of social life, and the Nomlaki appear to have been highly conscious of status and prestige in all of their interpersonal relationships. Nomlaki status was associated with the possession of wealth, the control of certain crafts and professions, the right to trade in and perhaps even to own certain types of goods, and prestige and importance in the community.

The recognition of rank was given verbal expression. Several terms denoted social position:

Tcabatu, rich man, chief. Further described as "a big wise fellow, a big man, like a chief. He doesn't have to be a chief. He is a rich man, a good, honest, straight-up man. He is a man who is wealthy and descended from chiefs. He is lucky about getting things. He doesn't work, because everybody provides for him. He is a man who can control his people; he is a man of means. He is a kind of clown too. He can do everything, for he is smart and can act like a fool (be a ceremonial clown) and speak sense in company.

Hehît, "a sort of clown who serves all kinds of purposes and can do all sorts of things. When they first start a big time, he yells a long he e e e, and tells the people what is going to happen. He is also a clown who does all kinds of foolish things — he falls down and spills things and gets scolded. He does things like this on purpose." It appears that this role served a ceremonial and a general function, that the *hehit* was a person of importance with considerable force in the community by means of his right and powers of ridicule.

Nêhkit, rich man. Also means "he finds it." "*Nehkit* is a rich man, not a chief or anything more. He is just a man who is worth a lot of property." We may assume that *nehkit* is the more general, and *tcabatu* the more specific term.

Watlamawîn, ordinary man, commoner, from *watlama*, ordinary; *wîn*, man. "*Watlamawîn* is just a common man — not a good talker, doesn't do anything, doesn't pay attention to anything. One would say of him, 'Aw, he is nothing.' " The word *watlama* is used to refer to anything ordinary, such as a plain meal.

Êlama, lazy person. "They gossip about these people."

The implication of status to daily life and social relationships may be appreciated through the following statements:

When they see a strange man, they would ask, "Is he a man?" meaning, "Does he belong to something?" A person might answer, "No, he is just a *watlamawîn*."

Specialists (i.e., Huta initiates) may hunt occasionally, but they do not do so ordinarily. They always have a lot of work to do and are well paid, so that they don't have to go hunting. Such a man's wife cooks, but she doesn't have to go into the hills to gather like other women unless she wants to. She is not supposed to go out and work. She has on good clothes, things that are silk and jewelry to the Indians. The wife of a tradesman doesn't have to go out, and may even have an aunt or a grandmother to cook for her. She would wait on her husband.

Women wear beads and such things only at big times, or when they are showing themselves, unless they have nothing to do except dress up and look pretty. A chief marries a well-to-do woman.

The more beads a man has, the more important he is. Those who have more beads than others feel rich and are what are called "big Indians" and go around acting proud like rich white people.

People who don't have anything at all usually come to a supper late — such people as boys living with girls who didn't have any relatives so that they couldn't get married in the regular way, or orphans, or someone of that kind. Such a person would come within sight of where the people were having their time but would not come in until invited. He would wait where he can be seen until he is called. If anything is left, the people might give him something to cook. If he puts something into the chief's basket (i.e., the common larder kept for later distribution by the chief), the people appreciate that and talk favorably about it. But if he is selfish, the people won't pay any attention to him.

How closely these distinctions in status were marked by the initiation is not entirely clear. Apparently the privileges of owning eagles and of access to the chief's house were so limited. Jones believed that a person could achieve a measure of status by personality traits.

A common man, if well liked by a "made man" and if he carried himself well and behaved right and built himself up with the rules, even if he didn't belong to the Huta group, even though he was an outsider, might build up a group of his own separately. He would have to be a good person and agreeable. Then he might start a new rancheria and might come to be of some importance.

Yet Jones and other natives expressed themselves in a manner that tended to deny a belief in social mobility. A constant expression was that "it was given to a man" to be or do something. In matters of social position the underlying philosophy seems to have been that a person's abilities, wealth, and social position were inherent in him — not by biological processes but by virtue of his spirit. Their attitude might be likened to an unformulated mana concept, with a note of predetermination if not fatalism.

The existence of a slave class is doubtful. The following suggests that war captives were either returned or killed:

(Jones:) Dominic's grandfather got servants by capturing them from another tribe. He used a couple of Yuki as slaves until they grew up. He was about the only one who had Yuki servants. He had to send them back because other people wanted to kill those two boys.

They take slaves in wars, but sometimes those who had lost the most relatives would kill the captured slaves. Sometimes they would send the slaves home at night. They don't hold slaves very long, nor do they keep very many.

SPECIALIZATION

The initiation was viewed as an experience through which youths acquired the ability to engage in a profession or special craft, and a prevailing attitude regarded that ability as a special talent presumably resting on a spiritual base. All this suggests a rather elaborate system of occupational specializing and division of labor.

Specific statements that certain persons were especially qualified for certain tasks, were made in connection with the following crafts or professions: shamanism, necromancy, message running, fishing, trapping squirrels, trapping rats, bow making, arrow making, flint chipping, breaking of flint blocks, stone-pipe making, stone-bead making, tattooing, cutting of ear and nose septum, haircutting, skirtmaking, climbing for pine nuts, preparing buckeyes, salt leaching (from a weed — used in the valley only), and fire making.

Most of the above occupations and processes are discussed elsewhere, and it is unnecessary to go into detail here. Occasionally specialization became almost ritualistic. One description said that three separate persons had specialized tasks for the act of breaking flint: one to heat the flint, a second to tend the fire in the heating process, and a third to do the actual breaking. It seems likely that this activity had ritual meaning involving the supernatural, although this was not explicit. Bear hunting involved several persons with special powers or abilities. Similarly, in gathering pine nuts one person climbed the tree and dislodged the cones, a second one sits under the tree and chants, and others pick up and shell the nuts.

The development of specialization and the concept of "calling" in this simple society was somewhat unusual. In many instances the specialization formed a source of particular power and prestige, and the specialists were evidently always persons of substance and importance in the community. Probably — although it is not certain — a man who had not gone through the Huta initiation could not act as any kind of specialist, with the possible exception of the shaman. In this connection it is noteworthy that specialized crafts did not exist among the women, except that some women were shamans. It was recognized that some women excelled in such arts as basketmaking, but never with the implication of a specialized functionary who had supernatural power and social privilege.

Although specialization of crafts is not usual among simpler societies, it was not unique to the Nomlaki. In fact their neighbors and close linguistic relatives, the Patwin, shared the concept of craft specialization, as has been ably set forth by McKern (1922: 235-8). Among the Patwin, craft specialization was associated with specific families, who held a monopolistic hereditary right over the particular activity. Although there is some evidence that the Nomlaki individual achieved his skill and his prerogative from an older relative, it was not defined as the family characteristic and not associated in any discernible way with the olkapna.

Control of a special craft or function in Nomlaki society occasionally freed an individual of the work involved in basic food production.

> (Jones:) Everybody feeds other people like the runners. Hunters give them food too. The tradespeople are fed by others. Such a person may go hunting if he has caught up with his other work, but he is taken care of while he is working. That is why they like to be big men and why women like to marry that kind of a man.

It is doubtful if specialization in activities ever completely freed anyone from the tasks of hunting, fishing, and food gathering.

Shamans and chiefs might be freed from such labors, but it is more likely that everyone engaged in these basic activities. Control over a craft or profession was, however, a source of special wealth, so that the specialist found his activity served his own economic and social advantage.

This would be possible only in a society in which material wealth was an established social goal and in which there existed a mechanism for the free transfer of goods by either barter or sale. For this reason it is necessary to an understanding of the structure of the society to examine also the nature and role of wealth and the characteristics of barter and trade.

PROPERTY AND WEALTH

Resource property. — Ownership of land resided in the olkapna. Each olkapna usually owned a valley territory and another area in the mountains. Since the control over usage rested in the hands of the village chieftain, informants occasionally made reference to individual ownership.

> (Jones:) The land does not belong to individuals. Dominic's grandfather, by being such a big and good man, was favored. He was left a big valley. He owned one big oak tree of a special kind. It was a singular tree called *nuis*. There was a rancheria nearby, but old Dominic's grandfather owned that tree and got all the acorns from it. He also owned a valley of about 2,000 acres of open land. It was two or three miles away from his home. This valley was staked off — each different division (olkapna?) got a different part of the valley for themselves. They had poles to mark the different persons' territories.

Personal ownership could apparently be claimed of certain favorable trees or fishing places. The term of ownership is not entirely clear, but it probably had reference only to the seasonal product. The following statements are offered as indicative of attitudes, although they do not give concrete institutional mechanisms.

(Raglin:) If a person has a good fishing or hunting place, he can keep it to himself. Men keep good hunting grounds away from other people. If a man isn't at his fishing place, someone else uses it. Everybody knew the trees that were his own property. There was no inheritance of trees.

(Jones:) Where there is a tree of small acorns, some family owns that tree.[3] He will lean a stick against the tree on the side toward which he lives. Thus the people know what family owns it. He may set up too many and will give away the others to his relatives. This person kind of owns the tree — like you would a fruit tree. In those days the families owned them. They own trees in the mountains too. They maintain border lines, but if you are friendly with them they may give you a tree in time of need.

The private ownership of land resources was limited and unimportant to the economy and social structure of the Nomlaki. For all intents and purposes, productive resources were held by the village olkapna. But private possession of various forms of chattels was significant. These can be divided into three categories: capital goods or equipment, wealth and ceremonial objects, and magic formulas. Important items in the first category included bows and arrows, pestles, baskets, and nets — especially the large and expensive deer nets. In the second category, the prime items of wealth were the hide of the black bear, beads of magnesite and shell, and feathers. Magic formulas of greatest importance were knowledge of "poisoning" magic and special "charm stones." Ownership of wealth items was particularly the mark of status, and there is evidence that such property could be held only by persons who had undergone the Huta initiation. This might be called a system of sumptuary laws or — perhaps better — sumptuary customs.

Wealth. — In native values the pelt of the black bear was the most valuable economic item.[4] No man of distinction would ever be

---

3. Cf. Nisenan usage, where land is held by the village but rights to trees are privately established (Beals, 1933: 363).

4. In 1906 Washington mentions the supreme value of the black bearhide, which was desired for purposes of burial. "(It) must be black and must be

buried without being wrapped in a fine bearskin he himself had obtained during his lifetime. He might, of course, obtain several and use some for relatives, but the finest would always be for his own interment.

The possession of feathers was similarly a sign of wealth. Especially desired were the yellowhammer quills, woodpecker scalps, and eagle feathers. Eagle feathers served both utilitarian and ceremonial purposes and formed a mark of distinction. The following account of eagle ownership indicates the value of these birds as well as the simple manner in which the wealthy maintained ownership of this form of property.[5]

(Jones:) If you have an eagle nest, that is yours. There is a special ceremony for killing and plucking the eagle, and it is buried with a string of beads around its neck. People who handle eagles are well-to-do. One man may own a couple of nests with birds, or he might buy birds for their feathers. After burial they gather the feathers, and the dancing feather man takes care of them. The tail feathers are for arrows, the wings for dancing, the down for caps (which distinguish the important warriors from the rest). Almost all the feathers are used, but not the beak or claws. Wristlets for dancers were made out of some of the feathers. The eagle is an important bird among the Indians. A man who finds a nest figures on getting money. A common man may own a tree. Thereby every spring he can get birds and sell them to the fellow, but it is against the rules for a common man to keep the eagles. If a person is poor they try to keep him down — they buy the stuff before he gets a start. They get the benefit. The rich people never get enough of anything. Those who can, get yellowhammers and then sell them.

---

perfect as regards eyebrows, whiskers, and claws. Forth years ago, a trader sold such a bearskin to an Indian of this region for commodities to the value of one hundred dollars . . . Next to a skin of a black bear were esteemed skins of the brown, . . . the grizzly, and the panther, in the order named" (Washington, 1906: 144).

5. Eagles elsewhere are considered important property. Cf., for example, Fewkes, 1900, p. 690.

Money. — Among the Nomlaki the form of economic wealth that can be defined as money was shell beads, which were used as currency throughout north-central California. These beads were strung, the string often measuring from finger tips to shoulder. It was considered bad form to count out beads in trading, because it was a sign that the person was penurious.

Several kinds of shell were known: the clamshell, a small bivalve used for earrings, abalone, and dentalia. Clamshells were traded from the Patwin and Northeastern Pomo, who, Wintun informants believed, lived near the sea. Their source was probably the several tribes of Coastal Pomo and the Coast Miwok. Only occasionally did the whole shell come into Wintun territory. More often the disk-shaped beads were already roughly tooled, but were improved by the native craftsmen.

> (Jordan:) Beads come from down south. They must be closer to the coast down there. They get the shells and chip them into pieces and break the corners and grind them on rough stones. Occassionally we get the rough shells.

> (Jones:) Our tribe didn't grow beads. The beads came from the Noimôk (i.e., Indian groups to the south). Sometimes they buy shells from these people; it is cheaper that way. The Noimôk get over to the sea and trade back and forth with the ocean Indians and sell the raw goods to the people to the north.

The earrings made of a small bivalve (*dao'têdê, lônôk*) were scarce and used solely for ornamentation, a matched pair being particularly desirable.

A few dentalia came into the area from the north, where, according to Du Bois (1935: 25), they were highly prized but did not function as currency. They were not considered very valuable by the Wintun.

> (Jones:) There were shells that the northern tribes (Trinity, Shasta) get, called k'obi. They are long and are

used for necklaces. We had a few in here. We never valued that ready-made stuff.

The abalone (*tcên*) was used in small rectangular and triangular pieces as a decoration on skirts and hides. Another type of bead was the baked magnesite, often referred to by informants as "Indian gold."

(Jordan:) Abalone shell is broken up and a hole drilled through the pieces to make ornaments for around the neck. Lônôk are small, round, twisted shells that are strung into a belt. They are used whole. Mempak, (*mêm*, water; *pak*, bone) are clamshells of which they make beads. I have seen them cut holes in small ones and wear them in the ears. I've seen two or three old fellows wear these shells. These earrings are called *ma·tlala*. Some mêmpak beads are small; some are large. The thickness increases the value. The best are about a third of an inch thick. Some of mine are about an inch in diameter, but the smaller ones look prettier. The big men wear the big ones.

Tulul (magnesite) is mined out of the ground. Whites have taken it over and we can't mine it any more. It grows in Lake County. They dig it out of the ground and wrap it in leaves; then they bake it in the ashes. It gets colored and is worth more. Some of it is clear and looks like meerschaum; and some is colored red or dappled like pinto, and this is the prettiest. It is prepared by wrapping it in leaves and placing it in hot ashes. This is usually done right where they get the magnesite.

The relative values of these several types of objects are best given in tabular form, even though the evaluations are only approximate. This table was compiled from the various informants' statements and from Kroeber's data (1932: 356-8).

TABLE 2

EVALUATION OF NOMLAKI WEALTH GOODS

Article	*Value*
Hides	
Black Bear	$50.00-$60.00
Brown bear	20.00
Grizzly bear	15.00
Silver fox	12.50
Otter	2.50
Beads	
Belt of 20 earring shells	40.00- 50.00
Pair of earrings	4.00- 5.00
Tulul (magnesite)	5.00- 25.00
Mêmpak (clam disks)	0.01- 0.25
Feathers	
Eagle (alive)	8.00
Yellowhammer headdress	4.00- 8.00
Practical	
Pestle	$20.00-$25.00
10-unit net	10.00
Bow	7.50
Bow and 20 arrows	10.00
Fish nets	2.50- 5.00
3 ft. loop sinew deer snare	1.00
25 ft. hemp rope	0.75- 2.00
Social values	
Chief's daughter (first payment as wife)	20.00
Weregild	120.00

TRADE, BARTER, AND EXCHANGE

Nomlaki society recognized wealth as a primary orientation for the patterning of behavior. They had a form of currency, and they secured certain items of culture from outside their own territory. Trade was therefore an important aspect of Nomlaki social life.

Trade etiquette. — The Nomlaki made a distinction between trading and the exchange of gifts, but the etiquette of trading demanded that the trade articles be offered as gifts.

(Jones:) They don't argue over the price. If a man refuses a cheap offer, he is not well thought of. One can't say no to a trade. This system evens out after a while. Whenever a fellow counts his beads close, they don't like to trade with him and might refuse to because it takes too long, even if his stuff is good. You have to sell anything that is wanted that you have brought with you. They make friends by trading in such a way. They can come across the border and trade. They come a-talking — saying that they want to see so-and-so, calling the man's name. Only a couple of the "big guys" will come up and listen to the trade. They talk as well as they can.

Ordinarily they come back to the same person to trade — they are sort of trading partners then. Hosts always give visitors a gift as a last present.

Formerly, if a man was trading he would put down a basket; the other has to take it. This man gives what he wants — he might give a string of beads. Now it is his time to throw down something and ask for baskets. They took turns in offering things to trade. If goods aren't suitable, they may make remarks but hardly ever back out of trades.

(Freeman:) If we come to the border line to trade, we go to the captain's house. All the captains (?) sit down on their heels. They all smoke a pipe and talk business and don't fight. While trading, Indians won't hand a foreigner both the bow and arrows at the same time.

Trading was not always amicable. "If some people felt cheated in a trade, the head chief might send some man to quiet things down. He always sends two men to settle matters of trading. He has special men who are good talkers, usually older men."

Types of trade. — There were three distinct types of trade: the internal or incidental trading; the east-west or river-products, hill-products trading; and the north-south or bead-pelt trading.

The first of these was of secondary but not minor importance. This type of trade was the purchasing of incidental supplies from neighbors — the barter that followed when one group ran out of seeds, tobacco, or various small objects that could change hands unceremoniously. Even fire was mentioned by one informant as an object to be purchased in an emergency. The chief apparently acted as a sort of clearing house in this form of exchange, maintaining a

supply of goods from which purchases could be made. ''If outsiders
come in or run short, they buy goods from the chief. The chief sells
some goods to outsiders. He keeps trading until he has more than
others. These goods belong to the chief, not to the tribe. They buy
tobacco from a headman, the same as going to a store. Sometimes
they go quite a way to buy it.'' Ropes or small strings of beads were
used as currency, but the trade often amounted to a temporary
informal loan. This trade afforded a means of distribution of
necessities when a group ran out of a supply that could not be
replenished except by mutual sharing.

The trading between the foothill Wintun on one hand and the
valley groups on the other was a transfer of the surplus produce of
one environment for the different produce of another. The
important articles of transfer in this east-west trading were pine
nuts, acorns, mountain seeds, and animals from the foothill people
in return for salmon and river animals from the valley. Trade was
not by direct barter between these goods, but was carried on by use
of shell money and exchange of other valuables.

Trading with the Yuki to the west, also in the second trade
category, was less active because travel was more difficult between
the two areas, and the two groups were for the most part enemies
(Goldschmidt, Foster and Essene, 1939). However, the Yuki desire
for sale was an incentive to trade.

In the third form of trading — between north and south — the
Wintun formed a link in the long trade chain that extended from
San Francisco Bay to the Shasta territory. Between the central
California coast and the Shasta, trade was an economically effective
activity, since there was a flow of clamshell disks northward in
exchange for their superior stone, pelts, and yew wood. As these
articles moved in the trade route, the value of each was enhanced in
proportion to the increased scarcity of each. Interestingly enough,
in this transfer of goods the Wintun added little, but profited chiefly
by their role of middleman, which resulted from their location
between the two producing areas. The Nomlaki had fewer pelts
than the peoples to the north, no valuable flint or obsidian deposits,
and of course no raw material for shell beads. Magnesite beads
were the major exception, and sale perhaps a minor one. The
Wintun increased the value of northward-moving clam disks by
working the crude clamshells or imperfectly formed beads to
greater fineness. They did no such improving of pelts, bows, and

flint blades as these goods passed southward. The informants themselves recognized their northern neighbors as superior in tanning fur and the manufacture of bows. One informant said, "We didn't furnish anything."

This trade route was so firmly established and the profits so marked that it was exploited by a white man who attached himself to Homaldo at the time of the northward movement of the Ghost Dance (DuBois, 1939: 64). The informants told of his buying shells and beads in the south and bringing them to the north, where he traded them for pelts that he traded in turn in the south. His profit, no doubt, lay in the extra pelts he could place on the white market.

The following account of native professional middlemen is of exceptional interest, but this activity was undoubtedly an unusual one.

(Jones:) Once there were two fellows who roamed around from place to place to trade. The folks kind of got after them. "Why do you go around to trade; why don't you let them come here?" they would ask. "If I stay home," they answered, "I won't learn anything. By going from place to place I learn more, I learn other people's ways and how they act and treat each other. If I stay here, I don't see anything and can't learn anything. By traveling around I learn more of different things, of talking." Probably this man was a good speaker, but he learnt how to act and carry himself and to treat things differently. "By going around I trade for things that I don't want, but I take them to the next place and trade for something else. When I get something that I care for or that would be handy to me, I keep it. I'm stingy with that." The people could not do anything with these traders. It was dangerous in those old days. There was no need of lying around like a bear or something, they thought. They were *pôxmalê* from Paskenta. That was long before the whites came into the country. They always got by; they got along. There were only three or four who could go any place and travel around. They were wise and would travel and were good speakers. They would go to the house of some good speaker first, have something to drink (soup), and say what they had come for. They would smoke and talk and

joke. The next morning the hosts would give them some
food to get to the next place on. They would go on for three
or four days. The old people objected, but these men
insisted that they could be treated no better by their own
people. They learned quite a bit and picked up a lot. They
got so that people would invite them from a great
distance.

Trade and war settlement. — Trading was also a concomitant
of warfare, taking place either after the battle or in lieu of fighting,
when the "peacemaker" prevailed upon the parties to come to
terms. This is reminiscent of the northwest-coast Potlatch and is
closely allied to the general practice of paying weregild, the
settlement of paying with goods instead of with a life.[6]

(Jones:) After a war, there would follow trading. The river
Indians would bring up salmon or river foods, while the
hill people might bring lots of acorns or pine nuts. They
would do a lot of trading after the peace was made. They
might trade a bearhide for otterhides. After the trading is
made they might mourn the dead. They would make visits
over the border line in order to trade and buy.

When enemies meet they call to one another. If the
settlement is friendly they approach closer and spread out
their goods. One man would throw something in the
middle, one man from the other side would throw in
something for it and take the traded material back. They
trade till one side has traded everything. The ones that
have some left make fun of those who have run out,
bragging about themselves. The first offenders have to
buy out the offended before they pay for the body of the
murdered man, whose death has first caused the dispute,
but they have already agreed to pay. This trade takes
place on the border line. The Paskentas out-traded the
river people by gathering up lots of things and having
more than the others. They got things together during the

---

6. Among the Hupa and their neighbors the development of peace trading
and the peace dance was apparently converted into a major ceremonial. Cf.
Goldschmidt and Driver, 1940: 126.

night. The offenders (Tehama, in this case) have to buy a
bearskin in which to wrap the corpse. This is payment for
killing a man.

Gift exchange. — A distinction was made between gift exchange
and trade. There were various occasions on which it was
appropriate to offer gifts, creating an obligation on the part of the
recipient but not a demand on the part of the donor. The obligation
was strong, and the rules of etiquette of gift giving were
formalized.

(Jones:) If you are getting acquainted with strangers and a
girl has a nice string of beads, you can ask her what she
wants for them. She has to sell them to you at your offer if
she wants to claim you for a friend.

They used to give to outsiders for the purpose of
making friends. You can trade gifts. It is an insult to
refuse a gift. If they later meet face to face, the fellow who
offered the gift will ask the other (belligerently) what he
meant by refusing the present. Then the other man might
start begging to be let go, and would give a string of
beads, maybe unwillingly.

(Freeman:) In order to remain friends, people give each
other presents. The gifts go back and forth. When a
person gives a friend something, it is because he thinks
that person needs it. The other man will give him
something in return without explaining what it is for. I
don't know how they got started doing that. They say
there were stingy Indians among the people too. I heard
them talk about my grandfather's brother. They say he
was stingy. If you were fishing with him and didn't catch
any, he wouldn't share his catch with you. The same with
deer or any kind of game. He was a good hunter but awful
stingy.

(Jones:) When you are given a basket of food, you refill it
with something else. If you return the basket empty, the
donor will dust it out and turn it bottom side up (as an
expression of distain). If you fail to return the gift it is an

insult, and the person will not visit you until you do return
it. Indians notice such things.

When a young man of importance comes to another
man of importance, the latter may ask someone in a
whisper who the stranger is. The man will answer, will tell
who the stranger's mother was too. The host will try to
find if there is any relationship between them through the
father or the mother. He might give the younger fellow a
present. The younger man's relation has to return this
present in some way.

A ceremonial gift exchange among the River Wintun
approaching the pattern of the northwest-coast Potlatch is
described by Powers:

Between the nummok (*Noimôk*) and the Norbos (a
southern group of Wintu) tribes there existed a traditional
and immemorial friendship, and they occupied a kind of
informal relation or cartel. This cartel found its chief
expression in an occasional great gift dance (*dūr'-uo-
pu-di*). There is a pole planted in the ground, near which
stands a master of ceremonies dancing and chanting
continuously while the exercises are in progress. The
visitors come to the brow of the hill as usual, dance down
and around the village, and then around the pole, and as
the master of ceremonies announces each person's name
he deposits his offering at the foot of the pole. Of course, a
return dance is celebrated soon after at the other village,
and always on these occasions there is great rivalry of
generosity, each village striving to outdo the other, and
each person his particular friend in the neighboring
village. An Indian who refuses to join in the gift dance is
despised as a base and contemptible niggard (Powers,
1877: 238).

Payment for services. — Services of others appear to have
been hired for pay. The services of a "talker" was occasionally
hired by an inarticulate chieftain.

(Jones:) A speaker for a chief who can't make speeches
will tell the chief at the end of a big time, "I guess I'll go

now.'' The chief knows about what he owes, and lays a string of beads by the speaker, who will wear these to show the people. He may get two or three ropes (of beads).

The hiring of shamans and runners is discussed below. I had two reports of hired labor.

(Jones:) A man might chop wood to get food for a neighbor. He might work for a bow to hunt with or for a set of arrows. He would have to ask for what he wants when he is through. His wife might help him.

When a man sends another man after flint, he pays for his service. A person might order flints of greater weight made for him. He might send six or eight miles to get someone to do this. The maker would send the first one he made as a sample to the man who wanted the arrows; perhaps he would haft the point.

Borrowing. — My informants made only one mention of borrowing.

(Jones:) If you borrow something, you borrow it for a specific time; and if it is not returned on that day, they will come after it the next and they won't come alone. They don't lend to strangers.

Origin of the wealth complex. — As discussed above, the wealth pattern was apparently derived separately from and later than the olkapna-village institution in the organization of Nomlaki society. Specifically, these particularly important aspects of the wealth complex were associated archaeologically with a Late phase. The connection between wealth and the Huta initiation suggests an association with the Kuksu system, which Kroeber has found to be a relatively late cultural manifestation in the region immediately to the south of the Nomlaki.

The Nomlaki were located geographically between the Patwin and the wealth-oriented societies of northwestern California. There were only one or two tribes intervening between them and the Hupa. It might be inferred, therefore, that the wealth pattern came southward from the coast of British Columbia, via the tribes of northwestern California, up the Trinity, and thus to the tribes of the Sacramento drainage. The central California development may have derived ultimately from the Northwest Coast, but it did not come to the Sacramento Valley via the Trinity Alps. If it was utlimately of northwestern provenance, it must have moved southward to the San Francisco Bay region and then back north.

There are two reasons why the Nomlaki must have obtained the wealth complex from the south rather than from the Hupa. First, the intervening Wintu to the north did not share the pattern in any important degree. Second, the details of cultural affinity point southward rather than to northwestern California. These details are itemized in table 3.

Table 3 shows that the Nomlaki shared with the Patwin the use of clamshell-disk beads as money and did not value the highly prized dentalia of the northwestern Californians. Nomlaki and Patwin wealth objects were closely similar but clearly distinct from the Hupa and Yurok. The Nomlaki social pattern relating to wealth was again in greater conformity with the peoples to the south than with those to the north. The central California tribes destroyed wealth at death (so inheritance was secondary); they tended to limit the acquisition of wealth by sumptuary regulations that were foreign to northwestern California legal theory; they did not recognize private rights to productive resources as did the Hupa and Yurok; and wealth appeared rather as an adjunct to status instead of the means by which status was acquired.

WARFARE

The Nomlaki recognized two levels of blood conflicts: fueds and warfare. In both cases disputes were between groups. In feuds the dispute was limited in extent and generally more personal in implication; in warfare a wider number of persons were involved and the grievance appears to have been against a group rather than an individual. Thus disputes over poaching would more likely lead to war, whereas disputes over women or murder would result only in a feud. Finally, warfare always involved separate tribal units, but feuds were fought between groups within a single tribe.

War stories have been the chief source for ethnographic data

TABLE 3
NOMLAKI WEALTH COMPLEX IN ITS RELATIONSHIPS

Culture Practice	Nomlaki	Patwin*	Hupa-Yurok†
Money	Clamshell-disk beads	Clamshell-disk beads	Dentalia
Important items of wealth	Black bear pelt, magnesite beads	Black bear pelt, magnesite beads	White deerskins, "flints"
Most valued feathers	Eagle, Yellow-hammer	Yellowhammer, woodpecker	Woodpecker scalps
Control of wealth	Limited to Huta initiates	Family monopolies	Theoretically open to all
Inheritance	Unimportant; property of deceased destroyed	Unimportant; larger part burned with dead	Chief means of acquisition of wealth
Acquisition of wealth through profession or skill	Apparently a means of wealth acquisition	Acquired by monopoly of skills and professions	Not a recognized means of wealth acquisition (except by shamans)
Land and resources privately held	Only trees, eagles, and occasional items	None recorded as privately held; but under authority of chief	All resource property held in private; no control through chiefs
Destruction of property	Most wealth destroyed at funeral of owner	Much property destroyed at funeral of owner	Little property destroyed at funeral of owner
Generosity	Generosity prime virtue		Generosity unimportant; close bargaining characteristic
Wealth as source of status	Important to status, but within ascribed group	Relation to status not clear, inherited chieftainship most important source of status	Wealth only source of social status

*Kroeber, 1932: McKern, 1922.
†Kroeber, 1925; Goddard, 1902; Goldschmidt and Driver, 1940.

on warfare. These stories, which purport to be accounts of actual conflict, follow a pattern of such uniformity that their accuracy as history is invalidated. But for the same reason they can be taken as an expression of native attitudes and cultural expectancies.

In 1939 there was published a group of nine stories of the wars between the Nomlaki and the Yuki, neighbors and traditional enemies across the Coast Range (Goldschmidt, Foster and Essene, 1939). Three of these stories were obtained from the Nomlaki by me, one was obtained by Essene, and five were obtained from the Yuki by Foster and Essene. The general pattern of the stories is as follows (figure indicates the number of stories using that theme): A small party is attacked (8) while camping (3), gathering (2), poaching (2), or trading (2). A woman or girl returns with the news (5), a war party is formed (7), and after a period of preparation (5) either a surprise attack is made (4) or a prearranged battle fought (2). The enemy is nearly wiped out (7) with little or no loss of life (2), scalps are taken (3) and a victory dance celebrated (4). Four of these accounts purport to refer to the last Yuki-Nomlaki conflict. These accounts always claim victory for the side of the teller and always place fault with the enemy. There is no individuation of heroes, although careful reference may be made to places. None of these stories is reprinted here, but some others given below show similar patterning.

The cause of war was usually transgression of property rights or occasionally a murder growing out of a dispute over a woman. "Fighting is usually over hunting grounds. Sometimes they fight over women." There was no clearly demarked warrior class. It was not necessary to be a Huta initiate to join the fight, but not all men engaged in warfare. Those who did fight underwent special practical and magic training, and it was said that warriors "uphold one another in a pinch" and call one another brother.

> A warrior is trained by being shot at with blunt arrows. He has to learn to dodge them. They practice that way. This dodging is called *t'eya*. Those who can't dodge are advised to stay out of the thick of battle. Such a man might go to war, but he would stay in the rear because they put the best in front. Good dodgers do this almost without moving. Some shots come quick and are hard to dodge, so it is necessary to turn one's side to the enemy. The

wobbling shots are harder to dodge than the straight ones.

They have good runners and fighters picked out for war. Those who can't run or shoot well can't get into war. They pick the men like they do a ball team. It takes a good runner to run with the elkhide armor. Warriors don't get anything for fighting. They have to practice to be good fighters. They hunt and have foot races, wrestle, carry wood, and practice lifting as training for warfare.

(Jones:) Newsboys can carry news from Paskenta to Tehama and back between evening and dawn. It is about thirty miles each way. They trot. They have free passage into enemy territory. It is necessary that they eat special kinds of food which is more preserving to the Indian body. The runners have to be careful of their diet. They are from twenty-five to forty years old, for they can't do this work when they are too young. They have to keep their wind. Special ones are picked for this — not just anyone. They try out on the plains — people say that that is the hardest place for runners.

The runner is in a dangerous position. He does no other work, for he must always be ready to go. When he isn't running, he practices. He doesn't hunt or fish, but is well taken care of. He gets paid for his trips wherever he goes and he accumulated quite a lot. Several people may pay him for one trip, and he might get as much as seventy-five dollars. There aren't runners at each village; they are pretty scarce. They are important for wars.

Old blind Martin had been a newsboy. He made trips from Paskenta to Tehama. He said he never shot at a man in his life. He carried news over and back and had to remember every word he heard. After the runner comes back, after he catches his breath, he tells everything that was said. Two fellows repeat what he said, so that everything is heard three times. Everyone listens, and when they are all through they discuss the matter.

In war times there are arrow carriers, who also carry the spears. Normally everyone carries his own, but in tight places they give the extra arrows to these carriers.

There is always a lookout on watch when a group of women are gathering seeds. If anyone comes to molest the women, the lookout will yell a war whoop in warning, and the people know what that means. They know by the way the watcher yells that fighting or killing is going on.

Warfare was not without its magic practices and practitioners. Each fighter utilized special springs for bathing. These were called *yuhkin sawal* (*yuhkîn*, "go to fight," cf. Yuki, "enemy").

There were two important practitioners: the seer and the poisoner. It was the business of the seer to determine the proper course of action and predict the outcome. The poisoners "will sneak through to the enemy on their bellies and do their work, and sneak out again, as quietly as possible. They kill people in this way." Details of poisoning will be found in the section on shamanism.

The actual conduct of war appears to have been of two kinds, surprise attacks or short pitched battles. Most war activity among the Nomlaki appears to have been devoted to preparation, travel, and the aftermath. There were generally one leader, a number of warriers of various skills, and the special functionaries already indicated. Certain of the warriors were protected by elkhide armor, not unlike a portable turret, from which they could shoot arrows with some degree of protection.

> They fight at close range. They let their fastest runner use the elkhide. He runs up close and then crouches down. The men come and stand behind this shield. The enemy can't hit the Huta members because they dodge the arrows and are good fighters. If a warrior wastes his ten arrows without any results, he doesn't fight any more. They never shoot back the enemies' arrows, but they might save them. A man who is being held at bay may shoot back an enemy arrow, however. They quit fighting just at sunset. The peacemaker will yell, "Quit, the sun is down."
>
> It is against the rules to throw rocks at an enemy who is being held at bay hiding under a bush. They won't shoot arrows at such a person unless they actually see him. It is too wasteful of arrows.
>
> They aren't allowed to club one another — they can

spear, knife, or shoot. They carry the *sen* with them, but aren't supposed to use it.

They never talk about wars except among themselves, and then only in a whisper. They don't brag about what they have done except at the place where they killed the man. If they want to disgrace a person whom they have killed, every person will throw a stone over his body until he is covered. That means hatred. They will leave the body there, and never tell where it was left, though they will send word to the people to get it.

They rob whomever they kill. Take away the bows, arrows, elkskin armor. They take a scalp if it is a bad war or if they hate the enemy and want to get even. After a war dance they cover the scalp with rocks. Each person brings a rock about nine inches in diameter. That makes the other side mad. They might use, sell, or trade whatever they took off the enemy.

Killing a common man isn't important, but they like to get a man with a lot of tattooing because he will be a "Big man." They don't take every scalp — just those of certain people, such as the headman or a person close to him. The brother of a chief would be satisfactory. They like to kill some "big man" and take his scalp.

If they get a warrior who has been a lot of trouble, they give a war dance. I haven't ever seen one. I don't know what they do with the scalp when they are through with it. They take a big scalp from across the forehead and temple and all the way around. The Tehama Indians (River Wintun) scalped Andrew Freeman's grandfather. He fell as if he were dead and they scalped him, but he lived through it and became an old man. He always wore a handkerchief around his head.

They put the scalp on a long pole so that everyone can see it. There is a bunch of straw on the end of this pole. The dance leader carries it around. When the dance is nearly over, everyone shoots an arrow into the straw.

People come from miles around to a war dance. They pass the scalp from one rancheria to another. The people follow the scalp as far as it goes. They say that a rancheria will pay to use a scalp. They pass it on to all the people who knew the man.

Powers (1877: 237) describes the River Wintun war dance as follows:

> The Nuimok (River Wintun) . . . have a magnificent costume for this (war) dance, which consists of a long robe or mantle made of the feathers of different birds, arranged in rings or bands, and the head surmounted by a plume of the longest eagle feathers, the whole presenting a brilliant and gaudy appearance. In the scalp dance (hupchuna) a scalp was hoisted on top of a pole, on the head of an effigy made in the human figure . . . After all the villages had assembled they danced around it together, yelling and discharging arrows at the effigy. That village was accounted victorious that lodged the most arrows in it.

The following stories add substance to the general discussion on warfare. In addition to the stories below, there are the several accounts of warfare with the Yuki already mentioned (Goldschmidt, Foster and Essene, 1939).

(Jones:) In antelope times they used to go down hunting and get across the border and get killed or get into a fight. If they kill somebody and the murderers don't stop and pay for the body, that means a fight. They don't say what the person did; they will just say, "You turned one down at such a place, we turned one down here. That makes us even. We'll meet you where you want." Then the river Indians go home and send the news by a messenger, who is not molested. Thus they arrange a meeting. They come about fifty yards apart and talk over the matter. The men will want to fight. There is always a peacemaker, like Dominic's grandfather, who doesn't believe in war or bloodshed. The peacemaker is always a chief. He might be from a neighboring place. The peacemakers will work to try to stop the men from fighting, saying, "It's always best not to lose any blood, not to fight, but to try to be friendly. Let's try to get along and live the right kind of

life.'' The people might take him at his word. There might
be one at each side, each keeping his side from too much
trouble. If they make peace the men come together, but
they remain wary because they take prisoners at peace or
any time. The offender may pay for the burial. The river
Indians would bring up salmon or river foods, the hill
people might bring lots of acorns or pine nuts. They would
do a lot of trading after the peace was made. Perhaps also
bearhides would be traded for otterhides, the bearskins
being used for caskets.

After the trading is finished they might mourn the
dead. Then perhaps some families might visit. They have
to watch out, keep inside the houses, and get away at
night. It is difficult to get anything across a border line.

These Indians ran the Tehamas away. It was the last
war they had among the Indian tribes before the whites
came into the country. The Tehamas had gotten the best
of our Indians who were fishing across the border line, but
they ran too far west. So our side went down and caught
the Tehamas on the plains and killed a lot of them. They
cut the Tehamas down just to get a few good warriors.

They gathered Newville and northern Nomlaki
together, and they sent spies to the east, who visited the
Tehama. The spies were fed; they were loaded with fish
before they went home. The spies found all the snares that
the Tehama had set out and all the strings across the
paths. They had a lot of trick stuff that they put out late at
night. The spies cut the snares down, and met their own
party halfway. The spies cut the trails wider too. The
warriors reached Tehama at the break of day. The people
there swam across the river, and our men shot at them. A
whole lot got across by swimming, but they left the
women. The Nomlaki people called out the women and
told them why they had done this. There were a few big
fellows left. The runner came out and told who he was.
Our people started to kill him but decided not to. Some of
our people who were related helped the women mourn and
then came back home. They didn't kill the children. After
that there were no big warriors among the river Indians.
They had to kill all to get the ones they wanted. Those who

had not swum across the river were those who were related to the hill people or those who were known to be peaceable. Some of our people wanted to kill these fellows, but others stopped them. They remembered this war after the whites came in and would get the Paskenta people drunk and kill them. They are related in a way, but the warriors get angry.[7]

One time a niece of Dominic's grandfather was killed, while gathering seeds, by some of the Shasta (Wintu) Indians from Cottonwood. There was a group of men out hunting. Most of the women got away from these men, but this girl was caught. As she fought all the way while they were returning, they had to kill her. Our men were near by but not close enough. They finally caught up with these Shasta and started fighting. The Shasta were good shooters too, and both sides were afraid. Our people ran out of arrows, and they had to send a messenger boy after some.

Our Indians' rule was to quit fighting as soon as the sun went behind the mountains. The sun was almost down when Dominic's grandfather came up. He took one shot and killed their leader, who was called Suywayha, just before sunset. He had called to this old *tcekôn*, "We are over our line and just about home," to which the old chief retorted that he had killed deer and bear with a single shot. He showed what he meant by pulling his bow and killing Suywayha then and there.

BLOOD REVENGE AND CRIMINAL LAW

The differentiation between war and vengeance was one of degree. Among the Nomlaki it was cause for vendetta when a member of a near-by group committed a crime; war was brought on when a person from a distance did the harm. Further, revenge was called for when the act was personal; war was necessary when the

---

7. Jones frequently expressed himself in hypothetical terms, as in this story, rather than give a specific account. Since specific accounts always partake of the general and since Jones's data always are based upon specific incidents, the difference is chiefly in mode of expression.

offense had more general implications. Vengeance was most frequently retaliation against invasion of sexual rights or gambling indiscretions; war was frequently caused by poaching and disregard of property rights. The distinction was not sharp, however.

Responsibility for action against legal offenses rested with the person harmed or his immediate family. No data exist to show clearly the range of obligations in legal matters or whether all olkapna members were called upon to support their olkapna brothers in legal cases. In narratives about legal disputes, the offended person usually handled his own private vengeance, acting alone or with a brother (presumably a blood brother). This vengeance was usually the murder of the offending party. Then the plaintiff became the assailant, and the family of the original offender demanded justice. However, there was no vested authority empowered to mete out justice; it had to be wrested by strength through vendetta.

The technique of settlement was similar to that of war settlement. One party (presumably the last aggrieved) demanded of the other that they meet in open battle. The two sides, mustering their full strength in manpower, came together in fighting regalia, bringing with them trade goods such as pelts and shell money. A "peacemaker" who was adept at public persuasion stood between the two hostile parties and harangued them to come to an amicable settlement. There may have been one such functionary from each side. If these speakers, who did not have any vested power, could not prevail in their peaceful sentiments, fighting ensued. If the peacemakers were successful in gaining a hearing, the opponents proceeded to a specific property settlement. By that time, fault had usually accumulated on both sides, and so payment would be forthcoming from both parties. The mere transfer of the net amount due would have been unthinkable; each offense had to be settled separately. The payment for the murder appears to have involved the costs of proper burial — black bearhide and all. This was no fixed sum, however, since it was Nomlaki practice to bury and destroy as much property as possible in the grave of the deceased. After the settlement for damages had been concluded, the two parties engaged in trade. Informants are agreed that these settlements did not succeed in allaying all ill feeling in the dispute, but grudges continued to be borne and each party awaited the opportunity for retaliation.[8]

The nature of feuds is more graphically described in the following accounts. The first two are divergent tellings of the same case.

(Jordan:) I heard of a man killing another man for sleeping with his wife. It was this way. One man took a woman away from another who had failed to pay him his gambling debt. The woman's husband went to his older brother in Newville and told what had happened. The older brother said that they would have to go after the man.

The girl's mother told her daughter's captor that they had better go out in the hills, but the man said that he wasn't afraid. He had been hunting for antelope all day and was tired. The old lady wanted them to go into the hills.

The two brothers went in the night to the woman's house. They came late in the night. The old lady was sleeping outdoors by the windbreak, in front of the house. The two brothers talked to the old lady. She tried to offer them something to eat. The younger brother had a spear in his hand. He sized up the house to see if he could handle his spear inside. He laid it over the fire in order to burn the handle down short. About midnight he walked in, put a little grass on the fire to make it blaze up so he could see. He found the man fast asleep. He gigged this man right above the diaphragm. The man grabbed for his bone knife and tried to fight back, succeeded in getting a few slashes on the other man's arm. The two brothers held the man pinned down until he died. The wife went into a corner and cried, but her husband yelled to her, "Shut up or I'll kill you."

The brothers went to their father who lived close by

---

8. In northwestern California, settlements were carried out in a similar manner, but there was a strong sentiment against reopening a dispute once settled. This sentiment received sanction, not only in strong community feeling, but also in the recognized principle of law that the person guilty of reawakening hostilities was liable to a fine double that originally agreed upon. Apparently no such sanction existed among the Nomlaki.

and told him, "We kind of crippled our brother-in-law (?)."

The old man knew from this that they had committed murder. He thought it would be all right if he got a bearskin and gave it to them to bury the dead man in.

The murdered man's relatives found out about the murder in a little while. They shot the brothers' father when he was bringing the bearskin, and then went after the two boys. They ran these two boys from morning until evening, until they began to get tired.

The older brother told the younger to get away; so he left and ran, while the older one hid in a willow thicket on the creek bank. He didn't have many arrows. He could hear the enemies talking. "Go in after him," one of them said. He shouted to them to come on.

The man who wore the elkskin came up. He shot and just scraped the hiding brother's shoulder. The brother shot this man in the neck and jumped out and got his arrows. After that the others begged to be let alone, and he agreed. The younger brother had believed that the older one had been killed, and was very pleased when they met. They moved down to Elder Creek, and the former husband never bothered to get his woman.

Once after that there was a group of men who were playing games. The younger brother almost threw another man into the fire. The next morning this man came out with his bow and arrow pretending he was going to shoot a hawk. As he took his bead he turned on the younger brother and killed him. Then he ran away. He belonged to another tribe which had been friendly. They say he had been hired. When he got out on a hill he yelled, "That wasn't my fight," and named the man whose it was. That must have been before the whites came in.

(Jones:) I heard the story this way. They were gambling, and when the young man lost everything he wouldn't give over his money, and the winner took the other's wife. The loser said, "If she wants to go, take her. I can't give you this money." The girl got ready and went with the man. The young man told his brother about this, and the brother said that they would have to do something about it.

They went after the winner, and this man fought against the brothers and wounded the younger. Soon the brothers were fighting a whole lot of this man's relatives, and they had to give up. They were ashamed about this. The man who lost his wife said that he couldn't stand it. His mother-in-law thought a lot of him and carried food to him. Finally he got well and decided he would take care of the matter himself. The old lady told him where the couple were in the house. He went in. His spear was too long, so he came back out and burned it off and then went in the house and pinned this fellow down to the ground. His woman ran outside. He took her back home.

At daylight they found the man lying dead. They figured out who had done the killing. They sent word that he would have to pay for the kiling, and he said that he should be paid for being crippled. They argued back and forth for a while until the man who lost his wife thought that he could lick the others; so he agreed to fight.

They came to the appointed place with their property on both sides, and all the people came to see what kind of a fight there would be. They talked and talked. The one said, "You can't collect a gambling debt." He said that he hadn't completely lost the game, that he had been angry. Finally he suggested, "You pay me for getting hurt, and I'll pay you for killing this man."

They paid off this way. Then they made their trades, and they buried the dead man. The killer furnished the bearskin and the nets and ropes with which to tie the corpse.

The following story presents another form of marital difficulty and the attendant settlement.

(Jones:) I heard a story about a man who married a girl he didn't want because both parents kept urging him to do so even though he loved another girl better. He lived with his wife for about a year and they had a child. He stayed away from her quite a bit and only slept with her occasionally. One day he decided to go to the other girl he liked best. He just started living with this girl.

His wife cried and cried for several days. Her brother said, "Why do you cry? He's not dead." But she kept crying. The brother got up one morning, straightened an arrow, and went to the brother-in-law's house, saying, "I'll give you something to cry about." He killed his brother-in-law while at breakfast and returned and told them what he had done. The family of the murdered man came over and demanded payment from the wife's brother, but he didn't pay. They sent word for him to meet them at a specific place and time, saying that otherwise they would kill a member of his family. So the brother-in-law came. Both parties went there with all their wealth and met at this place. A peacemaker was there and gave a big talk. He asked what was going to be done about the matter. The murderer agreed to pay the funeral expenses rather than shed more blood. The peacemakers do all the talking. They have a settlement, but the grudge always remains between the two parties. It won't really be settled.

SUMMARY OF NOMLAKI SOCIAL ORGANIZATION

The inevitable complexity of a description of the social organization makes it advisable to draw together the major features into a compact summary. The organization of social life revolved on two axes: the geographical-familistic grouping into village-olkapna units on one hand, and initiatory wealth-owning cult with its status implications on the other.

Daily life centered in a village with a population of from twenty-five to two hundred persons under the leadership of a chieftain who owed his powers more to force of personality than to any culturally established sanctions. His office was hereditary in the male line, although succession was subject to review by the men of the village. The village itself was a kinship group comprised of persons related in the male line together with their married-in wives (and a few outsiders, owing to temporary matrilocal residence). This kinship group was named and exogamous, and its members recognized kinship to any strangers who belonged to a like-named group. It was, therefore, a clan in all its major features. Within the village olkapna there was a series of separate families comprised of man, wife or wives, and minor children. These families were the food-producing and food-consuming units, but they shared food resources with their fellow village members (and olkapna kin).

Cutting across these spatial kinship groupings was another division, which distinguished persons according to social status. An initiatory rite introduced a limited number of adult men into a secret society. The members of this group were persons of status, having a disproportionate measure of authority in public matters and having certain sumptuary rights, especially those of engaging in trade in wealth objects that were the specific goals of this class. This group also controlled most of the skilled crafts and professions, which gave them a special source of profit and social position. Members apparently commanded the respect of their fellow initiates and obtained special privileges by their brotherhood in the organization.

The wealth objects recognized by the society included furs and shell beads, and the greatest desideratum was the pelt of the black bear, which served as a burial shroud. These goods served as goals to attainment, and their acquisition marked off distinctions in status. They were acquired in part by trade with neighboring tribes, the profit accruing to Nomlaki traders by virtue of enhanced value as the goods moved further from their place of origin.

There was a general absence of officialdom and legal authority with any vested powers. Disputes were adjusted by means of warfare and feuds. In the absence of legal authority, property played an important part in arriving at settlements. Wealth property was transferred to the offended party in payment for crime, not as a result of established system of fines for specific criminal acts, but by negotiation between the two disputant parties. Wealth therefore played an important part, not only in the establishment of status, but in the maintenance of law and order.

Yokuts-Mono
Chiefs and Shamans

by Anna H. Gayton

INTRODUCTION

The purpose of this paper is not exactly what the title perhaps
implies: it does not purport to be a discussion of social organization,
nor of religion as such. While descriptions of political organization
and the chief's place in it, of religious ideas, concepts of the
supernatural, and the shaman's relation to them, of ceremonial
activities, and of other cultural miscellanea, must appear here, they
are not offered as topics of primary interest, but rather as stage
settings and properties against which the chiefs and shamans play
their interacting roles. It would no doubt be simpler to define the
chiefs as legal officials in a static social setting, and to relegate the
shamans to their place as professional doctors; but in so doing we
would have only a partial picture, and that a conventional one, of
these functionaries. Native informants on first inquiry invariably
describe their chiefs as the official leaders of the political unit,
adding as other officials messengers, dance managers, and in some
instances, sub-chiefs. Shamans are never recognized as officials.
Yet all informants supply anecdotal evidence which shows that the
shamans, unofficially, were political factors of tremendous power.
To show the chiefs and shamans not as categorized functionaries,
but as individuals of elevated powers operating in a given social
setting is the purpose of this paper.

THE CHIEF

SOCIAL STATUS

The social organization of the Yokuts and Western Mono tribes was exceedingly simple. There was a complete absence of anything like a class or caste system. With the exception of the chief's and winatum's lineages, which were mildly aristocratic, any man was as good as his neighbor. This does not mean that there was a failure to recognize differences between individuals. But the differences of influential superiority or inferiority grew out of qualities inherent in the person himself, such as his abilities to acquire wealth or supernatural power, or to be an inspiring orator. Though wealth was regarded as desirable, and a wealthy man was respected for his possessions, the actual range of financial extremes was not great. There was no wealthy class. The annual mourning ceremonies at which much property was destroyed and more distributed among the attendants, dispossessed a bereaved family of such wealth as it might have accumulated. The casting away of gifts at mourning ceremonies had the further advantage of keeping money and coveted objects in circulation. One might say that among the Yokuts and Western Mono the per capita wealth had a low mean deviation.

To seek assistance from supernatural powers for success in gambling, hunting, or general good health and fortune was anyone's privilege. This was accomplished through dreams of animals and birds, as of Eagle for wealth, Mountain Lion for hunting, etc., which were acquired by the use of a tobacco emetic, a day-to-week-long meat fast, and praying to the animal both before and after its dream appearance. Relatively simple as were the rules for gaining supernatural help, many persons thought them too troublesome and preferred to ignore them. Thus it was that in south central Californian society an individual attained success by his own inherent abilities and energy; the intelligently industrious person, perhaps encouraged by belief that sacred powers were aiding him, would, other things being equal, find himself in a better social and financial position than his stupid or less enterprising neighbor.

As a citizen in the community the chief possessed social prestige based primarily on his revered totem and authoritative office, and secondarily upon the wealth that accrued to him because of his position. His position was acquired by heredity. Normally the office passed from an elder brother to the next younger, and then reverted to the elder brother's eldest son. This rule was not rigid, however, and was modified in accordance with circumstance. When a chief became too enfeebled with sickness or age to continue his duties he would say whom he wanted to take his place. If his choice was acceptable to the other chiefs and elder men of the village, a gift of money was sent to the nominee. The man chosen did not have to accept the office unless he wished to.

The chief's house was perhaps larger than that of others but not necessarily or markedly so. Neither was the dress of a chief or of the members of his family distinctive. Powers (1887: 371) states that chiefs wore their hair long, but so did all men, according to my informants. The food storehouses of the chief were always well filled. He did not hunt himself. Food was provided for the chief's family by young hunters in the village. Such men were not permanently appointed for the task, but would be dispatched by the winatums to get fresh meat or fish for the chief. Informants disagree as to whether the chief paid for his provisions or not, but the weight of evidence indicates that he did not. The chief had to have a plentiful food supply for it was his duty to offer a meal to every traveler, foreign messenger, or stranger, who entered his village. Furthermore, the chief or his wife gave meat to extremely poor people or those who had difficulty in obtaining sufficient food, as the aged or widowed. Such people would accept the food and if possible would return a little acorn meal to the chief when they had an extra supply. A basket might be given in return. Such a return was prompted by courtesy and gratitude, and was not compulsory.

While polygamy occurred among Yokuts and Western Mono it was not frequent. The chief was more likely than other men to have two wives. This was partly because of his wealth which permitted him to pay for and support them, and also because of the more numerous household duties in his menage. The chief's wives must have food ready for immediate preparation at all times because of the hospitality extended to visitors in the tribe; they cared for the poor of their village, and at the same time entertained socially in a more lavish manner than other families.

In monetary wealth the chief always surpassed his fellow-citizens. The manner in which his worldly goods were acquired is not completely clear but there are several known sources. One of these was through commercial trading of desirable objects such as eagle down, and of articles traded with trans-Sierra Mono, or between local tribes. The commerce in eagle down was controlled by the chief as the bird was sacred to him and could not be killed without his permission. On this matter a Wukchumni (Y) informant gave the following.

Only a chief could order an eagle killed. He paid the man who killed it three to five dollars for the bird. Some man or woman was then asked to prepare the bird; they were paid for their trouble. The large feathers were plucked off. The skin was removed with the down still on it. The leg bones were kept for making whistles. The meat was removed but only the fat saved for tallow salve. The feathers, down, leg bones, and tallow were kept by the chief, and these he sold to doctors or any other persons who wanted them for religious or ceremonial purposes. The carcass was given a special ritualistic burial, at which a mournful attitude prevailed.

This trade in eagle products brought some profit to the chief. The demand for eagle down was constant as it was used by the majority of people for religious purposes such as scattering during prayer, and to make ropes of down which had power in curing sickness. Such ropes were used by non-professional persons who had supernatural power as well as by doctors.

Further profit came to the chief through intertribal commerce. Traders who came from other tribes with baskets, pottery, salt, tanned skins, etc., would first go to the chief's house to state their business, as was customary with all outsiders, and to receive the welcoming meal. Hence the chief had first chance to buy the wares they brought and retail them to his neighbors if he so wished. As a man of wealth he could take advantage of this opportunity to purchase desirable articles. The chief's house was often made headquarters for buying and selling when foreign traders appeared. Winatums were dispatched to notify other villages if the traders did not intend to go further.

Chiefs shared in the payment received by doctors of this tribe when dances were given for purposes of entertainment. Thus at the annual mourning ceremony the doctors' contest, which was an indispensable part of the ritual series, was performed by four to ten shamans. Some of the shamans were of the local or host tribe, but the majority were invited for the occasion. At such times invitations, together with a gift of money, were sent to chiefs who were asked to bring their doctors to the ceremony. The shamans themselves were paid by the audience. Each person present at the contest contributed a little shell money, the equivalent of ten to twenty-five cents. This money was collected by the shamans' winatums, and the total was divided among the shamans, the singers who accompanied their performance, and the shamans' winatums.

Often a chief was asked to bring an especially talented doctor or dancer to give a performance for the specific purpose of making money. From the audience's point of view the spectacle was an entertainment which they gladly paid to see. The following account of the Huhuna dancer gives us an example of this method of making money: [1]

The Waksachi (WM) did not have a Huhuna dancer among their own people. There was one from the Wukchumni (Y) and one from Tule River reservation that came up to Waksachi villages with their chiefs. They came to the Michahai (Y), too. Their names are not remembered. They came to fandangos at Tucao (the central village of the Michahai with a heavy admixture of Waksachi). They made money for Pao'itc, the chief, but they were paid for doing it.

Huhuna could hear money. Before the dance began the chief had money hidden. He put up the most but anybody that wanted to could put up a little money for this. It was hidden in the ground, under a shrub, or up in the rafters of the shades around the dance space. Huhuna was brought in. Sometimes he wore a mask that covered his eyes. He danced around. As soon as he heard the hidden money he pointed to it with a stick he carried. He had his own winatum who dug it out for him and put it in a basket.[2] After the money was all found Huhuna continued his dancing in order to make money for Pao'itc. In the meantime Pao'itc had sent his own winatum for a doctor

1. The Huhuna dance was part of the mourning ritual series, but might be performed outside of its ceremonial context at any time.
2. This winatum might be loaned by the local chief or might be brought along with the chief and Huhuna.

who was to kill Huhuna with magic. He paid the doctor three or four dollars to do this. The winatum made a little fire in the dance space from which the doctor manufactured his magical "air-shot" (toiyuc). He also told Huhuna where to sit down when he was to be "shot." The doctor had a blanket which was laid down for his money to be thrown on. When the shaman was ready he danced around a bit and then cast the invisible "shot" at Huhuna. Huhuna fell over unconscious. Pao'itc's winatum was standing by ready to pick up Huhuna and carry him over to his own (Huhuna's) chief. Then all the spectators present threw down some money for Huhuna who had died. This was collected by Pao'itc's winatum and placed at Huhuna's side. It was this money which Pao'itc received. Then the spectators again gave money or acorn meal, which was presented to the visiting chief.

The doctor who had shot Huhuna now came forward and went through the process of reviving his victim. This ended the performance and Huhuna and his chief went off to their camp.

The money given by the audience at Huhuna's death and received by Pao'itc totaled more than his expenses in giving the ceremony. Similarly Huhuna's chief received a greater monetary value in the money and acorn meal paid in than he paid to his dancer. The informant was uncertain whether Huhuna's chief paid him on these occasions or not.

Thus chiefs, though always having to pay more than any ordinary citizen to entertainers or ceremonial performers, nevertheless often made a large profit from such affairs. It is difficult to find a basis for this reciprocal relationship unless it was that the dancer was more likely to obtain a larger audience when sponsored by his own chief. It was not possible to hold a dance or ceremony in any village without permission from the local chief. If a dancer such as Huhuna wanted to make some money by going about to various villages, it is probable that he would be more likely to get permission to give his dance if accompanied by his own chief than if he came alone. On the other hand, such performances, outside of their ceremonial context, may have as often been instigated by the chief in his desire to make money as by the dancer himself. A similarly profitable reciprocity between chiefs and shamans will be discussed in a later section.

No conventional system of taxation was employed by Yokuts or Western Mono but an equivalent method was in vogue. In the description of Huhuna's dance given above we saw that each person in the audience contributed a bit of money or foodstuff to pay for the entertainment. This was usual at all public functions. At an evening festivity, perhaps a purely social affair, a chief would tell his winatum that he wanted a certain dance performed. He would give the winatum some money which the latter took to a dancer with the request for a performance. This initial payment was all that the chief contributed. When the doctor or dancers gave a performance in which they were accompanied by one or more singers, the winatums collected a little money from all the persons who assembled to witness it. This collection was given to the dancers and out of it they paid their accompanists and winatums. Doctors who wanted to make money might offer to give an exhibition on these occasions. For this they first obtained the chief's permission. In this case the chief paid them a sum just as if he had requested the dance.

In defraying the expenses of annual mourning ceremonies the entire tribe contributed as usual. The largest sums of money were furnished by the chiefs, the subchiefs, and the bereaved families. Though it was not compulsory for every family in the tribe to subscribe to the mourning ceremony it was an expected obligation. Noncontributors would not attend the affair. The results of not joining in the annual mourning ceremony will be taken up in a later section.

The system of payment at this ceremony is extremely involved. As it has no bearing upon the present discussion a description of the method will be omitted here. However, this much should be said, that from this affair the chiefs profited not at all, in fact were sometimes reduced in circumstances by it. They received financial aid from the subchiefs whose duty it was to make up any deficit in the funds which were needed for the occasion.

What becomes apparent from this system of paying for the expenses of festivities is this: that the chief requested certain performances, sanctioned others, that cost money; doctors and dancers did not dance and winatums did not run errands for nothing. But it was the spectators who paid the expenses. The chief was, and was regarded as, the ceremonial leader of his community of whom it was said "he gave this dance," "he made that mourning ceremony," etc., in spite of the fact that it was the public at large who paid for them. No public taxes were levied and placed in a general fund, but the more simple expedient of having the persons present at any ceremony contribute on the spot produced the same result.

EXECUTIVE FUNCTIONS

There were usually two or three chiefs in a tribe, perhaps occasionally more. A village of any size boasted at least one or two. A Wukchumni (Y) informant states that his tribe had five chiefs when he was a boy. Three of them lived at Gutsnumi, the other two at Daiapnuca. He cannot remember their names, but knows that some of them were related to each other, i.e., they did not represent five different lineages. When a decision relative to a local group was to be made its chiefs had to act unanimously, and similarly all chiefs if the entire tribe were involved. The same informant continued:

> In a single village, if one chief suggested having a fandango, the others had to agree before he could go ahead with his plans. If one chief were thinking about something he wanted to do he would tell his winatum to get the other chief or chiefs. In the meantime he would go out to the fire which a winatum had built. A winatum notified the villagers that there was going to be a meeting. Everyone in camp who wished to go to the meeting could do so regardless of sex or age. The chief would start talking to the people as they gradually assembled. As he talked to the people, the other chiefs upon their arrival, talked among themselves, agreeing or disagreeing with what was being said publicly. The winatum of the chief who was making his speech would go to the others to see what they thought. If they all agreed to go ahead with the plan that had been suggested, all of them, including the instigator, held a low-voiced consultation about specific plans, for instance, the date of holding a fandango. Their decision was announced at once to the people, who were

waiting to hear it. If a chief, while addressing an audience, said something wrong one of the others would speak up and correct him.

The executive governing of the chiefs was of a paternal-judiciary type. That is to say, they were consulted for advice, and gave or denied permission for certain events to take place. Thus were preparations made for the annual mourning ceremony among the Wukchumni (Y) and Yaudanchi (Y):

Families who had lost relatives during the year and wanted to make the mourning ceremony would talk about it among themselves. They had been saving money, and getting or making baskets in preparation for it. When they decided that they were ready they sent for the chief's winatum and told him to tell the chief what they wanted to do. The winatum went back to the chief. If there were other chiefs in the village they were summoned for a conference (as described above). If the chiefs thought enough money and supplies were obtainable to carry through their plans they would set the date for the affair at twelve days in the future. Then they sent their winatums to those neighboring tribes that they wanted to invite.

There were minor variations in the procedure not given in the above account. A Wobonuch (WM) informant described it as follows:

The month in which a mourning ceremony was to be held was tentatively set a year ahead. During that time everyone saved up for the celebration, especially the bereaved families. When the month drew near the most influential chief sent for the other or secondary chiefs, and for the head members of the families who were to give the ceremony in order to decide whether the time was still acceptable to all. If the chiefs delayed in calling this meeting and the families concerned wanted the matter discussed they could approach the chief and ask for a conference. The choice of a date depended mainly upon the financial condition of the bereaved families, and the amount of food available. The affair was usually held in the late summer after the village members had returned from their summer camps. Game and vegetable supplies were most abundant at that time. This was important as the host tribe was responsible for the subsistence of all visitors for a six-day period, as well as for giving and throwing away quantities of food.

Those who talked over the coming ceremony were first the chief or chiefs of the village and their brothers who had to share the expenses. The chiefs' winatums were always present. This small committee knew the whereabouts of absent members of their own village who were expected to be present, and how long it would take to notify them of the coming affair. At this meeting the date was set for about three weeks away. If men were off working and sent back a reply that they could not be ready by that date then the date would be shifted a few days to meet everyone's convenience as nearly as possible. Also other tribes asked, especially the one having the reciprocal part in the ceremony, might alter the date if they felt that they could not be ready at the time suggested.

After the first meeting held by the chiefs and bereaved families the local chief's winatum would call the other winatums, both men and women. The men he would send to chiefs of other villages and tribes that were to be invited, and to local people who were away and should be notified. The women winatums were told to look to the food supply and arrange for the cooking during the week of the ceremony. The most influential chief's winatum was the head one; it was he who usually bore the invitation to the reciprocating tribe. There was a winatum who acted as dance manager, and supervised the camp assembly and food provisions. The doctors' winatums set about getting other doctors for the dances.

The round of ceremonials during the year was always the same: the jimsonweed ceremony, the snake dance, and the first salmon ceremonial took place in the spring, and the mourning ceremony, first seed and acorn rites, and the bear dance occurred in the fall. Everyone knew approximately when these dances should be held but the specific time was always decided by the chief. The procedure was about as above. If snake doctors or bear dancers wished to hold their ceremonies they sent a notice to the chief. On the other hand, a chief who thought that the time for ceremony was approaching and who had heard no report of the dancers' intentions, would send a winatum asking them to prepare for the ceremony. Thus among the Wukchumni (Y):

> My people all have bear poca on my father's side. The chief told them when to make the bear dance. This would be along toward Christmas time. The chief sent his winatum to my father's brother asking him when he would be ready. He said he'd be ready in twelve days. Then my uncle picked out some of us to dance with him.

The bear dance among the Wobonuch (WM) was determined as follows:

> The bear men remembered are Unurigan (bear dancer), Supana (the interpreter's maternal grandfather), and Tcineda, his half-brother. The oldest bear man thought about the time to hold the dance. Then he sent for the bear dancers from other camps. Only those persons of the bear lineage danced who had "taken" bear for a supernatural helper through a dream. Many other people were in bear lineages but did nothing in respect to their totem except to refrain from eating or killing it. The dance was held in September or October, for if it were not held before bears holed in for the winter, all people of the bear lineage would sicken and die. Furthermore, no one with a bear totem might eat of the new acorn crop until after the dance had been made. If the dance were properly performed, Bear, the totemic, supernatural patron of the lineage, would continue to function for his human protégés even during the period of hibernation.

> All people with a bear totem contributed money for the dance, but only the dreamers danced. Food was supplied by the bear lineages for all visitors (who stayed

not more than three days). Hunters and fishermen always brought game to sell at such festivals.

The Entimbich (Y) gave the snake dance yearly. It was attended by neighboring Yokuts and Western Mono tribes. The procedure in giving the dance was as follows:

A big snake doctor would think it was time to make the snake dance, which always took place in the spring. He would send a winatum after the other snake doctors in his tribe. They talked over the affair and set a date for it. Then they notified the chief. If he agreed to the plans, messages were sent to all villages and camps of near-by tribes. At Kitceyu, where the Entimbich were centralized, Chukaimina (Y), Choinimni (Y), Michahai (Y), Wobonuch (WM), and sometimes Waksachi (WM) came. Everyone had to attend this ceremony during which the doctors predicted who would be bitten by rattlesnakes during the coming season. A preventive "cure" was given these people then and there. In fact, participation in the ceremony at all was regarded as preventive . . . The doctors making the dance had to see that food was supplied for all visitors. Both chiefs' and doctors' winatums looked after the various details. (The doctors were of course generously paid for giving the ceremony, though they apparently did not profit by it. It was their civic duty to give the affair. The money paid by the spectators was theoretically in propitiation of the rattlesnakes themselves over which the doctors had control through dreams.)

A sweat-house could not be built without the chief's permission. If the men of a village thought a new sweat-house was needed they would consult the chief, who would decide when it was to be made. Usually every man in the village helped in its construction, which was directed by winatums. Among the Wobonuch (WM) the chief announced that a feast would be held six days after the work was finished. The chief was the first to enter the new sweat-house when the opening celebration was made.

In the late spring when the time approached for the villages to break up into summer camping groups, the chief would call his people together. He would tell them that his family was moving, that he thought it was time for all of them to go, and to return at a certain time in the late summer. After this most families would leave for their camps, but their departure and return was really a matter of their own choice. Generally members of a village moved about as they pleased. If a family wanted to move away, say to another village, or ahead of time to their summer camp, they were free to do so. The head of the family might tell the chief of his plans but in doing so he was rendering a courteous gesture rather than asking for permission. On moving into another village or camping in its vicinity, the chief of that place was notified by the customary call. Persons who camped about without advising a chief in the neighborhood of their business were open to suspicion.

Beyond the guidance of ceremonial activities the chief's legal offices were few. The settlement of quarrels between individuals or families was often but not necessarily brought to the chief. Small disputes between families, quarrels between women, or between husbands and wives, or cases of divorce did not come before him. Sometimes the chief would hear of a protracted interfamily feud and would send his winatum to the parties concerned asking them to come to some agreement. But difficulties resulting in murder or serious personal injury were usually brought to his attention for settlement. If a family wanted revenge upon a malicious shaman, poisoner, or murderer to the extent of taking his life, the case had to be laid before the chief before any overt action could be taken. However, hot-headed men occasionally sought vengeance upon an enemy without consulting anyone; in such a case the culprit's family was free to retaliate. When the chief gave permission for a person who was regarded as a public enemy to be done away with, no retaliation could be taken by the victim's family. The chief, however, did not usually make a decision of this sort entirely by himself. If there were no other chiefs in the village he would ask the advice of a few venerable men. An angered man might forestall the chief's veto of his plans by consulting men those opinion bore weight before going to the chief. Thus among the Wobonuch (WM):

> Men often had their wives or daughters taken by a shaman. If a woman refused to sleep with a doctor or go off with him he would make her fall ill and die. A man who

knew or suspected who the doctor was that had thus
victimized women of his family would take steps for
revenge. Instead of going directly to the chief he would
consult first the old and respected men of the village or
tribe. He would go to one old man like Joe ('Merican Joe)
and explain his case. If Joe thought the offended man was
justified he would say so; but he would then send him on
to another old man to get his advice, at the same time
telling him to express his (Joe's) views. The man would go
to four or five such prominent elders and have their
unanimous consent to action before approaching the chief.
When he went to the chief he would present his case and
say that all these men had advised a certain procedure.
The chief might disagree but could not refuse in the face
of contrary opinion. If the vengeful man had gone to the
chief first and the chief had disapproved of the proposal to
kill the shaman, that would have been the end of the
matter.

If a man knew positively that a doctor had killed a
member of his family he could take it upon himself to kill
the doctor. He would just get his bow and go out and hide
around until he had a chance to shoot the doctor.

Among the southern foothill Yokuts quarrels were settled by
chiefs:

In the early reservation days at Tejon a Yauelmani shaman
bewitched a Yaudanchi so that he awoke crazed, and soon
died. When the Yaudanchi slew the poisoner the
Yauelmani were incensed at the summary fate of their
compatriot. But one of their chiefs restrained them and
they laid down their bows, which seems to have been the
end of the matter except for talk (Kroeber, 1925: 516).

Among the North Fork Mono a chief gave permission for
revenge upon a murderer.

Sometimes a buzzard moiety medicine man might try to
poison an eagle moiety person. If the poisoner did not
confess and promise to save the person, the eagle captain

(chief) went after the poisoner and killed him.

The bohenup (chief) had power of putting people to death for wrong-doing. If a person is bewitched he complains to bohenup of person who he thinks bewitched him. The bohenup sends people after the wizard. They tell him there is to be a big time (as a pretext). They bring him to the bohenup and ask him to take the spell off the sick man. If he does not he is murdered in secret at a certain time. Perhaps the bohenup will say he is to be killed when the leaves come out on a certain tree (Gifford, 1915).

Neither among Yokuts nor Western Mono were there definite laws governing action or punishment for misdemeanors. Theft was practically unknown according to direct statements by informants, and none have ever been mentioned in anecdotal material. Food thefts need never have occurred as custom demanded the offering of food to anyone who came peacefully to one's door, and further, hungry poor were rare because of the chiefs' care for the needy.

Chiefs always decided matters of intertribal relation but on the powers of chiefs in intertribal wars we have little concrete data. On the whole the Yokuts and Western Mono tribes were peaceful rather than warlike. A few organized raids on villages are reported from the plains region but in the foothills only sporadic, unsystematized outbreaks took place. In such hostilities as occurred there were no war captains other than a man who took leadership upon himself or by general consent, because of his natural abilities as a leader and marksman. Good hunters took up arms when necessary simply as persons who were skilled in handling weapons. A typical account of intertribal hostilities and the chief's minor role in them is the following:[3]

The Wobonuch (WM) and Entimbich (Y) have always been friendly. Long ago unfriendly relations existed between these two tribes and those on the north fork of the Kaweah river, chiefly the Waksachi (WM) and

3. This war occurred in the childhood of Supana, a grandfather of George Dick, who was a very old man when Dick was a boy. 'Merican Joe said it occurred "long before the round dance (Ghost dance of 1870)." It probably took place at least seventy-five years ago.

Wukchumni (Y), whom the Wobonuch refer to collectively
as the Pasuaj. One time some Entimbich women were out
gathering seeds on Mill Flat creek. Some Pasuaj came
over there and killed all but one woman just for meanness.
The woman who escaped ran to a Wobonuch village,
Kadawinao, and told what had happened.

The Wobonuch men gathered together. A few of
them started southwest toward Aukland (Pasuaj territory).
There they met a young man and woman. Now there had
been two intermarriages between the Wobonuch and
Pasuaj and these young people were the respective
offspring. In the avenging Wobonuch party were relatives
of the pair. As they met they cried "Cousin!" to each
other at once. Then a long parley began. Some of the
Wobonuch said that the couple were Pasuaj and had to be
killed, but the relatives protested. The irate Wobonuch
said they should be killed no matter who they were. They
finally won out by threatening to kill the Wobonuch
relatives of their own party. Then they killed the young
couple and returned home.

Soon a Pasuaj named Wasomai, and his brother and
sister, came and set up a camp near Taobin. The
Wobonuch camp, Nimaiawe, was about two miles off. A
trail from it passed near the Pasuaj camp. An old
Wobonuch man was traveling along this trail. The Pasuaj
brothers shot at and wounded him. He succeeded in
reaching Nimaiawe. He told what had happened to him.
The best men were all off hunting deer. The chief (Pinoa?)
sent out winatums to bring them in.

The Pasuaj brothers knew by this time that they had a
war on their hands, so Wasomai got out by an obscure
route and went for help. He returned with a lot of his
people. The Wobonuch had come over from their village
and the two parties began to shoot at each other from
behind trees and rocks. The fight went on for several days.
The Wobonuch lost four or five men. At last the
Wobonuch chiefs decided to call a truce. They called a
meeting of the chiefs on both sides by sending winatums
(who were protected at all times) into the Pasuaj camp
accompanied by the Pasuaj who had previously married

into the Wobonuch tribe. The chiefs talked the matter over
and a truce was settled. Immediately a dance was held
which tribes from both sides, i.e., Wobonuch, Entimbich,
Waksachi, and Wukchumni, attended. This was the first
social intercourse between the tribes of Dunlap valley and
those of the Kaweah river drainage. They have kept up
friendly relations ever since.

The Wobonuch had no war leader or captain: at
Taobĭn there were two guards who stayed on the trail
where it came in between two big rocks. There was a
narrow approach of this sort on each side of the village.
When strangers appeared these guards would go out to
meet them and ask their business. If strangers came along
quickly, minding their own business and behaving as if
they had some purpose, they would not be harmed, but if
a man were seen lurking about in the bush he would be
shot at once.

The Chunut informant says that occasional intertribal wars
occurred but that there was "no special man to lead the fight." She
added that chiefs never fought. Any man who was good at fighting
would lead the hostilities. Such a man was likely to have raven as
his dream helper.

In warfare, then, the chiefs had no active part, but functioned
in their traditional role of advisors or judiciaries whose decisions
were accepted by common consent.

CEREMONIAL DUTIES

The chiefs had certain ceremonial duties which informants
seemed unable to define clearly. At apparently all public functions
the chief made a short speech. Informants sometimes call this a
"prayer." He always told the assembled people what the ceremony
was to be and why they were making it, but specific remarks for
individual occasions the informants could not or would not give.

The most important speech made by the chief was that at the
annual mourning ceremony. This was spoken on the last (sixth)
night of the celebration during the "cry" ritual. Among the
Wobonuch the chief addressed the mourners at the ceremony just

before the destruction of the images of the deceased; "he told them what they were doing and why, and he told them to quit worrying now. 'This is the end of your feeling bad.' "

The Choinimni informant said that the chief made a speech at the cry ceremony but "couldn't remember" what it was about. Another informant, Michahai-Waksachi, said he would repeat what the chief said in this speech "but my language is too short." As a matter of fact his English speech is exceptionally good, and he quite willingly gave the best rendition that he could of a chief's speech at a Ghost Dance ceremony (Gayton, field notes).

On the whole there seemed to be a distinct reluctance on the part of informants to provide this information. Whether this was due to the feeling that an ordinary person should not repeat a chief's address, or that they actually felt that they could not do justice to the chief's rhetoric it is impossible to tell. Stephen Powers had the good fortune to witness a mourning ceremony among the Chukchansi (Y). In his account of the Yokuts he gives in considerable detail the speeches of the chief and his herald on this occasion (Powers, 1877: 386-7). These are substantially the same as the description given by my informants. The substance of all informants' remarks on this subject was that the chiefs in addressing an assembly would tell the people why they were there, what was going to be done, and end by telling them to have a good time.

In the previous pages we have discussed the various functions of the chief. The chief, however limited in power, had a social prestige resting upon his position as a protégé of and surrogate for Eagle, the mythological creator-chief. He possessed more wealth than the average citizen in spite of the fact that his position incurred more than average expenses. His relations with his subjects had a distinctly patriarchal aspect: he provided food for the poor, settled quarrels, generously paid messengers and ceremonial performers, gave advice on debatable projects, protected public safety by permitting bad shamans and poisoners to be killed, and addressed assemblies in words betokening his desire for the well-being of his people. That this is the generally accepted aspect of the chief appears from the foregoing accounts supplied by a variety of informants. However, a chief who was not a good man at heart, and who had a desire for personal aggrandizement, attained it through illegitimate arrangements with malevolent shamans. This matter will be taken up after the shaman's functions and position in the tribe has been defined.

MINOR OFFICIALS

The winatum has been frequently mentioned in the previous pages and his duties incidentally described. The activities of this official were all important in the execution of the chief's instructions and the organization of tribal functions. He was an essential unit in the social machinery. There seems to have been no variation in his duties or position among any of the Yokuts or Western Mono tribes. While the duties falling to a winatum might, from our point of view, put him in the class of a servant, such was not the case. The office carried with it a certain prestige; informants of a winatum's lineage, as Sam Osborn or Mary Pohot, speak proudly of their parents' status just as do those of chiefly lineage. Though winatums were always paid for their services "they did not work to make money," and are never spoken of as rich men, as are chiefs and shamans. Whenever a winatum arrived at a house on an errand he had to be paid a small sum, usually the equivalent of ten to twenty-five cents, unless he had come from a distance. A chief paid his own winatum for every service rendered, as well as those who came to him bearing news from another tribe or village. The paying of winatums was not standardized: the chief or any other person making use of a winatum gave him what both considered a fair amount according to the employer's financial status.

The position of subchief and his functions are of an indefinite sort. Foothill Yokuts and Western Mono of Kings river had this official; Yokuts of the plains and upper San Joaquin river apparently did not. Among the Yokuts the subchief was called tuye'i. The Western Mono had no special name for this office which was filled by the real chief's brothers. The Wukchumni (Y) and Yaudanchi (Y) tuye'i was described as follows:

> The tuye'i was a kind of second chief. The position went in families, and both sexes were called tuye'i just as all in the chief's family were called tia'a. There were usually four to six tuye'i in a tribe. When a mourning ceremony was to be held, and the chief was arranging financial affairs so as to

cover the expenses, the subchiefs put up enough money to cover any deficit that might occur. Subchiefs who were about fifteen years of age or over contributed. If the chief were away or unable to attend to his part in a ceremony, the tuye'i took his place: they were the first to start eating at meals, made his speech, and also any decisions that were called for. On the evening of the fifth day of the annual mourning ceremony the subchiefs gave a supper to the chief. Money, baskets, and blankets which had previously been given them by the chief were returned to him at this time.

A Yaudanchi informant said:

"The tuye'i helped the tia'a at the mourning ceremony. If the tia'a put up five dollars the tuye'i put up three. If the tia'a had no money these men had to put up the rest."

The Wobonuch (WM) regarded the brothers of an active chief as sub- or secondary chiefs. They had no special term for these men, whose functions were as among the Yokuts.

Both Chunut and Tachi informants denied the existence of this official in their tribe or vicinity.

Some tribes had an official who took charge of the camp and ritual organization at large fandangos. He is called in English the "dance manager"; he was a kind of master of ceremonies. The Yokuts called this man the yate'itc. The Kechayi (Y) had the official and describe him as follows:

The yate'itc was a kind of winatum. He talked for the tiya and he worked at arranging meals. He made all announcements for the chief and often acted as a go-between, between the chief and his people. The chief often talked to people in person or in public but he seldom made announcements to a large gathering unless his yate'itc were away. The position was inherited from the father's side but could be of either moiety. The Kechayi yate'itc, Kotcon, was of the Nutuwic moiety, whereas the Posgisa yate'itc, E'ukiyi, was Tokeluwic. At fandangos or parties the yate'itc "prayed" before each meal. He said,

"Come close to this food. We are going to have a good feast. When supper is over we will play and have a good time."

On the Wukchumni (Y) dance manager we have the following:

This man was not called winatum. He was hired for a big fandango by the chief. The position was hereditary; it always had raven for totem. The man's duty was to keep order in camp and affairs running smoothly: he called to the people to get up in the morning, went out to meet new arrivals and told them where to camp, informed the chief of their arrival; he told people to be quiet, stopped children who were playing too noisily, or women who were quarreling or "getting mad over their cooking."

The dance manager among the Wobonuch (Y) had no special name but was called natinab (winatum), just as were the official servants of chiefs and shamans.

The occurrence of this official seems to be sporadic, and cannot be regarded as characteristic of the Yokuts and Western Mono. It seems to be a specialization of the winatum's office which is localized in the foothills and plains. Officials similar to winatums and dance managers occur in southern California among the Serrano, Desert Pass, and Mountain Cahuilla, and Cupeño (Strong, 1929: 26, 43, 62-3, 107-8, 165-7, 251-2).

There was no special official for the jimsonweed ritual. A "man of good heart" who knew how to prepare the poisonous plant usually conducted the affair.

THE SHAMAN

SOURCE AND USES OF POWER

The shaman, in the eyes of the Yokuts and Western Mono, was an institution as old as that of chief. In their mythology Owl appears as the prehistoric shaman whose duty it was, upon the creation of man, to sponsor and aid those human beings who took up the profession of doctoring. But neither in mythology nor in present reality does the shaman appear as a person having legal jurisdiction over his fellow-beings. His powers were exclusively occult. His supposed ability to manipulate supernatural elements for both good and evil purposes left him in an equivocal position. A doctor was both feared and respected; but whether he was more respected than feared or vice versa depended entirely upon his personal character.

The shaman's source of supernatural power was a dream helper, usually an animal. The creature appeared in a dream, often that of normal sleep during the night. It spoke to its protege, saying "Use me," or an equivalent phrase, and gave him a song. If the person thus approached wished to accept the offered power he took care not to forget the song, and would seek another encounter with his patron in a dream experience. If the creature appeared again it was to give the man further instructions: he was told what to use as a talisman in effecting cures, and perhaps given other songs. The dream helper, though often sought, might come voluntarily to any one. No one was obliged to "take" a dream. Many people felt that the rules of fasting, praying in an isolated spot, taking a tobacco emetic, basking in the sun, and so on, which were necessary to a successful relationship with the occult, were too troublesome. Others were afraid of attempting it lest they make a mistake and incur the ill will of the dream creature. Many people, both men and women, acquired a little power, sufficient to keep them from danger on strange trails, to cure simple illnesses of their children or friends, or to have luck in hunting and gambling. Relatively few persons, and these only men, became professional shamans. Probably many persons had sufficient power but did not wish to proclaim it.

Shaman's power was not of a peculiar sort nor was it inherited. It was merely a greater quantity, an accumulation of dream experiences, say six, to an average person's one or two. The more of such experiences one had the greater his knowledge of the occult would become, and the bond between the individual and the supernatural world increasingly strengthened. In other words, the difference between a shaman's power and that of a non-professional was one of quantity rather than of quality. As one informant expressed it: "A doctor was just a person who had too much power. They got mean, tried to see what they could do just to be doing it, and finally got so they thought they could do anything by means of their power. People would be here yet if the doctors weren't so mean."[4]

The reason some people were unwilling to become professional doctors, that is, cure any individual for the purpose of making money, was because of the danger of being killed if a patient died. The exercise of supernatural power for benevolent or malevolent purposes was believed to rest entirely upon the shaman's choice. Hence a doctor who attempted to cure a patient and failed was open to suspicion: either he had not sufficient power, or he had deliberately bewitched the person and was allowing him to die. Said the same informant: "If a man died his relations thought maybe the doctor didn't really try to cure him. They would get mad and talk about it. They'd say, 'he doesn't know much,' 'he is a bad doctor,' and like that. They'd get madder while they talked and maybe decide to kill that doctor. Some of the dead man's relations would kill the doctor. There was no special man to do this. They didn't always tell the chief."

A doctor who lost several patients but still continued to cure was definitely believed to be malicious. First of all he was causing illness in order to make himself rich through the fees gained in administering to the sick man, and secondly, he was allowing him to die out of sheer malice.

The usual method of securing a doctor was to send a fee with the request for him to come. Shamans of reputation were often sent for even when they lived two days' journey away. Doctors traveled about a great deal and might be here or there. If the doctor accepted the fee he came as quickly as possible and began his ritual of diagnosis and cure. The performance lasted about two days, longer if the patient were slow in recovering. The doctor received an additional fee after he began his curing. A doctor of repute received from thirty to fifty dollars for visiting a patient, occasionally more if he were extremely powerful. Ordinarily a shaman did not return any of the money received even if the cure were unsuccessful and death resulted. The Kechayi (Y) informant stated that a good doctor would return the fee in case of failure. If the doctor had come from a distance he kept enough to pay for his trouble. But this was unusual. People stood in such fear of a

---

4. From Sam Osborn, who himself has considerable power. He has cured immediate relatives and intimate friends but does not profess to be a doctor.

shaman, especially one of doubtful reputation, that they preferred to let him retain the fee rather than engender his ill will by asking for its return. This custom of retaining the fee increased the shaman's wealth and augmented the belief that doctors made people ill just to get their money. The usual excuse for failing to cure a patient was that the shaman who had caused the sickness had more power than the one who was attempting the cure. The name of the criminal doctor could not be disclosed even if the curing doctor suspected or knew who he was, for fear of his own life, i.e., the more powerful shaman would kill him. Only an eminent doctor who knew his occult powers to be supreme would dare to continue a cure against the animosity of another shaman.

The most common cause of illness was believed to be the intrusion into the body of some foreign object which had been projected by the evil magic of a doctor. The extraction of this object by cutting and sucking theoretically constituted a cure. The intruding object was always exhibited upon its extraction by the curing shaman; it might be a few hairs, finger-nail clippings, insects, a blood clot, the moustache of a mountain lion, and so on.

The art of poisoning was known throughout south central California and was clearly distinguished from supernatural causes of sickness. When known to have caused deaths, poisoners were killed just as were shamans. The case of a bad chief who used poisons from sheer maliciousness as well as to make money will be described in a later section.

People were often warned of coming sickness by a frightening experience devised by the doctor involved. In such a case the fright was considered the cause of death as much as the sickness itself. Thus a doctor would send a coyote to scare a man. The man seeing the coyote under peculiar circumstances would know at once that a doctor was after him and would bring on a self-inducing illness. Doctors often frightened people by sending owls to hoot outside their houses at night.[5] A doctor might send a dove to a group of people sitting outdoors. It would fall down and die near some one, and that person was doomed. It was certain that a doctor had sent it, as no ordinary bird would do such a thing of its own accord. Doctors' supernatural messengers, foretelling death, also visited persons in dreams.

5. Coyotes and owls were supernatural servants of shamans.

Two doctors might decide to kill another shaman. They took their basket trays and went off to some knoll which was their customary meeting place. Plain people did not dare go there. They would make a fire and talk the matter over. When they had decided what kind of death, that is slow or sudden, to inflict upon their victim, one of the doctors would get out his eagle bone whistle. He would run around the fire, whistling as he went. The other shaman would hold his tray up to the sun to get power on it. He talked to the sun. The magic ''shot'' that appeared he put on the tray; the shot is said to look like seeds or salmon eggs. Then the doctors exchanged activities, and the second doctor would get all the power that was left. Then they crashed the trays upon the ground and the shot flew off into their victim, no matter how far away. They would get a coyote to visit the house of the doomed man. During the night one of the doctors would go to the victim's house and walk around it. As he did so he would stamp on the ground, wave a talisman in the air, and say ''Now I've got you!'' (or an analogous phrase). The doctor within the house slept soundly: his own power was ''covered up,'' and his dream helpers could not come to his aid. In two or three days he would fall ill. The malicious shaman would repeat his circuit of the house on several nights. The sick man would call some other doctor to cure him but it would be of no avail. The shaman called in might be able to diagnose the cause of the illness but he would be afraid to tell who the criminals were lest he be killed by them. The two conspiring shamans would continue to go out every night and talk to their dream helpers, saying, ''I want that man to die!'' Usually a slow death was visited upon the unfortunate shaman. During his illness the sick man would call on all his helpers; he would try all his talismans but they would be useless. He would die anyway unless he were a man with extraordinary supernatural power.

MALICIOUS ACTIVITIES

The sinister activities of evil shamans are ever present in the native mind. The following series of anecdotes related by informants from various sections of San Joaquin valley are evidence of the baleful role which doctors played in aboriginal life.

A Wobonuch (WM) informant, 'Merican Joe, with George Dick interpreting, gave the following:

Cahaola (Charlie Pete) had a large family. They were living at Sief's below Mill creek. One of his girls got sick and died. Soon another had a similar attack. Cahaola got a doctor named Puca to cure her. He was a man of small stature, and "very, very mean." This was the doctor who was poisoning Cahaola's children. Puca sat down in front of the girl and cut her in several places. He finally sucked out a water weaver. It had been used as "air-shot."

Soon others in Cahaola's family died: the water insect went from one to another killing each. At last there was only one girl, Pahamo, left, and she too fell ill. Cahaola now was desperate. He came over to Kitceyu (Dunlap) and consulted Laotcu'i (Little Dick), the Entimbich chief, telling him that he wanted to kill Puca. Laotcu'i sent him to see Hamatc (Luckett). Both chiefs agreed that Cahaola was justified as it was well known that Pahamo had refused to sleep with Puca. Hence Puca was taking the usual doctor's revenge by making her sick. Puca was living over at Kitceyu at the time with a daughter of Haipuc (Samson Jack). He had two other women, one up at Hart's basin, the other in Drum valley. He always took barely nubile girls.

There had been a fandango at Kitceyu. Someone told Cahaola that Puca was going over to Ko'onikwe (No. 3 Mill Camp) the next day, so Cahaola went ahead on the trail to waylay him. When Puca was ready to start he sent some of his friends on before him saying that he was going down to Barton's saloon to get some whiskey and would catch up with them. Then he followed by himself.

Cahaola was waiting on the trail. He saw Haipuc and some other men coming along, so remained hidden. Then he saw Puca in the distance; Puca was riding a white horse and was plainly visible. Puca drew nearer; he was very drunk and was singing loudly. The song he sang as he rode was "You can take my heart (soul, spirit) away today." He had already been informed through a dream that Cahaola was going to kill him. As he came opposite, Cahaola jumped out and shot him through the body with a .44. Puca fell off his horse and landed upright on a rock; he sat up rigidly straight. Cahaola accused him of killing his family. Puca admitted the crime and said he was glad he was going to be killed. Then Cahaola shot him between the eyes.

When Cahaola reached home his last daughter was dying.

The activities of bad doctors among the Waksachi (WM) are best illustrated by anecdotes involving three generations of shamans. Of the following, numbers 1 and 3 were told by Sam Osborn, number 2 by Josie Alonzo:

1. A group of Waksachi were living at Tcitatu. There was a nice young girl there. A doctor named Wasic sent his winatum around to call a few of his shaman friends together. The winatum asked Wasic what he was going to do.

He replied, "I am going to kill that pretty young girl. I want these doctors to help me with some extra talismans as there is a beautiful woman at Kitceyu whom I am going to kill, too. I am going to make them sick. After they are dead I am going to skin them and stuff them like dolls. I have lots of money and baskets up at Tawatsanahahi in a big rock like a house; there is a lot of poison there, too. I am going to set those dolls up in there."

The winatum was aghast but was too afraid of Wasic to object. He told the other doctors that they were to meet that night at Tawatsanahahi (eating dead person; also called Tawatsa'asot'ho'i, dead person skinned), a hill above Kitceyu which was a customary meeting place for doctors. No ordinary person dared go up there.

When the doctors assembled they made a fire and

proceeded to make "airshot" in the usual way. The girl at Tcitatu got sick suddenly and died the next day. They made "shot" for the woman at Kitceyu. She died, too. Then the doctors went home. They were warned not to tell anything on threat of being killed by Wasic.

The girls were buried and stayed in the ground two nights. On the third night about eight o'clock Wasic went to the Tcitatu girl's grave. He walked around it twice, each time stamping at the head. The girl rose right up out of the ground and stood up. Then Wasic waved his talisman, a rope of eagle down, and the girl flew into the air and came to earth some hundred yards away.[6] Then he flew himself by the same means. They moved thus again and again until they reached Tawatsanahahi. Then he did the same thing to the young woman at Kitceyu. He had to call on his friends for more talismans for this as the power of his own was worn out. When both girls were placed on the rocks the doctors assembled and skinned them. They stuffed the skins with grass and dressed the dummies in beads and quail feather earrings.

"Doctors always worked at night on such business; in the daytime they were where they belonged."

2. A man named Tukatsi lived at Kitceyu. His wife was a Waksachi named Nellie. She became lame. The condition slowly grew worse until she was entirely crippled. Etak, a powerful doctor and the son of Wasic, was accused of causing the sickness. Etak was also accused of the death of two or three women and a man. When Tukatsi's wife died after being treated by Etak he went over to the doctor's house. Etak was just outside the door. Tukatsi shot him with an arrow. Etak began leaping all around and yelping, "Ai ii, ai ii i," just like a coyote. Tukatsi took up an axe and went after him but Etak escaped.

Tukatsi met another doctor on his way home. He shot him in the eyes. This doctor had not injured anyone so far as was known but Tukatsi was beside himself and was ready to shoot any doctor on sight.

---

6. This was a common feat of powerful shamans in the region.

3. Haloptca was a son of Etak. He was a "mean" doctor. His sister Tceyi married a man named Koikoi'itc. They had four children, two boys and two girls. They moved over to Owens valley to live, for some reason. Haloptca made an eagle down belt and took it over to his niece. Two days later the girl died from poisoning with which the belt had been treated. Her brother died one year later. Soon after that the other two children died, and finally Tceyi herself. Koikoi was beside himself. He came over to Kitceyu to kill Haloptca. The bad doctor knew from a dream that he was being sought so he kept out of the way.

Koikoi went to Haloptca's house. Etak was there; he was an old, old man now, and blind. Koikoi shot him. Haloptca heard of this and rushed down to Visalia to get the sheriff. Koiloi was still around looking for Haloptca when the latter returned with the sheriff who made Koikoi a prisoner. Haloptea went home and buried his father. Koikoi was taken to Fresno and then to San Quentin. He died there.

Doctors were generally feared by the Wukchumni (Y) as elsewhere. Mary Pohot told the following incident as a specific instance of a prevailing condition:

When Mary was a young girl she lived with her aunt. The old lady had a new blanket for which she had paid twenty dollars. A doctor knew about this and came to the house demanding that it be given him. He threatened to make everybody in the house sick. The old lady was frightened. The doctor gave her $1.50 for the blanket and went off with it.

That evening Mary's uncle returned. His wife told him what had happened. The old man was furious; in spite of his wife's protests he went to the doctor and demanded full payment. The doctor just laughed at him. He said, "All right, I'll pay," and gave the old man two worthless baskets. This kind of thing happened all the time.

Another Wukchumni informant, Jim Britches, told of his own experience at the hands of a bad Patwisha (WM) shaman:

A Patwisha named Tcitcen was Jim Britches' stepfather. Teitcĕn was a "big" doctor. When Jim was quite young, perhaps ten years old, his mother, Tcitcĕn, and himself were living at Naranjo (Wukchumni territory). Tcitcĕn disliked Jim; he wanted to kill him. He sent $10 up to Little Dick at Kitceyu asking him to help kill Jim. Little Dick refused. Then Tcitcĕn went ahead with his own power and made Jim sick. The boy became delirious.

Just at this time there was to be a big fandango at Ironbridge, near Naranjo. A powerful Choinimni doctor, Puclĭlĭn, and his winatum, Pony Dick Watun, came down for the celebration. Jim's mother sent for Puclĭlĭn to come treat her son. When he arrived Puclĭlĭn asked Tcitcĕn why he, who was a big doctor, did not cure Jim. Tcitcĕn demurred, saying that he had tried but had not enough power.

Jim's mother was weeping now; she had given up all hope of her son's recovery. He was very sick; he had pains in his chest, at the back of his neck, and between the eyes. Puclĭlĭn cut in these places and sucked at the wound. He sucked out hard lumps of blood. Jim began to get better at once. Puclĭlĭn knew all the time that it was Tcitcĕn who had been making Jim sick. It was only because he was a very powerful doctor that he dared to cure Jim.

The activities of a Wukchumni doctor among the Gawia, and his resulting death in Waksachi territory, were described by Sam Osborn:

A Wukchumni doctor, Camaka, killed several Gawia. He wiped out a man's entire family until there was no one left but a little boy, the man's father's sister's son. The man could stand it no longer, so he went to some white people and traded his little cousin for a gun. This was the first Indian in this region to possess a gun. Someone told him that Camaka had gone up to Tcitatu for a fandango. The Gawia followed him and camped in Eshom valley about a mile above Tcitatu.

Bob Osborn, who was the chief's son, Sam Osborn, and two other men saw the camp and went out to ask the Gawia what he was doing there. The man told them what had happened to his family, that he had come up to kill Camaka, and hence did not want to go directly to the village. The Waksachi did not feel it was their business to hinder this man, but they asked him to wait until Camaka had left Tcitatu as they did not want any trouble started at the fandango that might involve other people. They also told the Gawia that the shaman had a horse and could get away easily so to be on the lookout for him. The man agreed to leave Camaka alone until after he had left Tcitatu. He went over to Badger where Sam Osborn's uncle put him up.

The following morning Camaka and his family went over to Badger, too. He made his wife and daughter look after the horses as he was afraid to be seen alone far from camp. In the meantime a Choinimni and his family had gone to Badger. They were camping there. The Gawia told the Choinimni of his affairs, and winning the latter's sympathy, the two agreed upon a plan by which Camaka might be killed. The Choinimni was paid for his part. That night the Choinimni made a big fire and asked Camaka to come over for a visit. He told the shaman to sit down on one side of the fire while he and his family and Sam's uncle sat at right angles from him. He said that thus Camaka might address them all as he was relating the latest news from down Wukchumni way. When all was arranged the Gawia leaped out from a pile of rocks behind Camaka and shot him in the shoulder. Then he rushed in and cut his throat.

The Gawia still was so enraged that he wanted to go over to Camaka's camp and kill all his family. Sam's uncle and the Choinimni restrained him from doing this, pointing out that the doctor's relations were innocent and to kill them would be unjustifiable murder.

Bob Osborn tells of another Wukchumni doctor who caused trouble among the Yokod:

A mourning ceremony was being held by the Yokod at
Yokol. Bob Osborn and his brother George were asked to
come and bring some deer as they were hunters of
renown. They stopped at Ranchería Flat over night. They
got six deer on the way. They reached Yokol on Thursday.
The crying ceremony ended on Saturday night and the
rejoicing celebration started early Sunday morning.

Present at the fandango was a Wukchumni doctor
who was accused of sickening or killing several Yokod.
Several men had decided that the time had come to kill
him. On Sunday morning at the moment when the
mourners were all standing in a row waiting to be washed
the Wukchumni doctor was standing off at a little
distance. The conspiring men were ready. One of them
ran down and grabbed the doctor. Another shot at the
doctor but hit the man who was holding him. The doctor
reached for his bow and shot several times at his
assailants. Then he rushed into the nearest tule house.
The men cornered him and shot him to death. Neither
brothers nor other relatives took up a feud as the doctor's
death was regarded by all as justifiable.

A Choinimni doctor who made people sick and cured them just
to get money was able to cause sickness as much as a hundred miles
away, according to Josie Alonzo:

After Kosewa's death a Choinimni doctor, Tcokonik, came
down to the Nutunutu (Y) at Kingston to cure the sick
people there. At this time, Josie, her mother, and her
sister-in-law with her two little boys, were working near
Visalia. A winatum had come around telling them that
Tcokonik was going to make a visit to Kingston. The
family decided that they wanted to go over to see the
performance. On the morning when they were ready to
start they all heard a little clicking sound like someone
flipping his finger nail against his forehead. At the same
instant the mother fell down; blood ran from her nose; she
remained unconscious for several minutes. Her relatives
picked her up and put her in the wagon. They all drove
over to Kingston. Tcokonik treated Josie's mother by

cutting the skin between her eyebrows. He sucked out a finger-nail clipping. It was Tcokonik who had "shot" it into her from a long way off while he was at Piedra, on Kings river. They paid him $20 for his services.

Tcokonik was considered a very fine doctor because he could cure without cutting. Once a man died after Tcokonik had treated him and he was accused of killing his patient. But Josie believes someone else must have killed him. Tcokonik was put in jail at Hanford for this, and on another occasion at Visalia. Bob Tista intervened for him both times. On the first occasion the man who had poisoned Tcokonik's patient ran away and was later caught, so the doctor was exonerated.

Another Choinimni doctor caused Josie herself to fall ill:

About twenty years ago Josie was up in the Kaweah river foothills shearing sheep. There too was a Choinimni doctor named Tcukpa. He and Josie talked to each other occasionally; later he asked her to sleep with him. She refused, upon which he became very angry and threatened to make her sick. She told him if he did anything to her she would kill him. That night they were playing the hand game with several others. Tcukpa got mad because Josie was winning. He had his magic talisman wrapped in a handkerchief in his pocket. He pulled out the bundle and struck Josie across the eyes with it. She immediately had a headache and nose bleed. Haitcatca, a man with some supernatural power, was there. He cut, sucked, and cured Josie. He sucked out only blood. He told her she would be blind some day, but she still sees very well. (The scars from this, and no doubt other cuttings, are plainly visible on her forehead.)

Tcukpa was finally poisoned. If he had been a really powerful doctor he could have cured himself. Nowadays people will pay anybody who is hard up, and willing to do it, to poison undesirable persons like Tcukpa: "They just do it to see if he is mets antũ (strong doctor)."

A Nutunutu (Y) shaman who terrorized the Indians about
Tulare lake killed Josie's cousin:

> This story concerns Pokoi'ik, Motsa's friend. Josie had a
> daughter, Mukuyik, nine or ten years old. One day she
> developed a severe pain in her right side; she had
> convulsions and died the next day. Later Josie learned
> from an old man that she had been killed by Pokoi'ik. This
> shaman was young and wanted to prove his power. Josie's
> husband had been working up at Kingston where Pokoi'ik
> lived. The shaman asked him for some money. He
> refused, saying that he had no money, that Josie had it all.
> This was true for the couple had been working hard and
> saved all they could. But Pokoi'ik got mad. He told this old
> man, "They'll dig up their money when their girl gets
> sick." He didn't go to Josie to ask for the money but just
> made Mukuyik sick. He killed her just to prove that he was
> able to. Said Josie, "Doctors often did this; they just like
> to try it like we'd try anything."
>
> Pokoi'ik became more malicious as his power
> increased, and people feared him more. Once Josie's
> brother, Wepis, and her cousin went up to a fandango
> given by the Wukchumni. Pokoi'ik walked up to Wepis
> and said, "Do you want to die or do you want to live?" He
> had been making a practice of doing this, and people had
> to pay him for fear of losing their lives. He had been
> preying on these two boys for a long time. When the boys
> went up to this fandango they had planned to kill Pokoi'ik,
> who, they knew, would be there. But Pokoi'ik knew about
> this beforehand as doctors usually did. When the boys
> were on the way home a weird, invisible object made of
> hair frightened the horse which the two boys were
> riding. Pokoi'ik had sent it. The horse reared, fell
> backwards, and crushed Josie's cousin. He died before
> the night was over.
>
> Poikoi'ik finally died. Somebody poisoned him.

A typical case of a doctor's death due to intervention in another
shaman's plans is that of Poso'o (Bob Tista or Bautista). Poso'o was
a good doctor with much power, respected by white people as well

as the Indians. He was a Tachi, and spent most of his life at the Lemoore ranchería. Josie Alonzo, who recounted the following story, lived with him for the last several years of his life:

> At the Tule reservation was an old Humtinin ("southerner") named Tcehĕmsuk, a Koyeti (Y). He had some supernatural power but was a poisoner as well. He has always been at odds with Sam Garfield, a Wukchumni, who with his family lived at Tule River reservation. Tcehĕmsuk asked one of Sam's boys, Pete, a lad of about twenty-one, to come over to his house to drink some coffee. Pete did not want to go, but at the same time was afraid to refuse. Tcehĕmsuk gave him some cold coffee to drink. The following day Pete developed a bad cold, and complained that he "felt like he was burning up inside." They called a white doctor, but Pete's condition continued to get worse so they sent up to Lemoore for Poso'o. When the latter arrived Pete's neck was swollen up on the outside. Poso'o sang and danced for two nights. He cut and sucked the patient's neck but could extract nothing but blood. While he was doing his diagnostic singing none of his dream helpers spoke to him though he followed his formula perfectly.
>
> One of his songs was:

watinihe	tsatsana	añtawuhun
whose	chicken hawk down	belonging to a doctor

Now Poso'o himself began vomiting blood. Pete kept getting worse and died in a few days. Finding his efforts useless Poso'o returned to Lemoore. Josie in the meantime had been visiting the Pohots (Wukchumni). When she returned she found Poso'o very ill. He kept vomiting blood. He got much worse and went to bed. He knew that Tcehemsuk was making him ill. He tried to kill Tcehemsuk (from Lemoore) with his supernatural power but his power was gone. He depended on his own power and would get no other doctor to help him. He sang his songs while he lay in bed but nothing came to him. One of his legs became "nothing but wood"; it burned continually; he could not use it. Josie had him taken to the hospital where he died.

"This Tcehĕmsuk was a big doctor, so was his brother. He had poisoned Pete, but it was with his tipni (supernatural) power that he kept Poso'o from curing Pete, and finally killed him too."

In the southern part of the San Joaquin valley women doctors occur, though they are relatively rare. The only account of a woman shaman is that of Poi'in, and her son Watisti, told by Frank Manuel, a Bankalachi (WM) informant. All informants speak of her as a powerful but good doctor who took part in the doctors' contest against men shamans. Her son, however, to whom she taught all her knowledge, used it for evil purposes:

Wuni was the last chief at the Tule River reservation. He was a Yaudanchi; he was a good man respected by all; he had only a little money.

Watisti had a lot of power. He had "all kinds" of supernatural talismans and dream helpers. He could make rattlesnakes bite people at any time of the year, yet such snakes were not visible to the victim.

Now Watisti disliked Wuni; he was jealous of his popularity. He sent a magic "shot" at Wuni. Though the "shot" entered at one place it scattered sickness all through his body. He died in a few days while Watisti pretended he was trying to cure him.

Upon the death of this chief several men wanted to avail themselves of the opportunity to kill Watisti. The shaman had been accused of several killings but this was the first they could "get" on him. Wuni was the last chief, so they consulted no one. On a Christmas morning under the leadership of Pete Suhusa, Yaudanchi (Y), another Yaudanchi, named Poncho, Bill Waley, a Wobonuch (WM) visiting at the reservation, and Juan Tcinu went to Watisti's house. He lived alone. Tcinu was sent to the house to tell the doctor that some people up the creek wanted to see him. When Tcinu and Watisti reached the spot where the others were in ambush they all shot at the doctor. Watisti had a talisman with him. He pulled it out, waved it, and flew through the air for a little distance but he was shot again and was killed. Watisti's mother had been dead a long time. He had no relatives that anyone can recall except his mother-in-law, who was alive at the time. She was very angry over his death and went about telling relatives of the avengers, "You're going to get a red cane," meaning that the winatum, who carried a cane ornamented with red paint, would be going about announcing their death.

CHIEFS AND SHAMANS

The foregoing accounts give ample evidence of the baleful effect that shamans had upon native life in southern central California. That their success was largely due to what was doubtless imaginary powers does not matter; they played an awe-inspiring, dominating role whatever its basis. The penalty of death which was dealt shamans did not deter the strong-minded. The acquisition of wealth and power was worth the risk to the man who possessed the talents needed for the fulfilment of his ambitions.

The question naturally arises, what were the relations between the chiefs who wielded legal power, and these impressive non-officials of anti-social activities? As a matter of fact there seems to have been more harmony than conflict owing to a system of reciprocal services; a system which greatly increased the wealth of the chief on the one hand, and protected the shaman from the violence of avenging relatives on the other.

In every tribe a powerful shaman was the close friend and associate of the chief. This alliance operated in various ways as the following accounts show. (In an earlier section we referred to the fact that theoretically no one was compelled to contribute to the annual mourning ceremony, or any other ceremony, for that matter, but that dire results often befell those who did not do so.) George Dick, himself of chiefly lineage, and grandson and grandnephew of two powerful shamans, described instances of cooperation of chiefs and shamans among the Entimbich (Y) and Wobonuch (WM):

If a man, especially a rich one, did not join in a fandango, the chief and his doctors would plan to make this man or some member of his family sick. The doctor would sicken his victim with the "air-shot" (toiyuc) used in the doctors' contest. The doctor sees to it that he is called in to make the cure. He makes several successive attempts to cure his victim, each time being paid for his services. He withholds his cure until he has financially broken the man and got him in debt. If he then cures the patient he sucks the shot out and shows it to the bystanders, saying that Night or a spring has made him ill.[7] On the other hand, he may let the person die, in which case the family must perforce join in the next mourning ceremony.

The money which the shaman has collected as fees in the case he divides with the chief. Should the victim's relatives seek vengeance, for which they must obtain the chief's permission, the chief refuses his sanction on the ground of insufficient evidence. Hadn't the doctor shown that Night had caused the illness?

The machinations of chiefs and shamans were so well established that it was possible to make arrangements for intertribal killings:

A chief may be jealous of a rich man in his tribe. If he wants him killed he sends his winatum to several other chiefs of near-by tribes, including that of the ill-fated man, asking them to come to a certain place on a certain night. Tawatsanahahi (Baker's Hill) was a favorite spot for these meetings. The various chiefs together with their doctors come at the stated time. There might be ten to fifteen present, including the doctors and the chiefs' trusted winatums.

The chief who called the meeting addresses the group saying that he (and perhaps others) want to do away with this certain man, and asks those present for their opinion in the matter. The people who want the man killed put up a sum of money to pay the doctors who are to do the killing. If the doomed man's chiefs want him saved they have to double this sum and give it to the opposing chiefs.

---

7. Springs of water frequently made people ill, by sending sickness in the form of a water insect. Night and Water are both personified.

If they do not do so they automatically sanction the man's death. The case is decided right there at the time. Very often such a man is killed not because he is rich but because "he knows too much" (about doings of chiefs, etc.) or because some man wants the victim's wife, and has bribed the chief to have the man killed. If the man is to be killed the doctors start right in to do it. "No matter how far off that man may be the doctors will be able to kill him."

There was still another way in which persons were done away with through chiefs and their shamans:

If one man wanted another killed he would go to a snake doctor just after the snake dance had been held. He would tell the doctor what he wanted and would give him a trust fee. "He gets about $100 if he is a big doctor; $50 if not so big. He is pretty likely to get killed so he asks for a lot." Then the doctor goes and consults his chief. The chief usually gives permission for the man's death after accepting $25 or $30. The doctor again interviews his patron and tells him that he will kill the man whenever desired. The patron sets the date, usually for the fall of the same year. Eventually the victim of the conspiracy is bitten by a rattlesnake sent by the snake doctor, and dies.

The dead man's relatives go at once to their chief (or others, as the snake dance was an intertribal affair) demanding to know how it came about that this man was bitten after having participated in the preventive snake ceremony. If the chief questioned knows the truth he accepts money offered by the inquirers and tells all, even betraying the doctor — for sufficient money. If he knows nothing, or is loyal to the doctor, he refuses the money, and even gives the relatives a small sum to help them find the culprit.

When the doctor is at last discovered the relatives return home. They tell their chief that they want to kill the doctor. He tells them "to get their bows and go kill that doctor and all his brothers, even if they are innocent. If the brothers aren't killed they'll be sure to do something mean (retaliate). This is a good old Indian law."

A Wukchumni informant gives a briefer version of a similar condition in his own and the neighboring Yaudanchi tribe:

The chief always had money. People made him presents when he was going to give a ceremony. If he got short of money he would have his doctor kill somebody who was rich. If the victim chosen belonged to another tribe he would send a gift of money to the chief of that tribe asking that he have his doctor kill the man. If the chief accepted the money he had his doctor proceed with the process of sickening and killing the man. The money received was divided between the chief and the doctor. Doctors who killed this way made sure that the patient would finally send for him by making him more sick for every other doctor that the sick man sent for.

Usually we had good chiefs with good doctors, but sometimes even a good chief would bribe a doctor to kill some man he thought ought to be killed.

The Kechayi informant made a brief statement which hints at the guilt of chiefs in such matters:

Sometimes a doctor would be killed if he lost a patient. A doctor and his chief would meet the bereaved family and their chief for the supposed purpose of making an adjustment. A discussion was held and "often the family killed the doctor and his chief right on the spot."

Gifford's data on the North Fork Mono of the upper San Joaquin river show an analogous situation in regard to the powers and activities of chiefs and shamans (Gifford, 1915). In this region the moiety organization prevailed but did not affect this phase of social life. The chief was always of the eagle moiety. Eagle's supremacy was recognized here just as it was to the south. Likewise too, the chiefs were open to bribe: "If a buzzard (moiety) poisoner wants to kill someone on the eagle side, he may go to the eagle captain and pay him for the privilege. In such a case the poisoner may be immune from punishment.''

Another informant told Gifford that "the chiefs were bosses over the doctors," but such a statement has little specific significance.

The doctors' contest, the most spectacular ritual in the mourning ceremony series, offered opportunity for doing away with undesirable shamans. In brief, this contest consisted of the magical killing of shamans who were ranged in opposing rows and "shot" at each other with magic "air-shot." Only the doctor who projected the fatal shot into a fallen opponent could withdraw it. If the shot were not removed the victim would not regain consciousness, and would die within a few days. Thus it occasionally happened that a chief would want a rival chief's doctor killed, in which case the shaman who had power to revive this man in the contest would be paid to withhold the cure. A pretense at curing would of course be made.

Almost all informants in describing the contest speak of the deliberate failure, at times, to revive one of the fallen doctors. Of the other methods of killing people, given above, to which the chiefs had recourse, little is said by most informants. Those who did admit that chiefs were in league with shamans, were all men with the exception of the Kechayi informant. The only detailed accounts of the intrigues of chiefs and shamans are those given above by the Entimbich and Wukchumni informants. That chiefs were not always the benevolent officials which Yokuts and Mono ideals claim them to be, either was not generally known or was not readily admitted.

CONCLUSIONS

The political life of Yokuts and Western Mono as presented in the foregoing pages leaves one with the impression that the condition was unsatisfactory from the point of view of its average citizen. A discussion of this social system may be profitable: first, it should be viewed as a practical political scheme, and secondly, as a cultural mechanism.

1. By a practical political scheme I mean a system which kept social order to the advantage and comfort of the majority, not from a general, humanitarian, or idealistic point of view but in terms of

this particular culture. The civilization of the Indians of California has always been regarded as low, that is, extremely simple. It is, relatively speaking. And the political institutions of Yokuts and Western Mono were perhaps as simple as any in California. Clans were lacking. The moiety, where it existed, regulated marriage and ceremonial participation. Patrilineal families dwelt together in permanent villages but owned no land other than an ill-defined tribal area. The household group was not large; normally its personnel included a married couple, their immature offspring, and a possible orphaned sister of either spouse, or an aged relative. A husband and father was head of his own household affairs but bowed to the opinion of elder male relatives when the entire lineage was involved. These families were entirely free to go about their daily pursuits of hunting, fishing, seed gathering, basket, pottery, and tool making, seeking of supernatural experience, gambling, or idling, without interference from officials. There were none to interfere. The sense of right and wrong, of duty to one's relatives and neighbors, was instilled in children as they grew up. Truthfulness, industry, a modest opinion of oneself, and above all, generosity, were regarded not so much as positive virtues as essential qualities. Informants today condemn those who are greedy, jealous, or egotistical. It was largely upon the personal character of individuals that the peace of a community depended.

Legal authority over the people at large was wielded by chiefs and their henchmen, the winatums. The chief's power was expressed as a general jurisdiction having a paternal-judiciary aspect. He made decisions on village or tribal affairs such as holding fandangos, or building a new sweat-house, he settled interfamily disputes, and granted permission for death punishments. His judgment operated in place of fixed laws. The winatums were the coordinating element in the interrelationship of the people and their chiefs: they were the universal joint in the social machinery. Their official activities were many, as executing orders from the chief, making announcements, carrying private and public messages between individuals and tribes, directing camp organization, and managing all phases of ceremonial activity. The presence or absence of the minor officials, subchiefs, and dance managers, made little difference in the powers of chiefs or the freedom of citizens. In other words, the chiefs, with their winatums as manipulating instruments, constituted the sole legal authority in the political system of south central California.

We have spoken of the complete lack of formulated law in Yokuts and Western Mono society. This is scarcely overstating the case, for the life-for-a-life rule was the nearest approach to a definite law, and this was applied only when the opinion of chiefs and elders saw its justification. By what means, then, were peace and public satisfaction maintained? Largely by means of an influence which had no legal basis, the fear of sorcery. This factor in civil life worked for public good; it was an awe-inspiring force itself, and served as a tool for chiefs when used by them through their shamans. The fear of sorcery operated between any one individual and another. If, as we have said, the peace of a community depended largely upon the personal character of each person, the personal character in turn was determined or molded by belief in supernatural powers which could be turned against one. A man dared not cheat another at gambling or trading, commit adultery, or neglect any civil or ceremonial duty toward his neighbor, lest the offended person visit sickness or death upon him or some member of his family, either by his own power or that of a shaman hired for the purpose. On the other hand, a man could not take offense for no reason, and retaliate by this means unless completely justified, for the matter would eventually be aired before the chief. Thus sorcery as a deterrent of crime kept a balance of peace in everyday life.

This seems to leave shamans holding the whip hand. One tends to envisage the life of Yokuts and Western Mono as shadowed by the constant threat of witchcraft. It was; but this does not mean that an individual lived in a perpetual state of anxiety and dread. The idea of malevolent sorcery was a commonplace in their lives; one took care not to bring its force down upon oneself. But their attitude to it may be likened to our own to, say, bacteria, automobiles, or gas, dangers to which we are so accustomed that they are given little conscious thought though they unquestionably modify our behavior. And shamanism in native life was no less a necessity than these useful hazards of our own civilization. A doctor might be able to kill one, but at the same time he had the ability to cure sicknesses brought about by other agents such as Night, Springs, ghosts, or other supernatural creatures. It was hard to give up money, baskets, or a prized possession to him, but it was harder still to be sick unto death. And the majority of doctors were not malicious. It is only of bad shamans that informants tell their tragic tales, and these men were of course blamed for many misfortunes for which they were not responsible. A good shaman who found that his patient was not recovering would frankly say he had not the power, and suggest that another be called. If he met with one or two failures he gave up his practice entirely, or at least until he had strengthened his contact with the supernatural. Such a man was free of suspicion. The doctor who continued to cure after losing patients was the one to be feared for he was causing illness just to make money in curing, without regard for public welfare. But the doctor whose avidity led him to such extremes was done away with on slight evidence; he had but a tenuous hold on life. Hence the men who were willing to risk their lives in this manner for personal aggrandizement were more rare than informants' accounts would lead us to think. To sum up, shamanism as a factor in political life acted as a deterrent upon crime, was a force which preserved as well as destroyed life, and its misuse was restrained by the threat of discovery and subsequent death.

Turning to the intrigues of chiefs and shamans, it will be seen that there was some justification for the alliance. A chief who hired a shaman to sicken a rich man who did not join in the expenses of a fandango or mourning ceremony was setting a public example at the same time that he was enriching himself. To the chief and to his shaman, who shared the money paid in fees by the sick man, it was unquestionably a matter of financial profit. But from the point of view of the public at large it was a fair punishment. Thus: a man of money who neglected or refused to bear his share of a public expense was placing a heavier financial burden upon his fellow-citizens; furthermore, generosity was an ideal, and the man who failed to contribute his share was showing himself to be greedy, and hence received no sympathy if misfortune befell him. In the absence of any law or system of taxation, it behooved each citizen, especially those of wealth, to participate in the sharing of public expenses, lest he incur the displeasure of the chief and of the public, and sickness or death be visited upon him.

The chief, however, in his turn could not unrestrainedly make use of malevolent supernatural power. He was a public figure, and as such was open to censure. Though his position was acquired by inheritance, his retention of it depended upon his conduct. Simple as was the civilization of Yokuts and Western Mono, upon the chief, as official executor, devolved all manner of responsibilities — and these were not easy. Take for example, the management of a mourning ceremony in which the chief's own village, other villages, and even other tribes were involved. The financial resources of all persons concerned had to be determined, and the intertribal exchange of money and food so adjusted that there was no unexpected loss to any of the participants. These matters, together with the wishes of other chiefs, the bereaved families, and guest tribes had to be managed to the satisfaction of all persons involved. This in itself is not so difficult, save that it called for executive talents which every man might not possess.

The greatest responsibility of a chief was the settlement of quarrels and granting permission to kill a supposed murderer. This responsibility was increased rather than lessened by the absence of codified legal system. A chief making an unsatisfactory decision could not excuse it on the ground that he was simply reading the law; he was personally responsible for the results of his counsel. To this end, he did not always depend upon his own judgment but sought the opinion of another chief or of respected elders. The hearing of cases did not take place publicly, but in or before the chief's house. This privacy did not matter, for a man who left dissatisfied aired his grievance to his neighbors. The community was small: there was little chance for secrecy, what one man knew, everybody knew. Lacking newspapers, gossip was rife. Popular sentiment turned against the chief who gave unfair decisions, or was suspected of self-aggrandizement. Such a man was not deposed from office, but gradually lost prestige. He was ignored in favor of another chief. If necessary, a new chief could be selected from among possible heirs, as a brother, or son, or even a cousin. Such a drastic procedure was rare, unless the incumbent were insensible. The chief, holding the highest place of respect in the community, would not care to lose it. Loss of respect, loss of prestige, in turn meant loss of wealth, a combination of disasters which no normal man wished to bring upon himself. The intriguing chief could and did hold office, but his selfish enterprises were carried on in secrecy and curbed by public opinion.

The foregoing discussion has attempted to demonstrate the factors in the political system of Yokuts and Western Mono culture whereby orderly social activity was maintained. The activities of its citizens were at once protected and restrained by two forces, one, based upon legality, the traditional authority vested in the chief; the other, based upon belief in sorcery, the occult power wielded largely by shamans. Chiefs and shamans, who sometimes combined these two forces in intrigue were in turn restrained in their activities by the threat of loss of prestige, and of untimely death.

2. In the first part of this paper the elements of Yokuts and Western Mono political life were dealt with in a purely descriptive manner. These elements have just been viewed as functioning parts of a working social system. They are now to be considered as functioning parts in their particular cultural mechanism. By cultural mechanism I mean the cooperation of elements within a culture, which, once established, exercise a force of their own that makes the cultural conformation persist as it is or trend in a certain direction. This phenomenon is fundamentally psychological and may be expressed in terms of habit, association of ideas, and conditioned behavior. But knowing this to be true, the cultural mechanism may be dealt with as such in its own sphere without translation into psychological terms, just as psychological processes may be considered without reduction to physiological terms. Granted that for psychological reasons the mental content of an individual is furnished by his surroundings we can turn to features in the milieu, in this case those of political life, and see them as coherent, interrelating parts of the cultural mechanism. In the situation under consideration we have the following concepts as factors in Yokuts-Western Mono political life: (1) on the side of the supernatural, a belief in Eagle as creator-in-chief of a primordial world inhabited by superhuman, superanimal creatures, a belief that these creatures exercise a power over present-day humans and their activities, that their power can be propitiated for benevolent and malevolent purposes, and that certain individuals (shamans) have particular control over this supernatural power; (2) on the social side, a totemic lineage system, a chief and a winatum as legal officials, the control of chiefs over ceremonial activities, class equality, economic ease, and generosity as an ideal. Negative elements will be mentioned as we discuss the interplay of the above factors.

As concepts in the system of thought (behavior) of any Yokuts or Western Mono the above factors are interrelated in a variety of ways. Thus: (1) Eagle is believed to be the supreme creator-chief.

This belief is expressed in a series of tales which contain tribal lore, present the facts of history as these are believed to be, and at the same time show the precedent for the established social system with eagle as chief, dove as winatum, owl as shaman, and so on. (2) A totemic lineage system determined the kin group: each person was born into a family which had an animal or bird as its particular symbol; this association had tangible expression in the daily acts of the person, he refrained from killing or eating the animal, he prayed to it, dreamed of it if he wanted its protection and aid, and, during ceremonials he wore a paint-pattern representing its appearance. Furthermore, if he belonged to a certain lineage, eagle, dove, bear, snake, or coyote, he had certain functions to perform which were his prerogatives. It will be seen that these factors and their interplay made up the chief's position: Eagle was chief; a person with eagle totem should be chief; the totem was derived from lineage membership; lineage membership was expressed in a number of private and ceremonial acts. This series of interrelating factors fortified each other's persistence in the cultural mechanism. To put it differently, if the chief as an institution were regarded as unsatisfactory, and a conscious desire for a change sprang into existence, the change could not be made without flying in the face of established concepts expressed in other associations, as that of Eagle as chief in mythology and ritualistic practices, or of totem with lineage which occured in every family, or of function with totem and lineage which operated not only in the case of eagle-chief but was a fundamental factor in ceremonial activities, as the bear, snake, beaver, and coyote dances. Whatever is said here in regard to the chief in his position is equally true for the winatum.

The shaman's place in society was the result of some of the same concepts recombined with others. The lineage factor did not enter in his case. The concept expressed in mythology of Owl as a prehistoric shaman, plus the whole "constellation of ideas" surrounding the supernatural world and its relation to the real world, gave the shaman his place. Thus: the supernatural world was accessible through dream experiences; any individual might try to establish contact with it; some persons had more ability to do this than others; the more frequent the contact the more supernatural power was acquired; a few individuals accumulated so much power that they could use it to aid or injure others; such men made their livelihood by using this power, and these were shamans. The human organism being what it is, sickness and death attack it; these being undesirable states and attributable to supernatural causes such as the illwill of Eagle, Ghosts, Night, Springs, or Lightning, the shaman as a skilled practitioner with supernatural forces must be called upon to relieve them. Dangerous as an individual doctor might be, the institution of shamanism had to be endured; to do away with it would be unthinkable in the Yokuts-Mono system of thought. The fact that the supernatural world was available to any one, and that the average citizen sought and had dream experiences, simply strengthened extant conceptions of shamanism and the supernatural. There could be no doubt as to the shaman's experiences, since every one had them in milder or less frequent forms. The mysteries of shamanistic tricks may have been doubted by a skeptic or two, but the public shamans' contest was ocular evidence of their powers to kill and to revive. By such demonstrations was popular belief maintained and fortified.

The lack of codified law was related, I think, to two different factors, an easy subsistence and generosity as an ideal. These two factors themselves may have been mutually interactive. Before white intrusion, game, acorns, seeds, and tule root formed an abundant food supply in the San Joaquin valley; there are no famine tales from this area. It would seem that this condition may account for the lack of definite property areas. There was no need to set up a boundary if there were nothing of special value to protect. If a food shortage had occurred, or an unexpected invasion taken place, competition for acorn, seed, or game areas would have stimulated or necessitated property ownership. Besides the lack of property laws, the custom of giving food to visitors, of returning value for value if a present were received, reduced the chances for theft, against which a formal law might have been established. Viewed from another angle these cultural habits may be regarded as laws; they were such in effect, but were not verbally formulated. From the point of view of their own culture the giving of food at any time, the giving of gifts, and especially the casting away of both at the annual mourning ceremony, were customs of courtesy expressing the ideal of generosity. Equality of rank among the people at large, that is, the absence of a class system, expressed the nullity of codified social law.

The lack of clearly defined concepts in Yokuts-Western Mono life may itself be regarded as a cultural form, an expression of thought habits. There existed a coherent system of thought which appeared in their mythology, their social system, and their ceremonial life. But the system was not ramified by specific ideas; thus, Eagle created the world and flew off, but whether he flew north, south, east, or west is of no moment to the Yokuts mind. He went above say some, or possibly to the east, another says to the west. That Eagle and all his former companions still exist is attested by the dream experiences of dozens of individuals; it doesn't matter where they are. The same laxity of thought prevails in the legal system: a chief makes a decision in a quarrel, but his next decision may or may not follow the precedent set in the former case. The respected elders of a village exercise a practical control over the chief's decisions, or the activities of their younger fellow-citizens. But their position is not defined, they hold no office, their influence is entirely a matter of personality. This lack of interest in defining, in the specific, in analysis, or in marshaled ideas, constituted a strong factor in the cultural mechanism; it kept the other factors in their respective positions. Ideas of the supernatural world interlocking with political practices were not weakened by a critical attitude in the public mind. I do not for a moment mean that there were not skeptical persons who consciously questioned the values of their own culture, but rather that the chances for such minds to occur were rare since there was no stimulus to critical thought. They not only had little chance to develop, but were rendered ineffectual in a cultural setting whose norm of thought was non-analytical.

Ceremonial Integration and Social Interaction in Aboriginal California

by Thomas Blackburn

Many of us who have devoted at least a portion of our professional careers to the study of aboriginal California feel defensive, I suspect, when discussing our research with our counterparts in other areas, and I imagine that we often view ourselves, consciously or unconsciously, as stepchildren of North American anthropology. The California archaeologist, for example, is faced with a dearth of the ceramic sequences, massive architectural remains, or *objets d'art* that gladden the hearts of many of his professional fellows; the ethnologist, similarly, seems resigned to a general absence of those complex political forms or systems of social differentiation that comprise the basis for many an ethnographic treatise. The fact that many of my colleagues are somewhat apologetic about their areal specialization is perhaps understandable; how justifiable it may be is a major topic to be explored by those participating in this symposium.

A theoretical dialogue currently drawing the attention of many archaeologists may help to place the attitude outlined above in proper perspective by making explicit the philosophical bases for a majority of the anthropological research undertaken in California. The dialogue referred to is that between what Binford and others (e.g., Binford 1965; Struever 1971) have termed "normative" and "systemic" theorists. For the normativist, a culture is a historically derived system of shared ideas, values and beliefs underlying behavior; it is the anthropologist's task to abstract this ideational basis or set of normative concepts from the cultural products or behaviors which are their objectification. Within a normative framework, emphasis is placed on shared traits characterizing homogeneous units, and any discontinuities in the spatial or

temporal distribution of such traits become boundaries distinguishing naturally-occurring units or "cultures." The normative
view thus tends to call attention to similarities while masking
differences, to utilize a typological or trait-list rather than a
multivariate systematics, and to focus interest on internal as
opposed to external processes and interrelationships.

For the systemic theorist, on the other hand, a culture is an
adaptive system composed of structurally divergent but articulated
subsystems:

> . . . in the partitive sense culture is an extrasomatic
> adaptive system that is employed in the integration of a
> society with its environment and with other sociocultural
> systems. Culture in this sense is not necessarily shared; it
> is participated in by men. In cultural systems, people,
> things, and places are components in a field that consists
> of environmental and sociocultural subsystems, and the
> locus of cultural process is in the dynamic articulations of
> these subsystems (Binford 1965: 205).

Within a systemic framework, therefore, the anthropologist's task
becomes one of delimiting systems and subsystems, with the
ultimate objective of reconstructing the total configuration of
intersystemic articulations. The attainment of such a goal requires
the utilization of a research strategy of regional scope, employing a
multivariate systematics.

That the vast majority of anthropological research in California
has been based on a normative model of culture can be considered
almost axiomatic; this is readily observable in both the kinds of
concepts employed and in the nature of the problems explored. One
of the more striking examples of the normative view in California
ethnology, for instance, is Kroeber's concept of the "tribelet,"
around which most discussions of aboriginal social and political
organization have revolved since it was first proposed. The
"tribelet" or "village-community" is generally conceived of as a
sharply emboundered, sociopolitically autonomous cultural unit,
easily distinguishable from other such units by its sense of
community, common control of a recognized territory, and its
ecological and political independence (Kroeber 1925: 830-2;
1954: 19-58). California then becomes a mosaic of several hundred

such tiny, autonomous, and occasionally feuding groups, each differing from its neighbors only in minor details of speech or custom. It is little wonder that the anthropologist or archaeologist faced with such a prospect becomes defensive, for spatial and temporal problems on such a limited scale seem rather peripheral to the traditional concerns of culture history.

Like other normative concepts, the tribelet model tends to be centripetal in its effects; i.e., it focuses attention inward upon those internal processes that generate the differentiae used to characterize or distinguish cultural "units," while at the same time it tends to submerge external dynamics. A systemic approach, on the other hand, is by its very nature centrifugal in its effects, in that any analytically delimited system inevitably articulates with a variety of other such systems; since these articulations are viewed as crucial loci of cultural process, attention is invariably drawn to both the internal and external interrelationships of the system.

When viewed from the standpoint of the systemicist, aboriginal California acquires a glamour and excitement incomprehensible to the normativist. The rich and complex array of interacting and articulating ecological, economic, social, political, ideological and linguistic systems within such a limited geographical area comprises a virtually unique natural laboratory for the study of many kinds of cultural processes. It is no accident that the various Indian societies of California violate almost every glittering anthropological generalization about the nature of hunting and gathering peoples (e.g., Service 1966). But it is essential for the complete realization of the empirical and theoretical potential of the field of California studies that we critically reexamine our assumptions, methods, constructs and paradigms, and reevaluate the empirical data available to us in terms of whatever revisions in theoretical outlook we deem necessary. The present paper represents a tentative step in such a direction, utilizing as it does both published and unpublished data to reexamine a particular locus of systemic articulation — ceremonialism — in light of modern theoretical developments.

A deep interest in forms of ritual behavior is, of course, as old as the discipline of anthropology itself, for ceremonial activities of one kind or another are frequently among the more prominent, colorful, and affectively charged of any of those in which people engage. But it has been generally believed that such activities are often essentially maladaptive in a Darwinian sense, leading to the neglect or unbalanced exploitation of otherwise important resources, the reinforcement of economically unsound behavior, or the encouragement of social interaction not conducive to social equilibrium. The recent surge of interest in the kinds of problems generally subsumed under the rubric of "cultural ecology," however, has brought about a reexamination of this assumption, and several authors have been led to suggest that ceremonialism may have important ecological (Vayda 1967; Rappaport 1968; Bean 1972), economic (Chagnon 1970), or political (Bulmer 1960; Schwartz 1963; Crumrine 1969) functions or consequences. Rappaport and Bean in particular have stressed the adaptive value of ritual in systems maintenance, and have at least implicitly suggested a major theme of this paper: that ceremonialism comprises a significant nexus of intra- and intersystemic articulation, and is therefore an important locus of cultural process.

Parenthetically, I should like to draw attention to the fact that it is almost certainly not coincidental that specialists in both Melanesia and California are voicing a similar interest in cultural ecology, and a similar dissatisfaction with traditional paradigms (cf. Watson 1970). Anthropological research in both areas is in a state of flux, as normative concepts prove increasingly inadequate as explanatory tools for the analysis of what seems at first glance a highly unstructured field. It is probably significant that both Melanesia and California are frequently described as being characterized by "loose" or "flexible" forms of social structure, and that many of the attributes ascribed to one apply almost equally well to the other. In this connection it might very well be that Watson's suggestion that "a social system organizes a flow of personnel in space and time" (Watson 1970: 108) could be applied profitably, for example, to the considerable population realignments and relocations that seem to have occurred among the Chumash in late prehistoric and early historic times, and which are usually explained primarily in terms of warfare and/or disease-induced depopulation. Perhaps the most important realization stemming from a comparison of the two areas, however, could be that "a viewpoint limited to the static depiction of groups-on-the-ground, their composition, and the immediate social attributes of their membership" (ibid.) must, and can be, superseded by other perspectives.

Fiestas of one kind or another seem to have been a prominent feature of aboriginal life in Southern California, as numerous observers have attested; thus Boscana, for example, notes in 1822 that:

> . . . so great is the affection which they have for their dances that they will spend days, nights and whole weeks dancing, and it can be said that all their passion is given to dancing, for few days pass that they do not have a dance, without becoming tired of a thing that is continually of the same sort, the most insipid that one can imagine . . . That these Indians are so fond of the dance is in memory of their God Chinigchinix who as we have said above went away dancing to Heaven, and they were of the belief that those who did not dance (that is, of the dancers, who are only the chiefs, and Publem or wizards), and those who did not attend the dances, were to be punished and hated by their God Chinigchinix (Harrington 1934: 38).

Unlike certain other aspects of aboriginal culture that were rapidly eroded under the impact of massive acculturative influences, fiestas continued to be important contexts for both social and religious interaction until surprisingly late, although naturally subject to considerable modification in detail. The ethnographic notes of John P. Harrington, for example, which in most cases have reference to post-mission events, are full of data on fiestas, songs and dances, religious observances, ceremonial officers, and other kinds of social practices that are usually assumed to be the most sensitive to external disruption.

Any discussion of ceremonialism, at least in the southern half of the state, should probably begin with a consideration of the Mourning Anniversary, for as Kroeber has phrased it, "the anniversary or annual ceremony in memory of the dead bulks so large in the life of many California tribes as to produce a first impression of being one of the most typical phases of Californian culture" (1925: 859-60). Certainly the anniversary, as we shall see, provided the context for types of social interaction that touched upon almost every facet of aboriginal life. In the discussion that follows, I have summarized data contained in Gayton's detailed description of this ceremony as it was practiced by the Wukchumni

Yokuts and their neighbors of the Central Foothill region (1948: 124-31); however, much of what is described below would apply equally well to many other ethnic groups in California.

A mourning anniversary was normally held at one- to three-year intervals by every tribelet in the Central Foothill region. An annual celebration was the ideal, but only particularly large and wealthy groups could achieve this standard since great expense and considerable financial preparation was involved in sponsoring such a ceremony. At least three separate tribelets were usually directly concerned in the affair: 1) a host group sponsoring the ceremony; 2) a financial recipient group that provided money for the host group in exchange for equivalent amounts of food or gifts; and 3) a group having a reciprocal ceremonial relationship with the host group involving the ritual washing of mourners at the close of the six-day ceremony. When a host tribelet decided to sponsor an anniversary, a sum of money was raised by the mourning families, chiefs and sub-chiefs, and anyone else who wished to contribute or invest; this sum was then presented to the financial recipients, who were obliged (once they had accepted it) to return it with 100% interest at the ceremony to be held some months later (in the meantime, of course, they could invest it in various financial transactions at the normal interest rate of 50%). In addition, those individuals in the host tribelet that had originally contributed sums of money were obliged to provide the recipients with an amount of food or gifts equivalent in value to their initial contribution at the end of the ceremony. As Gayton comments:

> . . . in terms of value, no profit was made on either side; in terms of materials, the hosts received money in exchange for commodities. The money was required to pay the washers, singers, winatums, huhuna dancer and accompanying shaman, the participants in the Shamans' Contest, and entertainers on the final day of celebration, and, above all, to pay for the food provided and consumed throughout the week. The recipients who received the commodities could sell them on the spot if the transactions were possible. All informants agreed that a great deal of side trading went on during, and on the final day of the ceremony. Naturally, the opportunity was unparalleled throughout the year (1948: 124).

In addition to the economic reciprocity described above, every tribelet seems to have been involved in a traditional ceremonial relationship of a reciprocal nature with another tribelet; this consisted of the ritual washing and clothing of mourners in specific families of one tribelet by members of specific families in the reciprocating tribelet. The families that did the washing also supplied the special baskets and new clothing required, which the mourners kept; in return they received either money or valuable gifts, an exchange that apparently involved goods or services considered to be of equal value.

Although every mourning anniversary thus involved most of the population of a minimum of three tribelets, such occasions normally attracted spectators from an extensive geographical area and from a variety of other ethnic groups. Gatyon, for example, mentions ten Yokuts tribelets and four Western Mono tribelets of the Central Foothill region, members of which might regularly be found in attendance at ceremonies sponsored by any one of their number (ibid: 125-6). In 1819, Estudillo estimated the number of people participating in a mourning anniversary at Chischa to be somewhere between 2500 and 3000 (Gayton 1936: 18). Nor was this scale of interaction confined to the San Joaquin Valley area alone; Harrington's ethnographic notes contain abundant evidence that the spatial range of social involvement in coastal fiestas during both mission and post-mission times was considerable, a situation that probably reflects aboriginal conditions as well. An important Ventureño Chumash fiesta, for example, might be attended by sizeable numbers of people from as far west as Gaviota or the Santa Inez Valley, as far east as Malibu or the San Fernando Valley, and as far north as Tejon, while performances by Yokuts dancers were not uncommon on such occasions. To the east, among the Cahuilla and Luiseno, two different forms of ceremonial interaction appear to have survived into historic times; one of these involved an actual reciprocal participation in ceremonies, and was characterized by an exchange of long strings of shell money called *witcu*, while the other consisted of a considerably looser type of interaction involving only an exchange of small strings of shell money called *napanaa* (Strong 1929: 92-9). The geographical range of ceremonial participation among these Shoshonean-speakers seems to have been somewhat more restricted than that of their neighbors to the west, where attendance at an important ceremony was apparently frequent within a radius of 60 miles; however, ceremonial involvement was still extensive, as Strong indicates:

> It was customary . . . for all the clans north of Palm Springs irrespective of linguistic differences, on hearing of a death in another clan to send one string of shell money to the leader of that clan . . . Thus there would seem to have existed a loose ceremonial union between all the Cahuilla, Serrano, Luiseño, and Gabrieleño clans who inhabited the territory from the San Gorgonio pass west to the Pacific Ocean (1929: 98).

The type of ceremonial interaction described above was extensive not only in geographical scope, but in organization as well. One of Harrington's Kitanemuk informants, for example, as a child attended mourning anniversaries at San Fernando Mission, *mat ʔapxa ʔw* (in upper Piru Canyon), *kaštu* (near Piru), and Saticoy during the course of a single summer; during this period her family lived first at Newhall and then at Piru. The occurrence of several such fiestas during the same season was not accidental, as the following comment attests:

> The ancient custom was for capitanes of various rancherias to talk together and plan to give a series of fiestas all in the same year and three weeks to maybe a couple of months apart. The capitan of *mat ʔapxa ʔw* would plan maybe to give one first and El Piro to follow, etc., etc., till the last fiesta might be way down San Fernando way. Fiestas were not given as one gives a dance now, nor every year either. They were given by a captain in honor of his relative or relatives who had died and also for his people who had lost relatives — as an obligation. The people had to save for them long (years) in advance and work for them in advance, preparing food, etc. A series of fiestas like the above-mentioned would come off one year and then for 4 or 5 years there would be none anywhere (Harrington n.d.).

In the same connection, it is interesting to note that when Estudillo encountered the mourning anniversary at Chischa in 1819 the

Chunut and some Wowol were not present, having gone south to attend a similar ceremony at Buena Vista (Gayton 1936: 76).

Although the several ritual activities associated with the mourning anniversary were undoubtedly a prominent element in aboriginal ceremonialism, a wide variety of other ritual occasions also contributed to the complex social, economic, and political interaction that seems to have characterized the annual ceremonial cycle. These rituals ranged in both scope and importance from small, sporadic and relatively private rites of passage to large, annual public ceremonies involving considerable numbers of people from different local groups. Among the Chumash, for example, the kinds of occasions calling for ceremonial observance would include birth, the naming of children, adolescence, the drinking of *toloache*, marriage, illness and recovery from illness, wakes, a chief's birthday, the appearance of rattlesnakes in the Spring, the completion of the harvest in the Fall, and the summer and winter solstices. In addition, dances were frequently performed simply for pleasure, or as a means of raising money for a chief or as a source of income for the dancers themselves. The intensity of ceremonialism in aboriginal life must have been pronounced, and it seems likely that there were few occasions during the course of the year when the life of an average person was not touched, directly or indirectly, by its social or economic concomitants.

The political aspects of ceremonialism in both southern and southcentral California are especially interesting, as well as being of potential theoretical significance. The best exposition of this facet of ritual behavior to date is probably Gayton's excellent analysis of the "unholy alliance" between Yokuts chiefs and shamans (Gayton 1930); since a closely parallel situation also existed among the Chumash (and perhaps other groups as well), a brief summary of the operation of this alliance will be presented below.

The political power of the Yokuts chief, as is generally true for California as a whole, depended more upon the social prestige accorded him and the personal qualities he possessed as a wealthy and prominent member of the community, than upon any genuine coercive force available to him. His role was essentially paternalistic and judicial in nature, in that he provided for the poor, settled serious disputes, gave advice, contributed money to defray the costs of ceremonies and public performances by shamans, addressed important assemblies, and gave his stamp of approval to the execution of individuals threatening public safety. The position of chief, therefore, could be characterized as one of considerable moral authority combined with little apparent power.

The position of shaman in Yokuts culture was in many ways the converse of that occupied by the chief. The shaman was an equivocal figure in many respects, in that he possessed considerable supernatural power which he was capable of using for either benevolent or malevolent purposes; for this reason he was often regarded as a necessary evil, to be both respected and feared. The role of doctor was a dangerous one, in that a shaman who failed to cure a patient was open to suspicion of sorcery; several such failures might lead to the death of the shaman at the hands of a patient's family, either with or without the tacit approval of the chief. If the chief had given his approval, no retaliation by the victim's family was possible. The position of shaman could perhaps best be characterized as one of considerable coercive potential but little moral authority.

The development of an informal alliance between chiefs and shamans seems an almost inevitable progression in political sophistication, given the elements stated above. In every Yokuts tribelet, a powerful shaman was a close friend and associate of the chief; this man used his powers for the financial benefit of the chief, and was in turn protected by the chief from possible retaliation by aggrieved relatives. A wealthy man who did not bear his fair share of responsibility for financing an important ceremony might be poisoned by the doctor, who through successive treatments would eventually obtain the victim's entire fortune. The doctor might then cure the patient, or he might let him die, in which case the victim's family was obliged to participate in the next mourning anniversary. The money which the shaman collected as fees was then divided with the chief, who ensured his associate's immunity from retaliation. It was even possible for a chief to arrange the death of a man in another tribe. A secret meeting of the chiefs and shamans of several neighboring groups would be called to discuss the matter, and if no one objected or doubled the sum offered to the shamans who were to do the killing, the man's fate was decided on the spot.

While primarily a mechanism designed to benefit the participants, the type of alliance just described undoubtedly had latent social benefits as well. The peace of the community in many respects depended upon fear of the ever-possible sanction of sorcery. An individual who performed an anti-social act toward another might be subjected to the malevolent aspects of shamanism, which in turn was restrained by the ultimate sanction of death. The political power of the chief was enhanced, as was his fiscal standing, while social order was maintained in the community at large.

A more direct and open relationship also linked Yokuts chiefs and shamans in what might be described as an oblique form of taxation. No dance or ceremony could be held in a village without the permission of the local chief, who received a sizeable portion of the money or food-stuffs each spectator was expected to contribute during the performance. In addition, chiefs often took their shamans on tour for the specific purpose of raising money; both chiefs and shamans apparently profitted from the arrangement. As Gayton has pointed out:

> What becomes apparent from this system of paying for the expenses of festivities is this: that the chief requested certain performances, sanctioned others, that cost money; doctors and dancers did not dance and winatums did not run errands for nothing. But it was the spectators who paid the expenses. The chief was, and was regarded as, the ceremonial leader of his community of whom it was said "he gave this dance," "he made that mourning ceremony," etc., in spite of the fact that it was the public at large who paid for them. No public taxes were levied and placed in a general fund, but the more simple expedient of having the persons present at any ceremony contribute on the spot produced the same result (Gayton 1930: 377).

Among the Chumash, as previously noted, there existed a similar situation with, however, the addition of certain important new elements. Chumash religious beliefs, and their more important public (as opposed to private) rituals, revolved around the esoteric and metaphorical worship of two sacred celestial 'bodies,' earth and sun. The sun was perhaps regarded as supreme, a vivifying male force or entity that was also vaguely threatening, a possible bringer of death; the earth, on the other hand, was the generally maternal provider of food and other necessities of life, to be worshipped in her three aspects of wind, rain and fire. A fairly precise twelve-month lunar calendar, semi-annually adjusted by reference to the solar solstices, was employed in determing the proper times to observe a variety of occasions; the importance of such astronomical cycles to the Chumash is demonstrated by the fact that there was even a kind of astrologer called an *alcuqlas* whose duties included the naming of new-born children according to their birth-month, the administering of *toloache*, and the reporting of illnesses or other social problems to the chief. The dates of two of the most important ceremonial occasions, the late September harvest fiesta and the Winter Solstice ceremony, were directly determined by the phases of earth and sun.

Most ritual occasions involved one of two different kinds of ceremonial structure: 1) the *săwil* or shrine (often placed on hill-tops, promontories, or in other remote spots) in which sacrifices of money, seeds or down were made or ceremonies were held; and 2) the *siliyɨq* or small ceremonial enclosure (equivalent to the Kitanemuk *yɨvar* or Gabrielino *yobar*) especially erected at a fiesta, which only baptized ministers or ritual officers called *ʔantap* were allowed to enter. Although the Chumash had the usual variety of herb and sucking doctors, rattlesnake, bear and weather shamans, and many individuals with limited powers derived from possession of an *ʔatišwin* (a dream-helper or talisman), there was also a formal cult organization homologous to the Chingishnish cult as it probably existed among the Gabrielino and Luiseño. Members of this cult were referred to as *ʔantap*, and their primary responsibility seems to have been the performance of dances and other rituals at large public ceremonies. Members were baptized into the cult as children, and through a period of apprenticeship learned the esoteric language, sacred songs and dances, and other aspects of ritual that characterized it. The parents of children who became members apparently had to pay a considerable sum of money for the privilege; presumably, only high-status families could afford this, and it is interesting to note that the chief and all members of his family were required to belong. There were apparently at least twelve *ʔantap* in every major village, many of whom participated from time to time in ceremonies held in widely-scattered locations; since the chiefs, other important officers, and shamans were all members of what essentially was a ubiquitous, far-flung religious elitist society, the *ʔantap* cult acted as an important integrative mechanism throughout the Chumash area. Although it is too early as yet to do much more than speculate, it appears probable that some members of the *ʔantap* cult were also members of the various *gremios* or "brotherhoods" of occupational specialists (such as canoemen, makers of sinew-backed bows, etc.) that also cross-cut localized political and residential affiliations; thus the *ʔantap* cult may have provided a kind of supra-organizational framework for the integration of the kinship-chartered, economically significant sodality-like *gremios* with the political and religious hierarchy.

The same management of ceremonies and other public gatherings was the responsibility of an officer called the *alpaxa* (an important official second in authority only to the chief, and distinct from the *ksen* or messenger), the *wot* or chief among the Chumash was a prominent figure behind the scenes on every important occasion. Dancers and singers, for example, were kept on a steady salary by the chief, who received through the *alpaxa* a sizeable portion of the considerable offerings collected from spectators at their performances. Again, charmstones and other power objects were apparently considered the property of the chief, and anyone wishing to use such items for a time had to pay for the privilege. The financial transactions occurring in connection with the Winter Solstice ceremony are particularly illuminating; during the course of the ceremony a public meeting was held for the purpose of settling any and all outstanding debts contracted during the year by anyone present, before the beginning of the new year. The *alpaxa* presided at this meeting and received a portion of any money that changed hands. The *alpaxa* also received the large quantities of money and goods offered on this occasion in honor of *xutaš*, the earth; again, presumably, a part of this went to enrich the chief, the *alpaxa*, and other *ʔantap*.

The same "unholy alliance" that we noted before between Yokuts chiefs and shamans also existed among the Chumash, although in a somewhat different form. According to popular belief, a secret meeting of important chiefs and shamans was held some months prior to a mourning anniversary in order to select the date and location of the ceremony. At this meeting one of the *ʔantap* present was selected as an *ʔaltipatišwɨ* or "poisoner." The identity of this individual was apparently a closely-guarded secret, although he was an obvious figure at important ceremonies because of his actions. The *ʔaltipatišwi* wore bags of herbs on his legs or at his waist, and would get up beside the dancers while they were dancing and imitate their movements. It was generally believed that the *ʔaltipatišwi* selected a wealthy man from a rich and populous village and began to poison him some months before the fiesta was to be held; during the course of time the *ʔaltipatišwi* would extract large sums of money from his victim before either curing him or allowing him to die. In the latter case, the offerings presented at the fiesta would be even greater, and the *ʔaltipatišwi* would get a percentage from the local chief. How frequently shamans actually did poison people at the instigation of a chief is, of course, debatable; however, it is abundantly clear that the widely-held belief that such practices did exist (a belief strongly reinforced by the foreboding presence of the *ʔaltipatišwi* at Chumash ceremonies) provided a chief with indirect coercive abilities that undoubtedly augmented his political power significantly.

It is probable that social institutions existed aboriginally among the Gabrielino and Luiseño which were very similar to those just described for the Chumash; this can reasonably be inferred from comments made by such astute early observers as Geronimo Boscana and Hugo Reid. Boscana, for example, makes the following observations in 1822 about the Luiseño:

> . . . they do not understand the signification of their usages and customs; this knowledge being confined to the chiefs of their tribes, and the old men who officiate as priests; and when they reveal anything, to their children, it is only to such as they intend to rear for their successors, and these, are enjoined to keep fast the secrets . . . under pain of severe chastisement. A veil is cast over all their religious observances, and the mystery with which they are performed, seems to perpetuate respect for them, and preserve an ascendancy over the people (1947: vii).

> Very great was their veneration for the Vanquech, or temple . . . No one was permited to enter it on their feast days, but the chief, the Publem, and elders (1947: 17).

> Although the Captains did not exercise any power, whatever, in the administration of justice, or in any other way, still the people possessed great respect and

veneration for their persons, particularly the youthful part
of the community, who were early instructed to look upon
them, as well as upon the Publem and elders, with fear
and trembling . . . on this account no one dared to treat
them with disrespect, or to injure them by word or action,
for death would have been the consequence, and its
execution carried into effect as follows: —The case having
been declared in the council, an elder was appointed to
make public the crime, which he did by crying most
bitterly throughout the rancheria, saying, that "so and so,
has said or done this or that, to our captain," —that
"Chinigchinich is very angry, and wishes to chastise us,
by sending us a plague, of which we may all die. Arm
yourselves, then, both old and young, to kill the offender,
so that by presenting him dead to Chinigchinich, he may
be appeased, and not kill us." This was repeated several
times throughout the town. As the Indians were easily
influenced, they immediately went out, armed, in search
of the delinquent, and when they fell in with him, they
despatched him, and, together with the arrows with which
they killed him, he was borne to the presence of
Chinigchinich (1947: 21).

Similarly, Hugo Reid, writing in 1852 about the Gabrielino, notes
that:

The only ones admitted into the church, were the seers
and captains, the adult male dancers, the boys training for
that purpose, and the female singers. But on funeral
occasions the near relatives of the deceased were allowed
to enter (Heizer 1968: 21).

Their medical men were esteemed as wizards and seers
. . . They not only cured diseases, but created them; they
poisoned people with herbs and ceremonies, and made it
rain when required, consulted the good spirit and received
answers, changed themselves into the form of diverse
animals, and foretold coming events. All of this was firmly
believed by the people, and in consequence their seers
were held in dread and deep reverence (Heizer 1968: 32).

There have been several things implicit or explicit in the foregoing discussion which suggest that since ceremonialism provided a context for wide-scale social interaction involving several theoretically autonomous local groups, and since ritual involvement had important political implications and/or functions, the degree of political interaction existing aboriginally may have been greater than we have heretofore assumed. This suggestion is, in fact, supported by a certain amount of both published and unpublished data. Hugo Reid, again speaking of the Gabrielino, mentions that:

> Being related by blood and marriage, war was never carried on between them. When war was consequently waged against neighboring tribes of no affinity, it was a common cause (Heizer 1968: 7).

> All prisoners of war . . . were invariably put to death. This was done in the presence of all the chiefs, for as war was declared and conducted by a council of the whole, so they in common had to attend to the execution of their enemies (Heizer 1968: 15).

> If a quarrel ensued between two parties, the chief of the Lodge took cognizance in the case, and decided according to the testimony produced. But, if a quarrel occurred between parties of distinct Lodges, each chief heard the witnesses produced by his own people; and then, associated with the chief of the opposite side, they passed sentence. In case they could not agree, an impartial chief was called in, who heard the statements made by both, and he alone decided. There was no appeal from his decision (Heizer 1968: 19).

Geronimo Boscana provides further information on the Luiseño:

> In the event of the decease of their captain, or his inability to govern . . . a feast was prepared, and all the neighboring chiefs and friends were invited to attend. . . Upon their arrival, after all were collected together, the object of the invitation . . . was explained. If this were satisfactory, *their consent was given*, and a day specified for the event . . . (1947: 19; italics mine).

The new captain did not assume the reins of government, until his father died or resigned them to him, and then, the only ceremony necessary in taking the command, was, to make known the fact to the neighboring chiefs. . . On the day of transferring the government, all the neighboring chiefs were invited, and a grand feast was given on the occasion. It was the custom among these Indians, in all their feasts, to carry presents to the person who gave the invitation, and he in return, was obliged when invited, to give one of equal value (1947: 20-1).

Fernando Librado, Harrington's primary Ventureño informant, gave a fascinating description of chiefly interaction during the 1860's in an account which provides us with a tantalizing glimpse of aboriginal conditions. Wataitset was the last chief of *muwu* (the main village at Point Mugu), who when he died was succeeded by his son Mateo. After a time, though, it was discovered that Mateo was not Wataitset's real son; in addition, Mateo had already decided that he was too poor to properly fulfill the duties of chief, and wished to vacate the position. Therefore, a meeting was held at Ventura in 1862 to appoint Pomposa, who was related to the *muwu* chiefly lineage through her grandfather, as chief. A number of prominent people were present at this meeting, including Luis Francisco (chief of *sapwa* in the Conejo Valley), Marcelino (chief of *soxtonoqmu* in the Santa Inez Valley), Juan Justo (chief of *mikiw* or Dos Pueblos, north of Santa Barbara), and the *ksen* or messenger of Rogerio (chief at San Fernando Mission but, apparently, actually chief of *humaliwo* or Malibu). At Saticoy in 1869, sometime after the death of Luis Francisco, Pomposa gave her first and last fiesta as chief. This fiesta was held in late September, and was attended by Juan Justo from Santa Barbara, Marcelino from Santa Inez, and Rogerio from San Fernando. Each captain brought his dancers and singers, who performed during the five-day fiesta. A *siliyiq* was constructed by one of the dancers from San Fernando, and Juan Justo acted as *alpaxa* for the occasion. A number of traditional dances were performed, and there was a shaman's contest between a dancer from Santa Inez and another from San Fernando in which each supernaturally paralyzed or blinded his opponent and then cured him.

In the preceding pages I have presented data from a variety of sources which suggest that ceremonial exchange within and between social groups comprised a functionally significant context for a wide range of forms of social interaction in aboriginal California. Such interaction seems to have been frequent, intense and colorful, particularly among groups such as the Yokuts, Chumash and Gabrielino. But ceremonialism is of significance for more reasons than simply its readily observable, affective prominence in native life; thus several scholars, as was mentioned previously, have recently drawn attention to the important role ritual behavior may play in the maintenance of social systems, and have suggested some of the ways in which it serves to integrate differing subsystems. Vayda, for example, in an excellent discussion of trade feasts among the Pomo (1967), points out that such occasions served the dual purpose of delaying the consumption of subsistence goods, while reducing inequalities in such goods caused by local fluctuations in the environment. Thus groups with a temporary abundance of goods could "bank" their excess with less-fortunate neighbors through an exchange of money, a mechanism that ensured the widest possible distribution of resources in time and space, and one which effectively united apparently autonomous groups into a much more inclusive ecosystem.

Such institutionalized means of redistributing resources, of course, were generally present in one form or another throughout much of the state; but in the south most of the transfer of resources or other goods occurred in the context of reciprocal ceremonial exchange, so that a new element is added: regularity. Thus social interaction was no longer dependent solely on irregular environmental fluctuations; instead, social factors involving the demands of an annual ritual cycle as well as reciprocal obligations of a social, economic, or political nature, became the primary motivations for social action. Thus what began as an ecologically adaptive convenience becomes a socially catalytic necessity, stimulating the production, exchange, and consumption of economic goods, reinforcing interpersonal and intergroup relationships, and providing the context for political cooperation and integration. As we have seen, ceremonialism touched upon almost every aspect of life in California because it was in the context of ritual that the various ecological and social subsystems articulated; this point has been nicely demonstrated for the

Cahuilla by Bean (1972), who was primarily concerned with the regulatory functions of ritual. But if, as Binford has suggested, the locus of cultural process lies in the dynamic articulation of subsystems, then ceremonialism may be either an important regulatory mechanism or an important source of cultural change. It is probably no accident, for example, that the utilization of a general-purpose currency seems to have occurred most intensely in the context of ceremonial exchange, or that the increased political sophistication found in southern California appears to have involved new ways of integrating political authority with religious sanctions. Certainly the investigation of such possible interrelationships presents both a challenge and a promise for the future, and the same ecological and cultural variability that once relegated the study of California Indian societies to the curio shop of anthropological commerce may well be the key to the understanding of important kinds of cultural processes.

Flexibility in Sib Affiliation Among the Diegueño

by Katharine Luomala

The purpose of this paper is to present examples of the flexibility and looseness of the structure and functions of certain consanguineal, unilineal kin groups among the Diegueño Indians in southern California and adjacent regions. The examples, recorded in 1934 by Dr. Gertrude D. Toffelmier and myself, show tribal accommodations to individual deviations from the conventional rules of descent or from traditionally expected residence and affiliation with certain kin.

The willingness of the Diegueño at that time, and within the memory of the then living older generation, to tolerate these accommodations, however grudgingly, may reflect a comparable flexibility in the still earlier aboriginal period. This might account for the recurrent question among anthropologists whether to regard the social groups involved as sibs or as lineages in which the unilineal rule had deteriorated under Spanish and American acculturation. It has also been suggested as an alternative possibility that the social units in question were merely local groups in which a unilineal rule had not become definitely established before acculturation obscured old customs.

TRIBAL DIVISIONS

The Diegueño tribe is roughly classifiable into four main divisions — three in the United States and one in Baja California. Although they exhibit cultural differences, their similarities are numerous enough to make any statement of boundaries suggestive rather than definitive. The Western Diegueño, also called the

Northern Diegueño, who include both the mountain people and the little-known coastal dwellers, ranged from the eastern foothills of much of San Diego County west to the Pacific Coast south of San Luis Rey River. After the Franciscans established San Diego Mission in 1769 they slowly missionized some of the Western people. The name San Diegueño, however, came to be applied also to the three less missionized divisions.

The Eastern or Desert Diegueño, also known as the Southern Diegueño, extend east of the mountain people to Salton Sea and into Imperial Valley of Imperial County and southwest into Mexico. The Eastern and Western Diegueño are often jointly labeled the Kamiyai, but this term is sometimes limited to the Western division. The third division, the Kamia or Yuman Diegueño, is located in southeastern California, Arizona, and Mexico farther south and east than the Eastern people. The Kamia, Gifford (1934: 1) suggests, may originally have been a branch of the Eastern Diegueño of the Imperial Valley who through contact with the Yuma tribe of the Colorado River learned a little farming and other practices absent in the aboriginal culture of their kinsmen. The fourth division of Diegueño spreads across the international boundary into Baja California. Their United States kinsmen call them Xakuwak, Southern Water People, or, in English, the Mexicans. Still farther south are related tribes like the Akwa'ala, the Kiliwa, and the now extinct Cochimi.

DIEGUEÑO CULTURE

The Diegueño dialects belong to the Yuman division of the Hokan-Siouan linguistic superfamily. In aboriginal times the tribal economy of hunting, fishing, and plant gathering varied somewhat among local groups in their exploitation of the diverse resources of the mountains, foothills, deserts, and seashore. Each group moved seasonally within a familiar and restricted habitat. Although wild plants were occasionally transplanted, the economy was nonhorticultural until perhaps the late eighteenth century, when a few groups, imitating the Colorado River tribes, half-heartedly added gardening to their livelihood and missionized groups began to supplement their hunting and gathering economy with gardens and livestock.

With neighboring tribes like the Shoshonean-speaking Luiseño and Cahuilla and the Yuman-speaking Mohave, the Diegueño form part of a small nucleus of tribes which are set off from other California tribes, and from the Intermediate Culture Area generally, by their possession of one or more of a cluster of traits that signalize them as the western outposts of the Southwestern Culture Area. Among these traits are sibs, pottery, symbolism in color and direction, and sand paintings. The Western Diegueño have absorbed more from the geographically contiguous Shoshonean tribes than have other Diegueño; there are detailed similarities in the mourning ceremony and other rituals and — significant for this paper — in social organization. Missionization and later settlement on adjacent reservations intensified cultural interchange.

SOCIAL ORGANIZATION OF THE DIEGUEÑO
AND THEIR NEIGHBORS

The group which the Diegueño call *cimuL* (as recorded by Spier, Toffelmier, and myself) or *simüs* (as recorded by Gifford) is translated by Gifford as "clan" and by Spier as "gens." I shall designate it, however, as "sib" (cf. Murdock 1949: 47, 67) except in direct quotations. The field researches of Gifford, Kroeber, and Spier on the social organization of the Yuman and Shoshonean tribes of southern California and adjacent areas raise doubts as to the exact nature of this and comparable groups in the region. Precise determination was hampered, of course, by the decimation of the population and by the cultural changes which resulted directly or indirectly when large numbers of these Indians were assembled in missions after 1769 and on government reservations after 1870.

Gifford (1918: 216-217) suggests that five southern Californian tribes — the Yuman-speaking Diegueño and the Shoshonean-speaking Serrano, Cahuilla, Cupeño, and Luiseño — have exogamous, unilineal (patrilineal), localized sibs. They differ among themselves, he notes, in that the Serrano, Cupeño, and Cahuilla possess totemic, exogamous patrimoieties whereas the Diegueño and Luiseño lack them.

In surveying the Pima and the Mohave, Cocopa, and Yuma of

the Colorado River, Gifford observes that these tribes likewise have
sibs but that their sibs are nonlocalized and totemic and, except for
the Pima, are grouped into moieties. The difference between these
tribes and those of southern California in regard to localization
leads Gifford to question whether the social units of the Californian
tribes are actually true sibs or perhaps only local groups. Though he
raises this problem specifically with reference to the Diegueño and
the Serrano, he also sees its relevance for the Cahuilla, Cupeño,
and Luiseño.

With respect to the Western and Eastern Diegueño, Gifford
(1918: 167) writes that both

> possess non-totemic exogamous clans with paternal
> descent. In both dialects the word for clans is "simüs,"
> usually translated as "tribe." Each clan was probably
> localized, or at least regarded as localized by the natives.
> This fact perhaps renders pertinent the question whether
> these social groups are true clans or only local groups.
> Exogamy and patrilinear descent would seem to indicate
> that they are really clans. All members of a group consider
> themselves related, and often at the present day the clan
> name is added to, or takes the place, of the American
> surname.

Kroeber, writing on the same divisions, is also undecided as to
whether they have true sibs or not. After calling them "exogamous
patrilineal clans" in an introductory sentence (Kroeber 1925: 719),
he adds:

> Their system, like that of the Luiseño, is, however, a
> vestigial or rudimentary one, evidently because they are
> situated at the edge of the California area of clans.

Later (Kroeber 1925: 720) he says of the Eastern Diegueño social
organization, which has been "less disturbed by civilization," that:

> This is a gentile system reduced to a skeleton; the only
> unquestionable clan attribute is exogamy. Patrilinear
> descent proves nothing, since the wholly ungentile tribes
> of California reckon and inherit in the male line. It is not

unlikely that the scheme had its origin in pure village communities or small political groups among whom a prevalent exogamy hardened into a prescription, while the name of one of a number of spots in their habitat became generally accepted as their appellation. Only a slight readjustment in these directions would be required to convert the Yurok villages, the Pomo communities or the Yokuts tribes into "clans." In short, it is doubtful whether the term clan is applicable.

A footnote added by Kroeber after Spier's field work in the Eastern division concludes:

> Other than their names, there is little in all this to mark the "clans" as being more than local bands or miniature "tribes" of the usual California type.

The data on the Western (Northern) Diegueño suggest to Kroeber (1925: 720) "a more definite social system," presumably because one locality, Pamo, had a village or community chief in addition to a chief for each sib within the village. Kroeber qualifies his conclusion by adding:

> But the northern Diegueño were shuffled into the mission and mission stations and out again after secularization, and it would be venturesome to draw inferences from statements that may refer to conditions either 50 or 150 years ago.

Like Gifford, Kroeber leaves completely open the question as to whether or not either or both Diegueño divisions possess true sibs. The problem may perhaps be resolved by distinguishing what may be two different types of groups, not always coterminous, among the Diegueño: (1) the consanguineal kin group called *cimuL* and (2) a residential group for which no native name has been reported but which the Spaniards called the "rancheria."

DIEGUEÑO CONSANGUINEAL KIN GROUPS

Each *cimuL* or consanguineal kin group is named after an
object, a creature, a place, or a human peculiarity. Although
Kroeber (1925: 719) states, "Their names, so far as translatable,
give the impression of being place names, perhaps of narrowly
limited spots," I was unable to detect patterning of names in any
Diegueño division. The members of a *cimuL* owned tracts of
hunting and gathering land communally and shared much food.
Each *cimuL* is exogamous. A spouse is sought outside the sibs of
both the father and the mother, and in an acceptable sib all near
relatives must be excluded from consideration. Descent is
traditionally unilineal, through the father. Residence is traditionally
patrilocal; a couple usually lives in the territory of the husband's
father, although it may have its own hut near the main shelter. A
household consists of the active, adult head couple, their unmarried
children, and their married sons with their wives and dependents,
but it may also include the husband's unmarried siblings, his aged
parents, and any surviving dependent siblings of his father's
father.

Variations in residence occur when parents try to keep one
married daughter, "the best of the lot," at home. The *cimuL* of the
girl and her father, through the *cimuL* headman, sanctions a waiver
of the bride-price in such cases in order to induce the groom to
establish his new home with or near the bride's parents and to
assist them. If the son-in-law is a good provider, though his
brothers-in-law may tease him and order him around, he often
becomes a pet of his wife's parents. As a result, matrilocal
residence is common and is so frequently mentioned with approval
that one wonders whether the residence rule should not be
described as bilocal. Although her parents arrange at least her first
marriage, a woman can easily divorce an unsatisfactory mate,
usually with her parents' assistance, and remarry if she wishes.
Her parents will always take care of the children. Cultural values
emphasize respect of the young for the aged, of a man for his wife's
parents (but without respect taboos), and of all for the mother's sib
because, so people explain, the mother suffers in bringing children
into the world.

All four divisions of the Diegueño have some of the same
names for their *cimuL*. Individuals who belong to a *cimuL* of the

same name, no matter in which division they live and even though they cannot trace their exact relationship, nonetheless regard each other as kinsmen and address one another by kinship terms. For instance, Spier's Eastern Diegueño informant, in recounting names of *cimuL* that he knew for Baja California, one of which was the same as his own *cimuL*, voiced the belief that "those of the same gentile name are distantly related to him" (Spier 1923: 306). Gifford (1931: 10) reports that Kamia lineages extend their rule of exogamy "to include members of corresponding Diegueño lineages" whom they address by kinship terms. A Western Diegueño told Dr. Toffelmier and me that to marry into a *cimuL* of the same name as one's own, even in a different division, is "a shame and a disgrace" because the individuals, even without any known relationship or only a very distant one, are considered related and call each other by sibling or cousin terms.

Members of the four Diegueño divisions do not recognize themselves as a tribe. Even a single division has no sense of unity, as is indicated by the Diegueño custom of translating *cimuL* by the English "tribe." But the Diegueño do realize that the dialects of their own and other regions are mutually intelligible. The names of *cimuL* in other divisions are usually familiar, or at least are recognizable as of the same language. A stranger's claim to belong to a certain *cimuL* is accepted. If his *cimuL* is the same as his host's, the inability to discover any actual blood ties does not invalidate acceptance of his kinship with its associated privileges and responsibilities. This attitude enables a stranger to change his sib identification in a new locality with the assurance that his new sib members will accept, at least at first, his claim to kinship.

What we have described is a named, unilineal, exogamous, consanguineal kin group in which all those bearing the same group name derived from the father call each other by kinship terms, and treat each other as relatives, even if they cannot trace genealogically their common origin and even if they come from different regions. This seems to justify referring to such a group as a sib. Such qualifying adjectives as rudimentary, vestigial, and incipient, which others have used, may be warranted by the occasional irregularities in form and function. From information collected since 1925, however, while admitting the difficulty of evaluating the period to which the information refers, I shall be venturesome enough to suggest that rudimentary sibs of this type existed among the Diegueño prior to acculturation but assumed greater significance with the beginning of European contact, when dislodged natives or guides to explorers and missionaries discovered people of the same language and sib names as themselves in distant localities.

DIEGUEÑO RESIDENTIAL COMMUNITIES

Gifford implies doubt of the native claim that the kin groups are really localized, although later in the same study, when comparing the Eastern and the Western divisions, he seems to accept localization. He states (Gifford 1918: 174):

> The information from Northern (Western) Diegueño informants does not seem to indicate as definite a localization of the clans as do Southern (Eastern) Diegueño data. It is possible that removal to the missions and subsequent segregation on reservations has effaced the knowledge of the original distribution of clans from the minds of the Northern Diegueño. The more remote Southern Diegueño, less in contact with the missions, would certainly be more likely to retain such information.

Gifford's initial doubt is nevertheless well founded, I think, because a complex residence pattern is indicated by occasional reports of two or more *cimuL* living in the same locality. This overlapping, it seems to me, is not entirely to be explained by acculturative changes or by informants' ignorance about the localities occupied by particular sibs. Ethnographic emphasis on determining the localities occupied by each sib has tended, in my opinion, to obscure awareness and investigation of what may actually have constituted a Diegueño residential community.

Spier (1923: 299-308) determined that each *cimuL* is "definitely associated with a restricted locality which is probably its usual summer home." He learned the names of places associated with 21 Eastern Diegueño *cimuL* or "gentes." Of the overlapping in localities between two or more sibs which his informant reported more than once, Spier (1923: 301) states:

This may either be merely apparent and due to the indefiniteness of localization, or it may indicate the occupation of the same site by two or more gentes at different periods. It seems most probable, however, that such gentes, with others as well, lived in these localities either in single communities or within a small radius. My informant was told as a small boy that the gentes formerly lived in closely segregated localities, but were beginning to mingle . . . (A footnote adds:) Obviously this may be rationalization rather than fact.

Dr. Toffelmier and I supplemented Spier's predominantly Eastern Diegueño information and added localities connected with a few Western Diegueño *cimuL*. Our Western Diegueño informant knew of certain kin groups in other divisions which he said were localized, although he was not always certain of just where. He frequently identified individuals in terms of locality and of sib. Drucker (1937: 5) mentions Diegueño named kin groups which ranged over specific localities in Baja California and the state of California. For the Kamia, Gifford (1934: 12) reports the localization of an occasional Kamia lineage; when he pressed his informants for more data they referred to "shadowy legendary" localities in Imperial Valley. Within their memory, however, lineages had not been definitely localized. Gifford concludes that Kamia localization may have been destroyed or prevented by the necessity of planting where and when the Colorado River made it possible.

No reference to the term "rancheria" was obtained by Dr. Toffelmier and myself, nor do Spier or Gifford use the word. Yet all of us, it is clear, learned that two or more sibs might occupy the same locality in friendly fashion, ward off trespassers from it, and form a settlement, and that such overlapping of sib territories is not rare. In other words, there is implied a residential community, which might include male family heads of one or more *cimuL*, or sibs, with their dependents. More commonly perhaps, depending on the resources of its habitat, a community is made up of male heads of only one sib with their households. In a large community, a more or less hereditary headman, who is sometimes also a medicine man, acts as an informal leader, with an assistant to carry out orders. Pamo, the winter residence of several Western Diegueño sibs who summered at Mesa Grande, had an elected village chief in addition to hereditary sib chiefs (Gifford 1918: 174).

In a community with only one sib represented among its male members, if a couple succeeds in persuading a son-in-law to live with them, a foundation is laid for the infiltration of the community by a second sib, that of the son-in-law and his offspring. If the couple then takes home a widowed or separated married daughter with children, these children add representatives of a different sib — a third one if the two daughters now at home have married into different sibs and both have children. The prospect is that the male children of the two daughters will make their mother's father's locality their own for life, while retaining membership in their father's sib. Thus is created a three-sib community which breaks down the original strict localization of a single sib, lineage, or extended family.

When only two or three known localities have a certain food, such as mescal or fine acorns, many sibs assemble to process the food at a common campsite which has a water supply and natural protection against the weather. Later these sibs celebrate ceremonies together. An entire sib does not always move to such a spot. A few families with a temporary leader designated by the headman, we were told by our informant, go to gather and process the abundant food while the others remain at the settlement they are then occupying. Certain sibs have maintained fairly continuous friendly relations with each other, living in adjacent and eventually overlapping localities, visiting back and forth, and preferring to marry among themselves. Although they formerly helped one another against marauders and hostile sibs, they never organized in any way.

Rancherias are mentioned in the notes of Judge Benjamin Hayes (Woodward 1934) on his own observations and those of other American settlers and of Spanish officials concerning the Western Diegueño in the Cuyamaca Mountains and Valley from 1825 to 1884. The term rancheria, or occasionally village or establishment, is used in these records for any campsite occupied fairly regularly, although intermittently, by families of these semi-nomadic — or semi-sedentary — Western Diegueño. Some families apparently regarded a particular rancheria as a major home base, if we may judge from references to certain places as "principal rancherias," but they might occupy several different rancherias during a year.

Whether these "principal rancherias" were predominantly summer or winter residences is not clear; some seem to have been one, some the other. Unoccupied rancherias were easily identified by such signs as collapsing huts and granaries, or fireplaces where the dead had been cremated, or natural mortars in which acorns had been pounded.

The size of a group at any rancheria is generally reported as an indefinite "few" or "a great many," but an occasional reference (Woodward 1934: 147, 145-146) is more specific. About 1868, in the acorn season, at the place called Iguae there were "a few Indians . . perhaps eight or ten men with their families: they came from San Felipe to gather acorns." In 1870 the same place had only six or seven individuals — an old woman, an old man, a younger man, and "three or four other Indians," but this was in July, three months before the acorn season drew "numbers" to Iguae from San Felipe, Santa Ysabel, and elsewhere. The relationship among the residents of a rancheria is never reported. We can only infer that the "eight or ten men" at Iguae in 1868 were kinsmen, and the same for the "six or seven" there in 1870.

A Spanish officer, quoted by Hayes (Woodward 1934: 144), mentions very strong localization. In 1837 this officer passed near the territory of the Cuyamaca Mountain Diegueño who were then little known, unconverted, without contact with whites, and with very little contact with the partially Christianized Diegueño at San Felipe and Santa Ysabel. Of these people, the officer said: "They were cut up into several distinct rancherias, often hostile to each other, they were numerous at Guatay and Cuyamaca valley, and in every sense of the word, savage."

What is meant by the term rancheria as used in the early records for Diegueño residential groups? An answer comes from Aschmann, who reconstructed the culture and history of now extinct Central Desert tribes of Baja California from published and manuscript data by Spanish missionaries and explorers in the desert and by modern ethnographers in the Diegueño tribes surviving to the north. Aschmann (1959: 123) states:

> From the evidence that can be adduced, then it would seem that a typical rancheria consisted of one or more loosely organized clans which were probably patrilineal. An organization almost identical to this existed among the

Diegueño (Spier, 1923: 299-308), the Yuman-speaking
tribe closest geographically to the Central Desert from
which adequate modern ethnographic data are available,
and there is a strong suggestion of something very similar
among the Kiliwa and their neighbors (Meigs,
1939: 83-88).

Led by an older man, often a shaman, whose informal leadership
was tacitly agreeable to it, a rancheria, Aschmann estimates, had
between 50 and 200 persons, with a group smaller than that tending
to affiliate with another and a larger one tending to split.

Although individuals might roam over great distances, people
had, notes Aschmann (1959: 127), "a strong feeling of belonging to
a district, though not necessarily one as small as the territory of a
single rancheria." However, each individual seems definitely to
have been associated with a particular rancheria, for explorers and
missionaries always identified an Indian by mentioning his
rancheria, and blood feuds were expiated by killing any member of
the offender's rancheria. Aschmann (1959: 123) therefore
concludes: "The definiteness of the association supports the notion
that membership in a rancheria involved lineage rather than mere
residence with a particular group."

According to Aschmann (1959: 125-130), intergroup ceremonies brought together all or parts of many Central Desert
rancherias friendly to each other. These occasions also provided
opportunities to make population adjustments through informal
realignments between groups either too large or too small and to
scout unexploited food resources. Two rancherias invited each
other to private ceremonies in the intervals between large
assemblages. In a season of plenty, whole rancherias assembled at
a water place to exploit the food co-operatively. When food was
scarce, a single rancheria broke up into its constituent nuclear
families to scour the desert.

IRREGULARITIES IN DESCENT, EXOGAMY, AND RESIDENCE

Murdock (1949: 339) characterizes the Luiseño as a tribe
with "patrisibs . . . clearly incipient, being very small and strictly
localized." He does not suggest that the Luiseño have, in addition

to patrisibs, what he has called compromise kin groups or clans, in this case patriclans, yet Luiseño social reganization resembles that of the Diegueño where, it appears to me, both patrisibs and patriclans occur. Several households, headed by patrilineally related males of the same sib with dependents of their sib and spouses from other sibs, live as a collectivity, albeit haphazardly organized. The applicability of the term patriclan or compromise kin group (Murdock 1949: 66, 68-69) to such a community is strengthened by the married-in residents' identification in sentiment with it. Since residence and descent are traditionally paternal, the married-in residents are usually females, although a few are males who are deviating from the rule. These original outsiders, while retaining their sib affiliations, become emotionally and practically associated with the habitat and the community.

One of Gifford's Western Diegueño informants (Gifford 1918: 173) even said that a woman becomes a member of her husband's sib. After pointing out that, since descent is patrilineal, the result is the same as if a wife did change sibs, Gifford adds that his informant may, however, have interpreted living with the husband's sib as becoming a member of it. It occurs to me that the Diegueño may have had in mind a wife's nearly complete sentimental attachment with her husband's locality and sib if their marriage was one of the ideal but rare lifetime unions and if during a long life she had resided with and worked for the welfare of her husband's sib. A Western Diegueño mentioned to us that his mother's father's mother's sister was still living when he was a boy and resided with his maternal grandfather. Technically the old woman never changed her sib, but sentimentally she "belonged" to her husband's sib; she had taken care of four, if not more, generations of members of a sib different from her own, and she had spent much more of her life with them than with her own sib.

Reality, it seems, resists both defintion and reconstruction — especially in this southern California-Arizona area where a developmental continuum of social forms has been detected (Murdock 1949: 75-76). Ecological factors produce seasonal population adjustments. Residential groups vary in size, form, and composition of kinfolk from place to place, season to season, and year to year, according to the food supply. Diegueño residential groups, it appears, have a variety of forms ranging from a household made up of a small nuclear family or a sizable extended family to a large group of several families led by male heads of the same sib or of more than one sib, with the most highly organized having a political chief in addition to admonitory sib chiefs.

Diegueño social organization, it seems, may be a continuation in slightly more structured form, in combination with a rudimentary sib system, of loosely or little organized bands, so characteristic of the Intermediate Culture Area, in which descent is reckoned on both sides and residence depends more on family convenience than on rule because of the roughly equal contribution of both sexes to the food supply. The sib system, superimposed upon and intermingled with the old band and compromise kin group, on the one hand, crystallizes and firms a preference for patrilineal descent, patrilocal residence, and the recognition of those who bear the same group name in other localities as kin too near to marry, and, on the other hand, it responds with a relaxation of rules to tolerate the old freedom of the band in order to meet exigencies.

Flexibility in the size and composition of residential communities is associated with occasional irregularities in following the ideal rules of residence, of sib exogamy, and of sib descent. Although examples must come from the period of acculturation, they may in part illustrate what occurred earlier. Disruptive changes requiring new adjustments afflicted the Diegueño even before the Europeans arrived. Our informant insisted that people do not change their sibs, that a man keeps his sib when he resides with his wife's people, and that a woman keeps her sib for life no matter where she dwells. Yet from time to time he recalled variations in the past as well as in the present. A conflict of ideal patterns with behavioral patterns exists regardless of an elder's strictness about the observance of exogamy and other rules by his children — rules from which he himself may well have deviated in what seemed an emergency. These deviations from the ideal rules, incomplete as much as our relevant information is, will next be presented, beginning with patterned sib-changes.

SIB-CHANGE AMONG DRIFTERS

A most striking pattern of sib-change is reported as having existed when our Western Diegueño informant's maternal grandfather was young, i.e., in the early 1800s or perhaps even earlier, and it has continued well into the present century. The procedure is for a Diegueño from a distant region, usually a Xakuwak from Baja California, to wander into Western Diegueño territory where he is a stranger, selecting a well-to-do local family as his host and falsely claiming to be of the same sib as the family head. Such a drifter is called a *kwitxal*. Our informant, using the term "tribe" as the equivalent of sib, explained:

> A *kwitxal* comes over from Mexico to reform here, and so he changes his tribe. He picks out some big, rich tribe and says it's his. Nowadays a *kwitxal* tries to tell you he's a Quero, or Kwaxa, or Hulmawa because they're tribes on both sides of the line. If he's good and hardworking, people take him as their tribe. Even in my grandfather's time this happened. Nobody could check up on the *kwitxal* because people didn't travel much and didn't know. But if a man is good, and gets acquainted here, he does all right. Pretty soon he marries into some other good tribe. But no old *kwitxal* can do this because they're too well known here.

If the stranger proves to be a capable hunter or trapper, a hard worker, and an economic asset to the sib, his host may even help him choose and purchase a near, hard-working wife from another good sib. If either sib suspects that the stranger may be marrying into his father's or his mother's sib, they are not likely to voice their doubts and thereby embarrass everyone concerned, including a good hunter. The stranger further exhibits complete assimilation to the customs of his adopted community by calling in a medicine man when he or his new family has an illness or a death. An unreformed *kwitxal*, on the other hand, avoids medicine men for fear they may practice black magic to get rid of him.

A number of factors favor the success of a stranger's sib-change. People vaguely realize that sibs with the same names as those in their division occur elsewhere but are uncertain to what extent. Rapport is promoted by the fact that the Diegueño divisions speak dialects of the same language and by the skill typically exhibited by transients in picking up local speech peculiarities. Uncertainty about the exact kinship ties of a stranger is accepted since it is difficult to trace kinship between all members of the same sib even in familiar territory. The limited amount of travel in the old days reduced the opportunities for checking a stranger's claim, even if there were a desire to do so. In general, however, a sib-changer of good character and the sib he chose had little motivation to disturb a mutually advantageous affiliation.

We may ask how people know that a stranger is really changing sibs, that he is not a member of the sib he claims. The answer seems to be that to the Diegueño it is common knowledge, which by definition requires no proof, that any man who leaves home to settle in a new area wishes to obscure his past, and that one way of doing this is to change sibs. The stranger, to escape perhaps starvation in the desert, or a blood feud, or intra-sib trouble, has become a voluntary or involuntary stray from his local group. Either he turns over a new leaf and becomes an asset to his new group or he remains a lazy, quarrelsome parasite of his chosen sib.

The term *kwitxal* may also be applied to a family which for some reason breaks away temporarily or permanently from the social and local nexus of the sib of its male head and no longer participates in communal sib affairs. If such a family survives in isolation and increases, it may ultimately reaffiliate with the old sib as a new lineage or it may become a new sib with a new name, which is one way of changing sibs. The Kwinxitc sib, for instance, is described, whether correctly or not is unknown, as "a side branch, a side tribe, of the Neeix" sib. With reference to certain *kwitxal* of this segmentary type who were known to his mother's father, a Neeix, our informant said:

> These *kwitxal* weren't really a tribe (sib). Maybe it was a small family that broke off and then got big, a small family of cast-off Neeix that was Gypsylike, here today and gone tomorrow. They started to separate in my grandfather's time, and he used to fight them. They were cowards like all *kwitxal*, afraid of everything. They lived through Santa Ysabel and Warner's country.

Also mentioned was the consolidation of two or more sibs, which led some sibs to lose their own identity and names by absorption into another sib. Our informant remarked: "Certain tribes died off, they were joined together, and the languages got mixed.''

The aforementioned ''old *kwitxal*,'' who do not successfully assimilate into new sibs, have two principal origins. Some are lazy drifters who have found enough work-free hospitality to remain. Others are individuals who have so exhausted the patience of their sibs and communities that to escape punishment, even death, they are forced to keep moving. Both types give the word *kwitxal* extremely negative connotations.

A stranger seeking irresponsibility avoids large strong sibs whose medicine men might bewitch him. He selects a weaker sib to claim as his own, makes himself a crude shelter, and lets his sib host feed him. He may be too lazy to hunt, but he knows he will not starve, that someone will feed him, for the Diegueño abhor stinginess and are taught to be generous even if it means self-denial. A good man waits for others in camp to eat first; he is too proud to eat game he has killed, but waits until others are fed and he takes the scraps. But not the *kwitxal*! If hunters go for bear he may tag along to claim a share of the meat and of any honey obtained, for all who assist in any way are rewarded. He steals, i.e., takes without permission, produce from gardens he has not helped to plant, and he consumes stored supplies with no intent of replacing them later like a good Diegueño.

The two principal talents of a *kwitxal* are his gift for dialects and his ability to detect when he has completely worn out his host's welcome and should move on. Using his acquired familiarity with the region he may then marry an old woman, who soon discovers to her sorrow that he does not intend to reform and that she must feed him from her own foodgathering and from her neighbors' generosity. When these drifters kill someone or get into other serious trouble, they may return home and report that their former hosts are a rich sib, with many horses and pretty girls, thus inspiring a raid upon them. The raiders and the resident *kwitxal* of foreign or local origin who form temporary aggregates in the foothills have given the word *kwitxal* such connotations as thief and marauder.

Spier (1923: 298) states: ''The name 'kwităx'l (marauder?) was recorded for a local group, comprising several of their (Diegueño) gentes, living on the east slope of Cuyamaca Mountain, and ikwainiL tipai (blackwood people), for a similar group.'' The names of these two groups — neither of which, incidentally, is the name of a sib — were probably employed by Spier's informant in the same general directional sense that the Diegueño use Xakuwak for Mexican Diegueño and Kamiyai for Diegueño to the north. The Kamiyai distinguish among themselves the Kuwak, South People, and the TitLipa or ItLkipa, People from Over There, on the coast and in the mountains. Thus our informant when he lived at Santa Ysabel was a TitLipa but later, when he visited there after living at Campo to the south, he was called a Kuwak. Blackwood People is perhaps a designation for the residents of the forested slopes of the central range called IkwainyiL.

Kwitxal who happen to congregate together cannot properly be called a local group, for *kwitxal* typically have no sense of community. They are not regarded, according to our data, as ever having constituted either a community or a sib. Although the Shoshonean Luiseño (Gifford 1918: 204) have a sib named Oyot, "thief," and the Diegueño called the Cahuilla Yellow Jackets because they raided the Kamiyai, no Yuman neighbors of the Diegueño appear to have either the word *kwitxal* or a comparable nonconformist people.

The *kwitxal* group mentioned by Spier was perhaps a temporary, unorganized aggregate of nonconforming individuals, men with a few women of the same type, who lived together for a season, perhaps a winter, in the warmer foothills but did not permanently identify with any locality. An aggregate of *kwitxal* may include representatives of many different sibs and lineages, but sib affiliation is unimportant to the aggregate as such, for it puts itself outside the discipline of any sib. The sibs from which they come are not "interested," to use our informant's term, in the *kwitxal* except to be annoyed at or ashamed of the renegades.

That drifters who occasionally congregate for a season do not constitute a community is indicated by our informant's remarks:

> The *kwitxal* don't have a *kwaipai* (headman) or come under any *kwaipai*, though they might bunch together for a while . . . They never organize to have a real tribe. They're outside a *kwaipai*'s jurisdiction . . . It's each man for himself, that's their rule. They never settle down. One bunch of them lived over on this side for a while one winter in the foothills but they didn't stay there long. . . They either drift away, or marry into other tribes (sibs), or

> mix in with them, or die out because they never have children . . . They're on the move like Gypsies; only Gypsies have families and *kwitxal* don't . . . A *kwitxal* just picks up some old lady or a widow without children or some *kimilue* (man-crazy) woman too lazy to make *bellota* (acorn meal), and doesn't have children of his own . . . (The *kwitxal* have no medicine men of their own, no ceremonies, yet) they flock to all the fiestas for grub but never offer to help out . . . they never miss a fiesta.

The *kwitxal*, then, are completely individualistic, without organization and without identification with anyone else's needs or with any particular locality for long. They do not constitute a sib. Our informant said:

> They aren't a regular tribe (sib), just a pick-up tribe . . . a low-down tribe from all different tribes . . . not really a tribe . . . just broken-off bits of regular tribes that live in the eastern foothills to the Salton Sea, out of the way. They don't get married, or if they do, it's to other *kwitxal* like themselves. Families in good tribes don't want their children to marry *kwitxal* . . . There have always been *kwitxal* since people were alive . . . They are true-born tramps . . . They learn from each other, that's why there are always *kwitxal*.

The informant had never heard that the Xakuwak, from which many of the strangers come, have a sib named *kwitxal*, and he doubted that there was a sib of that name in Mexico.

Any aggregate of *kwitxal* is thus a temporary, outlaw, splinter group which easily breaks up into its constituent individuals, who have flouted or denied customary sib controls and duties. Occasionally one of them deliberately changes affiliation from the sib into which he was born to one which offers him more advantages. If the sib he has chosen finds him a desirable addition, doubts as to his origin are suppressed, but for generations so many drifters have exploited the obligation of a sib to look after its members that the name *kwitxal* has now become the most opprobrious epithet that can be applied to a man or a woman.

As an epithet, *kwitxal* can be used either as a joke or in serious criticism of a sib relative or a member of another sib. Our informant said:

> You can call anybody a *kwitxal* as a bad name. You can say about a no-good person, "He's stinkin' *kwitxal*." You can even joke this way with your brother-in-law, and he can't get mad even for this. If he does, the *kwaipai* will give your sister a divorce. But some people do get mad . . . You make fun of lazy people and call them *kwitxal* for fun, but that doesn't make them a real *kwitxal*. A lazy Neeix wouldn't run off and join the *kwitxal* bunch. If another Neeix called him a *kwitxal* because he acted like one he'd be so ashamed he'd go right to work. If you call a lazy woman a *kwitxal* she gets a move on fast . . . My grandfather used to put all the *kwitxal* to work, but there's no cure for laziness today.

Despite his inability to understand how a misbehaving sib member could escape from the long arm of the headman, or why a person should leave his familiar associates and habitat, the informant nevertheless believed that *kwitxal* of local origin had existed in the old days as well as *kwitxal* from more distant regions who changed their sibs and communities.

Nowadays, when the society is more individualistic and sib pressure against the nonconformist has weakened because of government rations and individual ownership of homesteads, a *kwitxal* remains in his own community unless he commits murder, steals livestock, or practices black magic and has to flee to escape the law or private vengeance. Of a harmless *kwitxal* of local origin our informant said:

> He's a regular *kwitxal*. Everyone says he's living with his sister, but I don't think that's true. But he says it's too much work to get married. He's a *kwitxal* all right. He don't know nothin' from nothin'. He's got a gun, and a doe and buck pass right by him . . . (Of another *kwitxal* he said:) I'd like to find a cure for his laziness, but there's no cure for that kind of thing. It's like the air — if it's blowing that way you can't turn it back. It's its course. If there was

a cure for laziness there wouldn't be *kwitxal* . . . Some tribes breed a lot of *kwitxal* . . . They always say they're too tired to work . . . A *kwitxal* is always on a steady trot, from one place to another. He might put up a load of wood and give it to the man before he goes into his house for a meal.

Needless to say, the informant identified all hitch-hikers, male and female, on the highways as *kwitxal*.

ONE-SIB FAMILIES

Sib-changes sometimes occur in connection with families all of whose members belong to a single sib. A nuclear family that is irregular in this respect arises when two people of the same patrisib marry each other or when only one spouse belongs to a sib and the other, a tribal outsider, is sibless. The offspring of a one-sib household necessarily inherit membership in this sib — in traditional patrilineal fashion in the first type of family and likewise in the second if the parent with a sib is the father, but if it is the mother, then descent must be traced through her. It is considered worse to have no sib than to acquire membership in one through irregular descent.

If the offspring, when adult, follow tradition when they marry, their children will inherit their father's sib, and the grandparental deviation from custom will become obscured. But oftentimes, it seems, one irregularity often follows another, like a chain reaction, in subsequent generations — whether through cause and effect or through sheer coincidence it is difficult to determine from our inadequate material. Our examples, though they come from the last three generations when Diegueño life was changing rapidly, nonetheless show the persistence of old attitudes.

Individuals who marry into either their father's or their mother's sib are still criticized, even though they may argue that they are not actually blood kin. An ambivalent feeling about incest remains strong, and the continuing use of native kinship terms for sib members and other relatives fosters anxiety. Our informant, a medicine man, has treated both cases and dreams of incest. In no instance did these involve persons of different generations.

Incestuous dreams on the part of young, unmarried persons who call each other brother and sister and may actually be either siblings or cousins, it is believed, will lead, if not halted, to the act itself. In one case where a pregnancy resulted the couple, who were cousins, were hastily married off to mates in other sibs. Despite the negative attitudes toward marrying into the sib of either parent and toward marrying anyone called brother or sister, such marriages do occur, and they show the contrast between ideal pattern and actual behavior. A similar contrast also exists, now as in the past, with regard to the duration of a marriage. Lifetime monogamy is the ideal. In reality, however, considerable changing of spouses results in a brittle monogamy, and there are occasional cases of polygamy. The kinship maze is intricately crisscrossed with half siblings and stepchildren. If a woman with a reputation for promiscuity contracts an intra-sib marriage, the offspring may find it difficult to obtain desirable spouses, or indeed any spouses, in other sibs. Irregularities in one generation may thus be followed by irregularities in exogamy, descent, and residence in subsequent generations and by some changing of sibs to hide the confusion.

Our informant happened to refer to three cases of intra-sib marriage among people of his parents' generation who came from normal two-sib families. The offspring of these intra-sib marriages naturally belonged to the sib of their parents. In the case of a marriage between two members of the Kwatl sib, no complications were reported among their offspring or descendants. The two members of the Miskwis sib who married, however, had a son and a daughter who have exhibited many psychological difficulties; neither sibling has married, and they are rumored, although falsely according to our informant, to be living incestuously. The rumor-mongers also add reminders of the mother's several marriages, one of them to a white man. One of the worst things a woman can be called is "white man's wife."

The third case of intra-sib marriage involved two members of the Neeix sib. Their son inherited the Neeix affiliation but, for some unknown reason, changed to the Kwatl sib, also known as Quero, the Spanish translation of Kwatl, meaning rawhide. This son married a Hulwa woman. Their daughter has been as independent as her father; she has affiliated neither with her father's natal Neeix sib nor with his adopted Kwatl sib but identifies herself with the Hulwa, her mother's sib. Among the possible reasons for the father's change of sib may have been uncertainty as to whether his Neeix father is his actual biological genitor, the wish to affiliate with a large sib widely represented in all the Diegueño divisions, and a preference for the Spanish form of the sib name, Quero, as a surname. In another connection our informant remarked that several individuals had dropped their inherited surnames based on Diegueño sib names in order to assume Spanish surnames; these have a special appeal if, like Quero, they are translations of indigenous sib names. By the assumption of a new surname the man in question was enabled to claim a new sib and at the same time, because of its more familiar sound, to assimilate more readily into the larger American scene.

A sib shift or some other irregularity is evident in the case of a Western Diegueño man, a survivor of the coastal group, of whom Drucker (1937: 6-7) writes that he was "Supposed to have been of the Marawir clan, but he disclaimed them, or they him, for some reason."

The other type of one-sib marriage occurs when a Diegueño with a sib marries a sibless non-Diegueño who is either non-Indian or an Indian from a tribe without sibs or with sib names meaningless to a Diegueño. In earlier times an occasional mother might be sibless because she was a woman stolen by Diegueño raiders from another tribe. Some sibs like the Waichen, for instance, have absorbed many Serrano and Cahuilla. Since descent is traditionally patrilineal, a sibless mother presents no more of a descent problem than does a mother from a different patrisib.

The sibless parent is usually the father. In such cases the children take the mother's sib; though this is contrary to tradition, it is less abnormal and disadvantageous than having no sib at all. A family with a sibless father usually resides with the mother's father unless the husband establishes neolocal residence. The non-Diegueño husband, if he is more than a transient *kwitxal*, generally becomes closely identified with his wife's kinsmen since his own are either not present in the area or, if they are, remain aloof from his family of procreation. From the point of view of his wife's parents, his inclusion in their family circle follows the old pattern of keeping one married daughter at home, if possible, to care for her parents.

A one-sib family limits the total number of the children's kindred. On the other hand, it gives them a wider choice of mates since only one sib is excluded. Even a single sib, with its ramifications, can provide the childen with plenty of kinsmen. Our informant, the child of a one-sib family with a sibless father, liked to boast:

> I have lots of relatives. I'm rich. I can go to fiestas all over, and it doesn't cost me a cent. I belong to Neeix, KwainiyiL, Kwaxa, Saikul, Paipa, Waichen, and more too.

In his family of orientation were a dozen siblings as well as many children and stepchildren of his mother's sisters, whom he called brother and sister. Even the kinfolk of his half siblings, who are really not his relatives nor members of the Neeix sib, are nevertheless counted in his kindred and welcome him as a member of their in-group when they hold fiestas.

The sib situation of our informant and his wife illustrate the point that irregularity of descent in one generation may lead to more irregularities in subsequent generations. Our informant's mother was a Diegueño of the Neeix sib, and his father was a non-Indian, foreign to the territory, who, when he was not away working on ranches, lived on his wife's homestead with their children and at least one of his wife's sisters and family. About five miles away was the ranch of the wife's father, her mother, her father's unmarried sister, and her father's mother's sister. Much visiting took place between the ranches, and the children moved freely between them. Later, when the older girls married and moved away to new homes, the younger children added the ranches of these sisters to their list of homes. Our informant was trained by his mother's father to follow in his footsteps as a medicine man; he had "doctor dreams" and had taken toloache root (*Datura meteloides*] as part of his education. He and his siblings all affiliated with the Neeix sib of their mother and her father. The older girls married into different sibs, ones favored by the Neeix for spouses. The younger siblings have mostly married outside the tribe.

His grandfather selected for our informant a suitable girl — a Kwaxa, the same sib as that of his wife — but the informant, being only twelve years of age, evasively moved with his younger brother to the ranch of a married sister until the grandfather abandoned the marriage arrangements. When he married in his late twenties, he chose a girl who, like himself, had a Diegueño mother and a non-Indian father, but who came from a local settler's family. Since both the young people were Catholics and not closely akin, their marriage met church approval. The bride's mother, however, disapproved violently because both she and the groom's mother belonged to the Neeix sib and called each other "sister." It was a long time before she and others who disapproved this intra-sib marriage forgave the couple. Even if the young people had had fathers with sibs and had inherited different sib names, the relatives would have disapproved of the marriage because marrying into the mother's sib is considered disrespectful to the mother. The bride's mother who had so strongly disapproved of the marriage seems never to have considered that she, as well as the mother of the young man, had started this chain of disregard for tribal tradition by marrying sibless men. Two one-sib marriages of one type in the older generation had been followed by a one-sib marriage of another type in the younger generation.

The independence of this young couple in defying the traditions of their elders is the more striking because both, though coming from mixed households, had been intensively enculturated in many classic aspects of Diegueño culture. Our informant was one of the last boys to take toloache, and his wife was one of the last girls to go through the "roasting" ceremony for young girls. Both, however, were mature when they married — both of them for the first time — and the groom had spent two or three years working and living in Arizona, some of the time among the Apache, so that he had considerable perspective on tribal differences.

His mother-in-law, our informant said, finally became friendly after she had been partially persuaded to accept the possibility that sib kinship may be "no real relation, it's just a tribe." Perhaps one of her husbands, a man of a different sib from herself and well known as an authority on tribal custom, helped to influence her. He is reported as having said that old customs were dying and that "if a man *wanted* to marry a girl of his tribe (sib), then that was all there was to it. They (the conservative sib members) just *think* there's a blood relation in there."

When we asked our informant, then nearly 30 years married, if he would object to his daughters marrying Neeix when they grew up, he said that he would not object, "but 40 or 50 years ago it wouldn't have been right." Though he was willing to accept the possibility of his children deviating from tribal tradition in this respect, he and his wife were transmitting pride in their sib and tribal heritage to their children, albeit with an almost anthropological perspective derived from his youthful excursion to Arizona among tribes with different customs.

CONCLUSION

This paper has illustrated how Diegueño society, possessing named, exogamous, patrilineal (and patrilocal), consanguineal kin groups or sibs, has accommodated to deviations from recognized traditional sib rules of exogamy, descent, and residence. As the result of this flexibility, which tolerates an occasional matrilineal, matrilocal, endogamous, or other departure from tradition, communities may have formed in which two or more patrisibs exploited the same restricted habitat but with each lineage or sib of that community tending to claim a particular section as traditionally its own. The flexibility possibly reflects the later addition of the sib system to an older band and compromise kin grouping, with the total structure extremely adaptable to ecological conditions. That the unilineal group within the larger residential community may properly be called a sib is suggested by the presence of branches of sibs in localities occupies by Dieguño speaking different dialects of the same language. Even distantly localized sib members, although complete strangers with no known genealogical ties, are regarded as relatives. This has made it possible for mobile individuals to change sibs for their own advantage. When their assimilation is unsuccessful they form, with dissident individuals of local origin, unorganized, impermanent groups of a parasitic type known as *kwitxal*.

The flexibility of the Dieguño sib system appears to have contributed to its survival even into modern life, when individuals still find it worth while to identify themselves with sibs, to take the mother's sib if the father is a sibless outsider, and by other irregularities to make adjustments so that sib membership is still highly meaningful to them, even though these may entail the eventual destruction of the sib principle.

The Pomo Kin Group
and the Political Unit
in Aboriginal California

by Peter H. Kunkel

MODELS AS MYTHS AND THEIR ALTERNATIVES

It has now been over ten years since Elman Service introduced into the folklore of anthropology the myth of the patrilocal band as the principal, logical form of social organization for food-collecting societies (Service 1962, 1966). Those of us who know California ethnology well have always known that this model was a myth. Yet the most effective rebuttals to Service's model have come from workers in other areas (Lee and DeVore 1968). These were mostly anthropologists who have been doing field research among recent or contemporary food-collecting societies. It is surprising how much opportunity there still is to carry out such field work. It is also surprising, perhaps, that there is still such interest in the food-collecting ways of life.

Of course, food-collecting societies of the Paleolithic period were ancestral, ultimately, to all subsequent types of human social organization. We have therefore some reason to be curious about what such societies were like and how they arranged their social interaction patterns. Service's quite positive and rather male chauvinist myth certainly had the merit of telling us quite specifically, logically, and in some detail how those Paleolithic humans arranged their marital, residential, economic, and kinship affairs. It replaced the three rather tentative models which Steward (1936, 1955) had previously proposed by telling us that two of them were merely acculturationally disoriented relics of the third — Steward's patrilineal band, which with some embellishments became Service's patrilocal band.

The many anthropologists who contributed to the Lee and

DeVore symposium presented abundant recently observed
evidence for the variability and flexibility of actual food-collecting
societies. Thus they destroyed the positive, universal character of
Service's formulation, reducing it to its present mythological
status. Of course, it is clear that the patrilocal band, or something
like it, can be one phase in the cycle of change and regrouping
which such societies act out. But the "logical inevitability" of the
model is rather effectively refuted. It has been replaced, for an
interim, by a "trial formulation" which Lee and DeVore label the
"nomadic style." This nomadic style, they suggest, has the
following characteristics:

1. Limited personal possessions.
2. Small group size, usually under 50 persons.
3. Usually no exclusive claims to resources.
4. Food surpluses not prominent.
5. Frequent intergroup visiting and shifts in residence.

The Lee and DeVore trial formulation does perpetuate one
implied assumption that is also part of the Service myth — namely,
that food-collecting societies have to be small and mobile. Those of
us who know the California data well have good reason to question
this assumption also. Of course, it has always been recognized that
the Indians of California and of the northwest Pacific coast of North
America were "exceptions" to many generalizations concerning
food-collecting peoples. (It is interesting that populations whose
total numbers may well have exceeded those of all the "classical"
food-collecting societies put together are characterized as
"exceptions.") I would like to advance the counter-hypothesis that
it is the nomadic food-collectors who were the exceptions, at least in
Middle and Late Paleolithic times.

The "classical band-level" nomadic societies of hunters and
gatherers are mostly recent or modern occupants of peripheral or
"internally marginal" territories with inferior resources. As
surviving examples of a once more widespread way of life they have
generally been pushed into these less favorable areas by
agricultural and "civilized" peoples. But there once were no
civilizations and no agriculture. In those days, food-collecting
societies had available to them most of the habitable parts of the
earth. To get some idea of what food-collecting societies could
accomplish when fertile lands were available to them we must turn

to two major well-documented peoples — the Indians of the Northwest Coast of North America and the Indians of California. For both there is a considerable literature, albeit with tantalizing gaps in the demographic and ecological information. I maintain, however, that these peoples represent more closely the "normative" food-collecting situations of pre-agricultural times than do the peripheral badlands wanderers discussed by Service and by most of the participants in the Lee and DeVore symposium report.

Why have California scholars failed to come forward with data relevant to the nature of food-collecting people? There are probably several main reasons. First, until recently there were few recognized experts in California ethnology actively engaged in such research. The few students who were interested were struggling to get through the crisis rites of our profession. We were definitely not the sort of people who got invited to symposia or came forward with manifestoes (to which anyone would have listened).

A second reason for the relative silence from California specialists is that California ethnology is based mainly on "salvage ethnography" — the mining of the memories of old people — not on contemporary, on-the-spot, participation-observation of on-going societies. Data obtained by salvage ethnography methods are generally regarded as inferior in quality to data obtained by participant-observation. The greater prestige of the latter is reflected in the Lee and DeVore symposium report; most of the contributors were participant-observers during their field work. We California ethnologists have probably tended to be overly inhibited about entering broad fields of controversy for both of the reasons I cite. (Though we have muttered in our beards — actual or figurative — or to each other.)

Whatever the limitations of the California data — or of those of us who have become the caretakers of the California ethnological tradition — there is pertinent information here, which should be brought to bear on general theoretical questions concerning hunting and gathering peoples who live in favorable, rather than unfavorable environments. This paper presents some conclusions I have come to concerning the nature of political organization among the tribes of northern California. I concern myself mainly with the nature of the basic political units, ambilateral residential kin groups. However, these units were involved in several kinds of more complex social, political, and religious systems, which reflected rather favorable ecological conditions and what may seem to be very "exceptional" demographic conditions. Most of these systems were characteristic of "tribelets" which were semi-sedentary, rather than nomadic; organized at the levels of tribes or chiefdoms, rather than just at the "band level"; and which had population densities running well above the one per square mile figure so often cited as the upper limit for hunting-gathering populations.

HISTORY OF CONCEPTS IN CALIFORNIA ETHNOLOGY

Important theoretical generalizations concerning California Indian political organization have been advanced by A.L. Kroeber (1925, 1932), E.W. Gifford (1926a), and Walter Goldschmidt (1948). I will briefly review the essence of their generalizations.

In his *Handbook of the Indians of California* (1925), Kroeber first advanced the concept of the "village community" as the basic, autonomous political unit within the non-political, ethnologically recorded "dialect-tribes" of California (e.g., Yuki, Pomo, Miwok, Yokuts — really linguistic units, not tribal entities). He originally conceived these units as consisting of quite small populations, averaging about 100 persons, bound together by kinship ties, and occupying a principal village plus one or more subsidiary hamlets. These populations exploited fairly specific territories for their subsistence (see Kroeber 1925: 161-163, 228-230, 830-834).

Kroeber later modified this concept in certain respects. In his monograph *The Patwin and Their Neighbors*, Kroeber (1932: 258-259) proposed the term "tribelet" as more appropriate for the autonomous political unit, since the "community" (i.e., the group of people within a given territory) seemed more important and more permanent than the village, which might in the long run be subdivided or moved from one locale to another. As Kroeber (1932: 257) put it, each tribelet was a homogeneous unit in matters of land ownership, trespass, war, major ceremonies, and the entertainments entailed by the latter. He also considered the possibility that his original estimate for average population might be low. In this he was largely influenced by Gifford's (1926b) census data from the Pomo village of Shigom, which appeared in a monograph *Clear Lake Pomo Society.*

Gifford's (1926a) most significant theoretical contribution to the political organization of aboriginal California is his paper "Miwok Lineages and the Political Unit in Aboriginal California." In his paper, Gifford suggested that the underlying basic unit of California political institutions was a unilineal (usually patrilineal) kin group, the "lineage." By the term "underlying" Gifford implied that, although evidence for the existence of lineages was not always clearly present in ethnographic data from many California Indian tribes, it seemed reasonable to hypothesize their former presence. He cited definite evidence for the presence of lineages among the Sierra Miwok and various southern California peoples — including the Cahuilla, Serrano, Diegueño, Cupeño, and Luiseño. He also attributed lineages to certain of the Clear Lake Pomo, a point I will presently challenge.

In a sense, Goldschmidt's (1948) general paper, "Social Organization in Native California and the Origin of Clans," is a further extension of Gifford's thesis. By this time, Duncan Strong (1929) had demonstrated the validity of the lineage concept for much of Southern California with impressively detailed data. Anna Gayton (1945) also had discovered the presence of lineages among the Yokuts and Western Mono, something Gifford had apparently only suspected. Goldschmidt thus marshalled evidence suggesting the presence of unilineal tendencies among various tribes of northern California. Moreover, he went beyond the bounds of Gifford's original formulation to suggest the prominence of clans in aboriginal California. This hypothesis seems to be based on the assumption that extended corporate kinship groups among primitive peoples must inevitably tend toward lineality. In 1948 this was possibly still a reasonable assumption. But, in the years since then, Murdock (1960), Davenport (1959), Goodenough (1955), and others have made us aware of the importance of ambilocal or ambilineal corporate kin groups — "cognatic forms of social organization" as Murdock terms them.

I wish now to propose the possibility that there were two widespread types of corporate kin groups present in aboriginal California. They may have been characteristic of geographically distinct parts of the state. Let us assume a line running east through the Golden Gate, thence north up San Francisco Bay, east again through Carquinez Strait and the joint delta of the

Sacramento and San Joaquin Rivers, thence north up into the Sierra Nevada foothills. South of this line there is no doubt that Gifford's thesis held true; political subdivisions seem generally to have been patrilineages. Occasionally these were also independent political units. However, Kroeber's tribelet concept applied in most areas; that is, the lineages were usually political divisions within tribelets.

Tribelets also occurred north of the Golden Gate-Delta line. But, with respect to corporate subdivisions, the situation is less clear, partly because the data are less clear. McKern (1922) claimed patrilineal "functional families" for the Patwin in the southwestern portion of the Sacramento Valley. These have been interpreted as lineages, although McKern himself disavows such an interpretation (personal communication 1966). He feels that: "The political structure of the community was wholly independent from both the functional activities and social status of such families." Furthermore, he points out that only certain families among the Pomo were specializing "functional families." Other families were not.

Gifford believed the Pomo had lineages at one time, some patrilineal, some matrilineal (Gifford 1926a; Gifford and Kroeber 1937). Goldschmidt (1951) in his *Nomlaki Ethnography* reported lineages and even clanlike units for the Nomlaki, a Hill Wintun division. In addition, Goldschmidt (1948) had already made the argument mentioned above for the predominance of unilineal tendencies throughout the state.

I wish to argue against the importance of corporate, unilineal kin groups in northern California. I will first present positive evidence that the Pomo had ambilocal residential kin groups as their basic political subdivisions. Then I will suggest that the best interpretation of evidence elsewhere is that similar residential kin groups were present in most of the other ethnolinguistic divisions of "tribes" of northern California. I use "tribes" in quotation marks because the units which are frequently labelled as tribes in California ethnology were not truly functional sociopolitical units. They were mainly dialect or language groups. Kroeber's "tribelet" is the true sociopolitcal tribe for most of the area, and these units were usually smaller than the ethnolinguistic divisions both in population and in territorial extent. The residential kin groups were, in turn, subdivisions within the tribelets.

The residential kin group is essentially the "local group"

which Linton discussed in the *Study of Man* (1936: 209-230). The usefulness of applying Linton's concept to California Indian political units was suggested some years ago by Ralph Beals and Joseph Hester (1955). However, they mostly saw it as applying to total, independent political units. I see it as applying in most cases to political subdivisions within Kroeber's tribelets.

I must stress the fact that this unit is basically a residence group. In northern California, as well as in many other "primitive" areas, such local political units consist largely of people who are also related. The relationships may tend to be predominantly patrilateral, matrilateral, or ambilateral. They are not properly to be conceived as lineal relationships. Their principal basis is co-residence, not descent. For this reason, I will stress the use of such terms as patrilocal, matrilocal, or ambilocal as the proper descriptive adjectives, and will use the "lineal" terms only in very restricted ways as when describing inheritance or chiefly succession. The next section of this paper discusses the Pomo residential kin group.

THE POMO RESIDENTIAL KIN GROUPS

The Pomo ethnolinguistic "tribe" occupied a considerable territory in the Coast Ranges, north of San Francisco Bay. The Pomo heartland was the Russian River drainage, but Pomo also occupied considerable areas to the west and east of this drainage. Three ecological habitation zones were long ago outlined by Barrett (1908): (1) the Valley Zone, essentially the Russian River drainage; (2) the Coast Redwood Zone, a mountainous and heavily wooded area between the Valley Zone and the adjacent coast, which included the coast; and (3) the Lake Zone, in the drainage basin of Clear Lake, east of the Valley Zone.

The Pomo were probably the most intensively studied ethnolinguistic "tribe" of native California. Ethnographers who have studied these people include Barrett, Kroeber, Gifford, Loeb, Essene, the Aginskys, Omer Stewart, and the geographer Fred Kniffen. From reading their various reports one gets the impression that Pomo political organization was very complex, but that only fragments of the total system have been reported by any one ethnographer. Some years ago I attempted to reconstruct Pomo political institutions by means of structural-functional inferences (Kunkel 1962). By this I mean that I tried to piece together the known fragments in terms of functionally consistent and reasonable relations among them. In doing so I devised four models which perhaps approximate the real aboriginal political institutions in different parts of Pomo territory, and which relate to the major Pomo ecological habitation zones set up by Barrett.

My four models may be as mythical as Service's universal patrilocal band. It is quite clear, however, that the Pomo area was characterized by constantly shifting political alignments with residential kin groups the most stable elements in the system. Tribelets were important but somewhat fragile political entities, breaking up fairly often into their component parts — the kin groups — which then recombined in new ways. Three principal factors seem to have been variables in this situation: (1) the politically uniting functions of men's societies (Ghost Societies) and secret societies involved in the Kuksu religion; (2) the nature of secular chieftainship and its prestige relationship to ceremonial chieftainship; and (3) the political relations among corporate kin groups. I am mainly concerned, in this paper, with the nature of the corporate kin groups, for these are the units which Gifford has characterized as lineages, but which I claim are ambilocal residential kin groups.

My disagreement with Gifford concerning the nature of these kin groups is based largely on census data for the multi-kin-group village of Shigom, which also constituted the Shigomba tribelet on the eastern shore of Clear Lake. Data from other Clear Lake communities found in text and tables of Gifford's monograph *Clear Lake Pomo Society* (1926b) reinforce my position. If Gifford had not been so conscientious an ethnographer I would have far less evidence against his lineage hypothesis as applied to the Pomo kin groups.

Gifford's census data indicate that, around 1850, the population of Shigom, some 210-235 persons, was divided among 47 hearth groups, which were essentially nuclear or stem families occupying 20 houses (1926b: 291-295). The 20 households belonged to three larger groups on the basis of chiefly allegiance (Gifford 1926b: 343). Allegiance to each chief was through kinship ties which were predominantly matrilateral in nature (Gifford 1926b: 344-346). However, matrilaterality was a statistical trend,

not an inflexible rule. For 53 individuals whose chiefly allegiances
are listed by Gifford, 51% of the allegiance ties were matrilateral,
13% were patrilateral, and 36% could not be determined (i.e., the
chiefly allegiance was known but kinship relationship to chiefs was
unknown).

Residence patterns showed similar statistical variability.
Viewing house residence in terms of the connecting links between
constituent hearth groups, 62% of the links were matrilocal, 27%
were patrilocal, 9% were "neutral" or "mixed," and 2% were
unknown (Gifford 1926b: 304). Here, the total sample consisted of
58 possible linking bonds between families. Oddly, when looking at
hearth group membership in terms of relationship between male
family head and persons (other than wives or unmarried children)
belonging to their hearth groups, the picture is reversed and there
is a predominant patrilocal pattern! That is, 66% of the cases were
patrilocal, 26% matrilocal, 4% avunculocal, and 4% "mixed"
(Gifford 1926b: 300-301). The total sample consisted of 70 cases.
Both the statistical variability and a matrilocal tendency are again
emphasized in figures on 44 Shigom residents whose parents were
from two different villages (i.e., one parent from some village other
than Shigom): 66% matrilocal, 34% patrilocal.

Now it may be argued that, although these figures indicate
ambilocal residence and ambilateral allegiance to chiefs, they are
not directly relevant to descent, hence do not disprove the existence
of lineages. However, it is precisely these residential clusters, with
their associated chiefly allegiance patterns, that Gifford claimed as
political lineages. His ethnographic and demographic data from
Shigom fully support the political significance of these units.

I can record that Gifford was aware of the possible non-lineal
implications of his demographic data. In 1926 (when he published
both his general paper on lineages and his Clear Lake monograph),
he did not see these implications as disproving his lineage
hypothesis. Instead, he took the position that the chiefly allegiance
groups were "modified lineages." However, in 1957, when I had a
brief interview with him in Berkeley, Gifford took the generous
position that I should interpret his published data as seemed best to
me, that he had no strong convictions on the matter 30 years later,
and no unpublished data to add.

My interpretation is that whatever their past these chiefly
allegiance groups were not lineages by 1850. Further, in view of our

present knowledge about the frequent occurrence of non-lineal corporate groups, I see no need to set up an assumption that these groups were ever lineages.

Gifford's Clear Lake data go beyond the village tribelet of Shigomba in respect to certain matters. Among other things, he records 23 contemporary chiefs of equal secular rank for the Lake zone, as of ca. 1850 (Gifford 1926b: 333-346). Thus 23 kin groups are indicated for the zone. My analysis suggests that these kin groups were single village tribelets like Shigomba; others belonged together in rather complexly confederated tribelets, at least in proto-historic times (according to unpublished notes of C. Hart Merriam on file with the Department of Anthropology, University of California, Berkeley), although most Pomo ethnographers have treated the villages in all cases as separate tribelets (e.g., Gifford 1926b; Kroeber 1925; Stewart 1943).

Gifford's scattered census data for other Clear Lake communities suggest the same ambilateral pattern for allegiance to chiefs as that indicated at Shigom (1926b). Moreover, the residence pattern is ambilocal as at Shigom. Furthermore, Gifford's descriptive ethnographic data indicate that residence was a matter of choice throughout the Clear Lake zone. This is, in fact, the key to understanding corporate kin groups of this sort. There is the possibility of choice, after marriage, between residence with the husband's joint natal family household and residence with the wife's. With the Pomo, such choice seems to have been tentative just after marriage. There was a good deal of moving back and forth, especially if the kin groups involved were in different villages. But, ultimately, a final choice was made, thus determining initial chiefly allegiance for children. Chiefly allegiance for in-married spouses remained ambiguous, a fact that is reflected in apparently inconsistent statements of allegiance presented in some of Gifford's tables.

The presence of the same types of ambilocal and ambilateral residence and allegiance patterns in the other two Pomo ecological habitation zones is inferred from general statements concerning chiefly succession and residence pattern in certain tribelets. Also, I have abstracted 35 clear cases of chiefly succession from the Pomo literature. Of these, 14 involved sister's sons as successors and 7 more involved other kinds of matrilineal succession. On the other hand, 9 cases involved chief's own sons as successors, 3 involved chief's brothers, and 1 involved some other kind of patrilineal succession. A single case involved some other mixture of both matrilineal and patrilineal connections, a succession by a sister's son's son. In summary: 21 cases were matrilineal, 13 cases were patrilineal, and 1 was mixed. Data on chiefly succession were abstracted from the following sources: Loeb (1926: 231-233, 240-241, 243-245), Gifford (1926b: 336-341), Gifford and Kroeber (1937: 196), Kniffen (1939: 384), and Stewart (1943: 50, 51).

Two other ethnographically recorded characteristics of Pomo culture are consistent with my thesis: (1) succession to various specialized economic or ceremonial roles was validated by sponsorship at Ghost Society initiations, and such specialization could be passed along by a sponsor who was either a matrilateral or a patrilateral relative; and (2) the Pomo could not marry cousins of any kind or degree.

COMPARATIVE DATA

I now wish to discuss evidence for residential kin groups as basic political units for other ethnolinguistic "tribes" of northern California. To a considerable extent, this evidence is negative in character. That is, except for the Nomlaki and perhaps the Patwin, there is really no definite evidence for the presence of lineages in the corporate sense in northern California. This is in contrast to the very full and specific evidence known from the southern part of the state. I must stress the implications of this contrast. Lineages involve more than just tendencies toward unilineal descent, unilineal inheritance, or unilocal residence. Lineages as corporate groups are always self-conscious entities and usually have specific symbols of in-group solidarity: collective representations such as sets of lineage-owned personal names; direct or indirect totemic terms used as lineage labels; more general terms referring to the corporate body as a category of group; lineage-owned ceremonial or political functions; and the like. Such things are well-known to have occurred frequently in most of the ethnolinguistic "tribes" south of San Francisco Bay and the Delta. North of the dividing line I know of only two good cases of such symbolism associated with possible corporate groups (and one of these is open to a different interpretation). One of these cases is suggested by the Patwin term *se're* for the supposedly patrilineal "functional family" as reported by McKern (1922). The other is the term *olkapna* applied to a localized clan as reported by Goldschmidt (1951) for the Nomlaki.

The Patwin term may not really refer to a unilineal group. According to data collected by Kroeber, and reported in his *The Patwin and Their Neighbors* (1932), *se're* could mean a family or any body of kin or other associates (Kroeber 1932: 273). For instance, it could refer to the people of a village. This suggests the possibility of a village population which consisted of one residential kin group. Kroeber (1932: 272-273, 291-292) further reports that Patwin residence, after marriage, was not always strictly patrilocal and that ceremonial functions or offices could sometimes be inherited from mother's brothers as well as fathers. Thus, one gets an initial impression that Kroeber's data contradict some of McKern's statements and certainly cast doubt on the possibility of Patwin lineages. McKern (personal communication) indicates that there is no contradiction, but that he too doubts the reality of Patwin lineages. He points out that he (McKern 1922: 238) as well as Kroeber (1932), describes variations in post-marital residence after marriage. With respect to lineages, I have abstracted the following statement from information provided by McKern:

> If I know anything about Patwin political structure and social concepts, and I believe that I do, the Patwin "functional family" can not reasonably be considered as a politically significant lineage, for the following reasons: (1) It was not the social unit of the community structure since it included only certain families, excluding others. Its existence derived from the family inheritance of certain properties consisting of ritualistic matter and charms which added persuasion of supernatural agencies to its chances of success in a specific social or economic function. The possession of such aids, inheritable within a family, exclusively, according to any prevailing rule of inheritance, would automatically produce a similar functional family in any society. (2) Although the possession of such functional assets added to the social prestige of a family, it yielded no political powers or influence as such. The chief of a village might or might not belong to a functional family. In any case, such

membership would have nothing to do with his political status. The special esoteric aids considered property by such a family related exclusively to a special social or economic specialty. The political structure of the community was wholly independent from both the functional activities and social status of such families. How can such a specialized group, not sufficiently representative to qualify as the social unit of the community structure, and entirely independent, as such, from political duties and responsibilities, be considered, even tentatively, as a lineage unit in the community social structure? (McKern, personal communication)

McKern, himself, never made a claim that the Patwin had lineages. Rather, that claim was made, at least implicitly, by Goldschmidt (1948) as part of his sweeping hypothesis concerning the emergence of clans in California. (I use "clan" here in the sense of "sib" as used by some American anthropologists.) Goldschmidt's (1951) best evidence for a type of corporate linear kin group comes from his own work on the Nomlaki. He gives persuasive evidence for interpreting the Nomlaki *olkapna* as a patrilineal corporate descent group.

The Nomlaki were a Wintun tribelet and the Wintun were closely related linguistically to the Patwin. Data summarized and tabulated by Goldschmidt indicate that these and most other divisions in the Sacramento Valley had patrilineal tendencies with reference to chiefly succession or other types of inheritance. Further, they had patrilocal tendencies with respect to residence.

Patrilineal norms with respect to chiefly succession and inheritance, along with patrilocal norms with respect to residence, would certainly be consistent with the existence of patrilineal lineages. But they do not of themselves constitute full proof of their existence. The general pattern for the Central Valley seems to have involved tribelets consisting of one or more villages, villages which consisted of one or more extended residence groups, which tended to have patrilocal, patrilateral ties to chiefs, and the patrilineal/patrilocal tendencies outlined above. However, there is no evidence for symbolic collective representations, such as totems, lineage names, and the like (except for the terms *se're* and *olkapna* as applied to categories of groups among the Patwin and Nomlaki, respectively). The residence groups of the Sacramento Valley may well be thought of as extended kin groups which were the structural expression of a lineal descent pattern. But the existence of lineages is doubtful.

Let us now look at data from "tribes" in the Coast Ranges and in the northernmost reaches of California. The Hupa, Yurok, Karok, Tolowa, and Wiyot of northwestern California all had patrilocal preferences with respect to residence. But such institutions as "half-marriage," formally defined illegitimacy, and slavery introduced alternative norms to such an extent that 20% or more of these populations must have been residing in a non-patrilocal fashion. Further, the emphasis on rich men as relatively informal power figures must have rendered patrilineal or patrilateral ties subject to so much exception as to be almost meaningless. The settlements among these peoples generally consisted of single residential kin groups or, in some cases, of clusters of such groups. It is a moot question whether these should be termed patrilocal or ambilocal units. No symbolic collective representations of a lineage-defining sort were present. Also, contacts with members of the Hupa tribe from 1962-64 yielded no clues whatsoever of present or past lineage-like groupings.

In the northeast part of the state, the Pit River tribelets had ambilocal and ambilateral residence and kin ties, according to Garth (1944, 1953). But Erminie Voegelin (1942) records patrilocal and patrilineal institutions. This difference may reflect variations among different tribes of the Pit River drainage. (To the east, perhaps, they were patrilocal; to the west perhaps ambilocal.) Ray's (1963) data on the Modoc suggest very definitely ambilocal residential kin groups.

Back in the Coast Ranges, the social organization of the Eel River Athabaskans is practically unknown. A few scraps of circumstantial evidence suggest that they had composite or patrilocal hunting bands that tended to settle down as small ambilocal or patrilocal kin group villages. The Yuki of the upper Eel River drainage had patrilineal and patrilocal preferences, respectively, to chiefly succession and residence, according to Foster (1944). However, the Coast Yuki as described by Gifford (1939) seem to have had ambilocal, single-kin-group villages and no larger political units. In the makeup of their villages, they were similar to some of the smaller Pomo villages of the Coast Redwood zone (though the latter were loosely linked into tribelets).

South of the Pomo territory, between the Russian River drainage and San Francisco Bay, dwelt peoples of the Wappo and Miwok "tribes." According to Barrett (1908), these peoples had social organizations similar to the Pomo. There is one bit of more specific information. This consists of census data collected by Driver (1936) for a Wappo village in the Russian River Valley.

This village, *Unuts-waholma*, had a population of 92, involving 21 hearth groups in 11 houses (Driver 1936:201). Various statistical tables indicate an ambilocal residential pattern (Driver 1936: 211, 201-204). Property inheritance was ambilineal (Driver 1936: 211). Marriage was proscribed among all known blood relatives. This last point strongly suggests that the village population was a single, exogamous, ambilocal, residential kin group, since all the houses seem to have been interrelated. There was one head chief and one assistant chief, a pattern quite similar to the chieftainship situation in a Pomo corporate kin group.

CONCLUSIONS

I have presented evidence for the existence of ambilocal corporate residential kin groups among the Pomo. In addition, I have in summary fashion indicated the nature of evidence for this residential type of corporate kin group elsewhere in the northern half of present day California. Negative evidence seems fairly strong against the existence of corporate lineages or clans. In many ethnolinguistic divisions or "tribes," especially in Sacramento Valley, it seems reasonable to suppose that patrilocal, extended family, residential kin groups were the key political subdivisions. But evidence for ambilocal political groups of the residential kin group type seems strong for peoples other than the Pomo: e.g., Wappo, Coast Yuki, Modoc, and some Pit River tribelets.

I have not used the term *ramage* for the Pomo type of group. At one time I considered this usage but have rejected it because the ramage concept seems to be basically applied to descent groups of an ambilineal nature (Murdock 1960) and only incidentally is such a group a residence group.

Most of the peoples dealt with in this paper were organized into tribelets numbering into the hundreds. Demographic studies have indicated population densities well above one per square mile for considerable portions of the area (Cook 1955, 1956, 1957; Kunkel 1962). Much of the area was characterized by a very complex type of religious system, the so-called Kuksu Cult, with very considerable ramifications of a political nature. The area was quite varied ecologically, but there were many very favorable local ecological niches available, and these were efficiently exploited by the people who occupied them without too much moving around. Permanent or semi-permanent villages with substantial houses are well-recorded in the ethnographic literature. All peoples in the area were food-collectors, and agriculture was quite absent in aboriginal times in the northern half of the state.

All in all, this is quite a different picture from the conventional depiction of hunting and gathering populations as small, nomadic, owning little property, and characterized by only "band-level" types of social organization.

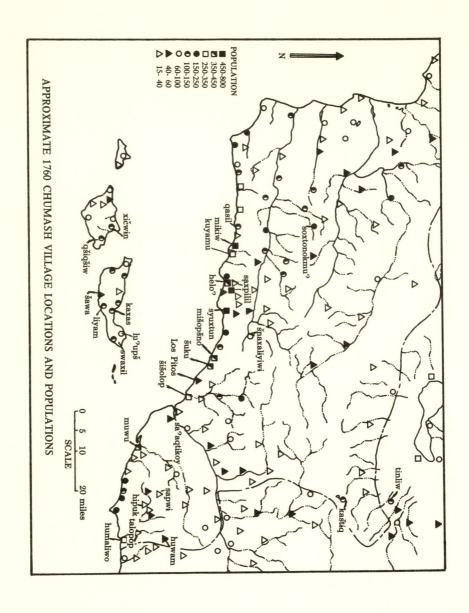

APPROXIMATE 1760 CHUMASH VILLAGE LOCATIONS AND POPULATIONS

POPULATION
- ■ 450-800
- ◨ 350-450
- □ 250-350
- ● 150-250
- ◒ 100-150
- ○ 60-100
- ▶ 40- 60
- ▷ 15- 40

N

SCALE
0   5   10   20 miles

xičwin
qšiqšiw

kaxas
ju?upš
swaxil
šawa
liyam

qasil
mikiw
kuyamu
helo?
saxpilil
šyuxtun
mišopšno
šuku
Los Pitos
sišolop

Soxtonokmu?

špaxalyiwi

muwu
sa?aqtikoy
sapwi
hipuk
talopop
huwam
humaliwo

tinliw
kašiq

Chumash Inter-Village
Economic Exchange

by Chester King

The Chumash Indians occupied areas on the coast of Southern California between Point Conception and Malibu, on the Santa Barbara Channel Islands, and in the inland valleys adjacent to the mainland coast. They maintained a market economy with standardized, portable mediums of exchange, frequently used to purchase subsistence materials, most manufactured goods, and some services. Many economic anthropologists have implied that no non-agricultural society like the Chumash, or even non-"peasant" or non-"modern" society can be expected to have such an economic system (Nash, 1966; Dalton, 1967).

In this paper I shall present a hypothesis which explains Chumash intergroup economic behavior. I shall then illustrate the hypothesis with geographic, historic, and ethnographic Chumash data. There will follow a description of how the operation of the intergroup economic system created archaeologically observed regularities. How the hypothesized relationships suggested in the paper can be tested, is treated in summary form.

A number of authors have recently explained differences and similarities between the economic behavior of different groups on the basis of environmental variation (Suttles, 1968a, 1968b; Yengoyan, 1968; Piddocke, 1968; Vayda, 1967, 1969). There are two types of environmental variability, which are here hypothesized to result in most or all differences in inter-group economic interaction. One form exists when neighboring groups are adapted to resource bases which have differing seasonal patterns. Exchange of materials between such groups can result in a more stable subsistence base, and thereby an increase in population, which in turn makes it necessary for the groups to maintain interaction. The more differences between the resource bases of adjoining groups, the greater the intensity of interaction. This first form of variability is requisite to all highly developed market economies.

The second form of variability results from the reliability of resources within each territory, and the number of kinds of resources being relied upon at any one time. Inter-group interaction increases (1) in relation to population pressure on the available resources; and (2) according to the degree of resource reliability, increasing when the resource base is less reliable, or relatively unpredictable. Inter-group interaction decreases when resources are more reliable. Averaging the effects of resource fluctuation charactertizes all economic systems to some degree.

Given the relationships between population size, resource variability, and inter-group interaction, it is possible to hypothesize that economic behavior varies between populations as a result of the efficient adaptation of each population to its particular environmental arrangement of critical resources. The degree different populations interact, and the ways in which this occurs, are therefore determined by differences and similarities in the environment of each group, and the extent to which population growth has resulted in the necessity for increased interaction.

Inter-group interaction results in harvesting more than the members of the local group can consume, the production of exchange goods, and the transportation and marketing of materials. All these activities require an increase in energy expenditure. Therefore the intensity of interaction is not normally greater than is necessary for group maintenance. Of considerable interest in this discussion is the fact that the village populations in the Chumash area spoke several related dialects. In 1769, the year of the first European settlement of California, the population density of this area was evidently greater than that recorded historically for any other non-agricultural area, excepting probably areas of the Chinook and certain other Northwest Coast groups.

There is a great deal of variability in the environmental settings of Chumash villages. In this paper, a simple classification of *Inland, Mainland Coast*, and *Island* is sufficient to illustrate the physical context of inter-village exchange.

The Inland area is characterized by a mountainous landscape, with small areas of relatively flat bottom-lands, which support valley oak and various grasses. As one travels from the valley bottoms, up the slopes of the mountains, the vegetation changes to a zone of sage and sage brush, or to chaparral, or (on some north-facing slopes) toyon and groves of live oak. Along narrow streams are found live oak, sycamores, bay trees, and *Prunas sp.* (wild cherry). The general environment has been classified as Upper Sonoran.

The Coastal area has almost all plants found in the interior, but in different proportions. Coastal sage usually covers large areas, and there are various microenvironments unique to this area, such as salt marshes and small lagoons. The seashores on the mainland have more variability in environment than do the shores of the islands.

The Island area has a cooler environment than the Mainland. The plant communities are more similar to those found in Central California than to those of Southern California. The islands have less than half as many plant species as the mainland. At the time of contact, the largest land mammal living on the islands was a species of small fox. These were the more important Chumash resources, the general areas in which they were found, and the seasons in which they were gathered.[1]

Wild cherry (islay) was gathered from July to September; acorns in October and November (in some areas, i.e. near Gibralter Dam, they were gathered in January as well as at other times), chia (sage seeds) in the summer, mescal (yucca) between January and May, and cacomites, or blue dick bulbs (*Brodiaea sp.*) were evidently collected in the early spring. Of these vegetable products, mescal and chia were not available locally on the Channel Islands. Mammals exploited on the mainland were deer, rabbits, squirrels, gophers, and rats. None of these animals were present on the islands. River fish were utilized in those areas where they were available (especially in the Santa Ines Valley); birds were also taken. The mainland area had most of the raw material resources used by the Chumash.

Sea resources were exploited by the coastal villages on the islands and mainland. Shellfish were also evidently gathered by inland groups, when they came to fiestas on the coast. Sea resources can be roughly listed on the basis of habitat.

---

1. It is apparent that the Islanders lacked some important vegetable resources, especially those obtained between the months of January and July.

Shore resources consisted of shell fish, other invertebrate animals, rocky shore fish, and sandy shore fish. The sandy shore fish are not common on the islands, which have mainly rocky shores. Some sea mammals such as seals and sea otters also frequent shore environments. Resources of shore environments were generally available at all seasons. They were therefore important in the winter, when other types of resources were scarce.

Food obtained in pelagic areas consisted of sea mammals and fish. Animals found in the pelagic environments were often seasonal and reached their highest frequency in the summer months. Evidently sea birds were also taken.

Island resources other than those on the shores were limited. Blue dick bulbs were probably among the most important. Acorns and wild cherry were also present on the islands, but seldom in quantities comparable to those of the mainland. Of the Santa Barbara Channel Islands, Santa Cruz Island is the only one with sources of material which can be used for small, well-made chipped-stone tools. The other islands have lithic sources which were used for ground stone artifacts.

Here listed are the goods traded between Chumash villages, categorized by direction of movement. There is a distinction in kind between goods which went from the mainland to the islands, and goods which came to the mainland from the islands. It is clear that the islands were exporting manufactured goods, whereas the mainland was exporting food resources and goods manufactured from materials which were lacking in the islands.

Items mentioned as moving from the islands to the mainland are these: each item is preceded by the name of the informant. Herrera 1542: beads of fish bone (Wagner 1929: 427). Costanśo 1770: coral beads (Hemert and Teggart 1910: 49). Font 1776: baskets (Bolton 1932: 272). Tapis 1803: beads of shell (Brown 1967: 9). Justo 1880's: dark stone digging stick weights (Heizer 1955;1544). Señora Welch at Dos Pueblos Ranch: stone ollas from Catalina Island (Schumacher 1879: 118). Fernando (Harrington's informant v.1) 1913: beads. There is only one reference which lists goods going from the mainland coast to the inland area. Martinez in 1792 recorded fish and beadwork as material going to the inland groups (Simpson 1939: 45). Several items are recorded as going directly from the island groups to the inland groups. Omsett in the 1880's said that shells for beads were traded to the inland people;

and Fernando said otter skins were traded to the inland groups. One of Harrington's informants said that acorns and islays, etc., were traded to the Islanders by the inland villagers.

The following references summarize the goods moving from mainland villages to the islands: Tapis 1805: seeds (Brown 1967: 9). Juan Pico 1880's: acorns, seeds, bows and arrows, etc. (Heizer 1955: 151). Juan Justo 1880's: grass seeds, furs, skins, acorns and roots (Schumacher 1879: 118). Fernando 1913: chia and acorns (Craig 1967: 83). Fernando 1913: *wo ʾni* (burden basket), and large baskets.

There are only two statements concerning goods going from inland villages to coastal villages. On May 18, 1782, Felipe de Neve wrote to Ortega, commander of the Santa Barbara Presidio:

> (The Channel Missions) have to vary in their methods from the rest (of the missions) of the Peninsula; this is required because of the location of the rancherias, the large number of heathen, their trading, and their stored food by whose abundance they maintain themselves. Their food is fish, game, seeds and other fruits that they trade for with the mountain Indians . . .'' (Calif. Archives 1782b: 26).

Martínez in 1792 recorded that seeds, shawls of foxskin, and blankets made from fibers resembling cotton traveled in this direction (Simpson 1930: 45).

The following statements given by Fernando to Harrington indicate that the Islanders brought goods to some mainland coastal villages. These villages were trade centers. Islanders and individuals from the surrounding villages met at these locations.

> At many of the villages on the coast of the mainland, as many as one half of the population talked the Santa Cruz Island language. The Santa Cruz Island people lived permanently in these villages, like permanent colonists. During the time of harvest, when the acorns, etc. were ripe, many Indians came from the islands to the mainland and went inland to gather the wild fruit. Santa Rosa Island was the richest in otter. The Indians would kill the otter with arrows. They would bring the skins to the mainland

at harvest time, and trade them for acorns, etc. The coast
of the mainland was where inland Indians, coast Indians
and island Indians mixed. That is why the *siliyiq*
(ceremonial enclosure used at fiestas) was on the coast.
There was commerce between inland and island Indians at
qasil (Refugio). Exchanged otter skins. *Šawa* was not
abandoned at large then. Refugio was a big village; it was
a center for it was a port of the Santa Cruz Island Indians;
a trail led to Santa Ines and there was much trade in
acorns, wild cherry, etc., from Santa Ines when the
islanders came. (Fernando to Harrington).

Governor José Joaquin Arrillaga wrote to the commander of
Santa Barbara in December, 1804, just after the abandonment of
the mainland coastal villages, indicating possibly related activities:

It shouldn't be your duty to transfer the mountaineers who
solicit at the Arroyo of El Capitan and at the Arroyo of
Casil (Refugio) (Calif. Archives 1804: 104).

Harrington's informant Fernando said: ". . . women and men
on the islands made the beads and came here to Ventura to sell
them . . . Pitas Point . . . was the place where the island Indians
came" (Craig 1967: 83).

Governor de Neve wrote to the commander of the Santa
Barbara Presidio on March 6, 1782, prior to the establishment of
the Presidio: "(At) the large rancheria of Asumpta (Ventura) . . . its
natives have since the first expedition manifested themselves as
good friends; they find themselves frequently insulted by the
heathen traders to whom they were obligated to abandon their
rancheria and to form it in the willow grove (*sauce*)". (California
Archives 1782a: 89-91).

Additional references indicate the transportation of goods by
Islanders to the mainland: "They (Santa Rosa Island Indians)
carried on considerable trade in shells with the Indians in the
interior" (Omsett in the 1880's; Bowers 1878: 319). Friar Antonio
de la Ascension, who was on the Vizcaino voyage of 1602, recorded:
"They (the Channel Islands) are well settled with Indians who trade
and communicate with each other and with those of the mainland"
(Wagner 1929: 239). Crespi of the Portolá Expedition recorded in
1769 at Ventura: "In the afternoon some chiefs came from the

mountains (Ojai Valley), having come from their country purposely to see us. Some Islanders from the Santa Barbara Channel who happened to be in this town, came also, and they told us that twelve canoes had gone to the islands to bring from there the people who wished to see us" (Bolton 1926: 147). Fr. Font, on the Anza Expedition, said on February 24, 1776: "They pointed out and showed me an Indian who was there at Rincon saying that he was from the large island of the Channel called Santa Cruz, and that he had just come for pleasure, for it is a marvel to see how they navigate those seas. Although his hair was reddish he looked to me very much like the Indians of the Channel" (Bolton 1931: 257).

Transportation of goods by mainlanders to the islands is indicated in these statements: "The Ventura Indians used to go to the islands two in each canoe; fifteen or twenty starting off at one time. When they returned, four men would be in one canoe and the other would be loaded with fish and towed behind" (Fernando, Craig 1967: 83).

The following statements indicate that mainlanders might have been catching the fish themselves, although it's also probable they obtained them from the islanders:

> Then in the morning they go (from Hueneme), where they have rested after following the coastline down (from Santa Barbara), to *éne:més*, arriving near to the island of *ányá:pax*, and they skirt along that island and the island of Santa Cruz, to the rancheria they are headed for . . . When they were going to take a canoe trip to bring a load of something that would be heavy in the bottom of the canoe, sometimes they tied a rope once around or several times around the middle of the canoe, when they left with the canoe empty or just before they loaded in a load, which might be a load of abalones from the *éné:mes*, so as to keep the walls of the canoe from spreading when loaded (Harrington's notes on canoes, informant unknown).

On the Portolá return expedition to Monterey, April 30, 1770, Crespi mentioned that the whole village at Ventura had gone to the islands, presumably for a fiesta (Piette 1946: 114). A reference to the conveyance of goods from inland to the coast, a distance of about thirty-three miles, is indicated in this report: "Once saw a man of the Piro region wearing an épsu (basket hat) with carrying net band over it in front. He was bringing a heavy load of shelled acorns to Ventura. It was a long way" (Fernando, V1, in Craig 1967: 96). These statements further indicate extensive trade between the islands and mainland, but do not describe who transported the goods. Costanso recorded, in his narrative of the Portolá Expedition of 1769-1770:

> They hold intercourse and commerce with the natives of the islands, from which they obtain the coral beads, which in all these parts take the place of money. They value, however, more highly the glass beads which the Spaniards gave them, offering in exchange for them all they possess, such as baskets, otter-skins, bowls, and wooden dishes. But above everything else they esteem any kind of knife or sharp tool, admiring its superiority over those of flint; and it gives them much pleasure to see use made of axes and cutlesses, and the ease with which the soldiers felled a tree to make firewood by means of these tools" (Hemert and Teggart 1910: 139).

In 1805, the missionary Estevan Tapis said, concerning the Islanders, that they lived " . . . in more than usual poverty . . . the men wholly naked, the women little less so, hungry, with no recourse but fishing and some seeds got in trade from the natives of the mainland in return for the beads they themselves made from shells" (Brown 1967: 0). Juan E. Pico, a Ventureño Indian, was briefly interviewed by H. Henshaw in the latter part of the last century. He gave the following information. "The Islanders were more skillful in the production of stone implements and these formed their stock in trade. From the mainland they received in exchange seeds, acorns, bows and arrows, etc." (Heizer 1955: 151.)

The organization of the inter-village exchange system seems to have been essentially an expression of the profit motive on the individual level, and the operation of the law of supply and demand. Effects of the system were to produce a common resource base for a large area at the expense of much work. These aspects of the economic system can be seen in the following quotations. Longinos Martínez described Chumash economic behavior while he was in the area collecting data on resources for the Spanish government, in 1792:

All these Indians are fond of traffic and commerce. They trade frequently with those of the mountains, bringing them fish and beadwork, which they exchange for seeds and shawls (tapalos) of foxskin, and a kind of blanket made from the fibers of a plant which resembles cotton; and they prefer these to their own which they make from sea otter. When they trade for profit, beads circulate among them as if they were money, being strung on long threads, according to the greater or smaller wealth of each one.

In their bargaining they use, as we use, weights, their *poncos* of strings of beads. This word *ponco* (Gabrieleno bead measure, Kroeber 1925: 565), is used for a certain measure of strings, two turns from the wrist to the extended middle finger. The value of the *ponco* depends on the esteem in which the beads are held, according to the difference in fineness and the colors that are common among them, ours being held in higher regard. The value depends upon the greater or smaller extent to which the beads have been circulated, the new values depending upon their abundance. The value which should be placed upon our beads is always estimated with respect to their own, and in everything they keep as much order as the most careful man who has accumulated some money.

They make their beads out of a species of small sea snail (*caracolito*), which they break into pieces, shaping them in the form of lentils, then drilling them with our needles and stringing them. After the strings have been made they rub them down until they bring them to a degree of fineness, for in their conception they have more value so. These strings of beads, and ours, are used by the men to adorn their heads, and for collars which they weave with beads of different designs, like a rope belt, etc. They all make a show of their wealth, which they always wear in sight on their heads, whence it is taken for gambling and trafficking.

. . . The liveliness of these Indians makes them more given to thievery than those of other parts, and to the possession of things of some value, the desire for which

causes them to engage in commerce with soldiers and
sailors (Simpson 1939: 45-6).

Accounts exist which indicate the frequency with which the
Chumash traded, and the degree of emphasis placed on the
ownership of goods. Fages recorded in 1775:

> They are inclined to work, and much more to self-interest.
> They show with great covetousness a certain inclination to
> traffic and barter, and it may be said in a way that they are
> the Chinese of California. In matters concerning their
> possessions, they will not yield or concede the smallest
> point. They receive the Spaniards well, and make them
> welcome; but they are very warlike among themselves,
> living at almost incessant war, village against village
> (Priestly 1937: 31).

In 1776 Gárces, after having stayed in some Chumash villages
in the vicinity of Castaic Lake, passed near the present town of
Tehachapi and made the following comments:

> There were here none but women and children; who made
> us presents of meat, seeds and even two baskets to take
> along with us. There are here firs, oak, and many other
> kinds of trees. I returned the favor with some small shells
> such as they prize, but the women told me they regaled
> me solely because we were so needy; that their nation was
> generous, not stingy like that on the west. I believe they
> are right about this, for those of the west are dealers
> among their very selves, and by so much the more do they
> value and take care of their possessions — though
> certainly I have not reason to complain of them . . (Coues
> 1900: 304-5).

On December 31, 1782 Lieutenant Ortega reported that "these
Channel Indians are very different from the ones I have dealt with
in the entire peninsula (the Californias). They have a particular
inclination towards work so that if I have enough beads to hand out
to them as gifts, I feel that I should be able to finish the presidio in a
short time" (Geiger 1965: 14).

In his confessionary, Fr. Señán provided a list of things people owned (Beeler 1967: 54,45). The list includes: alchum — beads; altacash — big white beads (Olivella cylinders and cups; chipe — white bone beads; eshqueluoy — colored bone beads or sea shells; yquemesh — small spotted beads; anmitmiti — small beads; sucupi -garnets (?); Alcaputsh — mortar; chucuyash — par (steatite bowl); chuniec — pestle; choshtou — frypan; tosho — tray; ayujat — seed beater; estapa — rush (or tule) mat; sutinet — fiber rope; majaquesh — rags (clothes). It can be noted that the objects owned by individuals or families are the same as those being traded. Other objects for which there is ethnographic information concerning personal or family ownership include: (1) Digging stick weights (used mainly on the islands) which were of dark stone, usually well polished, and belonged only to the wealthy (Heizer 1955: 154). (2) Canoes, which were owned by the wealthy (L. King 1969: 42). (3) Food stores, wealth, charmstones, ceremonial regalia, etc., which were owned by the chief, who rented or loaned them out (L. King 1969: 42). (4) Seeds, acorns, and trees, which were owned by households (Harrington 1942: 34). Presumably bows and arrows, pipes, wood bowls and plates, fishing tackle, pigments, tools, brushes and food were also individually owned. Deer meat was said to be owned by the individual who killed the deer (Fernando V 1).

Many of the objects traded and owned by individuals were made by craft specialists (Craig 1967: 84). Fages provided the following statement concerning craft specialization:

> The occupations and ordinary pursuits of these people are limited; some of them follow fishing, others engage in their small carpentry jobs; some make strings of beads, others grind red, white and blue paint clays, and a certain kind of plumbiferous stones, which serve to the men to paint themselves with when they are celebrating or dancing or when they go to war, and which are used by the women for their usual adornment. They make variously shaped plates from the roots of the oak and the alder trees, and also mortars, crocks, and plates of black stone (serpentine) all of which they cut with flint, certainly with great skill and dexterity. They make an infinite number of arrows. The women go about their seed-sowing (gathering), bringing the wood for the use of the house,

the water, and other provisions. They skillfully weave
trays, baskets, and pitchers for various purposes; these
are well made with thread of grass roots of various colors
(Priestley 1937: 35).

Money was also redistributed in the form of payment for
services. Fine dancers (*ʔantap*) were on salary under the captain;
but sometimes the dancers gave dances "just for love." On
baptismal or marriage days in mission times, a father might pay the
paha (master of ceremonies) $2.50, which he turned over to the
captain. Sometimes, when the dancers voluntarily danced at
baptisms and marriages, they made more than when on salary from
the captain, for then everyone gave them presents and the dancers
got more than otherwise (Fernando). Doctors were paid when they
effected cures (L. King 1969: 44). Buriers were paid for their
services (L. King, 1969: 47). The *alšuqʔlaš* (manet official) was paid
by relatives of the recipient for administering toloache.

Henshaw obtained the following information from an
informant in the 1880's, indicating that the Chumash used
standardized measures in economic transactions: "For measuring
reeds and articles bartered in bulk, baskets were used. These were
of several sizes and although doubtless the standard was not very
exact, they approximately approached a standard . . ." (Heizer
1955: 153.) Fernando informed Harrington that "the Indians
measured strung piñons around the hand precisely as they
measured beads. One length of strung piñons was worth three of
the bead strings" (Craig 1967: 97). Another informant stated that
"the *ʔepsu* was the means of measuring when you wanted to buy
islay or acorns, etc. I don't know the money value of an *ʔepsu* full of
chia or acorns. But I know that acorns, chia, pilas (?) and islay were
more valuable than other foods. The islanders came in order to buy
and they bought four *ʔepsu* or six *ʔepsu* or as much as they were
able to carry" (Harrington n.d.).

Other information on measuring money includes an illustration
of measuring bands (Harrington 1918: 94), measurement equiva-
lances (evidently for Olivella shell beads, possibly whole shells
because of the low value) (Kroeber 1925: 565), and counting
information (Beeler 1967); see also Henshaw in Heizer (1955: 150).

Fiestas were an important social context for the redistribution
of goods. "Priests discouraged fiestas usually . . . (they) said

Indians spent all their money on fiestas'' (Harrington's informant B 1). Most of the large fiestas in the Chumash area were on the mainland coast, but some ceremonies and games were held at certain inland and island villages. The largest fiestas were held at specific villages, according to a ritual calendar. Smaller fiestas could be held by village or lineage chiefs with the consent of village chiefs.

One of the functions of a village chief was to establish dates for fiestas and to invite other villages to attend (L. King 1969: 42, 43; Engelhardt 1919: 65). The duties of the chief included feeding visitors and the needy, and approving everyday ceremony (Harrington 1943). Gift giving, excepting providing somewhat for the feasts, was not evidently extensively engaged in by the host chiefs. The guests were expected to provide donations for most fiestas. According to Fernando (V 1), visiting captains at a festival would make donations on their arrival, so that the host would have enough for the festival and the rest of the year. There was an economic interest in having a fiesta in Indian times, for the captain would save some of the offerings, so that when his people were in distress he would have something with which to assist them.

Collections were also made at some fiestas, as for example at the *Zorra* (fox) solstice dance on Santa Rosa Island. The *paha* acted, on this occasion, as a sort of floor manager. During the "islay" passage of the dance, the people at the fiesta put islay and "nicer things" in a basket carried by the *paha* (Fernando). Other instances of collections being taken are indicated in the following statements: "Also in midsummer (solstice ceremony) had a big tray and all put valuables in it as offering for sun and for crop increases" (Fernando). "At the coyote dance, *awitsaʔaʔs, after* the dance the *paha* comes from the south and cries 'The Grandparents are hungry.' He does this three times and then all the women and girls come with their *bateas* (basket trays) full of fine and different eatables and after going around three times they deposit everything at the *siliyiq* (ceremonial inclosure) (Fernando). At the winter solstice ceremony on December 24 at 3:00 an "old man" (*paha*) with two helpers erected a sunstick and that evening the old man and twelve dancers (*ʔantap*) participated in further ceremony. The dancers heard the old man deliver a short address on the weather conditions, crops, etc. Then at 8:00 they danced while the old man received all of the offerings. Givers of baskets of chia, islay, corn, beads, money, would go around the fire three times, make a speech, and present the gifts to the old man" (Fernando).

Fines could also be exacted at fiestas. The following incident from Harrington's notes refers to this mechanism, resulting in the redistribution of goods or money. One San Francisco day at Cieneguitas, it had been arranged with the Santa Barbara Captain Francisco Solano, called in Chumash *sexpeweyo* (chief of Dos Pueblos), for Juan de Jesús to dance the *Nuqumpiyaš* (Barracuda dance). A relative of Juan de Jesús, and his grandmother, who had raised him, requested that he withdraw from the dance because of his inability to perform properly. The Ventura Indians had to pay the Santa Barbara chief with beads, etc., indemnity, because Juan de Jesús withdrew.

Some individuals did not help to provide for fiestas. Fernando, for example, described to Harrington a class of good-for-nothing vagabonds. While most of the visitors at a fiesta hunted or paid for their board in some way, the real vagabonds did not care what happened, and were the only ones that had to be paid for. The refusal of a chief to accept an invitation from another chief to attend a fiesta was grounds for war (Harrington 1942). Feasts were often attended by individuals from villages at great distances. Chiefs were especially obligated to attend.

An interesting unpublished account of Mugu fiestas by Bowers from information collected from Juan Pico suggests that the fiestas at Mugu functioned traditionally to integrate most, or all the entire central Chumash area (cf. Blackburn, 1974):

> Here (at Mugu) lived a great chief or king whose authority extended to Point Concepcion 100 miles up the coast, and to Newhall and San Fernando eastwardly. The chief of each town or tribe was a petty king, but subject to the Mugu rule. The town where the great chief lived was near a large spring of water (Simomo) which rises at the base of a basaltic hill two miles from the ocean and bordering the Santa Clara Valley. Here meetings of all the tribes were held once in five years to pass laws and transact business pertaining to the numerous tribes of the district. When the time drew near for the meeting, two men were sent to notify the nearest tribe of the time fixed upon by the great

chief for the national gathering. The tribe visited by these men notified the next, and they a third, each informing his neighbors of the contemplated meeting until all were notified. Each tribe started at a time that would bring them to Mugu on a certain day. When they came in sight of the capitol, they announced their presence by fire and smoke signals. Seeing these signals, the king, accompanied by some of his chief men, would go out to meet them, sending two or three men in advance, and on the arrival of the tribe they were accompanied into the town with music, singing, and dancing and assigned to their place during the gathering. When the tribes or their representatives were all assembled, dancing and feasting began, which continued for five days, at the close of which the chiefs of each tribe were called into council for the space of three days, when they would be dismissed. The Mugus provided food for all their visitors for the first eight days, but after the expiration of that time, if any desired to remain, they must provide food for themselves. The ocean being near and fish and clams abundant, this was not hard to do (Bowers 1897: 29-33).

In order to maintain the operation of the economic system so far described, it was necessary to eliminate goods at a rate similar to that of their production to prevent inflation. Food items were of course removed from circulation primarily by consumption, but many other goods, such as beads, had to be removed from circulation by other means. One such means was the burial of goods in the ceremony with their owners or as offerings, or their destruction at other mortuary related events, such as the burning of houses and belongings; destruction of mortars and killing of one's dog at death; burning of boats and houses, destruction of goods at the mourning ceremony, and destruction of offerings at shrines for the dead (L. King 1969:51, 52). Concerning the disposal of goods at shrines, Fages wrote:

> They are idolators like the rest. Their idols are placed near the village, with some here and there about the fields, to protect, they say, the seeds and crops. These idols are nothing but sticks, or stone figurines painted with colors

and surmounted with plumage. Their ordinary height is
three hands, and they place them in the cleanest, most
highly embellished place they can find, whither they go
frequently to worship them and offer their food and
whatever they have (Priestley 1937: 32-33).

Harrington's informant Juan de Jesús Justo gave the following
information concerning shrines:

At *he?lo?* (Mescalitan Island) there was a place for
throwing things. Justo never saw it but heard there was a
big square enclosure 35 feet or more square, made by
tying bundles of feathers to tops of poles so stood three
feet high. Poles were near together placed upright in the
ground. Old men sat in their and made beads. They were
very venerated. Not all know very much. They were like
interpreters, interpreting for god.

Tiquxšo — place of Sherman's slaughter house in
Sycamore Canyon, Santa Barbara. It is a small arroyo
above the sisters' house near the mountain. Indians had a
shrine for throwing things at that place.

Tilqo?y — Tucker's Grove, at the first arroyo crossed in
going from Cieneguitas to Goleta. Indians used to throw
things there.

Another means of removing materials from circulation was to
trade them to other groups as described in the following section. It
can be noted that the Chumashan groups were usually trading
beads and other durable goods in return for items which could be
consumed. Font, in his diary of the Anza 1776 expedition, recorded:

The Indians of the Channel are of the Quabajay tribe.
They and the Beneme (Gabrieleno and Serrano groups)
have commerce with the Jamajab (Mojaves; these are
ethnic labels used by the Mojave) and others of the
Colorado River, with their cuentas or beads, consisting of
flat, round, and small shells which they hunt for in the
sands of the beach, and of which they have long strings

hung around the neck and on the head . . . (Bolton, 1931: 250). Among the Indians who came to the camp I saw one who wore a cotton blanket like those made by the Gila Pimas, and I inferred that he must have acquired it from that great distance by means of the commerce which they have with others (Bolton, 1931: 257).

Garcés traveled April 26, 1776, from San Gabriel with some Mojave Indians to the Castaic area, where he stayed at two Quabajay (Chumash, see Font above) villages, the largest of which was probably near the village of *kaštek*. The Mojaves who went with him were in the area for trade. Garcés then went north and explored part of the southern San Joaquin Valley; he returned to the Chumash villages where he made the following observations on May 10, 1776: "I went over to the Rancheria de San Pasqual where I found two Jamajabs recently arrived from their land (the others who had accompanied me had already gone back leaving only Luis and Ventura): hence is to be inferred the frequent commerce that the Jamajabs held with these nations and those of the sea" (Coues 1900: 301). The structure described for the Rancheria of San Pasqual has many features characteristic of the *atisaderos* used for high status people at fiestas, and Garcés may therefore have been describing trading associated with a fiesta.

On the 29th of May, 1819, it was reported, "Twenty-one heathen Amajavas" (Mojaves) arrived at San Buenaventura for the purpose of trade and social relations. The soldiers of the guard generated an incident in which several soldiers and some ten Amajavas were killed. Interrogations of some of the Mojaves who were later caught provides some information concerning trade between the Chumash and Mojave. On foot, it was said to take fifteen or sixteen days to go from the Colorado River villages to Ventura. The Mojave brought red ochre and heavy, soft, black blankets. These were traded for beads, light rope and Mexican blankets. The Mojave had planned to trade at Santa Barbara as well as Ventura (Cook 1962: 159-161).

Harrington's informant, Luisa, said that the Mojave brought bright red ochre, and that her father had some of the Mojave ochre. Daniel Hill wrote the following concerning trade with Yokuts groups:

The Indians of the Tulare country generally came over
once a year in bands of from twenty to thirty, male and
female, on foot, and armed with bows and arrows. They
brought over panoche, or thick sugar, made from what is
now called honey dew, and the sweet carisa cane, and put
up into small oblong sacks made of grass and swamp
flags; also nut pines and wild tobacco pounded and mixed
with lime. This preparation of native tobacco was called
pispe swat (pespibata) and was used by them for chewing.
These articles were exchanged for a species of money
from the Indian mint of the Santa Barbara rancherias,
called by them ponga (Gabrieleno bead measure, called by
Kroeber *ponko*; Kroeber 1925: 565). This description of
money consisted of pieces of rounded shell . . . which was
brought in canoes by the Barbarians from the island of
Santa Rosa. The worth of a rial (real) was put on a string
which passed twice and a half around the hand, i.e. from
the end of middle finger to wrist. Eight of these strings
passed for the value of a silver dollar, and the Indians
always preferred them to silver; even prior to 1833. This
traffic the Padres encouraged, as it brought them into
peaceable intercourse with the tribes of the Tulare Valley
(Woodward 1934: 119).

Harrington obtained the following information from a Tejoneño
informant when he asked if the Tejon area Indians were
Christianized and taken away:

He said no, that they used to go from over here (Tejon
area), to attend fiestas at various missions on the coast,
e.g. San Fernando. When there those in charge would
baptize them and ask them if they did not want to live
there; they would tell them they had everything there they
had elsewhere. Thus many stayed. Some who did not like
it would run away at night and come back here. The
dancers from here at fiestas on the coast were paid by
coast Indians with various kinds of coast shell-money or
beads and the Indians brought these back with them here.

Fernando described trading *mulus* with the Tularenos. *Mulus* was sweet, yellower than the finest grade of old-fashioned brown sugar, and was brought in lumps. The *mulus* was in tule cases like *panocha*, but to conform to whatever shape the lump might have. The Tularenos brought these products in carrying nets suspended over the forehead. Candalaria said that the tobacco smoked by the Indians came from Tejon already prepared in packages. The tobacco, called *so ʔw*, grew wild in the mountains of Tejon. Other information for the Tübatulabal comes from Voegelin:

> In going to Chumash villages near Ventura, route lay through Walker's Basin to Caliente, thence to Yokuts village, Lapau, then to Tejon, thence via Comanche Creek to two Chumash villages, *makakak* and *alkolaupal'*, near Ventura. Trip took two days on foot to Tejon, two more days from Tejon to Ventura. From Chumash, Tübatulabal obtained shell money, shell cylinders, steatite, probably, and in later times horses; these exchanged for piñons. They also took advantage of trading trips to Chumash to collect lumps of asphalt from the beach and to fish in the ocean. Occasionally Chumash made reciprocal visits. In trading, 'a sack of piñons was left on the ground; the Ventureños came up; and took as many as they wanted, and laid shell money down in payment' (Voegelin 1938: 51, 52).

Martinez described the Chumash as having a rather closed interaction system.

> In this port of the Santa Barbara Channel, according to my argument, there landed some Chinese, or person of great skill in his own handicrafts and the rest. Because of this superiority the nation has gone on progressing as it increased, although its customs have not passed beyond its limits, owing to the scant commerce and trade among these nations. If any chief merely makes an attempt to pass through another's jurisdiction they start a war and quarrels, because of the distrust these nations have of one another (Simpson 1939: 49).

The Gabrieleño and Juaneño were described by Martínez thus: "These nations are given to having many small baskets of seeds and other foodstuffs. From this point (northward from San Juan Capistrano) they also begin to use strings of beads to adorn their throats, ears, and heads, and to give some value to such ornaments" (Simpson 1939: 51).

References in the previous section on trade with non-Chumash groups indicate that trade with the surrounding groups was limited to a rather small number of goods; and that the intensity of interaction was much less than within the Chumash area. Boundaries of the Chumash interaction system have a close congruence with the boundaries of the area in which Chumash dialects were spoken. Martínez describes the Chumash as being exclusive in their commercial activity, and Garces' account gives substantiating data for the northeastern Chumash villages. Archaeological research in the Southern San Joaquin Valley (Wedel 1941; Gifford and Schenck 1926), has been relatively extensive near the Chumash border, and few of the objects characteristic of the Chumash area (abalone spangles, Catalina steatite cooking bowls and comales) appear there; whereas they are common over the mountain in the Carrizo Plain (Finnerty n.d.), Cuyama Valley (Strong 1935) and in the Sisquoc River area (Grant 1964; Rogers 1937). To the south, the Gabrieleño (Tongva), groups may have been somewhat involved in the Chumash interaction system, but it appears from archaeological evidence that their main lines of interaction were between the mainland and the Southern Channel Islands, having close ties with the Chumash in the Santa Monica Mountain area. The Southern Channel Islands had the highest frequency of interaction with Chumash groups of any non-Chumash group.

The ethnographic and historic data presented above indicate that the archaeological record should have the following characteristics: (1) There should be localities, especially on the islands, where the production of artifacts used in the economic system occurred. Presumably these localities should be characterized by large quantities of industrial waste and manufacturing tools. (2) Cemeteries, shrines and mourning ceremony areas should have a large number of objects manufactured and used in the exchange system. (3) There should be regularities in artifact form related to standardization for trade. (4) Sites outside the Chumash areas should contain beads which were made in the Chumash area. Archaeological data related to the first three points will be briefly discussed, first describing details concerning the production areas, use areas, and disposal areas of triangular bladelets.

In the summer of 1967, while visiting Santa Cruz Island, the author observed a unique site defined by a small area of dense shell midden about 60 feet in diameter. There were three housepit depressions, each measuring about twenty feet in diameter equally spaced within the roughly circular midden. The entire surface of this site was covered with large numbers of chert cores, resulting from the production of a particular bladelet type. These cores were also noted in a small area of exposed profile. The site is located on the west end of Chinese Harbor. Off the shore in this area are extensive kelp beds. The land plant resources in the area are of minimal value as food. Approximately two miles east of the site is the source of the chert present at the site. This chert is found at the contact zone of a large mass of igneous rock with the basal or overlying sedimentary rock which is to the west of it. At the ridge in the center of the island at the same contact zone, there is a large chert quarry which Rogers described as " . . . a rather extensive and well developed site, high on the ridge of the highest hill in the eastern part of the island. This site is fairly littered with flint chips and cores. The bed from which the chert was taken is only a short distance from the borders of the village. The flint work was probably the chief reason for this settlement" (1929: 308).

At this site we did not find any cores which were similar to those found at the Chinese Harbor site, although we did note several platform cores. A total of 142 struck bladelet cores, 16 unstruck prepared cores, 2 crude bladelets, one point, one scraper, 2 utilized flakes, and 2 crude core tools were recovered during a surface collection of the Chinese Harbor site. These were all made from chert, ranging in color from black to white, most of it being brownish. To correct any possible error in the rough surface collection, a small square area measuring about 30 inches on a side was thoroughly surface collected and bagged separately from the rest of the collection. In this control collection were 19 chert flakes which resulted from trimming the cores, 9 struck cores and one unstruck core. Now to be described is the production of the small triangular bladelet from the cores found at the site. In doing so, I shall be describing the cores.

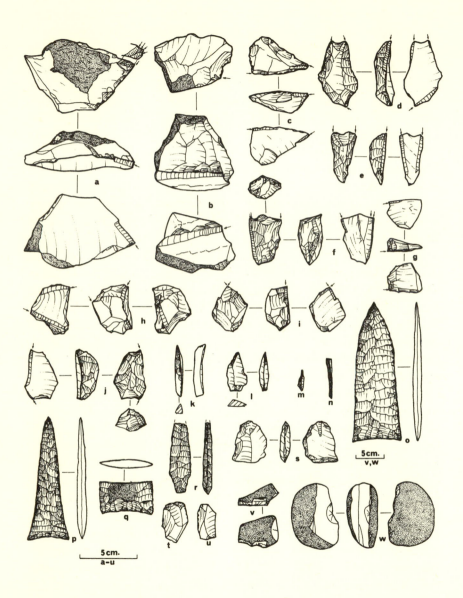

Figure 1. a-j Triangular Bladelet Cores; k, l Triangular Bladelet rejects; m Triangular Bladelet worked as dill, Triangular Bladelet from cemetery cache; o-q Well Made Chert Knives; r-w Other artifacts from Chinese Harbor site.

First a core was shaped before the removal of the blade. The range of size in these cores can be seen in the illustrations (Figs. la-j). A straight edge was flaked from a relatively flat platform. This edge is essentially like that of a "scraper." The edge is beveled and is at about 60° from the platform. A platform was made from which to strike the blade. This platform was at one end of the straight edge at a right angle to the straight edge. It was made in a number of different ways. One was the removal of a large flake which formed a notch (Figs. 1b, d, e, j); another was the truncation of the edge (Fig. 1f) or the removal of a series of what are technically burin spalls (Fig. la). The prepared platform was then struck by indirect percussion (probably with a punch), thereby producing a long, narrow bladelet with a cross-section which is usually equilaterally triangular. All are characterized by a surface which bears the scars resulting from the preparation of the straight edge (Figs. lm, n).

In 1962 Heizer and Kelly published an article describing several "burins" they had found in the Cessac collection from Santa Cruz Island. Many of these (Heizer and Kelly 1962), are in all features identical to the cores recovered at the Chinese Harbor site. Technically they are all burins; functionally they are not. Heizer noted that the burins he described were not previously described in the literature. He also noted that there are burins in Olson's collections from the Santa Barbara Mainland and Santa Cruz Island. He did not, however, describe these, and they may merely be simple burins of the kind used in the area for more than 7,000 years (King 1967: Kowta 1961). In 1966, at the Medea Creek Cemetery in the Santa Monica Mountains (LAn-243), a core and bladelets which had been removed from it, all heavily covered with red ochre, were found together in a rodent disturbed area. This core is the same type as those which were found at the Chinese Harbor site; a few cores used for the production of triangular bladelets as well as some triangular bladelets have been collected from the surface of a site at Orizaba Cove (Personal communication, Christopher Donnan 1970). It is not altogether impossible that the Chinese Harbor site is the only site at which triangular bladelets were produced. However, it is probable that several other sites in the area were centers at which triangular bladelets were produced.

Santa Cruz Island is the only island described as having sites where stone chipping was done in large quantities. Rogers

(1920: 301) is the only author who recorded most of the sites discovered on this island. There seem to be two centers where stone chipping was a major activity on Santa Cruz Island. These are associated with two sources of suitable material. The first area is on the north slopes of Mt. Diablo, and is described by Rogers (1929: 301). He was probably describing a site where large chert knives were being manufactured, since he treated such knives as weapons in his conclusion regarding Canaliño culture (Rogers 1929: 303). He also noted the presence of a manufacturing center at Prisoner's Harbor. This site is a fair distance from the raw materials and evidently was a center where large knives were being produced. Not far from Chinese Harbor, Rogers described a series of sites which he said were centers of flint chipping. He mentioned no other flint chipping centers on the island. Cessac in 1882 also reported the discovery of flint quarries and workshops on Santa Cruz Island in 1878 (Cessac 1951). As was previously mentioned, there are no recorded flint chipping areas on the other islands. For Santa Rosa Island we have the following negative statement from Jones, who did a good deal of work on the island in 1901: "I note many picks of roughly flaked stone and no flint or quartzite picks. This is probably due to the fact that but little flint or quartzite is found on the island, and that little only in the form of a few pebbles in the strata of cemented pebbles and sandstone which occur at the east end of the island" (Jones 1956: 213). From Anacapa Island a small platform core was recovered and illustrated by McKusick (1959). This core is a simple platform core, different from those recovered at the Chinese Harbor site.

On the mainland there are a number of areas which were sources of material for the manufacture of chipped stone artifacts. Rogers (1929) often mentioned finding chipping waste in the Santa Barbara sites. However, he never mentioned finding large numbers of cores in his Canaliño sites except one near Gaviota (Rogers 1929: 256). Cessac (1951a) also said, ". . . at Point Pedernal I discovered an important workshop for stone and jasper weapons." Many small utilitarian chipped stone artifacts found in sites on the mainland are made from fused shale, which was quarried in the vicinity of Grimes Canyon and possibly Cañada Larga. In the literature on the Santa Barbara area there is only one reference to a site in which there was specialized manufacturing of chipped stone artifacts. This is site SBA-60 at Goleta, the historic village of *saxpilil.* Kowta (1961) described the material recovered at a manufacturing area from this site, which included a series of small platform cores resembling the ones fround on Anacapa Island; this is the most common class of chipped stone artifact from the site. To the south in the Santa Monica Mountains no sites are known where specialized chert flaking activities have left noticed remains.

There appear to be three commonly occurring types of chipped stone tools made at a few villages in the historic Chumash area, often as burial offerings. These are large, thin chert knives, triangular bladelets from cores such as were recovered at the Chinese Harbor site, and small prismatic bladelets removed from small platform cores. It appears that only the last of these were made on the mainland, the others being made on Santa Cruz Island.

In summary, it can be stated that triangular bladelets appear to have been manufactured only on Santa Cruz Island. They are found in two contexts in the Chumash area: (1) At Olivella shell bead making stations where they were worked as drills and used to produce beads of types found in fair quantities in middens of late sites in the Chumash area, especially those on the Channel Islands. (2) With burials in late cemeteries (there are usually historic glass trade beads present in the same cemetery) where they are most often placed in a cache. The caches often have several hundred bladelets, and are always covered with red ochre. Most of them, and all of the large caches, are in cemeteries on the islands. Other bladelets were manufactured on platform cores, both on the coast and on Santa Cruz Island. They are found in middens and occasionally with burials in cemeteries. Large, well made knives such as are illustrated by Abbott (1879: Plate 10, 11: Fig. 4a-c) and Grant (1954: Plate 11a) were probably made on Santa Cruz Island. They are found in cemeteries at many historic Chumash villages.

In the discussion of triangular bladelets I have already mentioned the presence of centers at which beads were manufactured. On Map 1, the "B's" indicate location where triangular bladelets have been found, either in large caches in cemeteries, or in large numbers in the excavation of middens. The distribution of triangular bladelets suggests that they were manufactured at one cluster of sites and traded out to be used for bead manufacture at other site clusters. There were a large number of different types of beads produced in the Chumash area at the time of European contact. The beads made with triangular bladelets possibly include those made from the wall of the Olivella shell, and the inner whorl or callus (commonly found in both middens and cemeteries after around 100 A.D.), as well as clam and *Mytilus* discs and cylinders. However, long tubular beads of clam or columella shell could not be made with these drills. Tubular blanks and beads broken during drilling have been found at Burton Mound (Harrington 1928), Shishlop (Ven-3), (Greenwood and Browne 1966) and Medea Creek cemetery (LAn-243) (Linda King n.d.) and seem to have been made at many sites and to a lesser extent at large manufacturing centers (see also Latta 1949: 71 for data concerning the manufacture of this type of bead by the Yokuts). Finished tubular beads are found primarily in cemeteries. Besides disposal in middens and cemeteries, beads have been found covering the top of a hill near Ventura, the remains of the shrine described in L. King (1969: 51).

Mortar and pestle manufacturing centers have been found on San Nicolas Island (Bryan 1961) and on San Miguel Island (J. Beaton and B. Newman, Personal communication 1970; Heye 1921: 45-46). Rogers also described an area at Willows on Santa Cruz Island where mortars were apparently manufactured (1929: 313). An unfinished shaped mortar was discovered during the bulldozing of part of LAn-227. This is the most common type of mortar used in the San Fernando Valley area, the Southern California Islands (excepting possibly San Clemente), the entire Chumash area, and in the Southern and Central Yokuts area after around 900 A.D. Fragments of shaped mortars are occasionally found in villages and camp sites; whole or broken mortars are found in cemeteries.

Digging stick weights were evidently produced mainly on the islands. Rogers mentioned finding debris and drills indicating the manufacture of many "stone rings" at Prisoner's Harbor on Santa Cruz Island (1959: 307). Later he described the drills used to make "fossil doughnuts" as being in some instances as much as nine inches long and two inches in diameter. Jones illustrated several of these tools associated with burials (1956: Plates 96a, f; 97d; 123a,f; 124a). Digging stick weights are among the earliest manufactured artifacts found except beads, pigments, and projectile points (Orr 1968: 120). There seems to be a high correlation between the occurrence of digging stick weights (stone rings, usually dark, hard, and well polished), and manufacturing tools and/or unfinished bead blanks. These same burials usually have many objects with them, and are evidently found in proximity to other burials in the same cemetery which has large numbers of goods. Given ethnographic information concerning the ownership of dark, well polished digging stick weights by the wealthy (Heizer 1955: 154); statements indicating the chief's ownership of items (L. King 1969: 42); and the grouping of both adult and infant burials with many goods in Jones' sites, suggesting hereditary right of ownership, it can be hypothesized that the means of producing goods may have been owned by upper class members of each community. (See L. King 1969 for interpretations of clustering of wealth in another cemetery.)

Serpentine bowls were manufactured in the Santa Barbara area, probably in the vicinity of serpentine deposits found in the San Rafael Mountains — upper Santa Ines River area. These bowls have been found in cemeteries on the Channel Islands, along the Santa Barbara coast, and in the Sisquoc River area. Bowls and ollas made from Catalina steatite were made on Catalina Island and can be found in Schumacher (1879), Holmes (1901) and Finnerity et al (1970). Comals used for heating water and for frying were also made on Catalina Island. It is possible that the steatite bowls and ollas made on Catalina Island were mainly traded to villages in the Chumash area, since they are found rather infrequently in the Tongva (Gabrieleño) area. Fragments of steatite objects are found in middens, and whole or broken vessels are often found in mortuary contexts.

A number of other objects, which indicate trade, are found in archaelogical contexts. Fragments of pipes are found in middens of sites after 2500 B.C.; and whole pipes occur in cemeteries and ceremonial depositories (i.e. Burnett 1944). I know of no manufacturing centers for pipes; they are made of serpentine from the Santa Ines Mountain area, from schists in the Sierra Pelona area, from Catalina Island steatite and from porous red fused shale found in Oak Ridge. Charmstones of some types were evidently left in ceremonial structures or shrines and were placed with burials. There are a number of different types; some figurines were made on San Nicolas Island (Cessac 1951b). See Burnett (1944) for disposal areas on the Santa Monica Mountain coast. Molded ochre was both traded for from other groups and made at a number of localities for which no archaelogical data have been collected to date. Ochre was used up as paint or placed in cemeteries, often with high status individuals, and often along with other pigments such as fuchsite (L. King 1969: 37-38).

From Santa Rosa Island, Jones (1956), illustrated a number of forms of projectile points. These forms are the same as those found in sites on the mainland. A number of the points found on the islands are made of obsidian or fused shale which had to come from the mainland. Especially in the later time periods, the similarity of points dating at the same time throughout the area, and the extensive use of fused shale seems to indicate the trade of arrows or at least their stone tips. Most projectile points in late mainland sites are found in middens. Deetz suggests that differences between points in different Santa Ines Valley sites indicate patrilocality, but they probably indicate a temporal distinction (1968: 45, 46). Other objects mentioned ethnographically as being traded, whose remains have been found in cemeteries, are canoe pieces, wooden bowls, basketry, netting, and otter skins.

Another feature of the archaelogical record indicative of the exchange of food and raw material resources, is that the remains of these resources are found in regions where the resource was lacking. Thus, seeds of chia have been found on the islands in graves; and deerbone, often worked, is also present on the islands. Fish bones are common in many island sites and represent numerous species (Follet 1968), some of which would have to be taken from a boat. Shells are also common in inland sites (Levine 1968; Glassow 1965). These were probably gathered on trips to the coast, but shellfish may also have been traded for.

Some conclusions may be drawn from the above data and discussion. Following are the major features of the Chumash resource base: (1) There is environmental variability between adjacent geographical areas. (2) The local environment of every village had a large number of fairly productive food resources which could be exploited at different seasons. (3) The people in every local area exploited most of the resources available to them.

The exchange system had these features: (1) Constant flow of goods in a market economy. (2) Manufacturing of goods in areas with less constant food resource variability. (3) Craft specialization. (4) Frequent use of money (beads). (5) Centralized control by village chiefs of some aspects of inter-group exchange. (6) Goods which were produced and exchanged were regularly destroyed, thereby stabilizing the system by limiting inflation.

The Chumash inter-village system of exchange resulted in these regularities in the archaeological record: (1) The existence of sites or areas in sites, where certain individuals produced specialized products. (2) A uniformity of artifact types throughout the area at any given time. (3) At every site the existence of artifacts not manufactured locally. (4) The existence of sites of ecofactual materials from non-local environments. (5) Elaboration in the form of utilitarian household items. (6) The presence of different kinds of status markers and money in the form of artifacts such as beads, spangles, and pendants. (7) The presence of large quantities of goods in mortuary contexts. (8) Certain categories of items produced in the Chumash area are found in non-Chumash regions. (9) Graves of high status individuals containing high-status markers and utilitarian tools.

By randomizing the effects of environmental variability with frequent interaction, the Chumash were able to use more of their resources; the degree of their interaction was the result of the high variability in the resources used in the area. Their frequent use of money allowed them to average their many resources efficiently. The hypothesized relationships presented in the beginning of this paper can be restated in a dynamic form. Assuming that populations are normally close to optimum size (Birdsell 1968: 229-230):

A: Increased interaction results from (1) Variability in the environment of adjacent areas. (2) Decreased reliability of local resources.

B: Resources are averaged in the most efficient manner possible. (1) Increased use of standardized money occurs, and obligations tend to decrease (expensive gifts are less often given) when there are many important food resources or when there are many potential unreliable sources of a valuable resource, because frequently used money is efficient in averaging many variables. (2) Obligations increase (wealth objects are given), and the use of standardized money decreases when there are fewer important food resources or when resources are dependent on a few environmental variables (i.e. dry farming), because obligations (reciprocity) are efficient in averaging few variables.

The testing of these hypothesized relationships can probably best be performed by the use of a comparative method, since the degree of variability in environments, or the degree of use of money are relative. Differences in the primary exploitation of resources by different cultural systems and the degree of regularity with which resources can be exploited by the cultural system can be used to predict differences in inter-group exchange behavior on the basis of the relationships summarized above.

In this paper I have illustrated how the inter-group group-ownership group) exchange behavior within an area results in regularities in ethnographic, historic and archaeological data. It should be possible to test the hypothesized relationships with data derived from any of these sources. The prediction of information such as the location of trade centers, the types of goods being exchanged, etc., can of course only be done given specific data for a given area.

The Socio-Psychological
Significance of Death
Among the Pomo Indians

by B. W. Aginsky

The idea of the overt planned taking of one's own life which we find as an institution in our western civilization, in the orient (especially Japan), in the Trobriand Islands, and in other cultures, is mutually understandable to the individuals of those cultures (although the background for the acts is different in each case). The presentation of a society where overt planned suicide is foreign to the ideas of the people and where the concept is absolutely unintelligible seems worth while as an example for further study and understanding of the subject.

The Pomo Indians of Northern California cannot comprehend suicide as we know it. To them, every death and misfortune was the result of indirect or direct retaliation either from (1) the 'supernaturals', or (2) from some individual.[1]

There were many cases of individuals who would not have died when they did, had the psychological expectations been different.

(1) Death due to Retaliation from the Supernatural.

The supernaturals retaliated either for the infringement of a taboo or for the calling upon them for too much power. The power was essential for the successful accomplishment of any endeavor. Almost every masculine phase of Pomo life was on the status of a

---

1. "Sickness and misfortune are always believed to be results of the breaking of a taboo, or the work of a malicious enemy . . ." (Loeb, 1926: 305).

"The decrepitly aged are said to have been something strangled with a stick pressed down at each end. - - - Among the affluent Pomo the practice must have been rare" (Kroeber, 1925: 253). This is an exception as is the killing of twins and unwanted children at birth. Cf. Gifford and Kroeber, 1937: 150, Element nos. 680 and 693; and Againsky, 1939.

profession. Each member of a profession (some of which were money-manufacturing, gambling, fishing, deer hunting, and doctoring) had a collection of out-of-the-ordinary objects which were potent in their ability to store up power to be used for the successful participant in an undertaking, and the power and techniques, which he had received from an older relative. All the objects were kept in a "bundle". Any individual could increase the potency of his bundle by accumulating objects and putting more and more power into them (Loeb, 1926: 309).

Aside from the "poison men" (sorcerers), gamblers were the most fearless and at the same time most dangerous men in the community. Some gamblers made themselves so potent before a gambling match that their children died as a result. That is, the 'supernaturals' caused their deaths. Some of these men could not have children because they were so full of power. The same statements were also made concerning the other Pomo professionals, especially the hereditary doctors.

Retaliation from a 'supernatural' for the breaking of a taboo resulted in sickness which was followed by death unless remedial measures were set in motion (Barrett, 1908: 22-3). Connected with the bundle, there were numerous taboos which every professional had to observe (Gifford and Kroeber, 1937: 156).[2] The individual should never neglect his particular spirits who looked after him and who had to be given a dance periodically in conjunction with the opening of the bundle. The Pomo who owned bundles never would show them to anyone without giving the bundle a "big time." They were afraid that some terrible "accident" or death would befall them. What we call accident they call retribution from the 'supernaturals.' They explain a great many accidents as being due to the failure to observe some rule concerning their own or some relative's bundle. For example, one should never sell the bundle; one should never talk about such a thing. A daughter who told a man that her father might be prevailed upon to sell his bundle now that the old customs were falling by the way due to the westernization of the culture fell down a flight of stairs. The father who acquiesced and finally agreed to sell the bundle had a serious

---

2. "The bag" (outfit doctor's bundle) was thought extremely powerful: its shadow would kill a child on which it might fall" (Kroeber, 1925: 258).

accident. In another case a man fell out of an acorn tree and died because he had allowed a rat to get into his bundle.[3]

In addition there were a great many other taboos connected with such things as, for example, menstruation, the sun, the moon, various birds, thunder, death, birth, and sexual intercourse. In fact there is no phase of Pomo life that I could discover which did not have some taboos connected with it. The Pomo religion had a great many taboos which had to be observed. There were taboos concerning every bit of dress and paraphernalia. While Loeb — "was visiting the Northern Pomo an old man took sick and died. (Loeb) — listened in on the family discussion concerning the cause of the illness. The shaman (doctor) Bowen settled the matter. The man took sick because he had burned his ceremonial split stick rattle" (Loeb, 1926: 305).

During my field trips I continually endeavored to find a case of "pure accident" which had befallen a Pomo. A few times I thought I had come upon a case, but eventually found that the individual had broken some taboo or had accumulated too much power. Thus what we consider accident is explained by them as retaliation due to failure to comply with their religious precepts.

The Pomo were accomplished in woodcraft, hunting and fishing, but a Pomo was unable to cope with the world without his supernatural. On the other hand, to meet with a ghost or a supernatural creature (and the area was full of them) (Loeb, 1926: 303-5), meant death unless someone was at hand to drive away the "supernatural." If one saw a monster while alone in the mountains he frequently died because he could not reach home. The living things such as bears, rattle-snakes, mountain lions, etc., could be outwitted, controlled, killed, or escaped from. The individual used physical means in these cases, although there was always a definite reason for the occurrence, a forgotten taboo, or a neglect of the proper "supernatural." Nevertheless they relied upon themselves. But when they met with a monster or a ghost it was certain death unless a doctor took care of the patient (cf. Kroeber, 1925: 259; Loeb, 1926; Barrett, 1908; Gifford and Kroeber, 1937; Freeland, 1923).

---

3. Loeb states, "Among the Pomo if a man fell down and broke his leg while hunting, his misfortune was not attributed to bad luck but to the fact that he had broken a taboo" (1926: 305).

Powers, from whom we have our first report concerning these people in relation to this phase of their culture says, ''They are remarkable for their timidity. My host, Mr. Carner, related how a full-grown, vigorous Tatu in his employ was frightened to death in broad daylight by a belligerent turkey-cock. The poor fellow had never seen that species of fowl before, when one day he was walking through the yard the gobbler, being greatly blown out and enlarged in appearance, made a furious dash at him, and so frightened him that he straightway took to his bed and expired in two days. Another one of the same tribe unwittingly trod into a bear trap when hunting one day with a companion, whereupon he dropped all in a heap upon the ground, helpless and lifeless, with unspeakable terror, and died in his tracks in half an hour, though a subsequent examination revealed the fact that the steel trap had inflicted no mortal injury on him, and that he undoubtedly perished from fright. His comrade, instead of unclamping the trap, fled for his dear life, believing it was the devil they had encountered'' (Powers, 1877: 140).

These individuals' reactions to the turkey and the steel trap are perfectly understandable when other phases of the culture are taken into consideration. In the first place there are supernatural monsters whose descriptions so closely resemble turkeys that it seems as if the turkey itself was being described. Furthermore, the majority of supernatural monsters are birds who, at the order of the messengers, fly about the world seeking victims whom they kill and take to the abode of the dead at the southern extremity of the world. In the second place the entrance to one of the ''other worlds,'' is frequently found unexpectedly and in passing through the entrance, which is surrounded by sharp materials, the entrance suddenly closes upon the individual crushing him to death. In the former case death is sudden or lingering which might explain the time interval in the case of the death caused by the turkey; in the latter case the death is sudden. ''If Damatu so decrees, it is kept there and the patient never recovers; if not, the spirit is returned to the body and the person recovers'' (Barrett, 1908: 23).

In the vast majority of cases when a Pomo meets with a supernatural creature he loses consciousness. If he reaches home and faints and a doctor is called in, the doctor must reconstruct the man's movements in order to ascertain as nearly as possible which of the many ''supernaturals'' the man may have encountered. He does this questioning the members of the family: "Where was the man going? What was his purpose? How long was he away? Which direction did he take? Which direction did he come from?" Finally the doctor assembles the facts and comes to the conclusion that the man could have encountered certain of the "supernaturals." He then makes a composite costume using the most spectacular traits of the "supernaturals" he has decided upon. When all is ready, he has some assistants prop up the man in bed, goes outside the house, and at a signal comes toward the man in a menacing attitude while the assistants forcibly open the victim's eyes. The reaction on the part of the patient varies from a slight muscular reaction to violent struggling. In one case "her back went off like a crack of a gun and she began to shake all over" (Freeland, 1923: 63,67; Gifford and Kroeber, 1937: 157 and note).

The reactions point out to the doctor which of the many "supernaturals" the patient has encountered or whether it has been a ghost. According to the reaction treatment is instituted. Songs are sung, the patient is massaged and other treatments are applied. "Then the doctor takes off his costume or destroys the model before the patient's eyes to relieve his mind of fear. Recovery is said to be rapid" (Freeland, 1923: 63, 67).

The man who meets with a "supernatural," becomes ill, and is cured, sometimes becomes a sucking doctor and in turn cures individuals who become ill. However, he is in a different category from the "outfit or poison" doctor who will be discussed later (cf. Loeb, 1926: 303; Kroeber, 1925: 259; Freeland, 1923; Barrett, 1908; Gifford and Kroeber, 1937).

The Pomo were not afraid of a dead person, but after the dead body had been cremated (Kroeber, 1925: 253) which is done so that it "would go up into ashes and disappear into the air" they go through all kinds of purification rites and ceremonies to ward off the ghost. The ghost may be seen or heard when one passes by the place where the body was cremated. "It is doing some kind of work."

The Pomo were in great fear of ghosts. Special songs were sung to keep them away from the habitations because they came "wandering about." If a person has no ghost songs he hires someone who did have some to sing the songs and keep the ghosts away.

When a person sees a ghost he becomes very sick and faints. If

songs are not sung over him, or if he does not recover
consciousness and sing the songs himself, he dies. For this reason
the Pomo were afraid to travel at night, even in groups.

Jeff Joaquin was going to Yorkville to take possession of a colt
which his uncle (his mother's mother's sister's son) had given to
him. For some reason he was forced to travel part of a distance at
night, but he said the incentive was sufficient for him to overcome
his fear of night travel. He started on horseback from Hopland
about six o'clock in the evening. While he was passing through a
pine grove about halfway between the two villages he heard a group
of men talking. Jeff stopped the horse and listened, but heard
nothing. Then he started the horse and the noise started. He
stopped and the noise stopped. He remembered that his father and
grandfather had told him that some people were accustomed to
hunt in that vicinity in the past and he became frightened. His dog
had run ahead by this time and flushed some owls which flew
about. The man realized that the owls had been fooling him, so he
kept on gong (Gifford and Kroeber, 1937: 152-3, 202 and note
904).[4]

In a short while he came to a place where the trail went by a
spot where a cremation had taken place. About one hundred yards
before he got to that spot he heard an old woman crying and
pounding acorns. By this time it was about two or three o'clock in
the morning. Jeff did not stop this time. He kept right on going.
When he got to the noise it stopped. When he was about one
hundred yards beyond the place the same noise began again. Jeff
was very frightened. He kept right on going until he arrived at his
uncle's house. His uncle heard him coming, met him, took him
inside, and spread a blanket for him to sit upon, as was the custom.
As he was about to sit down he collapsed. He recovered
consciousness about three hours later. His grandfather was
"doctoring" him and singing ghost songs.[5] When the man had told

---

4. "The owl (bakuku, C) was considered a bird of ill omen" (Loeb,
1926: 167).

5. Loeb (1926: 306): "Kanu was a charm, and kaocal mana used to
counteract the effects of bad spirits and ghost fright." Freeland, (1923: 61):
"The healing songs for ordinary illness are addressed to Marumda, the
creator, and perhaps to the other great spirits, but the group called
"frightening" songs, used where a person is haunted by a ghost or monster,
call on this unfriendly spirit to remove its curse."

his grandfather what had frightened him his grandfather knew immediately that it had definitely been a ghost and became frightened himself. After many ghost songs had been sung the man recovered fully. The man stated that he would have died if a ghost-singer had not been present.

The majority of cases which I was able to collect pointed toward sudden visitations with the expectance of death always accompanying the illness because the "supernaturals" had always taken the "soul or essence" away. The doctors who were members of the community had a great deal of supernatural power in their control and were able sometimes to win the man back from the "supernatural."[6] However, it was institutionalized in this culture that death always followed unless a doctor of some kind intervened.

The taboos were so numerous that the individuals said that they often consciously neglected some of them, and frequently forgot some, and occasionally were ignorant of others.[7] When they were on a trip, out hunting, or for any other reason by themselves in the mountains, especially at night, they remembered their transgressions or omissions and they were almost overcome with fear of the "supernaturals' " striking them down.[8]

In the majority of cases the individual who was struck down by a supernatural was able to get to his destination before fainting. From the reports of informants it seems that their apprehension, anxiety, and fear became overpowering and when they finally reached their home or a relative's home they collapsed.

The Pomo also state that some individuals who had apparently encountered "supernaturals" were found dead in the hills. A few had been found unconscious. When they were badly mutilated the Bear doctors were blamed (cf. Barrett, 1908; Loeb, 1926; Gifford and Kroeber, 1937; Freeland, 1923; Kroeber, 1925: 259).

(2) *Death due to Retaliation from an Individual*

Every Pomo individual was constantly apprehensive that he

---

6. "Win" is used advisedly because there is a great deal of similarity between gambling and doctoring in this culture.

7. "Ignorance of the law" was no excuse here either. Occasionally an individual found out after his brush with death which taboo he had unwittingly broken.

8. "Seeing a ghost is not an accident; a ghost always comes for some purpose . . . nothing is nothing and something makes something, as the informant expresses it" (Freeland, 1923: 63).

was being the object of sorcery by the traditional enemies of members of his family and by the enemies he had made during his own life.9 The retaliation, and frequently it was only a fancied wrong that brought it about, was very drastic. Death, with but a few minor exceptions, was always the objective, and the objective was always attained unless the relatives of the stricken man called in a "doctor" to cure the ill person. This doctor had the ability to "take out" the "poison." He also was the man who had the ability to instill poison and in fact was one of the professional poison manufacturers to whom the people went for the means by which they could kill one another. Thus he could both cure and impregnate the people. This particular type of illness and death always came upon an individual by means of the "doctoring" of this professional class of death-dealers whose services were at the disposal of any individual or family who had sufficient goods with which to pay for the services (Gifford and Kroeber, 1937: 156-7).

Lingering illnesses, whether the inception was from breaking a taboo, or from poisoning, were explained as being due to the hiring of a doctor by the relatives of the stricken individual. Then there ensued a concentrated and intense battle between the group curing the patient and all the enemies of any relative of the sick man. The patient would be almost well and then have a relapse which was explained as being caused by the enemies injecting further "poison objects" into the endeavor.

When a person became ill he went to bed with the firm conviction that he had been poisoned and would die unless a curing doctor was hired to take out the poison and fight off the onslaught of the supernatural creature who was taking the "essence" of the man away. Under pressure by the doctor who was curing the individual, the situation when the man was impregnated with poison, was reconstructed. Usually another person had touched the patient at a dance, in the sweat house, or on a trip. The forces were immediately set in motion to retaliate, by impregnating that individual or a member of his family, with poison. This might be the prolongation of an old feud or the inception of a new one.

Feuds were continually going on throughout the Pomo

---

9. Loeb, 1926: 305; Gifford, 157 and notes. This sorcery was called poisoning although no actual poison was ever used. It was a paste made from the various parts of the bodies of potent animals or objects.

territory. Each member of every family was always apprehensive that he had been poisoned and at the first indication of illness, fancied or real, he collapsed. He had good reason for the collapse. It was the accepted pattern in the culture that when a person was poisoned by strong poisoners, death followed in every case. Many families had insufficient funds with which to pay for a long drawn-out battle which was frequently necessary to save the individual. Almost every mature individual had been instrumental, by contributions of money if nothing else, in procuring the death of other individuals. Every individual was cognizant of the fact that when a man was ill his enemies immediately all tried, individually, to place some object near his house to speed his death, and since every family had many enemies this was a considerable threat. Every individual knew that, in spite of the most expensive treatments, vows for cures, and careful watchfulness on the part of the victim's family, many individuals had died. All of these factors had considerable effect upon the individual when he became ill.

These institutionalizations must have brought about many deaths where recovery would have resulted otherwise, especially in view of the fact that no real poison was ever used and death from disease, accident and old age must have been the real reasons.

The Pomo deaths, which were not due to natural causes, are not comparable with the overt planned suicides of the cultures previously mentioned, but there are elements present in the Pomo death constellation which are found in the psychopathological deaths in our own culture.[10]

Although suicide, as we are familiar with it, did not occur among the Pomo, this form of "psychological death" occurred frequently. It was a form of self-destruction on the basis of mental processes.[11]

This psychological death was as real as death from any disease

10. It is not the province of the author to show how close a comparison can be drawn between the institutionalizations surrounding the Pomo deaths and the causation of the deaths of some of the psychopathics of our own culture.

11. "Benson, my Eastern Pomo informant, declared that an infringement of a taboo was always punished by the culprit's becoming afraid of something and turning sick. He illustrated this by a case in point. His people had a taboo on a man's giving meat which he had himself obtained to a woman if she had recently had sexual intercourse, or was menstruating, or was heavy with child. Benson himself once gave a piece of venison from a deer that he had just killed

known to man. There was no hope for a cure without the procurement of a doctor. Without his aid the man died as surely as if he had had his head severed from his body. The individuals were constantly under this terrific fear. In some of the cases of poisoning physical deficiencies appeared. These can be explained away as the diseases known to modern medical science. But in some of these cases recovery undoubtedly would have come about by itself if the man had not expected to die. The psychological reaction to the tradition certainly helped the disease triumph over the individual, especially where the family was economically unable to pay for the services of the better healers, and the sick man was conscious of that fact.

The varieties of anxieties which the Pomo indulged in were instrumental in bringing about psychotic states equivalent to what we call suicide. In our society we have cases of individuals "drinking themselves to death," of individuals taking their own lives, that is, being the cause of their own death due to emotional upsets. No one would say that the Pomo pattern of self-death was the same as ours, but nevertheless it was self-death if no one interfered.

As we have seen, there were two important categories concerning death. In the first category, the individual, by being full of anxiety and apprehension, brought about a psychological condition in himself whereby he reacted to a fancied meeting with a manlevolent supernatural which resulted in a state somewhat resembling catatonia, or had what we call an accident and fell out of a tree or fell down a mountain, etc. The illness resulted from the retaliation by the supernaturals for the negative or positive infringement of a taboo. The cure for this was a form of shock therapy (this includes the ghost cure) or medical cure. The illness resulting from impregnation by poison was the retaliation by a person for some real or fancied wrong and the cure was by means of

---

to a woman who was heavy with child. The woman at once vomited up the meat. From that time on Benson spent all of his time chasing deer which he merely imagined seeing. He never killed any and he grew quite thin. An old hunter came upon Benson while he was in this condition. The hunter questioned Benson and then informed him that he had broken a taboo and would die unless doctored up. The hunter took Benson into the boods, sweated him over a small fire with the aid of four sacred herbs, and bathed him in running water. After this Benson regained his health'' (Loeb, 1926: 305-6).

taking out the poison and driving away the supernatural who was taking away the "essence" of the ill man.

In both categories the man died unless a cure was instituted immediately. The individual was psychologically prepared to die, no matter which form of illness he had. He fell into the traditionalized acceptable mode of behaviour and helped death in coming. He could do nothing himself, as far as the cultural mode of behavior was concerned to fight death off. That was entirely in the hands of relatives who stood guard and hired a doctor.

Enquiries concerning suicide as we know it brought forth responses showing that the Pomo not only could not conceive of such a thing, but that they explained it as occurring in other societies because the supernaturals or the doctors in the cultures discussed, had caused the individual to do the act. As for themselves, they had never heard of anyone in their history who had ever committed suicide.

Mohave
Soul Concepts

by George Devereux

The present paper is based on three field seasons among the Mohave. References to other tribes are omitted because the data on the Mohave themselves are contradictory enough to make comparisons with other tribes undesirable.

All Mohave exhibit much interest in matters relating to the soul and its fate (Stratton, n.d.: 155); an interest quite in the general pattern of their culture, which has been described by Kroeber as a "dream culture" (A. L. Kroeber, oral information). This is only natural, since dreams are believed to be "real adventures of the soul." Interest in and knowledge of these matters is not limited to the more sophisticated or to shamans. Almost identically complete data have been obtained from two shamans and two lay informants.

From the point of view of immortality there are two categories of human beings. Except for certain accidcents they may meet with while in human shape the souls of twins are immortal. The souls of other persons are mortal.

Origin of souls. Souls spring from the state of "aliveness" after conception has taken place. The souls of twins, however, have always existed in heaven and have no father and mother. After cremation the souls of twins return to heaven using another branch of the forked road which they followed when they came down to earth to assume human shape. Only once in their disembodied existence do they enter the womb of a woman at conception, in quest of incarnation. "One life is all they want," the informant commented ironically. After the death of their human bodies they continue to lead a deathless life in heaven.

The souls (matkwí′ca·) All human beings have four souls, all of which resemble the body and duplicate its actions. They also have activities of their own. In the foetal stage they follow the actions of the mother and dream of "how to be born." The souls of foetal shamans, however, dream of how *not* to be born — that is, how to kill their mother during parturition. In other intro-uterine dreams they witness the origin of the world and listen to the instructions handed out to mankind by Pahó'tcate, "who does it all over for them" (Kroeber, 1925: 754). Thus they exhibit already in the foetal state their shamanistic propensities: the instinct to kill (Bourke, 1889: 175) and their nexus with the supernaturals.

These souls are occasionally visible to their owner and to shamans. Occasionally they may also appear in dream to other persons. It is impossible to tell however just *how* one known which soul one sees. "One just knows it." They can act independently of each other, as when one of the souls goes to visit the land of the dead.

The four souls. (a) Hlăkŭ'ytcitc. This is the "real shadow," the one whereby one is "proud" or "vain." It is the "second self" of a person, and in a way the core of his identity. It stands behind him as a rule. After death this soul alone survives and goes through three further metamorphoses. It receives the impact of the shaman's power when a person is bewitched. This soul of the bewitched person will see in dream the "real shadow" of the bewitcher. A shaman who wishes to divert suspicion from himself or cast suspicions of witchcraft upon another shaman, or to do both at one time, will kidnap the "real shadow" of the shaman he wishes to incriminate and make the bewitched person see this kidnapped "real shadow" rather than his own in his dreams. Furthermore, the "real shadow" will be the one to have commerce with the ghosts of the deceased — shamans always excepted whenever they send another soul to recover from the dead the abducted soul of a patient. The kidnapping of this soul, except for the purpose of using it for the above-mentioned deception, means death.

(b) Cúma'·tc mă hò'·tvetc is the "power soul." It is somewhat akin to a more personal "mana" and does not seem related in any way to the concept of the guardian spirit. "One is what one is through the power of this soul." It brings both good and bad luck to its owner, according to his dreams (cúma'·tc ála'·yk, dream bad; cúma'·tc áho'·t, dream good) (Kroeber, 1925: 754). It gives general good luck, special powers (especially shamanistic powers), luck in love, etc., but can also bring unhappiness and bad luck. It is not unlike the "sacrum" concept of Durkheim and Mauss: it is sacred and dangerous. Although it dies at cremation, its effects persist beyond the grave insofar that "one remains in the other world what one has been in this world" (i.e., a shaman will remain a shaman even in the land of the ghosts). It is this soul the shaman sends to the ghostland, when he tries to recover a departed soul. He must not tarry there, however, lest his own deceased relatives should try to induce him to remain with them (Kroeber, 1925: 778). This soul is seen when death is impending.

(c) Cúna'·kavokyé'ttcitc is the soul of "worldly wealth," and the soul through whose agency one acquires wealth. It never causes trouble and its sight augurs success. This soul also dies at cremation.

(d) Matmakwí'·ca: cúma'·tc mítce'·mvetc is seen only when one is about to die. Once it has been seen there is no recovery. It is either seen approaching or heard talking or coughing (or both) in the house. The ailing person will then think "It is like me." After this vision death is but a matter of hours or days. This soul too dies at cremation.

Twins also possess these four souls. Their immortality, however, is contained in their "real shadow." They strip off their other souls at death.

At cremation the "real shadow" changes into a ghost, known as the näväöí'·, and is carried away by a whirlwind either to the land of the ghosts — or into a rathole, if the chin of that person had never been tattooed (Kroeber, 1925: 729). In the latter case the ghost will never reach the land of the dead. The souls of twins return to heaven.

When a person dies of witchcraft his bewitcher takes away his soul "to his own place" and keeps it there until he himself dies. Then they both proceed to the land of the dead. If the bewitched person is a shaman his bewitcher will "exile" his soul until he himself dies. The exiled soul is released and can join the other ghosts in the land of the dead. A certain shaman told one of my informants that he exiled the soul of a rival shaman whom he had bewitched "far beyond Avi'kwamä'·."

The entrance to the "land of the dead" (càliá'·yt) is somewhere near Needles, California, almost by the Colorado River on the Arizona side. There is something that looks like a big

invisible "wash" containing a big invisible shed near a place called
Ahatcku·pi'lyk, which is but a few feet from the land of the dead.

For four days and four nights the ghost will visit his former
haunts and be seen by his relatives and spouse in dream without
any untoward effect to them, even if the wife or husband should
dream of intercourse with the ghost. After that period the ghost
settles down in the land of the dead and makes merry. According to
Bourke (1889: 174) this ghostland is near Bill Williams' Fork, and
when a man dies his relatives often request a shaman to visit the
land of the dead to check up if he reached it. Should the messenger
fail to find the ghost there, witchcraft is assumed to have caused the
death and the suspected shaman is killed to keep his victim
company.

Usually the ghosts leave the living alone. Should one dream,
however, of visiting or being visited by a ghost after the four days
and nights have elapsed, it is assumed that either the living long for
the dead or vice versa and that the dream represents a true
soul-adventure. Such dreams cause illness and death (Bourke,
1889), and a shaman is called in, either to bring back the patient's
departed soul, or to cure the disease known as ghost-wéyla'·k
(wéyla'·k näväθí'·). A curious form of this disease is the return of a
dead infant many years after its death to the womb of his mother,
wherein he makes himself a body from the clotting menstrual
blood, without the help of spermatozoa. Dreams of sexual relations
(especially incestuous intercourse) with ghosts are more fatal than
other dreams. Baths and fumigations with arrow-weed scare away
the ghosts.

One may visit the land of the dead with the help of a shaman
specializing in the cure of witchcraft, who must under no condition
let go the hand of the person he accompanies thither, lest the dead
should keep him in the land of the ghosts.

After a while the ghosts die and are cremated by their fellow
ghosts according to Mohave custom, since the ghostland is but a
pleasant replica of the land of the living (Bourke, 1889). From the
charcoal of the funeral pyre "some sort of a stink-bug, rough to
touch, not the gray one, but the black kind," will be born. The
insect is known as matka-úa'·n. It "faints" when a child picks it up
in play and is then revived by blowing warm breath on it. (Blowing
is a shamanistic practise.)

When this insect dies it becomes another kind of "bug" (?)

known as úhu'·lye, which has a long tail "like a rat." (According to verbal information from Mr. A. M. Halpern this word means "mole" in Yuma.) When this being dies life is completely finished.

The cycle of metamorphoses has been differently described by Bourke (1889: 180) who claims that the ghosts turn into three different kinds of owls successively, then into a "water-beetle," and then into air. This explanation was unacceptable to my informants, who claim that although owls are somehow associated with *death* (mainly as evil omens), they are not associated with the *dead*. Unusual activities of owls, such as entering houses or roosting upon the shoulders of human beings augur of death in the same way that certain dreams augur of death.

In view of the accurately timed successive metamorphoses later generations cannot catch up with those predeceasing them by several years (Bourke, 1889: 174). Shamans, however, can bring about a compromise for their own benefit by slowing up the first metamorphosis, and thus do away with the regret of never again meeting their predeceased beloved ones.

A shaman will thus bewitch a person of whom he is fond. He will seldom if ever bewitch those he hates, unless they be rival shamans. He segregates the ghosts of his beloved victims in an accessible place. He will visit them in his dreams, or else they will visit him, and sexual and other relations will occur between the dreamer and his disembodied captives. His victims are not seldom his own relatives with whom he cannot have commerce other than incestuous in the flesh. Berdache shamans have intercourse with ghosts of the same sex. The bewitcher keeps his victims in that place until he himself dies of a violent death. Should he fail to be killed, but die a natural death, he will lose his hold on them, and they will proceed to the land of the dead. Under these conditions they will "not belong to his group." "He does not bewitch people he dislikes. They would disrupt his nice group of followers." We already saw that if a shaman bewitches another shaman he exiles him until his own death to some far-away place.

In order to be able to maintain their hold on their ghostly retinue, shamans not seldom induce other people to kill them, by baiting them (Kroeber, 1925: 778; Bourke, 1889: 174). This is a form of vicarious suicide. Should a shaman who bewitched a number of people die himself of witchcraft, his bewitcher will exile his ghost in turn and "take over" the ghost-retainers of his victim, until he himself dies or is killed.

Should twins die of witchcraft or be killed for practising witchcraft, they lose their immortality and follow the pattern of simple humans. In no case can they take the ghosts of their victims to heaven.

There is a curious ambivalence of emotions toward the dead. The lure of the ghosts and the charms of the ghostland have been described above. Yet Hall[1] describes the case of a woman who was put on the pyre in what appears to have been a cataleptic state or apparent death and who revived on the pyre and was saved from the flames. After her unexpected revival she was treated with indifference. This incident mirrors the "ashes to ashes and dust to dust" aspect of the problem very adequately. Last of all this fear of ghosts is not unmingled with regret caused by the impossibility of joining those who died a long time ago. This is very apparent in the following custom: should a person exclaim in surprise or anger nápa·ua, meaning "father's father," one of his own relatives sitting nearby will "feel bad" and say "Sure, there he comes — now he stumbles; he has hurt his toe. He falls — he will not come."

The conflict between longing for the dead and the impossibility of catching up with them should one live too long after they died leads to an appalling number of suicides and attempted suicides (ordinary, funeral, and shamanistic pseudo-suicides or vicarious suicides).

On the other hand, the selfsame lack of belief in personal immortality (and perhaps their respectful envy of the immortality of twins) induces the Mohave, according to their own testimony, to stress tribal continuity and to treat children and twins with the utmost kindness, lest the sensitive ones should "make themselves sick and die." It may also be ultimately responsible for the kind, considerate, and jovial character of the Mohave, which stresses some of the finest values of mutual kindness and mutual help.

---

1. Yet Mooney (1896: 785) claims that resurrection and the return of the dead was the principal doctrine of the Ghost Dance religion among the Mohave. If so, no one today remembers it.

Emphasis on Industriousness Among the Atsugewi

by Thomas R. Garth, Jr.

The Atsugewi of Northeastern California place exceptional importance on industriousness. Work-ideals in connection with the food quest have become the dominant feature of the culture and the basis for an unusual cultural configuration, strongly influencing the criteria of status and prestige, the political organization, the subsistence economy and other phases of Atsugewi life. Some of the traits in this complex are shared with neighboring tribes and were undoubtedly borrowed. Others have developed in response to the rigor and poverty of the local environment. Although the Atsugewi were hardly innovators, they wove these environmentally determined and borrowed traits into a complex entirely their own. Here, as with the Dobu fear complex, the Zuñi social-mindedness, and the Kwakiutl megalomania, is a strong cultural personality which can only be understood in terms of a single drive (cf. Benedict, 1934). The trait the Atsugewi chose to emphasize is simple, prosaic, and one that is of necessity present in some degree in cultures the world over. Therefore its importance is less obvious and striking than if a more exotic trait had been chosen for the cultural theme. Nevertheless, this very fact gives the Atsugewi case added interest. This paper is the outgrowth of a general ethnographic study of the Atsugewi undertaken during the summers of 1938 and 1939. Its primary object is to demonstrate the existence of the work pattern and to show the functional relationships of the work-drive to the culture as a whole. As is so often true, the results suffer from dependence on informants' recollections of a culture that largely ceased to function sixty or seventy years ago.

The western Atsugewi (called Atsuge) inhabited the heavily

wooded area between Mount Lassen and the Pit River, particularly along Hat Creek. East of Hat Creek Valley the land soon becomes dry and almost devoid of trees except scattered stands of juniper. Here the eastern branch, the Apwaruge, occupied the more moist valleys, particularly along Horse Creek, where marshy grasses, tule and edible roots flourished. Most of the territory is open, rocky, sage-brush country, which supported a moderate amount of game, especially upland birds and some elk, deer and antelope. Although the presence of more abundant oak as well as salmon made the western area decidedly superior to the eastern, it too was mountainous, rock-strewn and much faulted and broken by lava flows, so that only the valleys supplied much vegetable food. Heavy snows and severe cold forced the settlement of only the more protected sites and made necessary the accumulation of large food stores which were kept in grass-lined pits or on platforms in trees. Although acorns and fish formed the staples, a wide variety of roots, seeds, and game was obtained during semi-nomadic summer wanderings. Starvation was known and fear of it was always a prod to activity. Subsistence, nevertheless, was probably much easier than the desert Great Basin. The rock-bound nature of the country as well as the cultural evaluation of industry is reminiscent of New England.

IDEOLOGY SURROUNDING THE WORK DRIVE

Work-ideals oiled the socio-economic machinery and provided the basis for the wealth-prestige system. The ideal individual was both wealthy and industrious. In the first grey haze of dawn he arose to begin his day's work, never ceasing activity until late at night. Early rising and the ability to do without sleep were great virtues. It was extremely complimentary to say of a person, "He doesn't know how to sleep," implying that he worked all hours of the day and night. Several informants boasted that their rich parent or grandparent frequently worked the whole night through, perhaps making string or repairing equipment. Interestingly enough, the nickname of one of these men was Nóhalal, translated "Going all the time." Sleepiness was anathema, and one who slept too much and was lazy was either sick or badly in need of a spirit guardian to give him energy.[1] Men prided themselves on their lightness of foot and ability to run long distances without tiring. Sometimes deer were run down in this way. A "good" man went about with a springy step and lively energetic manner. To increase his vivacity and obtain the favor of spirits he might run to the hills once a month, returning at the end of the day. Children were told to think about work and not about lying around. Every morning a dutiful father talked to his son as follows: "Get wood. Keep active. Go hunting whenever you can . . ." Children as young as eight or nine were expected to work, boys hunting small game which they added to the family larder, and girls digging roots and gathering seeds. Girls were expected to work all day under their mothers' guidance. Children did find time to play, however, especially in winter. Effects of the cultural tradition were apparent in several of my older informants, who were better workers than many of the younger people.[2]

The status system, too, was based on wealth and industriousness. There were three social classes; the industrious wealthy (saswahecar), the commoners (wikoi) — those in a rich man's entourage,[3] and the lazy despised paupers (brumui). The last-named, being improvident, frequently starved in winter usually depending on largess of a richer person to tide them through. Class divisions were not strict, although the rich did tend to intermarry, as a poorer family would not be able to keep up its end of the marital gift exchange. Theoretically even a poor man with skill and perseverance could accumulate wealth.[4] Neverthe-

---

1. A lazy lethargic condition was allied closely with the somewhat terrifying soul-loss symptoms, which led (unless a shaman interfered) to death. A victim felt little pain, but dreamt continually of the spirits who were persecuting him. Quite possibly the behavior of one of my informants was due to fear of such supernatural punishment. Although he was on a pension and was close to eighty years old, he worked almost incessantly around his small farm, building fence, chopping down trees, etc. He said he feared he would become sick if he lay around very much.

2. This was particularly true of Dave Brown, the informant mentioned in the previous note. The tribe is largely self-supporting today.

3. One informant referred to commoners as "hired men."

4. A favorite story tells of a poor orphan reared and trained by his grandmother. By exceptional prowess and perserverance in hunting he accumulated many buckskins which he traded for other kinds of property, so that he soon was wealthy and able to marry a rich man's daughter. An

less, it was a decided advantage to be a rich man's son and so profit by inheriting land and other capital goods.[5]

The Atsugewi apparently practised a Spartan work regime, requiring diligent year-around work. Men hunted and fished, cooked meat, and made skin clothing, while women gathered and cooked vegetable foods and wove baskets and mats. Men were expected to hunt (or fish) continually and even in the coldest weather.[6] There was no feeling that women worked harder than men, although they were said to produce more food, especially in summer. There was much competition among women in their gathering activities, for one who excelled gained prestige and was considered a very desirable wife. Rich men (the most sought-after husbands) were said to watch girls bringing home roots, selecting as wives those who had the most. Stopping work to gossip or rest was much frowned on. The ideal woman dug roots by herself to avoid gossip and ate none of her roots until that evening in camp. During spring and summer there were periods when members of several tribes worked the same root-digging ground or seed-gathering area. On such occasions men often gambled all day while their wives worked,[7] although according to informants only when sufficient animal food had been accumulated.[8] Not infrequently they wagered their wives' newly dug roots. This fondness for gambling seems to be the chief inconsistency in the Atsugewi work scheme, and one of which they seem to have been completely unconscious. Quite probably gambling served as a semi-ceremonial release from the everyday strain of the work drive. Certainly if the drive was as intense as facts seem to indicate some such emotional release or period of relaxation would be required.

---

alternate story concerns a poor orphan girl who acquired exceptional skill as a basketmaker and became wealthy thereby. Their skills were conferred by spirit guardians.

5. I doubt that there was much vertical mobility in the class system. Wealth was probably retained in certain families.

6. As it was a disgrace to return empty-handed, some hunters stayed out two or three days in order to have game to bring back.

7. Occasionally there would be a "Big Time," a session of general feasting and gambling in which both sexes participated. These were formal celebrations given by the local chief. Gambling was with members of another tribe rather than with village mates.

8. Quite possibly the spring fish runs supplied enough animal food so that hunting could be slackened for a time.

Another release mechanism was the rest day (yemĭwĭka), called by the chief every six days or so — "whenever he felt it was needed." This offered little more than a change of activity to women, who remained in camp preparing foods. Men either worked on equipment or gambled. In winter the rest day often preceded a communal hunt. The literature on surrounding tribes fails to mention such a village rest day, though it may have occurred among tribes nearby. Its occurrence indicates a well-organized and somewhat sophisticated work program, and further demonstrates Atsugewi work interest.

POLITICAL ORGANIZATION

Industriousness was a most valuable asset in acquiring political power. Certain men, because of extraordinary wealth and hunting and fishing prowess, became the leaders (Bawi) around whom a group of relatives and friends gathered.[9] In a large village of a hundred persons there might be several Bawi, each living somewhat apart from the others and having the houses of his friends and relatives clustered around his own large semi-subterranean earth lodge. Frequently the Bawi owned the land on which the group lived and other lands as well, all of which was an important source of wealth. He maintained his prestige by providing his followers with numerous "big feeds" and by helping them in time of need as illustrated below.

> Justĭcĭni, a rich man living in a settlement a short distance from the main village at Rising River, took his name from the land on which he resided and which he owned. According to Sarah Brown, he had more land than did the chief and was the wealthiest man in the village. He was an excellent hunter and fisherman, the best netmaker in the village and possessed many traps and several canoes. As second to the chief in authority, he sometimes divided deer meat among the villagers when the chief was sick or absent. Fifteen or twenty people lived with him in his large earth-covered lodge, where he called sweat dances

---

9. The *Bawi* belonged to the *saswahecar* class.

and feasts from time to time. His wife was blind and unable to do much work, and when he grew old he became lame. Then his relatives supplied him with food. Although he had an only daughter, his land and possessions went for the most part to his cousin, Buckskin Jack.

Nóhalal was a rich shaman who lived in a small settlement about a fourth of a mile east of the main village at Rising River Lake. In his lodge, the largest in the group, he occasionally held sweat dances. Johnny Snook, his son, gave the following account: "My father used to have big parties every once in a while. He went out early in the morning and obtained quantities of fish. Then he let the people help themselves and eat. He gave feasts and furnished all the food himself. He had manzanita cider, fish, and meat. His relatives and friends lived near his house, some of hem in small earth lodges. He talked for this bunch and was kind of head man. He was the only one who was wealthy. A man who was free with his food and who did all that he could to feed the people made a good name. Everybody liked him." Nóhalal made and sold nets and did much more fishing than hunting. When he grew old he gave most of his property to his two sons and to his step-son.

It was customary when deer or any large amount of game was brought in for it to be divided among everyone in the group. Occasionally Nóhalal brought in large hauls of fish at midnight and woke his followers for a feast. Thus the rich man's followers must frequently have benefited from his industry and hunting skill. The benefits were not wholly one-sided, however. A rich man's property, which might include several boats, nets, rope snares and other equipment, was in a sense a capital investment. In return for loaning it to his followers and others he received gifts of game or produce. The extent of this borrowing may possibly be judged by the fact that a simple, flat, bark sifting-board was said to have been owned only by the rich family — "others would borrow it." Similarly metates and comparable utensils were said to be owned only by the rich. These as well as other types of equipment were considered very valuable. All of this suggests that the rich man may have owned a very high proportion of the equipment used by his group and that his loaning activities may have been considerable.10 Probably an even more importnt source of food and wealth was the hunting and gathering lands and fishing places that he owned. Persons using these gave him a share of the produce gained thereon. He also could claim the fur of any animal killed on his land.

> My grandfather owned this side of Black's Mountain near the top. One time his wife was sick and he had no one to dig roots for him. When some people didn't ask to dig roots on his land, he became angry and took their roots from them, even from his relatives. They should first have asked him if they could dig.11

The above incident shows that the owner could demand all the produce from his land if he wished, although he customarily was generous in allowing others the use of it, especially if they asked permission.

Each winter-village had a chief, who was much like a glorified Bawi or rich man who had a measure of authority over the whole village, and controlled the village lands. He had his own group of relatives and friends living around his large lodge just as did the Bawi. Although wealth was important, it was by no means necessary that he be the wealthiest man in the village (as in Northwest California). Consistent with the general emphasis on work, his main duties were the organizing of communal hunts and fishing trips and telling the villagers when and where to go for various roots, seeds, etc. Consistent, too, was the requirement that a chief take an active part in the food quest. He was expected to

---

10. Gifts of food in return for borrowing apply chiefly to hunting and fishing equipment rather than to culinary utensils. If a man made a fine catch of fish using a rich man's boat, he gave part of his catch to the rich man. The loaning of a boat or other object was a favor for which one reciprocated with a gift. The whole system was based on gift giving. There was no idea of the gift being any prescribed amount, although one niggardly in his gifts was considered "like a poor man," being looked down on.

Near-exclusive property ownership by the rich is also suggested by the account of a poor man who wanted a share of the spoils after an attack on an immigrant wagon train. He was laughed at and told, "You are a poor man. You can't own things like that." In desperation he seized a copper kettle and ran off with it.

11. Given by Dave Brown.

work as hard as or harder than any commoner. Hunting, fishing, net making, skin tanning, etc., were chores performed by chiefs as well as by anyone else. Chief Petskuami of Dixie Valley was a noted hunter with sage hen "power" which enabled him to run long distances without tiring. He was a powerfully built man said to be able to carry two deer on his shoulders at one time. One of the Little Valley chiefs had twenty deer pits which he visited from time to time. Again, Wahánumca, a Hat Creek Valley chief noted for his liveliness, ran to the mountains once a month to enhance it. The only special consideration shown the chief was that after organizing a communal hunt he could stay home and participate in the division of meat afterwards. Even then he often took a smaller share than others to show his generosity. Like a rich man the chief enhanced his prestige by giving feasts, but on a much larger scale, members of other villages and tribes being invited.[12] These feasts were the only occasions when the villagers furnished the chief with food, and even so he supplied a large amount himself. Buckskin Jack of Rising River was said to have impoverished himself by too frequent feast giving.[13] He was noted for his generosity and his word was respected even as far away as Big Valley in Achomawi territory.

As the paternalistic caretaker of his followers, a chief was expected to keep affairs running smoothly, discourage strife, and in council make important decisions affecting the village as a whole. His influence was largely a matter of personality and prestige, he having no right to impose fines or to punish an individual. During the summer food-gathering period he aroused the camp at early dawn with a stentorian harangue, which if he were a good speaker could be heard a quarter of a mile away:

Get up and do something for your living. Be on your guard. Be on the lookout for Paiute. You have to work hard for your living. There may be a long winter, so put away all the food you can . . .[14]

---

12. Relationships with the Achomawi, Northeastern Maidu and Northern Yana were particularly friendly, these tribes often allowing reciprocal use of their root-digging grounds, fishing places, etc.

13. This was during later times when much of the food had to be bought at grocery stores.

14. An informant gave this as the usual nature of the chief's speech.

In this speech the basic ideological sentiments of the culture are well expressed.

MARRIAGE

Industriousness and the ability to make a living were prime requisites in choosing a mate, and it was then that an individual's status in the work-wealth system became most openly apparent. Marriage itself was a simple process which involved merely a couple's sleeping together all night. However, before a marriage could be consummated, parents carefully scrutinized the background of their prospective child-in-law, particularly his or her working ability and wealth. Sometimes a suitor visited a girl's lodge in hope of sleeping with her. If her parents thought he was lazy and incompetent they discouraged his coming into the lodge and might make their daughter sleep with them. Should be persist in his suit the girl's mother would disparage his hunting ability and might even drive him away with a club. Parents arranged most marriages and would ostracize offspring who married without consent. Yet should the pair prove to be capable workers able to make their own living, their parents might then accept them and commence the proper exchange of presents that was part of the marriage contract.

Marriage with a rich industrious man was every girl's ideal. Some of these men had three or four wives. Occasionally a girl was sent to a rich man's lodge with the expectation that he would take her to wife. Women were held to especially strict accountability in food production. If a man thought his new wife lazy, he divorced her and married someone else. The unfortunate divorcee, who was ridiculed by her fellows as an incompetent, might undertake a "power quest" to acquire gathering skill and a good husband. Some rich men were said to have tried and rejected four or five wives before finding one who was satisfactory. Divorces, which were common, were also caused by a wife's adultery or barrenness. Yet an industrious barren woman who was well liked might be kept anyway. A man might even divorce his wife and marry his brother's widow if the latter excelled at food gathering. In rare instances, by getting the chief's consent, a woman could divorce her husband, who thereby lost caste — especially if the cause were his inability to support his wife.[15] A very poor individual, usually lazy and incompetent, had a hard time finding a mate; some never married.[16]

RELIGION

Supernatural aid was considered extremely efficacious if not essential in becoming industrious and wealthy, and ceremonials are replete with supplications for liveliness and observances to insure it. The almost universal penalty for failure to comply with some supernatural regulation was to become sleepy, lazy and/or sick.[17] There was a host of humanoid spirits which affected daily life in countless ways. Almost any desire could be fulfilled by going to the hills for spirit aid. Men frequently sought hunting power or gambling luck, while women sought proficiency in root digging, seed gathering or basket making.

Spirit supplication began when children were old enough to talk. At every new moon they ran a short distance eastward and, mounting a stump, spoke to the moon thus: "Grandfather, see how tall I am. I am going to be big and tall. I am going to be tough." This was called *cǐneliwu weskume* (moon-power quest). A spirit might observe a child and if pleased with his industriousness plan to become his guardian at puberty. Frequently boys of from eight to fourteen were whipped with an animal tail or bowstring and made to dive into an icy pool to toughen them and make them energetic.

Puberty, however, was the most portentous period in regard to the spirit world, and much stress was laid on the adult initiation ceremony at this time. The high development of this ceremonial and the fact that it was the only ceremonial of any importance are entirely logical and consistent with Atsugewi ideology. There was no connection with wealth display which characterizes the ceremonies of Northwest California. Instead the ceremony played up the primary work drive — the desire to excel in the food quest.

15. The term for grass widow or widower, *yaxcowi*, was very derogatory.

16. Poor men were said not to know how to do things. They could not flake arrow points, make nets or hunt successfully. Often they went naked.

17. See footnote 1.

At a girl's first menses her father sent her to the hills, and asked the hill spirts to aid her. On returning that evening she donned an old buckskin dress, moccasins and a twined buckbrush headband and wristlets. After a round dance till near midnight, the girl's dance, *yokalbone*, began. The girl, carrying a cane and facing east, danced back and forth by a fire, being supported when she tired by her betrothed or by two girls. A male song-leader sat facing east and beat time to his song with a deer-hoof rattle. In short intermissions the girl gathered wood or rested a little, but never could she sleep. On her vivacity and industry during the dance depended her whole future character. Should she be sleepy and tire easily, she was certain to become a despised *brumui* (poor lazy person). At dawn an industrious woman lifted her up, handed her a deer-hoof rattle and sent her runnng eastward. There she gathered pine burrs assiduously to insure future proficiency at food gathering. In the daytime the woman's dance, *silmĭtsabone*, was performed to clean menstrual blood from the girl.

In summer the girl worked hard all day digging roots, which were given away, usually to the women singers.[18] She was expected to fill three pack baskets with roots before sundown. Although she could take short naps, on awaking she had to jump up instantly or she was liable to become lazy. The few sips of water allowed her were poured from a basket into her mouth. In winter she remained in the menstrual hut, occasionally fetching wood and sleeping very little. A scratching stick and a bark pillow were used. Meat was taboo, but she might eat most vegetable foods. The dancing lasted until the menstrual flow stopped four or five days later. The whole ceremony was repeated at several subsequent menstrual periods, one girl having danced eleven times before her ears were punched by an indsutrious woman and she was sent to the hills for the last time. Sometimes a girl spent the final night in the mountains building a fire and piling rocks. Two girls might go together for company. Frequently spirit guardians were acquired during the ceremony; in fact, it is quite possible that the ceremony was repeated until a spirit guardian was obtained.

---

18. In much of Northwestern California and in many central California tribes the pubescent girl was tabooed from all work.

A boy's first power quest was in some measure equivalent to the girl's puberty ceremony.[19] When a boy's voice changed, some proficient hunter, after giving instructions, inserted sharpened twigs into the boy's ear lobes and whipped his legs with a coyote tail or bowstring. He then sent the boy running to the hills and besought the hill spirits to treat the boy kindly and give him power. Afterward the sponsor performed tasks with alacrity to help the boys on the quest.[20] The boy fasted the two or three days of the quest and traveled from one spring to another, taking only a sip of water at each. At night he built fires and piled up rocks. After midnight he might sleep a little, but on awaking he had to jump up immediately or become lazy. Much depended on his active behavior during the quest. He threw rocks in all directions and if lucky he heard a fawn bawl, which meant that he now had hunting power, or he heard the groan of an old man, which meant he was to be a shaman. On his return and after his sponsor had given him a little water and vegetable food he ended his quest by diving into a stream.

After the quest the first of each species of animal killed was given away. Before eating epos roots in the spring the boy took a torch and ran up a high hill, lighting a series of fires on the way and a large fire on top.[21] On returning that evening he spit chewed bits of epos root over his arms and legs and chanted, "I hope I will be fast. I hope I will be light and healthy. I hope I will be here next year." The influence of the roots, which were said to carry sleep, was thus negated. A boy who consorted with girls before his first quest was certain to be lazy and worthless.[22] If lazy after the first quest, subsequent quests were undertaken for energy and hunting power. Youths especially desirous of success and health went to the hills every month, staying only for the day and returning at sundown.

Wealth or the skill which led to its acquisition was conferred by certain spirits. There were special "powers" for gambling,

---

19. He was said to be having monthlies, *aitxeĩki*.

20. Imitative magic.

21. This was reported only for the Apwaruge. It was performed each spring for about six years after the first quest.

22. This is similar to the Northwest Californian antagonism between money and sex.

flint-chipping, arrow-making, etc. These powers could be inherited, creating a situation reminiscent of the Patwin functional families, (McKern, 1922), each of whom practised a specialized craft. However, skill came from owning certain magic formulae instead of by spirit assistance. The following is an account of an Atsugewi flint-chipping power:

> A man dived into a spring and fell through the roof of a spirit's house in which there was a workshop. Here a spirit showed the man how to flake arrow points. When the man returned to his village he could make the points very rapidly and skillfully. A man without power works slowly and often breaks the points before he is half finsihed.

The Atsugewi seemed to be uninterested in any activity which did not relate directly to the food quest, and rarely did an individual derive the major part of his living from a craft. An exception was Oknarehe, an old Atsuge man who did little but make bows and arrows, which he traded for beads and other goods. He never hunted — probably because he was lame, and he fished only occasionally. His arrows were prized for their fine quality. One informant thought he had a spirit guardian that made him get up early. This again reflects the common habit of thought, the emphasis being not so much on skillful production as on intensive and sustained application to the task from early morning till late at night. Daylight power — a spirit that helped one arise early — was one of the most common spirit guardians.

Many of the same regulations applied to the birth ordeal as to the puberty ceremony. There was similar but not so sustained dancing after a birth, food taboos were much the same, etc. A new father (in puberty ceremony the girl's betrothed) had to travel in the hills all day. It was his duty to keep active and to collect wood by breaking off dead limbs, which he carried in a bundle on his back as if it were deer. This increased his hunting luck and helped the mother and child. After dancing all night he again ran to the hills at sunrise to continue his travels. This program ended when the child's naval cord dropped. During pregnancy a woman was expected to move about briskly and to work all the time. This would make the baby want to be born quickly. If the woman were lazy, the baby would grow large within her and might kill her. If the baby's feet began to emerge first, this was called *cĭnehwu Bokci* (the sun she met), and resulted from the mother's having slept past sunrise.

WARFARE

Even war attitudes seem to have been much influenced by work ideals. The Atsugewi had a more pacifistic attitude than the average Californian tribe. In marked contrast to such tribes as the Yuki and Nomlacki (Goldschmidt, Essene and Foster, 1939) they showed little pride in their prowess on the battlefield. Warfare was distasteful and was to be avoided if at all possible. A good chief kept his people out of war. His very name, *juswahecar*, meant "life saver." The following quotation is typical:

> The Dixie Valley people didn't fight. We did not go to war
> when one of our people had been killed. Only when two or
> three had been killed would be fight. I guess the Dixie
> Valley people were cowards.

However, the Atsugewi actually seem to have been as ready as any of their neighbors to seek revenge, although this was sometimes indirect, as by having shamans poison the enemy or by inciting a friendly tribe to attack.[23] It seems probable that the lengthy purification required of a killer throughout Northeastern California influenced the Atsugewi attitude. Certainly to be forced to abstain from hunting and fishing for a month — and even the time spent on the war path — would radically violate work-ideals. Rich men, I was told, never went to war.

It is revealing to note that not everyone accepted the cultural ideals. One informant voiced the heretical belief that rich men were unintelligent in allowing themselves to be hoodwinked into working incessantly to accumulate food, which as often as not was shared with relatives and friends. The "smart" individuals lay around much of the time and "sponged" off the rich. Whether this attitude

---

23. Although the frequent Klamath, Modoc and Paiute raids went unretaliated it was probably because these tribes had horses, which the Atsugewi were slow to get. The Atsugewi badly defeated the Klamath on their last raid, having been warned of their coming. The Atsugewi made revenging raids on the Yana, Maidu and Wintu on occasion.

was original or one prevalent among the poor it is difficult to say. Certainly none of my other informants mentioned it. If prevalent, it probably was not openly expressed.

DISCUSSION

Elements of the Atsugewi work-concept are not unique. The great majority are found, a few here and a few there, in surrounding cultures. Yet in none of these, to my knowledge, is there such a concentration of elements pertaining to industriousness. The Atsugewi puberty ceremony could be ascribed to other tribes without exciting particular comment as regards work emphasis. Similarly unnotable is the requirement that a pregnant woman throw her covers aside and jump up before sunrise to begin the day's work which she must do faithfully to insure an easy delivery. Yet taken with numerous afore-mentioned regulations about work it becomes obvious that the above instances are important expressions of an unusual ideological pattern.

The work ideology seems to have produced an intense absorption in the food economy and a stultification or non-acceptance of certain cultural elements such as ceremonials and dances. The only dances consisted of a simple round dance, a war dance, and those in the puberty ceremony.[24] Responsibility must be attributed to something more than environment, as the Northeastern Maidu in similar environmental circumstances had a series of elaborate dances and ceremonials (Dixon, 1905). Of these, as well as of Wintu dances, the Atsugewi must have been cognizant. Shoshoneans to the east also had several social dances. In recent times a few Atsugewi participated in some of the Maidu dances, but never did they adopt them. The ghost dances became intensely popular — possibly partly because there were few old ceremonials to compete — but this is atypical since the old culture had by then largely disintegrated.

Were Atsugewi work emphasis entirely the result of environment one would expect it to be more pronounced in the

---

24. There was also a sweat dance which was too unformalized to be called a true dance, as it consisted merely of gesticulations in front of a fire to show one's ability to withstand heat.

more rigorous eastern area than in the west. Likewise Shoshonean tribes in the desert-like Basin should strongly emphasize work, a situation which does not seem to exist.[25] More probably the Atsugewi situation resulted from the acceptance of northern wealth ideals, the expression of which was warped and limited by the unfavorable environment. Although the wealthy had an exalted position, they themselves provided much of the food and equipment needed to maintain and enhance it. Thus hard work was required, which itself came to have an exaggerated prestige value. Work-prestige served the added function of discouraging social parasitism, which might otherwise have flourished in this somewhat paternalistic social system. The valuation applied to treasure wealth in Northwest California was given by the Atsugewi — who lacked any considerable amount of treasure wealth for display — to utilitarian objects.[26] Even the simplest objects were given prestige value and were considered important forms of wealth. Thus a rich man could count his wealth in equipment and food, and need not have a fund of treasure. Wealth display took such form as having many deer skins drying on racks outside the house, giving notice that the occupant was wealthy and an excellent hunter. These skins were later worked into Plainstype shirts and dresses, the wearing of which gave prestige. A minor form of display also occurred at "Big Times" when property was brought for trade. Trading itself was usually in the form of gifts to a trading partner in another group and brought prestige to the giver. The bride purchase of Northwestern California became such in name only. Although wives were bought, there was no negotiated price, and the property paid her family was reciprocated. Status did not depend on the amount paid for one's mother, although a man

---

25. Studies of Shoshonean groups by Kelly, Steward, Lowie, Shimkin, Stewart, and others make no mention of an unusual emphasis on work.

26. The most commonly mentioned wealth objects were buckskins, otter and fisher furs — usually made into quivers, and clamshell beads. Northwest Californian items of treasure are rare or absent. Voegelin (1942: 90) reports woodpecker-scalp headbands as valuable among the Atsuge, but I got no mention of them, so they were probably not overly important. The Apwaruge denied having them. Dentalia were little esteemed, and long obsidian knives were absent, although in a myth a two-foot-long knife was a treasured possession. Possibly this is a memory of an earlier contact to the north (1942: 90).

derived considerable prestige by large gifts to his wife's family. Gifts were donated from time to time as long as the marriage lasted. In this concept of generous giving which pervaded all economic and social relationships lies a fundamental difference with Northwest California. The contrasting Northwest Californian attitude is one of cupidity, sharp bargaining, and definite prescribed prices and fines. Also comparatively minor attention was paid to industriousness as such. The only occasions when the Atsugewi demanded a fine on the Yurok pattern were for murder, adultery, and rape.[27] Both cultures stressed individual property rights, which formed the basis of a paternalistic order of which the rich man, the controller of property, was the head, dispensing assistance and food to his followers. Central Californian influences have, however, given the Atsugewi a true hereditary chief with some political authority, though his constituents did not provide him with food as was usual in Central California.

The intimate and functional relationship of the work-drive to the economy, political organization, marriage, and religion, and the fact that it is the basis for the cultural configuration has been demonstrated. It is evident that the basis for a strong cultural pattern of personality need not be dramatic.

---

27. For adultery and rape one or one-and-a-half strings of clamshell beads were demanded.

Religion and its Role Among the Luiseño

by Raymond White

That religion frequently shows great resistance to change and is deeply involved in the social structure as well as the psychological patterns of a culture has been repeatedly demonstrated in anthropology. This is also true for the Luiseño. A rich body of the central characteristics of the old native religion has persisted in spite of missionary influence for nearly two centuries.

Many features of the old Luiseño culture have been preserved, such as the names and uses of food plants, hunting techniques, geographical locations, and use of stone implements. But an outline of the old indigenous social organization has proved difficult to trace. The probable reason is that the modern Luiseño has not generally thought of his social organization as a matter apart from his religion. Any concerted effort to extract from informants data upon social organization, past or present, immediately becomes intricately enmeshed in problems of theology.

Where Luiseño tenacity in the maintenance of religion and religious organization has succeeded, some portion of the larger forms of social organization may be detected. These appear to involve moieties with dichotomous sets of religious officials and reciprocal ceremonial and economic arrangements. Indirectly there are also implications of moiety exogamy, village endogamy, and other important features that in practice had almost disappeared a full century ago.

Personal character studies made in the light of cosmological details reveal a complex structuring of society and the environment, preoccupation with supernatural adjustments between the two, and a rather Malthusian view of population density and the food supply. All these considered in terms of structurally ordered items of fragmentary information lead to the view that a separate nondichotomous "secular" organization of officials once also existed simultaneously with that devoted exclusively to religion. The disappearance of this secular group may be largely attributed to missionary practices, and is probably responsible for the sharp differences to be found in a comparison of the works of Fr. Boscana and modern scholars. Without the hypothesis of a nondichotomous group of "secular" officials (whose duties contained more emphasis upon economic and political than religious controls), any attempt to resolve the differences between scholars separated by a full century is extremely difficult, if not impossible. The information elicited in recent field work tends to confirm both early and late views.

That both the early and late studies of the Luiseño agree with a general reconstructable pattern is not immediately obvious. This lack is brought about through two basic characteristics of Luiseño religion: intricacy of religious structure, and secrecy. This is not to imply that in all instances secrecy results from a deliberate conspiracy of silence or misdirection, although it cannot be claimed that the Indians have *not* taken full advantage of the confusion existing upon the part of their protagonists. The secrecy issues from causes far deeper than any superficial evasions. It lies in the nature of the religious concepts, and the inadequate vehicles of "translation" conventionally used to convey Luiseño thought into English or Spanish. Fuller understanding has become possible only since the imminent extinction of his religious organization motivated religious chief (not[h]) Rejinaldo Pachito to make his knowledge a matter of history. The Luiseño community as a whole by no means unanimously approves his decision, but the rank-ordering system of the society is such that those who disapprove have no veto power.

As will become apparent in this discussion, comprehension of the Luiseño religious philosophy depends upon the acumen of the learner and the methods of instruction. The latter is not only systematic, but requires that comprehension be demonstrated by fairly accurate interpretations of interrelationships among the various clues given, and rapid adjustment made to the subtleties of corrective procedures. No one is permitted information beyond his *demonstrated* capabilities.

A preset philosophical background works to great disadvan-

tage in interpreting Indian thought and habit patterns. Not only did
it lead to an unfavorable description of Juaneño-Luiseño character
upon Boscana's (1933: 81) part, but seems to be responsible for a
curious error among the missionaries as a group. Failure to
interpret the Luiseño religious system correctly led to confusion
about the social system and features that were an integral part of it.
Apparently the Indian "secular" leadership was confused with the
religious chieftainships so that attempts to eradicate the former
missed the contemplated objective of destroying the latter (cf.
Jeffreys, 1956: 721-731). Some of this confusion is expressed in
Boscana's view of the character of these Indians (1933: 81):

> I presume that there may be some persons who will say,
> notwithstanding these (religious) accounts, that they are
> not satisfactory evidences of a total want of faith and belief
> for rare occurrences happen everywhere . . . This I
> concede, but exceptions are few. These accounts generally
> conform to each other in substance, and he who has
> perused them with attention, or is familiar with the
> character of these Indians, knowing that when they appear
> the most intelligent and entitled to the greatest
> confidence, they are the least to be trusted, he will I say,
> agree with me generally regarding their belief. As all their
> operations are accompanied by strategems and dissimula-
> tion, they easily gain our confidence and at every pass we
> are deluded.

The Luiseño were indeed people of strategems and
dissimulation, especially when crowded together into missionary
camps regardless of rank or rancheria. Further, the acceptance of a
new religion and ethic did not require them to abandon the old. For
the Luiseño, "religions" seem to occupy logic-tight compartments,
a feature that accommodated their acceptance of the Chingishnish
cult at about the same time as Christianity (cf. DuBois, 1908: 76).
The former has characteristics that suggest sources in one of the
world's great religions, yet seems to have propagated quite
independently of Christianity (White, 1957:20).

Secrecy, strategem, and dissimulation are bound up with the
concept that religious knowledge, formula, and ceremony possess
power and can be properly and safely exercised only by experts.

Further, the psychological characteristic that compartmentalizes religions or features of religion does not contradict Boscana's observations concerning the Luiseño character. When dealing with Christian matters, behavior and ethics were no doubt channeled into the Christian mold. Otherwise, however, the Indian behaved in a prescribed manner quite alien to Boscana's comprehension or expectations. This plurality of behavioral systems is clearly reflected among the Luiseño today, and is implicit in a clarification of many points contributed by Pachito. Once when confronted by an apparent fundamental conflict between points of religious philosophy, he explained: "But that is *another* religion," whereupon he proceeded to make clear that each religion must be understood concretely and explicitly in its own terms. They must not be confused or syncretized.

But in this study we are concerned with Luiseño character only as its various aspects become implicit in religion and ecological fundamentals. The old basic patterns of religious thought and their ability to reveal details of the Luiseño social organization are stressed.

The native Luiseño religion contains a cosmogony (cf. Kroeber, 1925: 677) that in its many parts delineates a set of concepts and precepts that are complex, moralistic, and largely consistent. Song was a Luiseño substitute for written history and laws; ceremony was its graphic reënactment. In large part, song and ceremony were devoted to selected cosmological subjects. Under these conditions, social organization and its controls were, to the Indian understanding, subject to the cosmogony. Luiseño life was mostly organized about it.

In some of its major features, the cosmogony describes occurrences and conditions resulting from human social and moral problems. Woven into the fabric of the tales is a set of human (and animal) characteristics dealing with sexual avidity, envy, insult and vengeance, as well as love and affection, loyalty, devotion to duty, and a rather fatalistic attitude toward the inevitability of misfortune.

The cosmogony is a tragedy that forms a primary theme of sadness and regret, hunger, and turmoil in Luiseño life, and provides a recurring set of subjects for the Luiseño forms of epic and lyric expression. At the same time it provides a self-validating explanation for unmoral and unwilling but necessary activities, and a rationalization for the unhappy state of affairs. Although it cannot be proved now, it seems likely that in pre-Spanish times nearly all the cosmogony was expressed musically, sometimes as esoteric ritual, sometimes as entertainment.

Luiseño music is far more complex in many of its characteristics than the casual ear might suppose. The ability to appreciate some of the subtle nuances of what otherwise might be mistaken for a monotonous pentatonic scale is not easy to acquire, and does not qualify one to appreciate the subtlety of the verse. The latter has been described by a young Indian who has spent years learning the language, and additional years collecting and seriously studying the music, as presenting an extremely difficult task. The verse pattern has a form unlike anything in the western-European world. The verses are hymns of a sort, but they may be sung only by those who inherit them and are instructed in their rendition or application, or those to whom special collection privileges are accorded — and this last only recently. The only times a song, usually sung only by qualified persons from a particular family, may be sung by other special individuals, is in commemoration of the "possessor" after his death. Compare Boscana on this subject (1934: 5-6):

> Since these Indians did not use writings, letters, or any characters, nor do they use them, all their knowledge is by tradition, which they preserve in songs for the dances which they held at their great feasts. But since these songs have their form or are in a language distinct from that which is spoken at the present time, no one, except those mentioned above (officials), understands the meaning of the song and dance; the others sing and dance but without knowing either what they are saying or what they are doing. I imagine that such songs are in a primitive language, and are not used or sung except in their feasts . . . They also have common songs and dances in their own language, which latter are sung and danced daily, and are understood by all, but these are nothing more than for the purpose of amusing themselves and idling about with one another.

A word-for-word translation of the songs yields gibberish. But to put the full meaning of a particular short song into English would require an essay. The subject matter is almost always cosmological; this is understood by the audience. The opening key expression alludes to a vast cosmological area of consideration — a limiting but extremely general statement containing all the implications, side issues, and so forth. The next expression or phrase imposes limits on the original statement but uses "loaded" words to bring forth new concepts in other dimensions. This continues until the end of the song when the new concepts have ballooned into a complex almost as great as the original key statement, and the original clue has been expanded until some incident, relating perhaps to the Earth Mother or Wiyot the culture hero, has been set forth. (There are considerable differences in information-content from rancheria to rancheria; each has a "history" of specific happenings enacted by Wiyot locally.)

These difficulties of translation are also found in the everyday spoken language, and make "translation" of terms by informants very precarious. The word "knowledge" is an example. It actually refers to ayelkwi, a mana-like power, the manifestations of which are only sometimes expressed as knowledge (cf. Kroeber, 1925: 679). Even in Luiseño, as Boscana (1934: 6) well knew, songs differ considerably in difficulty. One class is generally understood by everybody; another only by officials and profound thinkers. Today, some of the sacred songs in ceremonies are not even understood by the singers. On the comprehension of religious matters by the population in general as contrasted to that of the officials, compare Boscana's (1934:5) key statement:

> I confess that it is difficult to be able to penetrate their secrets, because the signification . . . is not known to all of them. This is only for the chiefs and certain satraps, who performed the work of priests . . . and when these taught it to their sons (and only to those who were to succeed them), it was always with the admonition that they should not divulge it . . . (otherwise) they would have many misfortunes, and would die, etc., instilling into them much dread and fear; and for that reason so little is known about their affairs, since those few who know and understand keep it to themselves.

Both song and language intensify the differences of understanding and magnify differences in philosophical depth displayed by various elements in the population.

Ayelkwi, "knowledge-power," and the consequences of its misuse among the immediate population is partly responsible for the "dread and fear" of spreading understanding. The potential use of ayelkwi by someone from an enemy rancheria made its public sharing unthinkable; and these features combined to make the secrecy, from which Boscana and others have suffered, more a consequence of circumstances than a directed conspiratorial affair. Yet these same features led to a rank-ordering of the society, the proliferation and specialization of officials, and an intensification of the causes of war. They also account for those aspects of character such as strategem and dissimulation that disturbed Boscana so greatly. Further, since in Indian eyes the missionaries were themselves dispensers of potent ayelkwi (in the form of religious formulae, skills, crafts, and so forth), the Luiseño leaders made every effort to "easily gain our confidence . . ." Acquisition of that ayelkwi was crucial in the ecological picture. All this serves to set the stage for an examination of the cosmogony, ayelkwi, and religious organization.

Ayelkwi is the Luiseño version of that power often called mana elsewhere. The general rules for its application are as follows: (1) It must be used specifically and unvaryingly according to a set procedure, and (2) it must always be used upon an appropriate occasion. Failure to follow the rules results in the loss of essential control over the particular kind of ayelkwi in question; the consequences are grave: deaths, accidents, disease, and so forth. No one knows how many kinds of ayelkwi exist, nor has it been possible to acquire a native system for categorizing them. Nevertheless, four general types may be discerned: (1) "Common" knowledge is that cultural and physical nature common to the Luiseño as distinguished from all other creatures and their respective forms of "common" knowledge; (2) "innate" ayelkwi is the differential powers with which individuals are born and that marks some of them as unusual and powerful persons; (3) "residual" ayelkwi comprises virtually all the unknown and unusual features of the Luiseño environment — a potentially procurable residuum of powers "thrown away" by Wiyot, the Luiseño culture hero; (4) "formulated" ayelkwi is represented by

ritual forms and procedures considered to have been promulgated
in decisions made either in cosmogonic times or later. All types of
ayelkwi in possession of a Luiseño must be treated according to the
general rules; hence, aberrant behavior upon the part of individuals
is expected if not encouraged under some circumstances. But by
the same token, ayelkwi-laden information is transmitted only very
reluctantly. Inappropriate application on the part of a novice may
bring disaster to the teacher; injudicious teaching may bring
consequences upon one's own people in the form of sorcery,
warfare, destruction of food crops, and so on.

There are several extant versions of the cosmogony, most of
which are garbled. This is especially true of Boscana's earlier
manuscript (the "Robinson" edition republished in 1933, written
about 1820); the variant version prepared by Boscana in 1822, and
published for the first time by Harrington (1934), is quite different
and conforms much more closely with information collected since
the turn of the twentieth century. The causes of garbling are
relatively easy to understand. They result from (1) informants of
lesser rank who do not actually know the full content and proper
order of events; (2) the tendency of informants to follow some
particular Indian theme after the fashion of the religious songs
rather than a chronological and linear historical manner of
presentation; (3) the use of two or more informants from different
villages; (4) difficulties arising from sheer size and complexity of
detail; (5) linguistic and philosophical problems; (6) the absolute
loss of knowledge following the breakup of the culture; and (7) the
fact that power may inhere in the content and be elicited in the
telling of information.

Since a full study of the cosmogony would require a lengthy
examination of all these features, a condensed, foreshortened
version of it offered by Pachito will be discussed here. It is
abbreviated, but contains the core of the materials to be
considered.

Concerning the general nature of the cosmogony, Krober
(1925: 677) has this to say:

> First, the concept of prime origins by birth, instead of
> process of making, is more thoroughly worked out than by
> perhaps any other American tribe except possibly some of
> the Pueblos. Secondly, there is a remarkable attempt at

abstract conceptualizing, which, though it falls short of success, leaves an impression of boldness and of a rude but vast grandeur of thought. The result is that the beginning of the Luiseño genesis reads far more, in spirit at least, like the opening of a Polynesian cosmogonic chant than like an American Indian tradition of the world origin.

It is difficult to avoid adopting a position even stronger than Kroeber's, especially in regard to his second point. With the discovery of ayelkwi as a systematic means of relating all parts and events of Luiseño existence, "rudeness" of concept is difficult to accept. Further, there arises a question of how far "short of success" Luiseño attempts at abstract conceptualizing fall.

Specialization by an officialdom in the presence of intense competition provides conditions for abstract thought. This is especially true in the presence of a thesis like ayelkwi, when coupled with some "leisure." (Officials were "paid" for their work in performing ceremonies, were accorded frequent "gifts" by members of the community, and possessed several wives — some of whom may have been "transvestites" (cuŭt) — to gather and process food [Boscana, 1934: 27].) Moreover, important possessors of major ayelkwi usually established individual personal workshops at some distance from the village where various special powers could be exercised in secret and frightful new forms be completed in private.

The major elements of the cosmogony are as follows: (1) genesis and the nature of things, (2) the Wiyot epic, and (3) addenda. The last is concerned mostly with a "god," Chingishnish, and the cult associated with him, and is properly not a part of the cosmogony; Luiseño religion is additive but not syncretistic. The concept of mana-like ayelkwi (knowledge-power) permeates the cosmogony, and the language, and no element may be considered except in these terms. Chingishnish may be passed over here. He has become merely the spirit personification of the functioning of ayelkwi; his approval or disapproval is an expression of whether the ayelkwi in any event functioned properly or miscarried.

The Earth Mother, Tomaiyowit (or -wut), in long succession gave birth to the prototypes of all things (cf. DuBois, 1908, and Kroeber, 1925). These $ka^hmel\breve{u}m$, ancient "people," include animals, such as Bear, Rabbit, Deer, Wood Rat, and Rattlesnake; birds, especially Eagle and Hummingbird; Indians; *Tamyush* (certain stone bowls used for ceremony), *Wiyalŭm* (also called *not*[h]-stones — small "effigy" heads imbued with power); plant life of all varieties, and so forth. Wiyot, the culture hero, was the last of these births. Among these births was also one who seems to have been called *Tovĭsh* (spirit ?). All these beings lived happily together, playing, reproducing themselves without limit in an indefinitely expanding living space, subsisting on an unlimited supply of clay, and thoroughly enjoying themselves in an Eden-like existence. All, that is, except Tovish. He seemed strange, and when the others noticed it and asked him about it — his form of play included unpleasantries — he hung his head and began to cry. Here is the first in a long series of tragedies. Tovish, or *towĭsh* (?), could not act in any other manner; it was his nature. So the others drove him away. In Christian times this entity seems to have been identified as the Devil, but some confusion exists in terminology and concept. Whether Tovish and towish truly equate is conjectural. Since the latter also refers to soul or ghost of the deceased, a rather different idea from that of a personified evil spirit, some question exists. Both can be dangerous, but certainly no Luiseño would confuse one with the other, if he had the means of differentiating.

Each of the ka[h]melum was unique by birth; each was endowed with unique powers and abilities. Wiyot, the last born, was also the greatest in power and knowledge. Upon him devolved the knowledge of how to make clay nourishing and how to make the living space expand indefinitely to accommodate an increasing population. It is said that *"he knew everything."* Because of this, he became the chief of the "people," whom he led and instructed. (Seeming inconsistencies in this part of the story may involve level rather than contradiction; they suggest that Wiyot was possibly a real person, conceivably an ailing chieftain who led some elements of the Uto-Aztecan migration into the area.) The Eden-like existence came to an end when a "woman," Frog, slowly killed Wiyot through witchcraft (cf. Reid, 1926:36). During this process, he traveled from place to place. Each rancheria seems to have a story of how he was helped there. At Pauma, while dying, he named the seasons, thus generating the calendar. On the third day after his death, he rose again in the form of Moila, the moon.

The death of Wiyot brought catastrophe. Clay was no longer nourishing. Living space no longer expanded. Wiyot had "thrown away" this knowledge-power along with most of the rest of his ayelkwi without having imparted it to anyone. This brought about a residuum of "knowledge" lying about in the environment which can be acquired by any competent person — that is, "residual" ayelkwi. Hunger brought about "cannibalism" among the people; the symbolic act of eating a piece of human flesh from the deceased by an official called the *Eno* and/or *Tacue* (Boscana, 1934: 47) is apparently related to this circumstance. Eno is identical with Ano, coyote; Tacue is the same as *Takwĭsh*, ball lightning. Both are eaters of human flesh, but the latter seems not properly a part of the cosmogony (cf. Kroeber, 1925: 680). Coyote was the first eater; it was he who ate the heart of the dead Wiyot. As Wiyot died, so everybody was required to die; his resurrection as the moon implies resurrection of other "people" as stars. Overcrowding brought the necessity of death as the price for having offspring.

Eagle is a special "person" who escaped this fate. Yet he "gave up" his children, all of whom die or are eaten by other "people" as the price of his perpetual youth. There was a cycle of ceremonies concerned with Eagle (cf. Boscana, 1934: 39-42). Even his name, Ashwŭt, suggests fertility. *Ash* probably signified puberty or first menses among young women (Kroeber, 1925: 673); *-wŭt* in nouns generally seems to mean "imbued with," hence, "capable of giving the life principle." Ceremonies involving Eagle and eagle feathers concern fertility and longevity, for example the girl's puberty ceremony contained a foot race said to have determined greater longevity among the successively fleeter of foot. The meaning of the symbol painted on a large boulder at the terminus of the race was in each instance known only by the individual girl, but possibly was representative of some form of bird, animal, or other ayelkwi object with which she identified.

The crises of overpopulation, restricted living space, diet and food supply, and death brought on by the murder of Wiyot, all involved ayelkwi. A Great Conclave of the "people" was called to solve these problems through discussion and a power-struggle process. It was "decided" that Wiyot was to be cremated, an act that was successful except for Coyote's eating of the heart. Cremation by the Luiseño was continued until the padres put a stop to it. These power "decisions" of the Conclave became binding throughout nature, and since ritual was evolved there, it constitutes a form of ayelkwi as effective and unalterable as any other form in nature. Thus, ritual and ceremony may be labeled "formulated" ayelkwi.

The living-space problem was partly solved by adopting arrangements like those found today: Gophers live underground, birds fly in the air, fish swim the waters, and so forth. Death and resurrection was another way out. Cannibalism, however, was one of the most important solutions.

Each of the ka^hmelum had been born with unique powers, and many of them had acquired additional ayelkwi from Wiyot. At the Great Conclave (*ka^hmelŭm pŭm yunach*), after it was decided that the people would have to eat each other, questions arose as to the hierarchical arrangement of such eating. The present arrangements concerning who is the eater and who the eaten were worked out after the discussion and power struggles. The outcome largely fixed the intricate relationships existing today among "people." The term "people," as stated earlier, includes a wide range of flora, fauna, and even minerals.

The ecological relationships observable within the environment clearly do not exist upon a one-to-one basis. This is reflected in the cosmological stories concerning the hierarchical organization of nature. The eater is not necessarily directly responsible for having cosmologically overcome the eaten. For example, Deer is a principal food animal for the Indians, but humans are not directly responsible for the plight of Deer. Deer Fly is one of the "people" who, through the Great Conclave, accomplished it. "Naming" things apparently constituted one form of sorcery, because this is the means used by Deer Fly in the cosmological power struggle. Each organ of Deer was named and in each instance Deer "knew" (ayelkwi) about it, except for the gall bladder, and in this area of ayelkwi Deer was at the mercy of those who did "know." "Naming" it therefore defeated Deer, and to this day the deer fly will lead a Luiseño hunter to his quarry.

The hierarchy in nature established by the cosmology is not a simple linear affair with each creature allotted a single position. The forms of "cannibalism" are not so arranged, nor are other characteristics of the "life-forms" involved. While it is true that, for the Luiseño, Eagle, Coyote, Deer, Bear, and others occupy places of high emphasis in nature, their relative hierarchical positions lie in different dimensions. For the Luiseño, all "life-forms" in the total environment belong to a structured existence of which the Indian himself is an element. His cosmogony provides the general outlines and rationale of the system. It is an elaborately tragic pattern in which every kind of creature has a social organization according to its nature, and these are interrelated in a complex manner so that they form a single total social organizational structure. The hierarchical arrangements by "species" are based upon "innate" ayelkwi according to prototype and to solutions to the various crises worked out in the Great Conclave of the people. Understanding such a system, the individual Luiseño may not always "know" the precise reasons why a hummingbird is seen to eat only blossom nectar and the human finds the lizard a tabooed food, but he has a generalized rationale for it.

All the intricate ecological phenomena of nature thus become a matter for intensive observation upon the part of the Indians. The behavior of every "living" thing depends upon its individualistic personal "knowledge," as well as its hierarchical characteristics. The most acute observation of every detail becomes necessary if one is to have sufficient food in the face of the internecine warfare existing throughout nature — nobody wants to be eaten; everybody strains his utmost to avoid personal catastrophe in a cannibalistic existence. Death is resented; achieving extreme age is a mark of great personal power. It is clear that simple anthropomorphism is transcended in this Luiseño explanation of his *weltanschauung*, even though an unusual form of "ethnocentrism" intervenes. Yet how much more imaginatively, elaborately, and comprehensively can a theory of ecology be apprehended?

Although the cosmogony provides something of a master plan for an understanding of the nature of things and is replete with examples, it does not directly deal with the philosophy underlying individualism and individual diversity or aberration extending into postcosmogonic times. The nature of ayelkwi is implicit rather than explicit in the cosmogony.

The idea of ayelkwi is not greatly different from that of mana, orenda, manitou (cf. Kroeber, 1925: 679). The Luiseño render this concept into English with the term "knowledge," although "knowledge-power" would approach it more closely. It is omnipresent, imperishable, and immutable. It is not corporeal, but is somehow involved in the nature of all things. Every detail of existence and event in nature, past, present or future, corresponds to an expression of ayelkwi in some form. It is present in the animate and inanimate, in spirit and secular being, in ceremony and habitual act. Ayelkwi is causal, and establishes both a firm basis for precedent and a reason for the unexpected. In the one sense it provides the forms and meanings of social organization, and in the other a rationale for the unpredictable. It is seen or otherwise apprehended in all natural phenomena as well as in human personality and behavior. It may "flow" with or without diminution from one character or event to another (cf. Harrington, 1933: 161). There is an infinity of types of ayelkwi. Above all, it is dangerous and difficult to manage.

Although ayelkwi (knowledge-power) is in some sense basically the same in all instances (power), it may appear to be fundamentally different in intensity and type of manifestation (knowledge). All things that manifest or are suspected to possess ayelkwi are considered "persons." Among them are certain shaped or incised stones called not[h] (religious chief, i.e., "repository of great ayelkwi"), various small stone bowls called tamyush, "statues" — outcropping boulders with shapes endowing them with legend — all species of birds, animals, insects, plants, spirits, the stars, planets, moon, and humans. All these things are "persons." But all members of the various categories of persons are not clearly, specifically, and immutably members of their own form category. For example, various mysterious lights seen at night (possibly ball lightning which occurs in the vicinity, St. Elmo's Fire, or phosphorescent emanations from bacterial decay in swampy areas, or from fungus) cannot always be clearly defined as one "person" or another. Such a classification, if it is ever made, must depend upon an understanding of the ultimate character of the ayelkwi possessed and manifested. The entity exhibiting the ayelkwi in question may be a spirit manifesting human as well as spirit powers, or vice versa. Which one he ultimately turns out to be is less important than the nature and meaning of the ayelkwi he possesses and exhibits.

In a sense, the categorization in the instance in question is academic, for transmorphism among "species" or categories of being is conceptually common. Here transmorphism is used in a broad and peculiar manner. The senses cannot be believed. That perceived has no necessary or immediate relationship to conceptual imperatives, whatever these may be. Wiyot, the culture hero, became the moon; the spirits of the dead form the Milky Way; Eagle (except for the young) is immortal so that no matter how often he is killed, nevertheless he is still alive and exists only as a single pair. This applies no matter how many eyries may be seen to be inhabited or the "simultaneity" with which more than two eagles may be observed (the power of his *wanawŭt* — a kind of magic cloak — is the instrument of his ayelkwi). Deer may turn into a seductive woman; the aunt of Nahatchish (praying mantis), a great chief in legend, is the mother of the spirit Takwĭsh (cf. Harrington, 1933: 180 ff.); some pula (witch doctors) could turn themselves into bear. In every instance, the identification or lack of it depends upon the characteristics of the ayelkwi involved. Although such a state of affairs makes clear the reasons for Fr. Boscana's (1934: 58, 1933: 84) confusion between whether something was classified as animate or inanimate, it also suggests that ayelkwi itself possesses some sort of a classification system.

The ambiguity of classification of "beings" or "persons" discussed above does not necessarily extend itself to all members of any particular "species." Clearly Deer is not confused with Hummingbird, nor Stone with Oak. But if a deer possessed the same ayelkwi as Hummingbird, he could assume and exercise the powers and characteristics of a hummingbird in a manner that would be entirely confusing to anyone except another possessing the same powers or some sort of counterayelkwi. Hummingbird's ayelkwi possessed by a deer would permit the deer to appear as a hummingbird at will. Thus, while ayelkwi is immutable, perception of "species" is not. Since ayelkwi can "flow," it is possible for an individual in one "species" to come to possess and to "know" that ayelkwi peculiar to another "person" or "species." From all this it becomes clear that not only are there many kinds of ayelkwi, but that individuals differ from one another by virtue of this fact. Apparently there are quantitative and qualitative differences in the forms of "innate" ayelkwi involved. This distinguishes pulum from the common "people," no matter what the "species."

As in the cosmogony, each child born is regarded as unique. Even today, the potentialities of each child are considered at some length during his earliest years. The uniqueness of each member of the society applies even though the person is an integral part of the whole. The innate humanness of each Indian is recognized, and his acquisition of common ayelkwi (the canons of ordinary, everyday behavior) is accepted as being relatively mundane. Nevertheless, it is also a matter of much concern that any particular birth might bring forth an individual with peculiar powers. Formerly this could often be directly determined and appropriate steps taken to "take out" the strange powers, should they be adjudged dangerous (cf. Harrington, 1933: 161). Obviously, the concept of flow of ayelkwi is present whatever its source or type. Thus ayelkwi is not distributed uniformly among "species," nor among individuals within any species. Hence children are given great care and consideration, and trivialities such as legitimacy and primogeniture have little bearing.

The principle of innate ayelkwi enters kinship considerations in a dual manner. The bestowal of viability, of human-life ayelkwi, seems to be the function of the female. The degree of differentiation of this life-ayelkwi among "species" is not clear. The male feature seems to be the bestowal of some particular and specific form of innate ayelkwi. This determines the patrilineage. Such is the principle involved in the case of Wakaterat of Pechanga, and also of Sheiyutl, the founder of Pachito's religious chiefly line. Sheiyutl was tormented by the other children of Pauma to the point of having an eye destroyed, and his mother was unsuccessful in having the chief rectify matters. This extraordinary situation suggests that Sheiyutl had no other representatives of his patrilineage at Pauma (nor presumably elsewhere). Nor had the child been accepted by his mother's consanguineal relatives, either male or female. Further, it is to be remembered that parallel cousins are termed siblings. The mother and child retired from the village and lived alone until the boy reached maturity. When the mother died, the young man returned to the village as a superlatively powerful person and subsequently married the daughter of a religious chief. The male offspring of this marriage was the first chief of the Pachito line.

The possibility that a female, while gathering food, might be impregnated by a spirit or some powerful "foreign" pula from another rancheria was considered a constant danger. Boscana describes this as follows (1933: 48):

In their excursions for the collecting of seeds, or for other purposes should they (young women) unfortunately meet with one of the sorcerers . . . they were to comply with any desire which he might express without manifesting the least reluctance on their part.

Elsewhere he adds (1934: 53):

And if the Indians, when going from one place to another see or imagine something extraordinary, they say that that is the soul of some dead person and they hold it a bad omen, fearing some misfortune, for they are of the belief that if a dead person shows himself to someone, it is to do injury to him, and particularly to the women, and there are some imposters who pass themselves off as these ghosts, in order thus to attain their desires.

The *wakenish* (girl's puberty ceremony) was designed in part to prevent such mesalliances. The exact nature of offspring could not always be certain. This led to a ceremonial or ritual form of "putting" and "taking." Its object was to "take out of" the child any exotic male principle, and "put into" him that of his sociological father or sponsor. In this way, the male lineage could usually be made determinative in spite of any biological involvements. But, it is said, the ayelkwi form within the child sometimes proved too powerful to be "taken," or the proper procedure for "taking" was not known. In this event, the child, if male, might found a new lineage in the manner just reviewed for Sheiyutl.

For the female child, the male principle seems to have been less important. Emphasis was upon her ability as a giver of the life principle. She does not seem to have endowed her children with the male principle she herself inherited from her father except, perhaps, in special cases. Her children, through a ceremony called the *scholahish*, were generally "confirmed" to the lineage of her husband. Whether this involved "taking" and "putting" depended upon the nature of the circumstances. In the event that an important patrilineage was in danger of becoming extinct, the patrilineage of the mother's father could be "confirmed," and "taking" and "putting" be performed as desired. According to Boscana (1934: 31) this presumably was a practice in the instance of some chiefly lineages:

In the succession of these chieftainships, women also
entered, when males were lacking. She could marry
whoever [*sic*] she pleased, though he were not of the race
or lineage of chiefs; but the husband, be who he might,
though he were the son of another chief, was never
recognized as such nor did he have command, but they
only recognized the woman. But she did not govern or
perform the functions of chief, but the government was
exercised by another, an uncle or a grandfather, the
nearest of blood. But the first male whom she bore,
immediately was declared chief . . .

In the cases of Wakaterat of Pechanga, and of Sheiyutl, it seems
that the "putting" and "taking" either was not performed, or was
unsuccessful. The former may have usurped the chiefly rank
position; the latter became the transmitter of great ayelkwi and the
founder of a new patrilineage. The principle of inheritance of
differential ayelkwi through family lines — usually male in the case
of offices — is conducive to the establishment of a nobility. But
there are also reasons for believing that this principle was involved
in the selection of the cuut (cf. Boscana, 1934: 27), sex inverts, or
transvestites. There is a rumor to the effect that the Cahuilla used
to select male children for survival according to penis size. The
Luiseño were richer and may have relegated their "weaker" male
youngsters to the status of cuut. This selection may have been
regional, for Torquemada (cf. Harrington, 1933: 112) mentions the
"robusticity" of the "Canalino" (Channel of Santa Barbara). At
any rate, this agrees with the concept of innate ayelkwi and with the
factual materials available upon the subject.

For pulum, ayelkwi conferred high status. But it was also a
frightful force with which to reckon. It is here that the "knowledge"
interpretation of the term begins to contrast sharply with the
"power" meaning. To acquire ayelkwi was to be duty bound to
"know" its characteristics and all formulae for its exact and specific
application if the power were not to run wild and cause incalculable
harm to both the novice and his kin and village as well. Put another
way, there are two primary points concerning ayelkwi that must be
remembered by all Luiseño: (1) ayelkwi is extremely dangerous,
and (2) ayelkwi must be used at times and places in exact accord
with its nature, and without fail, regardless of the anticipated social

consequences. Misuse certainly brings drouth, famine, flood, disease, death, and other disasters. Therefore, any ignorant social disapproval must be disregarded or met with courageous equanimity. These points serve both to provide supernatural sanctions for the social order in general, and to excuse certain "excesses" upon the part of those possessing high rank.

Why should ayelkwi confer high status? First, the vicissitudes of an environment in which starvation, famine, disease, death, and so on, were not uncommon, led to a development and refinement of magic arts designed to be preventive, and possessors of these arts were bound to be looked up to. For example, success in the food quest was dependent upon "knowledge," hence, any superior ability concerning increase or procurement of food made for high status. This led to the cultural habit of maintaining an extremely sensitive and penetrating observance of detailed occurrences within the immediate natural and cultural milieu by emphasizing attention to details concerned primarily with the rancheria and its population. Further, the attitude of acute watchfulness led directly toward the acquisition of "knowledge" concerning occurrences of a regular character in nature and magnified concern over irregular happenings. This tended to reinforce the philosophy of ayelkwi, and to stimulate an all-out effort to acquire it.

A second reason why ayelkwi conferred high status is found in the defense required by the rancherias. Any food shortage on a nearby rancheria would encourage raiding and warfare from that quarter. Ayelkwi was used in both defensive and offensive warfare. Failure to mount a strong front of highly skilled pulum as the first line of defense against failure of the food supply and disaster in warfare would lead to catastrophe; but incorrect pursuit of, and fumbling attempts to use, ayelkwi were similarly perilous. These features agree well with the hypotheses of population pressure and the limiting geographical nature of the rancheria discussed earlier. Thus, it seems that the philosophy of ayelkwi tends to create at least three classes of male persons within the Luiseño community — the pulum, the rank and file, and the cuut.

There were many grades of pulum, based upon the kind of ayelkwi mastered and probably upon the forms of innate ayelkwi inherited lineally. At the present, Pachito insists that the terms pulum and pupulum are identical in meaning and usage. The latter, however, is a reduplicated form *pu(1)-pul-um, suggesting the superlative. Pupulum may have designated the permanent hereditary officials who formed the core of the war council, and who exercised the traditional formal ritualistic ayelkwi (formulated), as contrasted to upstarts (pulum) who acquired some type of residual ayelkwi. The term seems to have applied also as the name of the council.

Parallel to this conception is the term pumelum, applied to the membership of the secret war society. It is fairly certain that with the probably exception of the cuut, "transvestites" (ordinarily the Luiseño males wore no clothing at all), the entire male population of the rancheria was organized into a permanent secret war society. Boys who were not yet seven were sometimes initiated, depending upon the ayelkwi faculties demonstrated by the child, and possibly upon the desire of the parent to insure inheritance of rank and office (cf. Boscana, 1934: 16 and 31). Upon admission, the candidate became *pumel*, plural *pumelŭm*. This plural form seems to be a diminutive *pul-mel-(a)-um. In order of declining rank, the statuses thus were: Pupulum, pulum, and pumelum.

During early mission times the secret society may have been divided according to moiety, for it had at least one paired official rank, the *paha'ŭm*, disciplinarians, with duties confined exclusively to the ceremonies of the society. On this subject, Tac (1952: 16) says:

> Thus they are in the house (adjacent to the wamkish, sacred enclosure) when immediately two men go out, each one carrying two wooden swords and crying out (a footnote says in part: . . . leaving the house they cry out, meaning "make way" . . .) without saying any word, and after stopping before the place where they dance, they look at the sky for some time. The people are silent, and they turn and then the dancers go out. These men are called by us *Pajaom*, meaning crimson snakes. These do not bite but lash out at those who come near them.

All paired formal religious officials were, of course, members of the secret society, and all functioned to some degree, but probably not always in an official capacity. The society seems to have possessed a considerable number of special unpaired officials.

This pairing of paha'um mentioned by Tac (cited above) may have resulted from various problems associated with the traditional activities of the war societies, the assumption of the Chingishnish cult by them, and a large, ill-amalgamated population at the mission. To the extent that similar moiety designations may have applied throughout the region, this pairing may also signify that the inflated number of warriors were reclassified into the natural divisions for disciplinary purposes. The old intervillage warfare patterns and rivalries were thus partly controlled, and the paired paha'um could, in an orderly manner, exercise specialized powers associated with the Chingishnish cult. Supernatural sanctions could enforce proper population behavior, meeting the letter if not the spirit of the imposed Spanish peace.

Knowing something about the philosophy of ayelkwi, the disruption of Luiseño society through the uprooting of villages, and the impact of European diseases, it is clear that the combined pumelum societies must have exercised, to the full, every method of warfare that remained available to them. After all applications of native ayelkwi had failed, various forms of foreign ayelkwi were adopted and practiced in the guise of what we call the Chingishnish cult. The purposes were to rectify the disasters to the population, and very likely constituted an early nativistic movement designed to drive out the Spanish invaders themselves. Tac's comment that "after stopping before the place where they dance, they look at the sky for some time" is very provocative, especially when it is recalled that the stars are the ghosts of departed ancestors who presumably retain all their great, ancient ayelkwi powers unimpaired.

Some general characteristics of ayelkwi have been enumerated and discussed above: Ayelkwi is indestructible, immutable, is found in all things, may flow, is dangerous. Further, the requirement that ayelkwi must always be used in exact accord with its nature, and without fail should circumstances demand it, is a cornerstone of the philosophy. It has been shown that ayelkwi is responsible for the nature of all things, and since it can flow, things are not always what they seem. In addition, "living" forms or "species" are in some fashion hierarchically ordered according to the power they possess. Forms close together on the ayelkwi scale have the potentiality of acquiring the powers of adjacent forms more readily and hence with greater frequency than forms widely separated. For example, a man might more readily acquire the ability to transform himself into a bear than, say, a rabbit, for of all "species," Bear is most like man. These characteristics of ayelkwi and the hierarchical ordering of nature are implicit in the Luiseño cosmogony, although they are not explicitly stated, nor readily understood.

Common ayelkwi accounts for that similarity in behavior and culture common to the various members of any particular "species." Innate ayelkwi is responsible for inborn similarities among various members of a particular "species," but is also responsible for differences in appearance, intelligence, personality, and the like, both among individuals and lineages. Residual ayelkwi constitutes the unknowns of the environment and is potentially acquirable by an individual in any "species" whose innate ayelkwi fits him for the acquisition. All three varieties have important bearing upon status and role as well as on the larger issue of the nature of the society and culture. But it is in a study of the function of formulated ayelkwi against the background of the other three that the characteristics of Luiseño social organization become clearer.

Formulated knowledge is always the exclusive "possession" of the official upon whom proper exercise of ritual is incumbent. In this sense, formulated knowledge (ritual tradition) is similar to residual ayelkwi; it must always be employed precisely where and when required. But beyond this basic similarity the parallel begins to break down. Residual ayelkwi accrues to individuals primarily, and to the particular lineage only incidentally. It may disappear upon the death of its immediate possessor, or be transmitted to any person at all who shows the innate capacity to exercise it. Since residual ayelkwi is subject to immediate use in warfare and the food quest, and is consequently the means by which the individual may change his status, it is avidly sought. Hence, residual ayelkwi is responsible for the rapid diffusion of some traits among the Luiseño.

Formulated knowledge, on the other hand, is as rigidly prescribed as religious conservatism can make it. In the main, it constitutes the means by which relations between the living and the dead are regulated, deals with the rites of passage, and establishes social controls among the Luiseño as well as the broader society of all the ''species'' who have important bearing upon the lives of the Indians. . .

The Development
of a Washo Shaman

by Don Handelman

This paper presents the life history of the last shaman among the Washo Indians of western Nevada and eastern California. This man, Henry Rupert, presents us with a unique case of the development of a shamanic world view through time. More specifically, he offers us an opportunity to examine the shaman as an innovator and potential innovator, especially with respect to the curing techniques and personal idealogy relating him to the supernatural, the natural environment, and other men. While the anthropological literature is replete with descriptions of shamanic rituals and cultural configurations of shamanism in particular societies, as well as functional explanations purporting to explain the existence of shamanic institutions, little attention has been paid to the shaman as an innovator, although the idea was presented by Nadel (1946), exemplified by Voget (1950) in a somewhat different religious context, and briefly touched upon by Murphy (1964: 77). Henry Rupert exemplifies the shaman as a creative innovator and potential "cultural broker," and his life history will be presented as an essentially chronological sequence of events, situations, and ideas.

In the period before White contact, the Washo occupied territory between Lake Tahoe, on the border of present-day California and Nevada, and the Pine Nut Mountains east of Reno and Carson City; in the north their territory extended to Honey Lake, and in the south to Antelope Valley (Merriam and d'Azevedo 1957; Downs 1963: 117). In terms of social organization, the Washo were composed of three bands, although the family, sometimes nuclear and sometimes extended, was the primary unit of social organization; and the family unit decided the yearly round of

hunting and gathering activities, sometimes under the leadership
of antelope shamans and rabbit "bosses." A high prevalence of
witches and sorcerers has also been reported among the aboriginal
Washo (Leis 1963; Siskin 1941) in much the same configuration as
has been reported for the neighboring Northern Paiute (Park 1939;
Whiting 1950), with all shamans suspect as potential sorcerers.
With increasing White occupation of their territory during the late
nineteenth century, their seasonal round was disrupted, and the
Washo settled around White habitations and ranches, working as
seasonal laborers, ranch hands, lumberjacks, and domestic
servants. It was into this disrupted cultural milieu, and
disorganized social situation, that Henry Rupert was born.

THE BECOMING AND BEING OF A SHAMAN

Henry Rupert was born in 1885, the son of Pete Duncan
and Susie John, both Washo, in Genoa, Nevada. Genoa was an area
of lush farm and ranch land amidst the arid Nevada semi-desert
which had been first settled by Mormon emigrants from Utah. In
the shadows of Job's Peak, a 9,000-foot mountain in the Sierra
Nevada range, the Mormons had farmed the desert and
transformed it into the rich grassland it still is today. When Henry
Rupert was still very young, about two to three years old, his father
deserted the family. Henry did not meet his father again until he
was twenty years old and his father, a complete stranger, was
working as a handyman in a Chinese restaurant in Carson City. By
this time Pete Duncan had remarried; and father and son remained
strangers until Pete Duncan died.

Henry's mother, Susie John, worked as a domestic servant for
a ranch in Genoa. Most of her time was taken up with her domestic
chores, and Annie Rube, Henry's older sister, organized and
managed the family household and acted as a family disciplinarian.
Her husband, Charley Rube, worked as a ranch hand and
fisherman, but he was also an antelope shaman, a man who in
aboriginal times was entrusted with the task of "singing" antelope
to sleep during the annual Washo antelope drives. Near the
encampment of Henry Rupert's family lived Henry's mother's
sister's husband, Welewkushkush, and his wife. Until the age of
eight, when he was taken to school, Henry divided most of his time

between Genoa during the winter and the shores of Lake Tahoe during the summer, usually in the company of either Charley Rube or Welewkushkush.

During his early years, Henry had a series of dreams which he still remembers with clarity, and which probably marked him early as having shamanic and mystic potential. As he describes the situation, he would go to sleep on the ground inside the family lean-to and dream of a bear who came and stood in the lean-to opening and stared at him. When he looked at the bear, it would vanish, and then Henry would fly up into the sky toward the moon. This dream recurred frequently over a fairly long period. As a youngster, Henry was also subject to spells of dizziness and fainting. These spells also occurred at bedtime, and both the lean-to and ground would whirl around in a circular motion. Henry would then tell his family to go outside the lean-to and build large fires to stop the ground from whirling about. However, no one paid any attention to his demands, and after awhile he would recover.[1]

Welewkushkush, a well known shaman among the Washo, was already between 60 and 70 years old when Henry was born, and on a number of occasions Henry was able to watch him healing. During one of these curing sessions, Henry observed Welewkushkush dance in a lean-to fire barefoot and emerge unscathed. Not surprisingly, the youngster respected his uncle greatly both for his curing feats and for his generous kindly attitude and demeanor toward his patients, relatives, and acquaintances. Henry maintains that he harbored similar feelings of respect toward his brother-in-law, Charley Rube, and that the same general attitudes prevailed in his family relationships. He was never severely disciplined at any time, and only his sister, Annie Rube, scolded him. Nevertheless, even within this milieu, Henry exhibited strong feelings of hostility and aggression, as well as independence, as exemplified by the following incident, quoted verbatim:

> Someone, I don't remember who, gave me a little puppy. I liked it very much. One evening that puppy made lots of noise, and he stealed some of the food we were going to

---

1. In this account there is an interesting conjunction of elements of bear, flying, and fire, which Eliade (1964) maintains are basic to the shamanistic complex, especially in North America.

have for supper. My elder sister gave me hell about it. She said: "You don't need that puppy in here; it's no good; get rid of it." I made up my mind to kill that puppy. I took it to a fence made out of rocks and I threw a big rock on top of the puppy and killed it. My mind was made up. When I make up my mind, I don't change it. The next evening they asked me where the puppy was. I told them I killed it, because they told me it had been no good.

During these early years Henry had few friends. He spent much time by himself wandering over desert and mountain for days at a time, living off the land when he could, and going hungry when he could not. Given the laissez-faire attitude within his family, he had to report to no one, nor did he even have to be home at regular intervals. While not self-sufficient, he was able and independent. On one occasion, he "hopped" a frieght train to Sacramento to see what lay on the other side of the Sierra Nevada Mountains. He also exhibited a boundless curiosity about the natural world around him, a world filled with strange forces and beings, and their existence was often manifested to him. He still remembers sleeping in an abandoned campsite one night and seeing a strange object which resembled a cloud pass close by his body while he was awake, and wondering what it represented. On another occasion, while walking down a deserted path at dusk he saw a white object ahead of him. As he walked forward, it moved. When he stopped, the object also halted. He began to sweat heavily and was extremely frightened. Finally he gathered his courage, walked up to the object, and found an old nightshirt flapping in the evening breeze. Yet he wondered that the object flapped only when he walked forward, and stopped when he desisted. Such incidents were not simple coincidences; they suggested an importance and significance that he was not yet able to unravel.

In 1892, at the age of seven, Henry received the first conscious intimation of what his future powers might be. A relative of his mother died; his mother was deep in mourning and quite despondent. Henry dreamt of the event which would follow, and the event came to pass during that winter. His mother went from the family encampment to a slue on the frozen Carson River, and there she attempted suicide by trying to break through the ice and drown herself. But the ice was too thick, and her attempt failed. This was the first time that Henry began to feel that he too might be gifted in the manner of his beloved uncle, Welewkushkush.

Without becoming unduly analytic at this point, it is pertinent to indicate that during these first eight years of Henry Rupert's life many of the elements which resulted in his becoming a shaman were present. During these early years Henry was a Washo, but a Washo who camped on the fringes of the dominant White society upon whom his mother depended for her livelihood. He spoke no English, only Washo; his mother worked as a menial, a domestic servant; and his father had forever deserted the family encampment. There is little doubt that these factors engendered much hostility in Henry. Yet, because of the great degree of freedom allowed him, much of this hostility was dissipated in his extensive and lengthy wanderings, which at times almost take on the attributes of a rudimentary vision quest. As a child of a culturally disrupted and socially disorganized Indian group, he differed little from many other Indian children in the area, but even at this early age his dreams, visions, and fantasy world were beginning to coalesce around the conception that he might have unusual abilities. Also, he had no peers with whom to identify. His models of socialization and learning were much older and more important; they included a shaman and an antelope shaman, both very well versed in Washo lore and tradition. Both of these men, and in fact his whole family, presented him with models of behavior based on kindness and sympathy, and to a lesser extent understanding. The aforementioned incident involving the puppy was apparently the one occasion that Henry's hostility was expressed within the family milieu, and even here it was met with sympathy. Up to the present time, Henry Rupert exhibits strong loyalties and deep affection toward his immediate family, their children, and grandchildren.

In the phase of his life just described, Henry had models of behavior, models of affect, that he admired and respected, and on the whole this outweighed his aggressive and hostile sentiments. But even more important in the long run were the personal qualities that he exhibited at an early age — his curiosity, independence, and perseverance which overcame his strongest fears. We shall find these themes recurring again and again throughout his life.

Some ten miles north of Genoa and two miles south of Carson City is the Stewart Indian School. Today it is a boarding school primarily for Indian children from the Southwest, but in 1893 it was a center for the "forced acculturation" of Indian children from the Great Basin under the supervision and control of the United States Army. As part of its pacification program in the area, the Army required all Indian children to attend and board at Stewart until they had completed the equivalent of an eighth grade education. Children held back by their parents were forcibly removed from their families by the cavalry. At the age of eight, Henry Rupert was taken from Genoa to Stewart, where he lived until the age of eighteen. It was here that he received the "power dream" which marked him as a potential shaman; here, too, he met his future wife, and here he began to formulate the basis of his philosophy of healing and his rationale for becoming a shaman, both of which were to be greatly expanded in later life.

At Stewart Henry experienced an environment vastly different from that of his years of freedom and independence. Stewart was highly regimented and often brutal. This was Henry Rupert's first sustained contact with White society. Discipline was harsh, and every effort was made at forced acculturation. Order was maintained with a rawhide whip and detention cells. Children were not allowed to return home for short respites until they had completed three full years at Stewart. Classes were held in the mornings and in the evenings. In the afternoons the children were taught a trade. If a child was late for meals, he did not eat. Here also, Henry was introduced to White religion through a profusion of Catholic, Baptist, Methodist, and Anglican proselytizers. All the children were forcibly baptized. Every morning, before breakfast, the children attended services. At breakfast, prayers were sung in Latin. On Sundays the children went to church in the morning, and in the evening they attended Bible classes and sang hymns. Some proselytizers even came on Saturdays and preached all afternoon.

The day after Henry arrived he ran away, but he was quickly returned. All told he ran away three times. The second time he was severely whipped on his bare back. However, Henry did well in school, and learned to set newspaper type. He found a friend in the school cook, who often gave him extra food to supplement the bare school rations. He also developed his own techniques for maintaining some symbolic degree of independence. On one occasion he accidentally broke a spoon and in consequence was forbidden to eat with a spoon for the next month; he then stole a spoon and used it. He resisted the blandishments of his schoolmates with regard to alcohol. The temptation was probably great, since his schoolmates went so far as to place a bottle of liquor under his pillow. At Stewart Henry made his first close friend, Frank Rivers, another Washo; only to Frank did Henry confide his potential powers. It was also at Stewart that Henry first came to know intimately Indians from other tribes in the Great Basin — Northern Paiute and Shoshone — and his first girl friend was a Paiute. One of Henry's strongest assets was his ability to absorb selectively those aspects of White culture which he felt were beneficial to him; thus he was able to master academic subjects, notably reading and writing, and learn an occupation, while resisting Christianity, regimentation, and alcohol.

In 1902, at the age of seventeen, Henry experienced his power dream, the event which marked him with certainty as shamanic material and which conferred certain abilities upon him. He described it to me as follows:

> I was sleeping in the school dormitory. I had a dream. I saw a buck in the west. It was a horned buck. It looked east. A voice said to me: ''Don't kill my babies any more.''
> I woke up, and it was raining outside, and I had a nosebleed in bed.

Henry interpreted the dream in the following way. The conjunction of buck and rain suggested that he could control the weather, since the buck was the ''boss of the rain.'' The buck was standing in the west, but looking east. The Washo believed that the souls of the recently dead travel south but that, soon after, the souls of those who have been evil turn east. The buck looking east was interpreted as a warning against developing certain potentialities which could become evil. The voice in the dream was that of a snake warning against the indiscriminate taking of life; previously Henry had killed wildlife, insects, and snakes without much concern. The rain, as he awakened, indicated that his major spirit power would be water. Awakening with a nosebleed placed the stamp of legitimacy upon the whole experience, since the Washo believed that this kind of physical reaction is necessary if the dream is to confer power. The fact that his spirit power was to be water was unusual, since most Washo shamans had animate rather than inanimate objects as their spirit helpers. Thus, while water baby was a fairly common spirit helper, water was not. In addition, weather control was highly unusual among the Washo, being more prevalent among both the Northern Paiute and the Shoshone.

The dream stressed certain potentials, specifically a Washo calling, that of shaman. It also confirmed the validity of Henry's early behavioral models, Welewkushkush and Charley Rube, and their philosophy of living in harmony with the natural world. In so doing, it de-emphasized those aspects of White society and culture which contradicted Washo values and behavioral expectations, but it did not forbid Henry the continuation of his quest for knowledge in the White world. Rather, it suggested that he pick and choose his way in relation to earlier models, thus serving as both a warning and a promise of greatness. That it was a power dream was congruent with Henry's aspirations and expectations concerning himself and his future.

At this transition point in Henry's life, shortly before he left the Stewart School, the dream served as a guidepost which integrated both his childhood years and his years at the school. His indecisions regarding the future were resolved, and his aspirations of becoming a shaman were crystallized. But his idealogy of healing remained inchoate, for he had not yet acquired the requisite shamanic techniques. He felt the need to help his people when they were ill, but he knew not how. Nevertheless, he was aware and insightful, and in learning through what he called the "law of nature" he set the stage for years of thought and introspection, aware also that discoveries came slowly: "One little thing may come every eight or ten years; you can't grab it in one bunch."

When Henry graduated from Stewart, he took a job as a typesetter with the Reno Evening Gazette, and he lived in Reno for most of the next ten years. During this period he mastered hypnotic techniques and began curing. But the most immediate power conferred on him by his power dream was control of the weather, and in 1906 he exercised this power for the first time. During that summer, Henry went to visit his family in Genoa. While there, he used to hang his pocket watch over his bed. One evening, before retiring, he had a vision in which snow slowly, but completely, covered the face of the watch. That winter the snowfall was very heavy and too deep to enable him to cut firewood. One day, Henry concentrated on removing the snow. That night and all the next day it rained, resulting in fairly widespread flooding. Although he had told no one of what he had done, his older sister, Annie Rube, accused him of causing the floods.[2]

In the winter of 1908 he once again called down the rain, but in doing so he lost this power forever. The winter was again difficult, and one day he constructed a medicine bundle and dropped it into the Truckee River, which flows through Reno. That evening the weather turned warm and it rained. However, in tying his medicine bundle, Henry used the buckskin from his shamanic rattle and replaced the buckskin on the rattle with a length of thread. This offended the spirit of the buck, the "boss of the rain," and Henry was never again able to control the weather.

During this time, Henry attended an exhibition of hypnotism at the Grand Theater in Reno. He was greatly impressed and did think the performance had been rehearsed. He told his friend, Frank Rivers, that he too could master the requisite techniques, and he ordered from Chicago a book entitled "The Art of Attention and the Science of Suggestion." In the evenings, and on Sundays, Henry would go into the sandy hills surrounding Reno and there practice his techniques on the stumps and rocks "as if they were human beings; I imagined they were alive; if somebody caught me at that they would put me in the crazy house." He mastered hypnotic techniques and held regular monthly sessions in the Reno Press Club, where he hypnotized people to the amusement and enjoyment of the assembled reporters. Interestingly, he felt no contradiction between acquiring power in a dream visitation and acquiring it from a book.

In 1907, Welewkushkush suggested that Henry hire another shaman to help him train and control his powers. The Washo believed that when the power, or spirit helper, first comes to a shaman he becomes ill, and that the novice shaman then hires an older experienced shaman to teach him how to extrude and control the intrusive spirit-power. Although Henry had experienced only a nosebleed in 1902 and did not consider this as a "sickness," he followed his uncle's advice and hired the well-known Washo shaman Beleliwe, also known as Monkey Peter. The experienced

---

2. This may be indirect evidence that his family expected Henry to gain power and were quite ready to attribute the cause of unusual events to him.

shaman could also help the novice to renounce his power, if such
was the latter's desire.[3] I do not know what the customary period of
time was between the power dream and the hiring of another
shaman to control the power, but in Henry's case some five years
elapsed.

Beleliwe, instead of giving Henry specific advice, told him
what he could accomplish with his power. He spoke of the two old
women who had first brought the power of healing to the Washo,
and he warned that the power of blood is evil. He also described
some of the feats which shamans could accomplish, citing the cases
of an old woman who had walked up the perpendicular side of a
cliff, of Welewkushkush who had walked under the waters of Lake
Tahoe without drowning, and of Southern Washo who danced in
campfires. Then he told Henry: "All kinds of sickness will look
pretty tough, but it will melt; it seems like you can't do anything
with it, but it will melt." However, the actual content of the
shamanic ritual had to be learned by observing other shamans at
work. Significantly, Henry's attitudes toward Beleliwe were very
similar to his attitudes toward Welewkushkush — respect and
admiration for both their personal attributes and their work. He told
me, "Beleliwe was a great man; he knew more than the rest put
together." While Henry's feelings toward Welewkushkush
changed somewhat during the next few years, Beleliwe's stature
continued to grow. And when Lowie visited the Washo in 1926,
Henry not only wished him to meet Beleliwe, but referred to him as
a philosopher (Lowie 1939: 321).[4]

---

3. According to Welewkushkush, the recipient of a power dream who
wished to reject the power covered himself with ashes, prayed to the intrusive
spirit to leave him, and then washed the ashes off with clear water. This ritual
was repeated daily over a four-month period under the direction of an
experienced shaman. It should be noted that Henry did not become ill after his
power dream and that he waited five years before hiring Beleliwe at the
suggestion of Welewkushkush. This may suggest that Henry performed the
Washo ritual mainly to appease his family and not because he believed it to be
necessary.

4. Beleliwe died as a result of curing a tubercular patient in Carson City.
He was able to take the tuberculosis "germ" out of the patient's body and into
his own, but the germ lodged in the back of his neck, affecting his speech and
bodily movements, and finally killing him. I do not know how Welewkushkush
died, but he told Henry that he could cure anything but the common cold and
that it would be the common cold which would finally kill him.

Henry performed his first successful cure in 1907. A brother of
Frank Rivers had died of alcohol poisoning. His mother was deeply
grieved and became very depressed. A White doctor was called in
but was unable to calm the woman. A few days later Henry, as he
was passing by, heard the old woman crying. He went in, washed
her face, and prayed for her. She recovered. It is significant that
this first cure was performed on the mother of his best friend —
within a milieu where his confidence would be bolstered. It is also
significant that Henry's family, with the exception of Welewkushkush, knew nothing of his shamanic power or his achievements with
weather control until after this first cure. His reticence is an
example of the self-doubt that always plagued him — doubt in his
abilities and fear that he would not find the answers his curiosity
demanded — but which drove him to greater efforts.

In his first cure, Henry used techniques generally similar to
those utilized by other Washo shamans. Traditional Washo curing
rituals required a shaman to work for three consecutive nights from
dusk to midnight, and a fourth night until dawn. In the course of the
ritual, repeated every night, Henry used tobacco, water, a rattle, a
whistle, and eagle feathers. He began by smoking, praying,
washing the patient's face with cold water, and sprinkling all his
paraphernalia with cold water. He then blew smoke on the patient
and prayed to come in contact with water. A peace offering
followed, in which he paid for the health of the patient by scattering
grey and yellow seeds mixed with pieces of abalone shell around
the body of the patient and into his own body, whence it might be
repulsed and captured by the whistle. Then he sat down again and
blew a fine spray of cold water over the body of the patient. This
ended the first half of the curing ritual, which was repeated each
night.

At some time during the course of the ritual, Henry would
receive visions relating both to the cause of the illness and the
prognosis. They usually involved either the presence or absence of
water. Thus a vision of damp ground suggested that the patient was
ill but would live a short while; muddy water suggested that the
patient would live but would not recover completely; ice suggested
that Henry must break through the ice and find water; burning
sagebrush suggested that the patient would die quickly unless
Henry could stamp out the fire. Over the four-night period the
content of these visions, or occasionally dreams, tended to change.

Thus, Henry might see a fire or a burned-over hillside on the first
night, damp ground on the second, muddy water on the third, and
on the fourth night a stream of clear, cold water or the Pacific Ocean
rolling over the Sierra Nevada. The portent of the vision of the
fourth night overrode those of the visions seen on the previous
nights.

During 1907-08, Henry Rupert acquired his second spirit
helper, a young Hindu male. He used, at infrequent intervals, to
visit a high school in Carson City which contained the skeleton of a
Hindu, and on one of these visits the spirit of the Hindu "got on"
Henry. Since the Hindu was a "White power," this precipitated a
major conflict in Henry's fantasy world and in the most important
area of his life, his healing. As a spirit helper, the Hindu demanded
to be used in curing sessions. Henry's problem was how to
reconcile the opposing demands of his Indian and Hindu spirit
helpers. The confrontation and its resolution came in a dream:

> I saw this in a dream. The Hindu's work says: "You will
> do great things if you make us the leader in this kind of
> work." The two Indian women say no: "We started this
> with Henry Rupert; we were the first. He (the Hindu) has
> no right here; this work belongs to us." I didn't know what
> to make of it. I pondered on it for a long time. Finally I
> decided, and I told them what I decided: "We all do the
> same work; let's help each other and be partners." And
> that is the way it works today; nobody is the leader. The
> Hindu wanted to be the leader in this kind of work. The
> two women said no. I fixed it.

This dream dramatically illustrates the basic conflict between
opposing themes in Henry Rupert's life: his desire to expand his
potentials for learning and healing by utilizing non-Indian
resources and his desire to follow the childhood models he loved
and respected. His resolution of this conflict was highly
sophisticated; he utilized a more complex level of conceptualization
and synthesis in which both opposing themes were subsumed
under a common rubric, that of healing, which applied to both
categories of spirit helpers. This rubric was neither Washo nor
"White" but constituted an ethic which cross-cut different ethnic
and racial categories. I prefer the term "ethic" to "principle"

because the synthesis had definite moral connotations of aiding and succouring others, and because to Henry the fact that he had become a healer was more important than either his being born a Washo or his forays into non-Indian knowledge. It was the Hindu who first gave Henry his insights into the components of the "law of nature" and offered him the code of living which he has since followed: to be honest, discreet, and faithful; to be kind and do no harm. These conceptions often ran counter to the behavior of traditional Washo shamans, but they were consistent with the models of Welewkushkush, Charley Rube, and Beleliwe. The ethic of healing which Henry developed was an integrated and complete synthesis; he was never troubled again by this kind of acculturative conflict.

After Henry acquired the Hindu spirit helper a number of changes occurred in his curing techniques — the first of his innovations of which I am aware. Before beginning a cure, he would now place a handkerchief on his head to represent the Hindu's turban, and when he blew water on the patient he prayed to the Hindu to come and rid the patient of his illness. He also began to place his hands on the patient's head, chest, and legs in a symbolic attempt to encompass the whole being of the patient with his power. He also began to envision himself differently while curing; while sitting by the side of the patient he saw himself as a skeleton with a turban on its head moving quickly around the body of the patient.

Henry did not perform his second cure until 1909, two years later. It was this cure which established him as a legitimate shaman among the Washo. The patient was a Washo whose family was camping on the Carson River near Minden, Nevada. This man had been treated by both shamans and White doctors without success, although the doctors had diagnosed his case as typhoid fever. Henry, although as a novice shaman he had been consulted as a last resort, was successful in curing the patient.

In 1910, when Henry was working as a gardner and general handyman for a banker in Reno, he suffered from rheumatism and from broken ribs which had never healed properly. He went to his uncle, Welewkushkush, to be cured, but the latter merely presented him with a warning:

He didn't work on me long. He just blew smoke on me,

and we talked. He said: "The thing that is causing it is
right here in your head, and you will forget all about your
stiff joint; you don't have rheumatism. You might be very
sick and your mind will go into the White people's world,
and I can't go there and bring you back." He blew smoke
on my forehead; that thing traveled in the smoke out of
me, and I got well. The thing he drew out was a piece of
printed matter. I didn't see it; he wouldn't show it to me.
It was what I had in my head from studying books. He took
out the Hindu's works. The printed matter belonged to the
White people's world.

Welewkushkush suggested that Henry would receive no aid if he
pursued his interest in the knowledge of White society and implied
that he would become ill if he continued; the two worlds, Indian and
non-Indian, must remain separate in terms of both intellect and
affect. But the ethic of curing which Henry had synthesized from
Indian and non-Indian elements prevailed over Welewkushkush's
thinly veiled warning. His independence established Henry as a
mature adult prepared to continue to develop his own philosophy of
living and ultimately to restructure Washo cosmogony.

In October, 1910, Henry married Lizzie, a Northern Paiute
woman whom he had first met at the Stewart Indian School. Her
father, Buckeroo John, a ranch hand and maker of rawhide lariats,
had been a devotee of Jack Wilson, the apostle of the 1890 Ghost
Dance. Buckeroo John did not approve of Henry as a prospective
bridegroom, nor did he think highly of Henry's curing abilities. It
was, neverless, significant that Henry should take a Paiute wife at a
time when intermarriage was infrequent and generally viewed with
disfavor, especially by shamans and other conservative Washo. The
union produced four children, three of whom today live with their
offspring in the same community as Henry. After his marriage,
Henry returned to work with the Reno Evening Gazette, melting
linotypes. But he soon came to suspect that the lead fumes were
poisoning him, and he returned with his family to Genoa, where he
worked as a ranch hand until 1924. During this period he continued
his healing, becoming increasingly well known.

In 1924, with all their children away at school in Stewart, by
now operated by the Bureau of Indian Affairs, Henry and Lizzie
decided to leave Genoa. Rather than choosing Dresslerville, the

major Washo community of that time, Henry decided on Carson Colony, 40 acres of land bought for the Washo in 1916 but unoccupied except for a few transient Northern Paiute and Shoshone families. In making this move, Henry isolated himself physically — and later also socially, when Lizzie died of tuberculosis in 1933 despite Henry's attempts to cure her. He became more of a recluse with greater opportunity to meditate the problems of healing. "Rupert, the sophisticated young Washo . . . was a mystic credited with shamanistic ambitions," says Lowie (1939: 321) of him at this time.

Henry also worked hard, planting and raising an acre of strawberries as well as a flock of turkeys. In the Depression years he earned as much as $100 a week during the summer months, and his flock of turkeys was later sold for $5,000. He also spent many evenings digging a large irrigation pond, which he later filled with goldfish.

But these were essentially years of thought, introspection, and self-examination. As a child, and later as a novice shaman, Henry had learned the tenets of traditional Washo religion. This included a conception of a spirit world populated by the departed souls of all animate beings which had populated the natural world. The spirit world resembled the natural world; it had the same people and a comparable round of activities. The age of a person in the spirit world was that at which he had died. The spirits of evil persons were segregated in one section of the spirit world, but they underwent no particular punishments because of their earthly transgressions. The spirits or ghosts of animate beings were feared as potential causes of illness because of their ability to intrude into the bodies of the living or to project inanimate disease-producing objects into them. When an individual died, consequently, his dwelling and possessions were burnt so that his ghost would be unable to retrace his path to the natural world.

The Washo had no coherent religious philosophy or theology, but they did have a number of creation myths and creator figures. Among the latter were the two old women who fought the Hindu in Henry's dream. However, these creator figures played but little part in the placation of the supernatural. In this respect the Washo dealt with the ghosts of animate beings, and these had the same motivations as living Washo, including revenge for present or past misdeeds and curiosity which brought them back to the world of the living. Hence, for example, parents avoided striking or spanking a child for fear of angering a dead relative, whose ghost might kill the child to punish the parents (Downs 1966: 60).

In the process of evolving a general ethic of healing, Henry Rupert reformulated some of the traditional conceptions of Washo cosmology. According to his new formulation, the substance and composition of the spirit world is very similar to electric waves or pulses of energy. These are everlasting and everpresent, and all objects in the natural world are also partially composed of them. To Henry, therefore, spirit and mind are the same, both being composed of what he called "ethereal waves." When an individual dreams, his "mind-power" travels to the spirit world, remaining connected to his material body by a thin lifeline of energy. If this thin thread of energy breaks, the individual's "mind-power" is unable to return to its material shell, and death results. According to Henry, when a person dies his departing spirit or "ego" remains temporarily encased in a weak body shell, the "astral body," but within one month the "astral body" falls away and the "pure" ego or spirit returns to the spirit world.

The spirit world itself has three planes — the first a "coarse" level, the second a finer level, and the third was the finest or purest level. Normally, when a person dreams, his spirit or mind-power travels to the first level. Passage into the second level, either in dreams or death, is impossible unless the individual has been pure in mind and heart and has followed "the law of nature." The third level is the domain of "God," "creator," and "omnipotent life." All spiritual life from the highest to the lowest is a manifestation of some kind of energy which has its ultimate source in the third level of the spirit world. This energy is an essence found in all animate life and inanimate objects in the natural world and may, in Henry's terms, be called "soul," "ego," "spirit," or "mind-power." The same energy is also the essence of all spirits, in which it coalesces into certain forms found in the natural world, thereby forming a connecting link between the natural and spirit worlds. While there is no actual separation of good and evil spirits in the hereafter, only those spirits which are "purer" in essence can reach the second level. No spirits, however, can reach the third level, the ultimate energy source.

We thus find, in conjunction with Henry's general ethic of healing, a general conception of "power" or "energy" which is the basis of healing. Henry makes no distinction between the miracles performed by the Old Testament prophets, those performed by Christ and his disciples, the healing powers of shamans, and his own work, since the basis of the power is in every case the same, though manifested at different times and in different social situations. All these people learned to tap the same source of energy and to channel it for purposes of curing and miracle-working. This power or energy is not, however, ethically neutral. It is positive and "good," and this accounts for Henry's disavowal of witchcraft and sorcery, which will be described later. Henry is aware that his conceptions are an act of faith. As he stated to me: "In my line of work I see it that way. Nobody told me this. Nobody can prove it. That is what I believe . . . the power is everpresent; it never wears out."

Because Henry's ethic of curing was based on contact with the supernatural or paranatural, it was necessary for him to develop some conception of a general source of power for curing. His personal restructuring of the spirit world did not rest on a dichotomy of good and evil but rather on a conception of differing degrees of "good." In his idealogy, no person or spirit could be completely evil, thus precluding belief in active malevolent supernatural agencies. It was no longer conceivable that ghosts, for example, could cause illness by intruding their spirit essence into humans. All mindpower derived from the same source, and both the source and the power it represented were beneficent and could not be utilized for malevolent designs. Consequently, traditional Washo beliefs in malevolent ghosts, witchcraft, and sorcery no longer had a place in Henry's world view. However, while human ghosts could not cause illness, the spirits of animal life and inanimate objects could and did.

How did Henry explain this possible contradiction? Everything, animate and inanimate, has been formed of life, "ego," or "soul." All living things require water as a minimal basis for existence. So, for example, when feathers are not sprinkled with water at regular intervals, they take water from the person owning them, "drying" him out and making him ill. Henry did not consider this a malevolent action, but he held that a person who transgressed, consciously or through ignorance, was accountable, since if the feathers were given water, the patient would recover. In one case I recorded, that of an old man who could neither speak nor eat, Henry had the following diagnostic vision on the fourth night of the curing session. He was sitting at the eastern end of a valley hiding from a whirlwind. Seeing it coming straight toward him, he was frightened and hid in the willows. The whirlwind stopped in front of him, and a magpie flew out and lit on a nearby willow. After he emerged from the trance state, Henry was told by relatives that the patient had at one time made feather headdresses and that he still kept a trunk of them in a deserted cabin. Henry said to me:

> The trunk of feathers made him sick. I prayed to the feathers and the birds not to be angry; he thought he was doing right, but he didn't give them water. I said: "I will give you water; don't dry this fellow up." Next day he spoke and was okay.

Although the Washo attributed rattlesnake power, the power to sorcerize, to Welewkushkush, Henry maintained that Welewkushkush had been taught to handle rattlesnakes without personal harm, and that the Washo feared and mistrusted phenomena which they did not understand. In another case, an old female shaman was accused of killing both a Washo political figure and a promising young shaman because she coveted their positions of leadership. According to Henry, however, she was a fine old woman who understood "the law of nature" and lived under it, and she could not be evil since her power was derived from a beneficent source. "They said she was a witch, but it was just coincidence. They blamed her for heart failure when she passed by. They couldn't prove it."

As Henry's fame as a healer spread he began to receive patients from a wide variety of ethnic groups. Though not common, it was not unknown for Washo shamans to treat Northern Paiute and Shoshone patients, but Henry treated these and Hawaiian, Filipino, Mexican, and White patients as well. In this trans-cultural healing he was successful, doubtless because his ethic of healing gave him increased confidence in dealing with non-Indians. His status as a healer grew continuously, and he became known and respected as a successful shaman from the Shoshone Yomba reservation in central Nevada to Mexican enclaves in Sacramento. His increasing renown attracted non-Indian patients who had exhausted other alternatives. A number of cases will illustrate the diversity of his clientele.

In curing a Protestant minister, who came to him with severe headaches, Henry received the following diagnostic vision. He saw a large auditorium in which were seated on one side a group of Whites and the minister, and on the other a group of Indians representing various tribes. Between the two was a large stage on which dressed steers were falling, forming a large pile of meat ready to eat. Everyone in the auditorium ate of the meat, except for the minister. Henry told the latter that he would lose his headaches, but that he had made one mistake. The minister had been in the habit of serving tea and cakes after his sermons, but while his congregation ate, he did not. This, said Henry, was the cause of his headaches, and the minister admitted the correctness of the assessment. The vision was a sophisticated reflection of the interrelationship between Henry's ethic of curing and his restructured cosmology. As he explained to the minister, the latter's absention, in a congregation of both Whites and Indians who broke bread together, was inconsistent with both Henry's ethic of curing and the minister's status as a servant of God.

In 1942, Henry journeyed to Sacramento to treat an old Mexican woman who had been diagnosed as having a malignant tumor of the abdomen. On the first night, Henry was unable to find water. On the second night he saw a burned-over hillside of which a section had remained untouched. On the third night he saw a small lake between two hills, and on the fourth, a stream of running water. On the morning of the fifth day the lump had disappeared from the woman's abdomen, and she later recovered completely.

A number of other cases dealt with psychosomatic disorders. In one of these, a Shoshone boy from Austin, in central Nevada, was brought to Carson Colony to be treated by Henry. The boy had auditory hallucinations in which he heard three men, who were following him, constantly threatening to kill him. The cause of the illness was discovered to be a tooth of a spirit which had projected into the boy's head. At the end of the curing session the boy no longer heard voices. In another case, an ex-soldier who had fought in World War II was brought to Henry with severe lacerations around his neck. This man had visual hallucinations in which two German soldiers were attempting to strangle him with barbed wire, so that he tore continuously at his neck in the attempt to remove the wire. Henry treated him successfully. In the case of a White storekeeper from Fallon, Nevada, with an apparent history of heart trouble, Henry found a butterfly in the man's chest and removed it. This man states to this day that he will not be treated by any other doctor than Henry.[5]

In 1942, at the age of 57, when Henry Rupert was working as a general handyman and night watchman at the Stewart Indian Agency, he decided to retire to Carson Colony and devote full time to healing. He was acutely aware that "reality" in healing and living is a matter of relative perception, psychological set, and social situation. The Hindu spirit helper had told him: "What appertaineth unto one, another knoweth not." And on one occasion he stated to me: "You don't know what I am talking about, and the same is true for anybody who reads this thing you write. What is real for me is not real for you." As an example, he cited an occasion when he was walking across a bridge over the Truckee River in Reno. He saw a woman who wailed to him that her son had fallen into the river and pleaded with him to save the boy. Henry was about to plunge into the water when the woman's daughter appeared and told him that her mother had periodic hallucinations and there was no one in the water. Henry concluded: "It was real for that woman; she thought her son was in the water; but it isn't real for me. What I know is real for me, but it isn't real for anybody else."

We must remember, in considering the phenomenological basis of Henry's conception of "reality," that he was an adept hypnotist cognizant of the importance of gaining and holding a paient's attention during a curing session by the use of such instruments as a rattle and eagle feathers. "I use them" he told me, "only to gain the attention of the sick person, nothing more," When Henry was treating a sick old Washo woman in Woodfords,

---

5. An interesting conclusion emerges from these and other cases. It seems possible that in a situation of culture change the doctor-patient relationship depends more on the faith inherent in the relationship than it does on common cultural background, cultural context, or cultural symbolism. In none of these cases did the patient know what Henry was doing; they accepted his efficaciousness as a matter of faith. It also seems likely that such doctor-patient relationships would not have been countenanced in traditional Washo society, where patients and their relatives were generally familiar at least with the techniques used, the paraphernalia required of a shaman, and the length of time required for a cure.

California, his Hindu spirit helper told him that her illness was being caused by the spirit of a dead mole which the woman kept as a gambling charm; the mole spirit wanted repayment for having been killed. The Hindu came to an agreement with the mole spirit: the woman would have to lose the sight of one eye, but she would live. Henry described what followed:

> As I prayed, I looked to the mountains. One of my eyes started to get dim. It started to close. I couldn't see out of it. At the same time, one of her eyes started to close and started to dim, and that's the way she left. She could only see out of one eye for the rest of her life, but she lived a long time . . . Funny things happen in my line of work, but it's true.

"Suggestions" made by the shaman in the context of the curing session are clearly an important factor in the efficacy of certain cures. A case in point was that of a young Washo who was brought to Henry. He had been unable to walk for a week and believed that he was stricken with polio. Henry worked on him for a few hours and then, during a rest period, told the young man that he did not have polio. He cited a personal experience of his own as an example. When he was working in Reno he had attended a medicine show, where he was examined and told that he had "heart trouble due to indigestion." Henry bought a bottle of medicine and drank some of it, after which his heart began to beat quickly and his breathing became irregular, but he then threw the bottle away and felt normal. After this illustration he again told his patient that he did not have polio, that his muscles were simply overworked, and that he should forget the matter. A week later the patient returned, saying that he had followed Henry's advice and felt fine.

In the course of his meditations and his dialogues with the spirit world, Henry also consciously restructured traditional Washo conceptions about the acquisition of shamanic power. The traditional Washo belief system required that an individual receive shamanic power involuntarily, through a dream or vision, after which he had the choice of either accepting or rejecting the power. While shamanic power tended to run in particular families, where children were socialized in an environment charged with the importance of dreams and the supernatural interpretations of events, shamanic power was never conciously transmitted from one person to another. Only after receiving power did a novice shaman hire an experienced practitioner to help him master and control it.

To Henry, however, living by "the law of nature" meant being closely attuned to the forces that created and controlled all beings and things of the world. Since power derived from a common pool of "energy," anyone who could tap this pool could use the resultant power for purposes of healing. In order to accomplish this, however, an individual had to possess certain personal qualities; he had to be honest, faithful, and discreet and live a pure life. It is significant that Henry first learned this possibility of the transmission of power from the Hindu, a non-Washo and non-Indian spirit helper. According to Henry:

> Anybody could learn it, but you have to come under these three things, and be like a recluse, and follow the law of nature. You can't be happy-go-lucky. If you live by nature, you can understand a little of nature and help nature do her work. I had to live just so to get what I was looking for. You can't get it by being foolish. I got it just by thinking. It took me over sixty years to learn that. If I had a teacher, I could have learned that in a month.

Even if a person was not pure enough to tap the power source himself, he might still borrow another's power for the purpose of effecting minor cures. Henry lent his power at least twice, once to a sister and once to a daughter-in-law, with the clear understanding that their use of the power was only temporary.

During the years when Henry was developing his own philosophy of healing and conceptions of cosmology he also continued patiently to search for new techniques and more efficacious curing methods. But he had little success until 1956, when, at the age of 70, he undertook to cure George Robinson, a Hawaiian, who had married a distant relative of his and was living in Hayward, California. Robinson was also a curer and had been a personal friend for a number of years. Henry regarded him with much the same affection and respect in which he had earlier held Welewkushkush and Beleliwe.

George Robinson had asserted that nothing was impossible

and that nothing could hurt him, and he paid the price of hubris. He gave a large feast for his children. Juanita, furious at this slight, decided not to live with George any longer. She began to fast and said she would die. She told George not to give her an elaborate funeral but to dispose of her body in the hills for the animals and birds to devour. He tried to cure her with all the methods at his disposal, but he failed and she died. Henry attended the funeral. George buried Juanita with a gold ring, erected a headstone, had a cement curbing built around her grave. But he did not follow Juanita's instructions, and he fell seriously ill. Henry described his condition as follows:

> He was dying; he was like a block of wood. Kids jumped on his belly and he didn't feel it. He couldn't pass food; he couldn't feel pain.

On the first night of the cure Henry was unable to receive any visions of either diagnosis or prognosis. On the second night he saw the cement curbing around the grave. On the third night he saw the brass medal on the headstone bearing Juanita's name. On the fourth night he saw the gold ring and received the following vision of prognosis. He was walking along the bottom of a deep gulch and saw coming toward him a herd of stampeding cattle. Frightened, he labored to climb the steep hillside. He saw one clump of sagebrush, grasped it, and sat down beside it. One steer galloped up the hill, jumped over the sagebrush, and said: "Tomorrow you gonna eat meat." George Robinson recovered, and on the following day he was again able to feel pain and eat. Henry warned him to stay away from Juanita's grave for four years, lest the grave dry out the water in his body and again make him ill.

In return for being cured, Robinson made Henry a gift of some of his power, in the form of a Hawaiian spirit helper named George. Although George lived in a volcano in Hawaii, his power was at its maximum in the vicinity of Henry Rupert's home. Consequently, Henry now preferred to cure at home and would no longer journey to visit patients except in emergency cases. Henry received from George a new set of instructions. The most important of these — "Everything comes quick and goes away quick," — emphasized the speed and efficacy of the new Hawaiian techniques. The content of Henry's dream themes also changed. He saw a dead and desiccated chicken which returned to life, and the skeletal remains of a horse which also came alive. Robinson had claimed that he could bring the dead back to life, and these dreams showed Henry knew that this ability might also be his.

A curing session utilizing the techniques now took place in daylight, and it lasted no longer than four hours and sometimes as little as a few minutes, depending on the nature of the ailment. Henry no longer needed visions of diagnosis or prognosis, and he could also eliminate chants, the blowing of smoke and water on the patient, and the use of the whistle to capture disease objects. Instead the patient was asked the location of the pain or swelling and was seated in a chair facing west, the direction of the Hawaiian Islands. Standing behind the chair, Henry twice called upon George for help, each time placing his fingers on the patient's neck, with thumbs on spine, for about ten seconds. Then, with his hands again on the patient's neck, he called out: "Wake up my body, wake up my nerves and circulate my blood; let my whole body be normal; and give me strength." Next, standing in front of the patient, he stated: "This person says he was sick here; he had pains here; it's not there now; it's gone." Then he placed his hand on the "pain spot" for some five seconds and asked the patient to take a deep breath and move his head from side to side. Usually the pain departed, but sometimes it moved to a different part of the body, in which case Henry again invoked George and repeated the procedure three or four times. Then, placing his left hand on top of the patient's head and his right hand at the patient's feet, he called to George: "Please mend this." Finally, he removed his hands and said: "We will close this."

According to Henry, the key to these techniques is contained in the following statement by his Hawaiian spirit helper: "We help nature, and nature does the rest." The above is a description of "Hawaiian curing" in its simplest form, as applied by Henry to ailments which he regarded as easy to cure.

Henry did not discard his previous techniques completely. Though he worked for briefer periods in his cures, for severe ailments he would use both the Hindu and George, and would search for visions of prognosis involving the presence or absence of water, as well as employing his newer methods. In effect he had developed a set of functionally streamlined curing techniques, involving less reliance on ceremonial artifacts, from which he could pick and choose according to the nature of the ailment. At the advanced age of 70, Henry relinquished willingly, without personal conflict, techniques that he had used for almost 50 years.

George posed no problems of integration for Henry. As a spirit helper, his power derived from the same general source as that of the Hindu, water, and the two old Indian women, and his curing functions were incorporated into Henry's general ethic of healing which overrode ethnic, racial, and cultural differences. The potential for innovation had not ended. From George he learned of a new way to stop bleeding in serious wounds quickly by placing his hands on the wound. However, the occasion to test this technique has not yet arisen, and Henry has doubts, not unreasonable or neurotic, as to his capacity to utilize it:

> I am kind of afraid of it; I don't have enough confidence. I have the idea it can't be done. I don't try it because I don't have enough confidence.

Today, Henry Rupert lives quietly in Carson Colony, continuing to cure, meditate, and tend a flourishing orchard in the desert. The Washo, despite their traditional fear and mistrust of shamans, regard Henry in a different light, recognizing, perhaps indirectly, the changes he represents. Leis (1963: 60) states:

> Only one (shaman) remained when we studied the Washo . . . and he was trusted and not feared by anyone. In other words, the sole remaining shaman was "good" as opposed to the "bad" Indian doctors who practiced witchcraft.

My own experiences confirm this completely.

Exactly what the social consequences of Henry's personal innovations are likely to be is uncertain. It is clear that the Washo have little knowledge of either the extent or content of these innovations, although they recognize that he does not doctor in the traditional Washo manner. At present there are no budding young shamans among the Washo, and it is unlikely that future shamans would take the traditional path to gaining supernatural power. Although Henry does not proselytize, he offers an alternative, but the regimen and qualities required are either unappealing or rare.

Nevertheless, the potentiality exists, and this could open a fascinating new chapter on shamanic healing among the Washo.

CONCLUSIONS

The most striking fact, in this life history, to me, is the coherence and integration of the innovations considered. The conceptions, both of an ethic of healing and of a coherent cosmology, are congruent with each other. Within this framework, Henry has been able to incorporate heterocultural spirit helpers, new techniques of curing, and proficiency in trans-cultural curing, as well as to explore the possibility of transmitting and teaching his healing abilities. Although his childhood models have greatly influenced his development, he has been able to resist their strictures and to reconceptualize his thinking on sorcery and witchcraft as causes of illness in terms of his reinterpretation of Washo cosmology. Throughout the material presented run themes of curiosity, experimentation, and perserverence, balanced by uncertainty of success. Henry's personality unfolds, through the years, slowly and positively with few contradictions. It takes the form of learning, testing, and integration, of working for maximal organization of all potentials within the framework of sophisticated general principles flexible enough to admit defeat in areas where spirit helpers are unable to operate. Thus Henry has recognized, through experience, the illnesses he cannot treat, and has accepted these limitations while delving into potentially more fruitful areas.

It is highly inadequate to suggest that Henry Rupert adopted shamanism as a neurotic defense against personal aggression and instability, or simply that he made a successful adjustment to the acculturative situation in which he lived. The shaman has often been analyzed and typed as a neurotic or borderline psychotic who performs valuable social functions in a deviant role to which he is shunted to meet his own neurotic needs (cf. Kroeber 1940; Radin 1937: 108; Spencer and Jennings 1965: 151; Boyer 1962: 233; Lantis 1960: 164; Devereux 1956, 1957: 1043, 1961a: 1088, 1961b: 63-64).[6] The neurotic defense of the shaman is

6. There are, of course, anthropologists who disagree with this formulation, e.g., Opler (1959, 1961), Honigmann (1960), Murdock (1965). Possibly the anthropologists' often ungenerous view of the shaman as a person

conceptualized as unstable, transitory, and inadequate; the experience of becoming a shaman is also often described as a revitalization experience.

These conceptions are not applicable in the case described. Henry Rupert presents us with a case of continuous psychological development, growth, and innovation throughout his individual life span. His first innovations included both a complex philosophical statement about the nature of the supernatural and natural worlds and a sophisticated approach to transcultural curing. All his other innovations were integrated into this psychological matrix, and this has remained stable through time and space. While his uncertainties and fears are considerable, Henry knows that one cannot face the unknown with certainty, unless it be rooted in rigidity. While man is fallible, Henry believes that the only path to knowledge is through experimentation, and his fears have never stopped him from experimenting.

Unfortunately, in anthropology, we have few ways of describing or analyzing the ego strength or ego integrity of individuals in the cultures we deal with, and ordinarily this does not concern us. We have good evidence of both social disorganization and psychological disturbance among acculturating peoples, and we can tentatively suggest that in many ways cultural processes have overwhelmed individual defenses in these cases by destroying traditional alternatives and failing to provide new ones. But what of the creative individual? What of the individual with great ego strength who is able to choose and combine traditional and new alternatives, not merely integrating them but developing new syntheses which may be both personally satisfying and socially transmissible? Of such persons and the roles they play we know little. And the same is true of the shaman who, as Nadel has suggested, can play a creative and innovative role. In the case of Henry Rupert we gain a glimpse of what the quality and content of such a syntheses can be in an acculturative situation.

---

is related to the way in which they often tend to identify and sympathize with a whole culture, and thus with the attitudes the majority have toward the shaman, rather than treating the shaman as a legitimate subcultural variant. It is ironic that these anthropologists can then return to their own culture and their own subcultural niches and complain about how society treats the "egghead" and the artist.

Power and its Applications in Native California

by Lowell John Bean

This paper presents a general description of supernatural power as it was perceived and used by California Indians prior to European contact. The principal existential postulates relating to the concept of power which were shared by most native California peoples are outlined, and the normative postulates (values) which regulated the use of power are briefly discussed. Specific ways in which power might be acquired, and the conduits or pathways to its acquisition are reviewed. Finally, some of the social implications deriving from the concept of the presence of power and beliefs about its characteristics are suggested. The description of power presented here is cross-cultural, and the author fully recognizes that not every aspect of power described in this paper can be strictly applied to each ethnic group in the state. Beliefs about power varied from group to group, but for the most part the ideas presented here were widely shared.

THE SOURCE OF POWER

The source of power is sometimes clearly explained in native California cosmologies, and sometimes it is not. Nevertheless, two principal patterns emerge in the cosmologies: (1) power is created from a void in which two forces, usually male and female, come together in a cataclysmic event that forms a creative force; or (2) power and creators appear simultaneously in the universe without explanation, and a creative force begins thereupon to form or alter the world. In both cases, various acts are accomplished through a use of power by a creator or primary creators that leads to a series of creations — among which is man. The outcome of these acts (narrated in dramatic episodes in the native cosmologies) is the creation of a hierarchically structured social universe — a cosmological model in which the nature of power is defined and rules are established for interacting with power sources. Although accounts in individual cosmologies may vary considerably from group to group in depicting this universe, throughout California there appears to be at the least a tripartite division of the universe into upper, middle, and lower worlds.

The upper world is occupied by powerful anthropomorphic beings — usually seen as the primary creators — with whom humans can interact to their own benefit. The upper world may also include astronomical personages such as the Sun, Moon, and significant stars or constellations, theriomorphic creatures who are the forerunners of animal species, and other spirit beings who have no counterpart in the real world. Often the dwelling place of the dead is associated with the upper realm, although it is sometimes located in a distinctly different place.

The middle world is inhabited by both men and various non-mortal beings with considerable power. Most native Californians view the middle world as lying at the geographical center of the universe. Usually, it is conceived as circular, floating in space, and surrounded by a void or by water.

Finally, the underworld is inhabited by superordinary beings who are usually more malevolent toward man than those of the other two realms. Such beings take many forms and are often associated with water, springs, underground rivers and lakes, and caves. Frequently, they are reptilian or amphibian in nature (e.g., serpents or frogs) or have a distorted humanoid appearance (e.g., dwarfs, hunchbacks, giants, cyclopes, water-babies).

THE NATURE OF POWER

The nature of power in the universe is best understood in terms of four basic philosophical assumptions shared by most native Californian groups in their world view (Bean 1972; White 1963; Blackburn 1974; Halpern 1955). These assumptions are as follows: (1) power is sentient and the principal causative agent in the universe; (2) power is distributed differentially throughout the three realms of the universe and possessed by anything having "life" or the will "to act"; (3) the universe is in a state of dynamic equilibrium in relation to power; and (4) man is the central figure in an interacting system of power holders.

First, power is assumed to be the principal causative agent (energy source) for all phenomena in the universe. Power is sentient and possesses will. At the beginning of the universe or some later stage in the creation, power was apportioned throughout the three realms in various degrees or quantities. Thus, power is potentially extant in all things. Power may remain quiescent and neutral, choosing its own time or place to manifest itself. Some things possess more power than others, but anything in the universe which has "life" or demonstrates the will "to act" possesses some amount of power. Even seemingly inanimate things may possess power. A rock which suddenly moves downhill may thereby demonstrate an ability "to act" and therefore reveal itself to be a power source. An animal may be normal or possess some extraordinary degree of power, or, most awesome of all, prove to be a were-animal. Nothing can be judged to be without power until it has been tested by empirical indicators. Since man is never absolutely certain whether or not anything is a power source until it is tested or reveals itself, he lives in a constantly perilous world fraught with danger. Power sources remain a continuous threat or advantage to man until his soul enters the land of the dead, where presumably all is well and power vis-à-vis an individual soul is permanently controlled.

All power beings are personalized and akin to man in their nature (capable of such emotions as anger, love, hate, pity, and jealousy). Because power beings are capricious, unpredictable, and amoral, they may manifest themselves in many ways which perform for or against man's benefit. It seems that only in historical times has power been viewed as disparately good or evil. Although power is omnipresent in the universe, it is not always omniscient, which means the beings possessing power can be deceived like humans.

The universe exists in a state of dynamic equilibrium with power. While there is constant opposition between power sources and a struggle among them to acquire more power, no one source of power has the ability to obtain ultimate superiority or to alter the condition of the universe irrevocably so long as man conducts himself in a manner which aids in maintaining the equilibrium.

Man is viewed as the central figure in an interacting system of power holders. As the articulating link between all expressions of power, man has been provided with guidelines for acquiring, keeping, and wielding power. Since power is sentient and personalized, man can interact with power or conduits of power much as he would with humans. Power can be dealt with rationally through a system of reciprocal rules (expectations), which were established or handed down to man in early cosmic times. Without individual or community action by man through such rituals as world renewal ceremonies, the balance of power in the universe would be upset, and one side of the system might be disproportionately favored over another. Individually acquired power (knowledge) and traditionally acquired power (held by priests or shamans) must continually be employed by man to maintain the dynamic equilibrium or harmony of the universe.

Since man occupies the geographical center of the universe, he is in an ideal location for bringing power from the upper and lower universes into play in the middle world. Religious persons such as priests or shamans are extremely important socio-political figures in native society. They are the boundary players of power, since they possess knowledge which makes it possible for them to travel safely to distant and hence dangerous places — often in any of the three worlds. Through interaction with power sources in all three worlds, men possessing a knowledge of the rules governing power are capable of receiving, manipulating, and controlling power throughout the universe with various degrees of success.

Form, space, and time are mutable and malleable under the influence of power. During rituals, when power is being exercised, past, present, and future may be fused into one continuous whole. A shaman may use power to bring sacred time into the present so that he can interact with beings from that time. He may transcend space, shortening or lengthening distances through the use of power. Or he may draw a land form toward him or travel speedily across space transformed into another creature, such as a bird, bear, or mountain lion.

Within the middle world of man, power can exist anywhere, and anything occupying space may contain power and be beneficial or dangerous. For this reason, the central place occupied by an Indian group — the village — is more sacred and safer than anything beyond its perimeter. Such a central place is viewed as "tame" or safe because it is controlled by men of knowledge who can protect the inhabitants from other power sources (Halpern

1955; Blackburn 1974).

If security, predictability, and sociability are associated with one's home base, everything beyond is associated with danger. The forest and other places not inhabited by man are unsafe because they are defined as uncontrolled — as are the other two universes. Thus, travel away from one's home base increases the chances of encountering danger. The danger of uncontrolled power is believed to increase in a series of concentric circles the farther one moves away from one's immediate social universe. For this reason, the presence of strangers in a community may represent a source of danger and must be viewed with suspicion. They may, because they live at a distance, possess greater power for ill use than one's own people.

Although power operates in a dynamic equilibrium in the universe, one of its major characteristics is that it is entropic (Blackburn 1974; Bean 1972; White 1963). Power has gradually diminished since the beginning of time in quality, quantity, and availability. Such a diminishment of power has occurred because man has at various times treated it or its conduits improperly, failing in his reciprocal responsibilities within an interdependent system. Consequently, as man struggles to reestablish the power balance of the universe in the face of forces seeking to create disequilibrium, power always seems to be restored at a lesser level than in the past. A very rapid loss of power is believed to have occurred after European contact as knowledge concerning the means of regulating power was lost. Nevertheless, power is always partially retrievable as new rules are established for obtaining and maintaining it.

VALUES AND THE CONTROL OF POWER

The concept of power is integrally related to several normative values concerning its use which are common to most California Indian groups. To maintain a viable world, it is considered mandatory that man acquire knowledge about the universe. Knowledge has value for its own sake as well as for being an instrument in the manipulation of power. Thus, persons who acquire knowledge are considered powerful and treated deferentially. Often it is assumed that knowledge is in part a product of advancing age. Very advanced age (without senility) among south central and southern California groups is an indication of greater power. In contrast, power decreases in north central California with advanced age (loss of physical strength before the onset of senility), and offices associated with power are passed on to younger adults.

In order to acquire power, one must behave honestly, prudently, moderately, and reciprocally in relation to others, and possess the ability to maintain confidences. Honesty is qualified by the understanding that deceit can be used by the weak when dealing with powerful beings or persons who have an unfair advantage. Self-restraint, industriousness, self-assertion, and self-respect are other qualities necessary for the proper use of power (Bean 1972; Blackburn 1974).

The rules for handling power and using its conduits (such as ritual paraphernalia) function to control the power holder and prevent his misuse of power in two ways. First, power can be used only at proper times and in proper places, and it must be used in accordance with set procedures (e.g., in combination with various power acts such as smoking tobacco). A failure to exemplify in one's conduct those moral values associated with the use of power (such as reciprocity and prudence) leads to automatic disenfranchisement of the power holder and possibly punishment from a tutelary spirit or other persons of power. Secondly, persons having power and knowledge may withhold from unworthy candidates information on procedures for acquiring and maintaining power. Thus, if a candidate's deportment in daily affairs is such that it is believed he will not use power safely or productively, he is kept away from the principal conduits of power. Sometimes, however, among certain groups a "troublemaker" was drawn into the circle of power to "tame" him. It was thought that his acquisition of an awesome responsibility might transform him into a better man.

In addition to the moral virtues described above, men of power adopted an eclectic and highly pragmatic view of the universe. Because power was seen as omnipresent and completely malleable, all phenomena were potentially useful as sources of power. The fact that potential power residing in an object was not immediately obvious could simply signify a failure on the part of an observer to have the requisite knowledge to recognize and use it. Thus, it was important to preserve an empirical attitude toward all new

phenomena or ideas and cautiously test them against the
framework of cultural realities which were already known. To the
native Californian, the diversity and unpredictability of power was
consistent with an ecosystem that was equally diverse and
unpredictable, although often kind and bountiful in the resources
provided by nature. Because it was understood that the sources of
power were so diversified, an eclectic and experimental attitude
toward power existed in California. Man was not dependent upon
one source of power, but attempted to acquire power from as many
sources as possible. Since power was unlimited in its potential for
acquisition, one shaman might have as many as ten or more
guardian spirits.

Finally, because this empirical and eclectic attitude toward
power was pervasive throughout California, new ideas developed
and spread rapidly and were readily molded into unique, culturally
specific styles of power control by different Indian groups. One
example of such a diffusion of new ideas was the Chingishnish
religion, which appears to have arisen in the late eighteenth
century either on Santa Catalina Island or among the Gabrielinos
(White 1963: 94). This religion spread south to the Luiseño and
Diegueño, who uniquely grafted it onto their own religions, and
even reached as far into the interior as certain Cahuilla groups, who
adopted specific features of the cult.

POWER FROM OTHER WORLDS

Power that existed in the here and now of man's middle
universe was viewed as left over from the sacred time of creation.
This residual power (White 1963) was conceived as lying about,
rather free floating, obtainable and manageable by those born with
sufficient innate abilities to handle it or those who otherwise had
acquired the requisite knowledge. The principal sources of power,
however, lay in the upper and lower worlds, residing in the "sacred
beings."

Among some Indian groups in California, every individual
sought a connection with power. In other groups, only specifically
recognized persons or those who wanted extraordinary power
sought it out. Since power was believed to be ubiquitous and
continually available, its presence and influence in the events of
daily life were constantly appreciated by all members of a culture.

Man was connected with the power available in the upper and lower worlds in very specific ways. Direct contacts were possible with tutelary spirits who instructed one in the use of power; souls and ghosts transcended the space between worlds and could be contacted during ghostly visitations to the middle world; and some humans — through ecstatic experiences — were able to transport themselves to the other worlds or to bring from them supernatural power. Some of the means through which power might be acquired include the following: the vision quest, the calling upon of power sources, dreaming, the inheritance or purchase of knowledge or ritual equipment, and prayers and offerings. Individuals might be instructed in the knowledge, acquisition, and use of power by a power giver itself (sacred being), or they might receive such knowledge through training from a shaman or other ritual specialist.

Various techniques also existed for making the individual more open to the acquisition of power by altering his mental or bodily sensibilities. These included the use or combined use of hallucinogenic plants, the handling of power-containing objects, and various forms of sensory deprivation or acts designed to concentrate attention, such as meditation, fasting, imposed periods of sleeplessness, isolation, induced sweating, listening to music, singing, drumming, chanting, and hyperventilation.

One of the principal routes to acquiring power was the vision quest, and the induction of an ecstatic condition to receive spirits having power was a common preliminary act. Several means were used to induce ecstasy on the vision quest, the most dramatic being the use of hallucinogenic plants with or without accompanying ritual. In California, the most frequently used plants containing hallucinogens were *Nicotiana* (tobacco) and *Datura* (jimson weed). The California poppy and formic acid from ants may also have been used by some groups. It was believed that such hallucinogens altered the user's perceptions and level of awareness, making him more receptive to perceiving sacred beings and other power sources.

Power could also be tapped and acquired through many channels that brought it into the human sphere of activities. These included rocks (such as quartz crystals) and other unusual objects, human and animal bones (especially predators among animals), human and animal hair, various animal parts (such as the heart and entrails), non-mind altering plants (such as angelica and pepper-wood), and all ritual paraphernalia.

Any unusual phenomenon or event might serve to bring power into the middle world of man or prove to be an omen which could be read for predicting the future (e.g., astronomical events, any peculiar behavior of humans or animals, multiple births, people with unusual marks or physical characteristics, etc.). Power could also be concentrated in specific places in the environment, such as in a pond (water being the great transformer), on a mountain top, or in a particular tree or grove of trees. Power might also be put into a place by those having power. A shaman, for example, might protect a sacred place outside his village where ritual paraphernalia was stored by putting power there.

Within the community, power was invested in or accumulated at various private and public places, most commonly the ritual center where the religious, political, economic, and social lives of the people came together. Such ritual centers were considered sacred places where cosmic or sacred time and space and spiritual beings met with secular time and space and human beings. In such ritual centers, elaborate rites of intensification were carried out as necessary to maintain the equilibrium of the universe or to aid in cosmic rebirth at the end of each year or when the balance of the universe was endangered. Such rituals were particularly critical during times of cosmic imbalance, usually the result of man's failure to perform rituals properly or to act reciprocally with other beings in the universe.

Sacred places could also be divested of power, however, and some places contained power only at appropriate times, such as during religious ceremonies or on those occasions when supernatural powers were closer and more accessible to man. During certain times or periods (such as at night or in winter), power was considered closer to man than at other times and simultaneously more dangerous unless checked and kept under control. In particular, during times of life crises (such as menstruation, birth, illness, and death), power might be in a highly chaotic state and very dangerous to the community. On such occasions, malevolent outside powers entering the village or emanating from the individual experiencing the crisis could harm both the individual and the community. Thus, ritual action, both public and private, was necessary on such occasions.

SOCIAL AND POLITICAL IMPLICATIONS OF POWER

The nature of power as described in native California cosmologies provides an explanation for certain socio-cultural organizational modes only recently becoming clear to researchers (Bean and King 1974; Bean and Lawton 1973). One of these modes is reflected in what Blackburn (1974) has called an assumption of the inevitable and inherent inequality of the universe. Just as power is distributed differentially and hierarchically throughout the universe, so is it distributed for acquisition and use by human beings.

Inequalities in social rank, intelligence, social prerogatives, wealth, and skills can all be explained by reference to the differential distribution of power. Certain individuals are naturally born with power or inherit it, others possess the capacity to seek it out, and in some instances power itself seeks people out. In a hierarchically ordered universe, it is not surprising that a hierarchical ordering of power is also accepted as part of the structuring of man's middle universe. In the middle or "real" world, some humans have more access to more power than others, and humans in general have more access to power than other species. A similar hierarchy exists in the plant and animal kingdom. Carnivores, for example, are more powerful than plants. In most California Indian cosmologies, there is a clear-cut chain-of-being in the biotic world in which man stands near the top of the power pyramid in the middle universe. He is also at the center of the entire universe, receiving power and using it to maintain the universal equilibrium.

Society itself is similarly hierarchically structured — characterized by the presence of classes of people with inherent power and with it privilege and wealth. Like cosmological beings, humans with power are regarded with ambiguity by others in their community. Power holders are "necessary evils" performing vital functions. They are treated with respect and awe, but also with considerable caution, since they are potentially amoral in their relationships with others. Their allegiance is to power, both the maintenance of power and the acquisition of more power, and thus primarily to other persons of power, even as much as their allegiance may be to the community they serve as administrators and boundary players. In effect, men of power stand somewhat

above and outside the social system in which they live — not
entirely responsible to the claims of the local social order. For
example, a shaman may not be as dependable in his conduct toward
his relatives as ordinary people would be. His higher calling
sometimes transcends his secular obligations.

In societies fraught with uncertainty, a person who can control,
acquire, or manipulate power is absolutely necessary. While the
social price required for his presence may be great, it is necessary
to pay it. Generally, throughout California, chiefly families were
those which had many priests and shamans. In economic matters,
the elite families controlled the principal means of production and
distribution of goods, owned monopolies on many valuable goods
and services (e.g., eagle down and ritual positions), possessed the
power to levy taxes, fines, and establish fees to support
institutions, and were able to charge exorbitant interest on loans,
thus amassing further wealth. In legal matters, they were the final
judicial arbitrators with the power of binding decisions involving
life and death within the community.

Just as there was a constant conflict between those with innate
power and those seeking to acquire it in the myths and cosmologies
of the California Indians, so did such a conflict exist in human
society between the elites holding power and newcomers seeking to
acquire it. The elites, with their inherited power that brought
wealth and privileges, were in continual conflict with individuals
from beneath their ranks who sought to acquire power, since power
was potentially available to anyone. The elites, however, possessed
control mechanisms for the licensing or sanctioning of power such
as secret societies, initiations, and inheritance of rank, knowledge,
and control of ceremonial equipment. These mechanisms provided
a means by which persons of lower rank, possessing skill and
ambition (sometimes even those who were socially disruptive),
might enter the system. Through such a licensing of power, bright
young people of lower ranks were able to move upward, yet the
power structure was always kept safe from serious disruption by
malcontents with talent.

Since power could always be destroyed, men of power who
misused their abilities or endangered the community could be
reduced in rank or power through ritual disenfranchisement or, if
necessary, assassination.

Empirical indicators of status held by elite families, such as symbols of political office (e.g., ceremonial bundles), were also cosmological referents to the most powerful supernatural beings in sacred positions of the upper world and therefore symbols of power as well. The main social implication of power was that elites lived a life and shared a knowledge system which clearly separated them from their people.

Chiefs and to some extent shamans and other specialists were usually men of conspicuous wealth, who had inherited their offices — patrilineally in southern California and bilaterally in Northern California. They wore expensive clothing, lived in larger houses than ordinary people, often were polygamous (certainly having greater sexual access to women), and married within the higher ranks (usually within their class, thus compounding wealth among ruling families). Such people were relieved from the day-to-day routine of hunting and gathering life and were often totally supported by the populace. This was also generally true of the higher ranking craftsmen. Unquestionably, the elite families received better medical care (because the best medical practitioners were in their ranks), the best diet, best living accommodations, and the least amount of risk in daily life (since they weren't required to carry out sometimes dangerous activities such as hunting or fishing). Such persons were generally relieved from fighting during warfare, serving instead as the arbiters who determined who would go to battle and as negotiators of peacemaking.

Thus, the distribution of power within a community played the primary role in determining all social acts and interrelationships, whether these were between close kin, members of the community, or between different political groups. Even warfare and conquest could be justified in terms of the need to acquire or maintain a power balance. Understanding this allows us to better appreciate the complexity of the social, economic, and political institutions of native California.

CONCLUSIONS

We have seen that understanding assumptions about power is central to understanding the nature of man and his relationship to the universe in native California. Power explains the operations of man's social universe within which all beings are potentially hierarchical, but competitively and reciprocally. Each part of the system through man's intercessionary role at the center of the universe performs a task vis-à-vis the other parts that will create or strive for a state of balanced equilibrium and the maintenance of a viable ecosystem.

The congruency we find between the philosophical assumptions in native California culture about power and the social realities by which the culture functions should encourage us to delve further into the nature of "power" as it is defined by other cultures. We should take seriously each culture's cosmological view of the universe and the role of power within the universe, because this may tell us more about the social rules for behavior than any other aspect of a cultural system.

In further studies of native California, I hope to explore the assumptions concerning the role of power in the universe and the rules for using power as they vary from one ecosystem to another. Clearly there are differences from group to group which I have glossed over in this generalized sketch. In particular, the different sorts of strategies for using power should be examined for all hunting and gathering societies to determine what rules (and I suspect they are very few) equip man to cope with specific types of ecosystems, levels of technology, and social and political conditions.

In another context (Bean 1974: 13), I suggested that native Californians achieved a level of socio-cultural integration not unlike that of many horticultural and agricultural societies — a level which may be more indicative of the normal levels reached within the limitations of hunting and gathering technology than those contemporary hunting and gathering societies which anthropologists have studied in the twentieth century. The California case continues to suggest that our evolutionary models for hunting and gathering societies are inadequate. It also suggests that the process by which cultures switch over to more advanced forms of economic achievement are yet to be understood, since native Californians had the opportunity and knowledge to make such a shift, but in most cases failed to do so. Such an opportunity existed in California because the philosophical assumptions about power provided for *all* possibilities of change. And, most especially, they provided a justification for centralized and hierarchically structured power, for the exploitation of individuals and other societies, for conquest, and for other variables necessary to political and economic expansion.

Bibliography

Abbott, C. C.
  1879 Chipped Stone Implements. Report upon U.S. Geograph-
          ical Surveys West of the 100th Meridian, Vol. VII:
          Archaeology, F. W. Putnam (editor), pp. 49-69. Washing-
          ton: U.S. Printing Office.

Aginsky, B. W.
  1939 Population Control in the Shanel (Pomo) Tribe. *American
          Sociological Review*, Vol. 4, No. 2.

Aschmann, Homer
  1959a The Central Desert of Baja California: Demography and
          Ecology. *Ibero-Americana*, Vol. 42, pp. 1-315.
  1959b The Evolution of a Wild Landscape and Its Persistence in
          Southern California. *Annals, Association of American
          Geographers*, Vol. 49, No. 3, pp. 34-56.

Bancroft, H. H.
  1883 *The Native Races of the Pacific States*. Vol. 1. San
          Francisco: A. L. Bancroft & Company.

Barrett, Samuel A.
  1908 The Ethno-geography of the Pomo and Neighboring
          Indians. *University of California Publications in American
          Archaeology and Ethnology*, Vol. 6, pp. 1-332. Berkeley:
          University of California Press.
  1917 Ceremonies of the Pomo Indians. *University of California
          Publications in American Archaeology and Ethnology*,
          Vol. 12, pp. 397-441. Berkeley: University of California
          Press.
  1952 Material Aspects of Pomo Culture. *Bulletin of the
          Milwaukee Public Museum*, Vol. 20, pp. 1-508.
          Milwaukee: Milwaukee Public Museum.

Barrett, S. A., and E. W. Gifford
  1933 Miwok Material Culture. *Bulletin of the Milwaukee
          Public Museum*, Vol. 2, No. 4. Milwaukee: Milwaukee
          Public Museum.

Barrows, David Prescott
  1900 *The Ethno-Botany of the Coahuilla Indians of Southern
          California*. Chicago: University of Chicago Press.
          (Reprinted 1967 by Malki Museum Press with Intro-

ductory Essays by Harry W. Lawton, Lowell John Bean,
and William Bright.)

Baumhoff, Martin A.

1958   California Athabascan Groups. *Anthropological Records*,
        Vol. 16, pp. 157-238. Berkeley: University of California
        Press.

1963   Ecological Determinants of Aboriginal California Popula-
        tions. *University of California Publications in American
        Archaeology and Ethnology*, Vol. 49, No. 2, pp. 155-236.
        Berkeley: University of California Press.

Beals, Ralph L.

1933   Ethnology of the Nisenan. *University of California Publi-
        cations in American Archaeology and Ethnology*, Vol. 31,
        pp. 335-410. Berkeley: University of California Press.

Beals, Ralph L., and Joseph A. Hester

1955   *Ecological Analysis of California Indian Territoriality and
        Land-use.* Los Angeles: Department of Justice Indian
        Land Claims Project. Mimeo.

1958   A Lacustrine Economy in California. *Miscellanea Paul
        Rivet, Octogenario Dicata.* Mexico.

1960   A New Ecological Typology of the California Indians. In
        Men and Cultures, Anthony F. C. Wallace (editor). Phila-
        delphia: University of Pennsylvania Press.

Bean, Lowell J.

1972   *Mukat's People: The Cahuilla Indians of Southern Cali-
        fornia.* Berkeley: University of California Press.

1974   Social Organizations in Native California. *ʔAntap: Cali-
        fornia Indian Political and Economic Organization.* Lowell
        John Bean and Thomas King (editors). Ramona: Ballena
        Press.

Bean, Lowell J., and Thomas F. King (editors)

1974   *ʔAntap: California Indian Political and Economic Organi-
        zation.* Ballena Press Anthropological Papers 2. Ramona:
        Ballena Press.

Bean, Lowell J., and Harry Lawton

1973   Some Explanations for the Rise of Cultural Complexity in
        Native California with Comments on Proto-Agriculture
        and Agriculture. In *Patterns of Indian Burning in Cali-
        fornia: Ecology and Ethno-history* by Henry Lewis.
        Ramona: Ballena Press.

Bean, Lowell J., and William Marvin Mason
    Diaries & Accounts of the Romero Expedition in Arizona and California, 1823-1826. Palm Springs: Palm Springs Desert Museum.

Bean, Lowell J., and Katherine Siva Saubel
    1972 *Temalpakh: Cahuilla Indian Knowledge and Usage of Plants*. Morongo Indian Reservation: Malki Museum Press.

Bean, Walton
    1968 *California: An Interpretive History*. New York: McGraw-Hill.

Beeler, Madison S.
    1967 The Ventureño Confesionario of José Señán, O.F.M. *University of California Publications in Linguistics*. Vol. 47. Berkeley: University of California Press.

Benedict, Ruth F.
    1934 *Patterns of Culture*. New York: New American Library.

Bicchieri, M. G.
    1972 *Hunters and Gatherers Today*. New York: Holt, Rinehart & Winston.

Binford, Lewis R.
    1965 Archaeological Systematics and the Study of Culture Process. *American Antiquity*, Vol. 31, No. 2, Part I, pp. 203-10. Washington, D.C.: Society for American Archaeology.
    1968 Methodological Considerations of the Archaeological Use of Ethnographic Data. In *Man the Hunter*, R. B. Lee and I. DeVore, (editors), pp. 268-73. Chicago: Aldine-Atherton.

Birdsell, J. B.
    1968 Some Predictions for the Pleistocene Based on Equilibrium Systems Among Recent Hunter-Gatherers. In *Man the Hunter*, R. B. Lee and I. DeVore (editors), pp. 229-40. Chicago: Aldine.

Blackburn, Thomas
    1974 *Chumash Oral Traditions: A Cultural Analysis*. Ph.D. dissertation, University of California, Los Angeles.
    1975 *December's Child*. Los Angeles: University of California Press.

Boas, Franz
    1916 *The Mind of Primitive Man*. New York: Macmillan.

Bolton, Herbert Eugene
   1911   Expedition to San Francisco Bay in 1770: Diary of Pedro
          Fages. *Publications of the Academy of Pacific Coast
          History*, Vol. 2, No. 3, pp. 143-59.
   1926   *Historical Memoirs of New California by Fray Francisco
          Palou, O.F.M.*, Vol. 2. Berkeley: University of Cali-
          fornia Press.
   1927   *Fray Juan Crespi, Missionary Explorer on the Pacific
          Coast, 1769-1774*. Berkeley: University of California
          Press.
   1930   *Anza's California Expeditions*. Vol. II. Berkeley:
          University of California Press.
   1931   *Font's Complete Diary, Anza's California Expedition,
          1774-1776*. Berkeley: University of California Press.
   1967   *Spanish Exploration in the Southwest, 1542-1706*. New
          York: Barnes & Noble, Inc.
Boscana, Fr. Geronimo
   1933   Chinigchinich. In *Chinigchinich, a revised and annotated
          version of Alfred Robinson's translation of Father
          Geronimo Boscana's historical account of the belief,
          usages, customs and extravagancies of the Indians of this
          mission of San Juan Capistrano called the Acagchemen
          tribe*, P. T. Hanna (editor). Santa Ana: Fine Arts Press.
   1934   *A New Original Version of Boscana's Historical Account
          of the San Juan Capistrano Indians of Southern California*,
          J. P. Harrington (editor), Vol. 92, No. 4, Smithsonian
          Miscellaneous Collections. Washington, D.C.
   1947   *Chinigchinich*. Part II of Alfred Robinson's *Life in Cali-
          fornia*. Oakland: Biobooks.
Bourke, John G.
   1889   Notes on the Cosmogony and Theogony of the Mojave
          Indians of the Rio Colorado, Arizona. *Journal of American
          Folklore*, Vol. 2, pp. 169-89.
Bowers, Stephen
   1878   Santa Rosa Island. *Annual Report of the Board of Regents
          of Smithsonian Institution for Year 1877*, pp. 316-20.
          Washington, D. C.
Boyer, L. B.
   1962   Remarks on the Personality of Shamans. In *The
          Psychoanalytic Study of Society*, W. Muensterberger and

S. Axelrad (editors), pp. 233-54. New York.

Brockett, L. P.

1882 *Our Western Empire or the New West Beyond the Mississippi.* Philadelphia: Bradley, Garretson & Co.

Brown, Alan K.

1967 The Aboriginal Population of the Santa Barbara Channel. *University of California Archaeological Survey Reports,* No. 69. Berkeley: University of California Press.

Bryan, Bruce

1961 Manufacture of Stone Mortars. *Masterkey,* Vol. 35, pp. 134-9. Los Angeles.

Bulmer, Ralph

1960 Political Aspects of the Moka Ceremonial Exchange among the Kyaka People of the Western Highlands of New Guinea. *Oceania,* Vol. 31, No. 1, pp. 1-13. Sidney.

Burcham, L. T.

1959 Planned Burning as a Management Practice for California Wild Lands. *Proceedings, Society of American Foresters, Division of Range Management,* pp. 180-5.

California Archives at Bancroft Library

1782a Felipe de Neve to the Commandante of the Santa Barbara Presidio, March 6, 1782. *Prov. State Papers,* Vol. 3, pp. 89-91 (CA 2, pp. 89-91).

1782b Felipe de Neve to Ortega, Commandante of the Santa Barbara Presidio, May 18, 1782. *Prov. State Papers Benicia,* Vol. 1, p. 27 (CA 62-28).

1804 Gov. Orrillaga at Loreto to Commandante at Santa Barbara. Dec. 31, 1804, *Prov. Rec. Bol. 11,* p. 104 (CA 26:104).

Castetter, Edward F., and Willis H. Bell

1951 *Yuman Indian Agriculture: Primitive Subsistence on the Lower Colorado and Gila Rivers.* Albuquerque: University of New Mexico Press.

Caughey, John Walton (editor)

1952 The Indians of Southern California in 1852. *The B. D. Wilson Report and a Selection of Contemporary Comment.* San Marino: Huntington Library.

Cessac, Leon de

1951a Report on Activities in California. *University of California Archaeological Survey Reports,* No. 12, pp. 6-12. Trans.

by R. F. Heizer.

1951b Observations on the Sculptured Stone Fetishes in Animal Form Discovered on San Nicolas Island (California). *University of California Archaeological Survey Reports*, Vol. 12, pp. 1-5.

Chagnon, Napoleon A.

1970 Ecological and Adaptive Aspects of California Shell Money. *UCLA Archaeological Survey Annual Report*, Vol. 12, pp. 1-25. Los Angeles: University of California Press.

Clapham, W. B., Jr.

1973 *Natural Ecosystems*. New York: Macmillan.

Clar, C. Raymond

1959 *California Government and Forestry: from Spanish Days Until the Creation of the Department of Natural Resources in 1927*. Sacramento: Division of Forestry, Department of Natural Resources, State of California.

Cook, S. F.

1943 The Conflict between the California Indian and White Civilization. *Ibero-Americana*, Vol. 21. Berkeley: University of California Press.

1955 The Aboriginal Population of the San Joaquin Valley, California. *Anthropological Records*, Vol. 16, pp. 31-80. Berkeley: University of California Press.

1956 The Aboriginal Population of the North Coast of California. *Anthropological Records*, Vol. 16, pp. 81-130. Berkeley: University of California Press.

1957 The Aboriginal Population of Alameda and Contra Costa Counties, California. *Anthropological Records*, Vol. 16, pp. 131-56. Berkeley: University of California Press.

1960 Colonial Expeditions to the Interior of California, Central Valley, 1800-1820. *Anthropological Records*, Vol. 16, No. 6. Berkeley: University of California Press.

1962 Expeditions to the Interior of California, Central Valley, 1820-1840. *Anthropological Records*, Vol. 20, No. 5. Berkeley: University of California Press.

Coon, Carleton S.

1971 *The Hunting Peoples*. Boston: Atlantic-Little, Brown.

Costanśo, Miguel

1910 The Narrative of the Portolá Expedition of 1769-1770. Adolph van Hemert-Engert and Frederick Teggart (editors). *Publications of the Academy of Pacific Coast History*, Vol. 1, No. 4, pp. 3-69.

1911 The Portolá Expedition of 1769-1770: Diary of Miguel Costansó. Frederick J. Teggart (editor). *Publications of the Academy of Pacific Coast History*, Vol. 2, No. 4, pp. 4-167.

Coues, Elliott
1900 *On the Trail of a Spanish Pioneer: Diary of Gárces.* New York: F. P. Harper.

Craig, Steve
1967 The Basketry of the Ventureño Chumash. *UCLA Archaeological Survey Annual Report*, Vol. 9, pp. 78-149. Los Angeles: University of California Press.

Crumrine, Lynne S.
1969 Ceremonial Exchange as a Mechanism in Tribal Integration Among the Mayos of Northwest Mexico. *Anthropological Papers of the University of Arizona.* No. 14. Tucson: University of Arizona Press.

Cuero, Delfina
1968 *The Autobiography of Delfina Cuero as Told to Florence C. Shipek. Interpreter Rosalie Pinto Robertson.* Los Angeles: Dawson's Book Shop. (Reprinted in 1970 by Malki Museum Press).

Curtis, Edward S.
1907-30 *The American Indian*, Vol. 13. Norwood.

Dalton, George
1967 Primitive Money. In *Tribal and Peasant Economies*, George Dalton (editor), pp. 254-81. Garden City, N.Y.: Natural History Press.

Davenport, William
1959 Nonunilineal Descent and Descent Groups. *American Anthropologist*, Vol. 61, pp. 557-72. Menasha: American Anthropological Association.

Davis, James T.
1959 Further Notes on Clay Human Figurines in Western United States. *University of California Archaeological Survey Reports*, No. 48, Paper 71. Berkeley: University of California Press.

Deetz, James
1968 The Inference of Residence and Descent Rules from

Archaeological Data. In *New Perspectives in Archaeology*, Sally R. Binford and Lewis R. Binford (editors), pp. 41-8. Chicago: Aldine.

Devereux, G.

1956   Normal and Abnormal: The Key Problem of Psychiatric Anthropology. In *Some Uses of Anthropology, Theoretical and Applied*, J. B. Casagrande and T. Gladwin (editors). Washington.

1957   Dream Learning and Individual Ritual Differences in Mohave Shamanism. *American Anthropologist*. Vol. 59, pp. 1036-45. Menasha: American Anthropological Association.

1961a   Shamans as Neurotics. *American Anthropologist*. Vol. 63, pp. 1088-90. Menasha: American Anthropological Association.

1961b   Mohave Ethnopsychiatry and Suicide: The Psychiatric Knowledge and the Psychic Disturbances of an Indian Tribe. *Bulletins of the Bureau of American Ethnology*, Vol. 175, pp. 1-586. Washington, D.C.

Dimbleby, G. W.

1967   *Plants and Archaeology*. London: John Baker.

Dixon, R. B.

1905   The Northern Maidu. *American Museum of Natural History Bulletins*, No. 17. New York.

Downs, James F.

1961   Washo Religion. *Anthropological Records*, Vol. 16, pp. 365-85. Berkeley: University of California Press.

1963   Differential Response to White Contact: Paiute and Washo. In *The Washo Indians of California and Nevada*, W. L. d'Azevedo (editor). Salt Lake City.

1966a   *The Two Worlds of the Washo*. New York.

1966b   The Significance of Environmental Manipulation in the Great Basin Cultural Development. In *The Current Status of Anthropological Research in the Great Basin: 1964*, Warren D'Azevedo (editor). Reno: Desert Research Institute.

Driver, Harold E.

1936   Wappo Ethnography. *University of California Publications in American Archaeology and Ethnology*, Vol. 36, pp. 179-220. Berkeley: University of California Press.

1937   Culture Element Distributions: VI, Southern Sierra
       Nevada. *Anthropological Records*, Vol. 1, pp. 53-154.
       Berkeley: University of California Press.

1961   *The Indians of North America.* Chicago: University of
       Chicago Press.

Drucker, Philip

1937a The Tolowa and Their Southwest Oregon Kin. *University
       of California Publications in American Archaeology and
       Ethnology*, Vol. 36, pp. 221-300. Berkeley: University of
       California Press.

1937b Culture Element Distributions,   V: Southern California.
       Anthropological Records, Vol. 1, pp. 1-52. Berkeley:
       University of California Press.

DuBois, Constance G.

1908   The Religion of the Luiseño Indians. *University of Cali-
       fornia Publications in American Archaeology and
       Ethnology*, Vol. 8, pp. 69-173. Berkeley: University of
       California Press.

DuBois, Cora

1935   Wintu Ethnography. *University of California Publications
       in American Archaeology and Ethnology*, Vol. 36, No. 1.
       Berkeley: University of California Press.

1936   The Wealth Concept as an Integrative Factor in Tolowa-
       Tututni Culture. In *Essays in Anthropology Presented to
       A. L. Kroeber*, B. Meggers (editor), pp. 67-87.
       Washington: Anthropological Society of Washington,
       D.C.

1939   The 1870 Ghost Dance. *Anthropological Records*, Vol. 3,
       No. 1. Berkeley: University of California Press.

Eliade, M.

1964   *Shamanism: Archaic Techniques of Ecstasy.* New York.

Erikson, Erik H.

1943   Observations on the Yurok: Childhood and World Image.
       *University of California Publications in American
       Archaeology and Ethnology*, Vol. 35, No. 10. Berkeley:
       University of California Press.

Essene, F.

1942   Culture Element Distributions: XXI, Round Valley.
       Anthropological Records, Vol. 8, pp. 1-97. Berkeley:
       University of California Press.

Evans, Col. Albert S.
    1873   *A la California: Sketches of Life in the Golden State*. San
           Francisco: A. L. Bancroft & Co.

Fewkes, J. Walter
    1900   Property Rights in Eagles among the Hopi. *American
           Anthropologist*, Vol. 2, p. 690. Menasha: American
           Anthropological Association.

Finnerty, Patrick
    n.d.   *A Burial Site on the Carrizo Plain, San Luis Obispo
           County, Calif.* Ms. on file at UCLA Archeological Survey.

Finnerty, Patrick, D. Decker, N. Leonard III, T. King, C. King, and
L. King
    1970   Community Structure and Trade at Isthmus Cove; A
           Salvage Excavation on Catalina Island. *Pacific Coast
           Archaeological Society Occasional Paper No. 1.* Costa
           Mesa, California.

Follett, W. I.
    1968   Appendix IV: Fish Remains from Century Ranch Site,
           LAn-229, Los Angeles County, Calif. *UCLA Archaeolog-
           ical Survey Annual Report*, Vol. 10, pp. 132-43. Los
           Angeles: University of California Press.

Forbes, Jack D.
    1963   Indian Horticulture West and Northwest of the Colorado
           River. *Journal of the West*, No. 2, pp. 1-14.
    1965   *Warriors of the Colorado*. Norman, Oklahoma: University
           of Oklahoma Press.
    1966   The Tongva of Tujunga to 1801. Appendix II of Archaeo-
           logical Investigations of the Big Tujunga Site (LAn-167).
           UCLA Archaeological Survey Annual Report, Vol. 8. Los
           Angeles: University of California Press.

Foster, George M.
    1944   A Summary of Yuki Culture. *Anthropological Records*,
           Vol. 5, pp. 155-244. Berkeley: University of California
           Press.

Freeland, L.S.
    1923   Pomo Doctors and Poisoners. *University of California
           Publications in American Archaeology and Ethnology*,
           Vol. 20. Berkeley: University of California Press.

Garth, Thomas R.
    1944   Kinship Terminology, Marriage Practices and Behavior

Toward Kin among the Atsugewi. *American Anthropologist*, Vol. 46, pp. 348-361. Berkeley: University of California Press.

1953 Atsugewi Ethnography. *Anthropological Records*, Vol. 14, pp. 129-212. Berkeley: University of California Press.

Gayton, Anna H.

1930a Yokuts-Mono Chiefs and Shamans. *University of California Publications in American Archaeology and Ethnology*, Vol. 24, pp. 361-420. Berkeley: University of California Press.

1930b The Ghost Dance of 1870 in South Central California. *University of California Publications in American Archaeology and Ethnology,* Vol. 28, pp. 57-82. Berkeley: University of California Press.

1936 Estudillo Among the Yokuts: 1819. *Essays in Honor of Alfred Louis Kroeber*, pp. 67-85. Berkeley: University of California Press.

1945 Yokuts and Western Mono Social Organization. *American Anthropologist*, Vol. 47, pp. 409-26. Menasha: American Anthropological Association.

1946 Culture-Environment Integration: External References in Yokuts Life. *Southwestern Journal of Anthropology*, Vol. 2, pp. 252-67. Albuquerque: University of New Mexico Press.

1948 Yokuts and Western Mono Ethnography. *Anthropological Records*, Vol. 10, Nos. 1 and 2, pp. 1-290. Berkeley: University of California Press.

Geiger, Maynard

1965 *Mission Santa Barbara, 1782-1965*. Old Mission Santa Barbara.

Geiger, Maynard (editor)

1970 *Letter of Luis Jayme, O.F.M. San Diego, October 17, 1772*. Los Angeles: Published for the San Diego Public Library by Dawson's Book Shop.

Gifford, Edward W.

1915 Unpublished field notes.

1918 Clans and Moieties in Southern California. *University of California Publications in American Archaeology and Ethnology*, Vol. 14, pp. 155-219. Berkeley: University of California Press.

1922   California Kinship Terminologies. *University of California Publications in American Archaeology and Ethnology*, Vol. 18, No. 1. Berkeley: University of California Press.

1923a   Pomo Lands on Clear Lake. *University of California Publications in American Archaeology and Ethnology*, Vol. 20, pp. 77-92. Berkeley: University of California Press.

1923b   Western Mono Myths. *Journal of American Folklore*, Vol. 36, pp. 302-67.

1926a   Miwok Lineages and the Political Unit in Aboriginal California. *American Anthropologist*, Vol. 28, pp. 389-401. Menasha: American Anthropological Association.

1926b   Clear Lake Pomo Society. *University of California Publications in American Archaeology and Ethnology*, Vol. 18, pp. 287-390. Berkeley: University of California Press.

1931   The Kamia of Imperial Valley. *Bulletins of the Bureau of American Ethnology*, Vol. 97, pp. 1-94. Washington, D.C.

1939   The Coast Yuki. *Anthropos*, Vol. 34, pp. 292-375. (Reprinted by The Sacramento Anthropological Society, Spring 1965.)

Gifford, Edward W., and A. L. Kroeber
1937   Culture Element Distributions: IV, Pomo. *University of California Publications in American Archaeology and Ethnology*, Vol. 37, pp. 117-254. Berkeley: University of California Press.

Gifford, Edward W., and W. E. Schenck
1926   Archaeology of the Southern San Joaquin Valley, California. *University of California Publications in American Archaeology and Ethnology*, Vol. 23, No. 1, pp. 1-122. Berkeley: University of California Press.

Glassow, Mike A.
1965   The Conejo Rock Shelter: An Inland Chumash Site in Ventura County, California. *UCLA Archaeological Survey Annual Report, 1965*, Vol. 7, pp. 19-80. Los Angeles: University of California Press.

Goddard, Pliny E.
1903   Life and Culture of the Hupa. *University of California Publications in American Archaeology and Ethnology*, Vol. 1, pp. 1-88. Berkeley: University of California Press.

Goldschmidt, Walter R.
  1948 Social Organization in Native California and the Origin of Clans. *American Anthropologist*, Vol. 50, pp. 444-56. Menasha: American Anthropological Association.
  1951 Nomlaki Ethnography. *University of California Publications in American Archaeology and Ethnology*, Vol. 42, pp. 303-436. Berkeley: University of California Press.
  1951 Ethics and the Structure of Society: an Ethnological Contribution to the Sociology of Knowledge. *American Anthropologist*, Vol. 53, pp. 506-24.

Goldschmidt, Walter R., and Harold E. Driver
  1940 The Hupa White Deerskin Dance. *University of California Publications in American Archaeology and Ethnology*, Vol. 35, No. 8. Berkeley: University of California Press.

Goldschmidt, W. R., F. Essene, and G. M. Foster
  1939 War Stories from Two Enemy Tribes. *Journal of American Folklore*, Vol. 52, pp. 141-54.

Goodenough, Ward H.
  1955 A Problem in Malayo-Polynesian Social Organization. *American Anthropologist*, Vol. 57, pp. 71-83. Menasha: American Anthropological Association.

Gould, Richard A.
  1966a Archaeology of the Point St. George Site, and Tolowa Prehistory. *University of California Publications in Anthropology*, Vol. 4. Berkeley: University of California Press.
  1966b The Wealth Quest among the Tolowa Indians of Northwestern California. *Proceedings of the American Philosophical Society*, Vol. 110, pp. 68-89. Philadelphia: American Philosophical Society.
  1968 Seagoing Canoes among the Indians of Northwestern California. *Ethnohistory*, Vol. 15, pp. 11-42. Tempe: American Society for Ethnohistory.
  1972 A Radiocarbon Date from the Point St. George Site, Northwestern California. *Contributions of the University of California Archaeological Research Facility*, Vol. 14, pp. 41-4. Berkeley: University of California Press.

Grant, Campbell
  1964 Chumash Artifacts Collected in Santa Barbara County, California. *University of California Archaeological Survey*

Reports, No. 63, pp. 1-44. Berkeley: University of California Press.

Greengo, Robert E.
   1952   Shellfish Foods of the California Indians. *Kroeber Anthropological Society Papers,* No. 7, pp. 63-114.

Greenwood, Roberta S., and R. O. Browne
   1966   *A Coastal Chumash Village: Excavation of Shisholop, Ventura County, California.* Ms. filed at Department of Beaches and Parks, Interpretive Services, No. 282, Sacramento, California.

Grinnell, Joseph, Harold Bryant and Tracy Storer
   1918   *The Game Birds of California.* Berkeley: University of California Press.

Guinn, J. M.
   1917   Some Early History of Owens River Valley. *Annual Publications of the Historical Society of Southern California,* No. 10, pp. 42-6. Los Angeles.

Gunther, E.
   1926   An Analysis of the First Salmon Ceremony. *American Anthropologist,* Vol. 28, pp. 605-17. Menasha: American Anthropological Association.

Hall, Sharlott
   1903   The Burning of a Mojave Chief. *Out West,* Vol. 18.

Halpern, A. M.
   1955   A Dualism in Pomo Cosmology. *Kroeber Anthropological Society Papers,* Nos. 8 and 9, pp. 151-9.

Handelman, Don
   1972   Aspects of the Moral Compact of a Washo Shaman. *Anthropological Quarterly,* Vol. 45, pp. 84-101.

Hardy, Osgood
   1929   Agricultural Changes in California, 1860-1900. *Proceedings of the Pacific Coast Branch of the American Historical Association, 1929,* pp. 216-30.

Harrington, John Peabody
   1913   Studies Among the Indians of California. *Smithsonian Miscellaneous Collections,* Vol. 68, pp. 92-5.

   1928   Exploration of the Burton Mound at Santa Barbara, California. *Forty-fourth Annual Report of the Bureau of American Ethnology, 1926-1928,* pp. 23-168. Washington: U.S. Government Printing Office.

1933 Annotations. In *Chinigchinich*, P. T. Hanna (editor). Santa Ana: Fine Arts Press.

1934 A New Original Version of Boscana's Historical Account of the San Juan Capistrano Indians of Southern California. *Smithsonian Miscellaneous Collections,* Vol. 92, No. 4.

1942 Cultural Element Distributions: XIV, Central California Coast. *Anthropological Records*, Vol. 7, No. 1 Berkeley: University of California Press.

n.d. Ethnographic and Linguistic Notes on File at the Smithsonian Institution, Washington, D.C., and with the Department of Linguistics, University of California, Berkeley.

Hayes, Benjamin

1929 *Pioneer Notes from the Diaries of Judge Benjamin Hayes.* Los Angeles: Privately printed.

Heady, Harold

1972 *Burning and Grasslands in California.* Paper presented to the Annual Meeting. Tall Timbers Fire Ecology Conference, Ms.

Hedgepeth, Joel W.

1962 *Introduction to Seashore Life of the San Francisco Bay Region and the Coast of Northern California.* Berkeley: University of California Press.

Hedges, Ken

1973 Hakataya Figurines from Southern California. *Pacific Coast Archaeological Society Quarterly*, No. 9, pp. 1-40.

Heintzelman, S. P.

1857 Report of July 15, 1853. 34th Congress, 3rd Session, *House Executive Document*, No. 76, pp. 34-58.

Heizer, Robert F.

1958 Prehistoric Central California: A Problem in Historical Developmental Classification. *University of California Archaeological Survey Reports*, No. 41, pp. 19-26. Berkeley: University of California Press.

1964 The Western Coast of North America. In *Prehistoric Man in the New World,* Jesse D. Jennings and Edward Norbeck (editors), pp. 117-48. Chicago: University of Chicago Press.

1968 *The Indians of Los Angeles County: Hugo Reid's Letters of 1852.* Los Angeles: Southwest Museum.

1974   Were the Chumash Whale Hunters? Implications for Ethnography in 1974. *The Journal of California Anthropology,* Vol. 1, pp. 26-32. Riverside: Malki Press.

Heizer, R. F. (editor)
1955   California Indian Linguistic Records. The Mission Indian Vocabularies of H. W. Henshaw. *Anthropological Records,* Vol. 15, No. 2. Berkeley: University of California Press.

Heizer, Robert F., and Richard K. Beardsley
1943   Fired Clay Human Figurines in Central and Northern California. *American Antiquity,* Vol. 9, No. 2, pp. 199-207. Salt Lake City: University of Utah Press.

Heizer, R. F., and Harper Kelley
1962   Burins and Bladelets in the Cessac Collection from Santa Cruz Island, California. *American Philosophical Society Proceedings,* Vol. 106, No. 2.

Heizer, Robert F., and David M. Pendergast
1955   Additional Data on Fired Clay Human Figurines from California. *American Antiquity,* Vol. 21, No. 2, pp. 181-5. Salt Lake City: University of Utah Press.

Heizer, Robert F., and M. A. Whipple
1971   *The California Indians: A Source Book.* Berkeley: University of California Press.

Helbaek, H.
1960   The Paleoethnobotany of the Near East and Europe. In *Prehistoric Investigations in Iraqi Kurdistan,* R. Braidwood and B. Howe (editors). Chicago.

Hemert-Engart, A. von, and F. J. Teggart (editors)
1910   The Narrative of the Portolá Expedition of 1769-1770. *Publication of the Academy of Pacific Coast History,* Vol. 1, No. 4, pp. 9-159. Berkeley: University of California Press.

Hewes, Gordon W.
1942   Economic and Geographical Relations of Aboriginal Fishing in Northern California. *California Fish and Game,* Vol. 28, pp. 103-10.

Heye, G. G.
1921   Certain Artifacts from San Miguel Island. *Museum of the American Indian, Heye Foundation Indian Notes and Monographs,* Vol. 7, pp. 1-184. New York.

Holmes, W. H.
  1900 Anthropological Studies in California. *Reports of the U.S. National Museum*, pp. 181-7. Smithsonian Institution. Washington, D.C.
Honigmann, J. J.
  1960 Review of *Culture and Mental Health* by M. K. Opler. *American Anthropologist*, Vol. 62, pp. 920-3. Menasha: American Anthropological Association.
Hooper, Lucile
  1920 The Cahuilla Indians. *University of California Publications in American Archaeology and Ethnology,* Vol. 16, pp. 316-80. Berkeley: University of California Press. (Reprinted in 1972 by Ballena Press.)
Howard, Hildegard
  1929 The Avifauna of Emeryville Shellmound. *University of California Publications in Zoology*, No. 32, pp. 378-83. Berkeley: University of California Press.
Howay, F. W.
  1940 *The Journal of Captain James Colnett Aboard the Argonaut from April 26, 1769 to Nov. 3, 1791.* Toronto: The Champlain Society.
Jacobs, Melville
  1936 Texts in Chinook Jargon. *University of Washington Publications in Anthropology*, Vol. 7, pp. 1-27.
Jeffreys, M. D. W.
  1956 Some Rules of Directed Culture Change under Roman Catholicism. *American Anthropologist*, Vol. 58, pp. 721-31. Menasha: American Anthropological Association.
Jennings, Jesse D.
  1956 The American Southwest: A Problem in Cultural Isolation. *Society for American Archaeology Memoirs*, Vol. 11, pp. 59-128.
Johnston, Bernice Eastman
  1962 *California's Gabrielino Indians.* Los Angeles: Southwest Museum.
Jones, P. M.
  1956 Archaeological Investigations on Santa Rosa Island in 1901, R. F. Heizer and A. B. Elsasser (editors). *University of California Anthropological Record*, Vol. 17, No. 2. Berkeley: University of California Press.

King, Chester
   1974   Explanations of Differences and Similarities Among Bead
          Use in Prehistoric and Early Historic California. In
          ʔAntap: California Indian Political and Economic
          Organization, Lowell John Bean and Thomas King
          (editors). Ramona: Ballena Press.
King, Chester, Tom Blackburn, and Ernest Chandonet
   1968   The Archaeological Investigations of Three Sites on the
          Century Ranch, Western Los Angeles County, California.
          UCLA Archaeological Survey Annual Report, Vol. 10.
          Los Angeles: University of California Press.
King, Linda
   1969   The Medea Creek Cemetery (LAn-243): An Investi-
          gation of Social Organization from Mortuary Practices.
          UCLA Archaeological Survey Annual Report, 1969,
          pp. 23-68. Los Angeles: University of California Press.

   n.d.   Medea Creek Cemetery Artifact Descriptions. Manu-
          script in possession of L. King.
Kniffen, Fred B.
   1939   Pomo Geography. University of California Publications in
          American Archaeology and Ethnology, Vol. 36, pp.
          353-400. Berkeley: University of California Press.
Kowta, M.
   1961   Excavations at Goleta Part 2: Artifact Description:
          Chipped Lithic Material. UCLA Archaeological Survey
          Annual Report, 1960-1961, pp. 349-84. Los Angeles:
          University of California Press.
Kroeber, A. L.
   1907   Myths of South Central California. University of Cali-
          fornia Publications in American Archaeology and
          Ethnology, Vol. 4. Berkeley: University of California
          Press.
   1908   Ethnography of the Cahuilla Indians. University of
          California Publications in American Archaeology and
          Ethnology, Vol. 3, pp. 29-68. Berkeley: University of Cali-
          fornia Press.
   1909   The Classificatory System of Relationship. Journal of the
          Royal Anthropological Institute, Vol. 39. London.
   1923   Anthropology. New York: Harcourt Brace and Co.
          (Second edition, 1948).

1925 *Handbook of the Indians of California.* Washington, D.C.: Bureau of American Ethnology.

1929 The Valley Nisenan. *University of California Publications in American Archaeology and Ethnology,* Vol. 24, No. 4. Berkeley: University of California Press.

1932 The Patwin and their Neighbors. *University of California Publications in American Archaeology and Ethnology,* Vol. 29, No. 4, pp. 253-423. Berkeley: University of California Press.

1936 Karok Towns. *University of California Publications in American Archaeology and Ethnology,* Vol. 35, pp. 29-38. Berkeley: University of California Press.

1939 Cultural and Natural Areas of Native North America. *University of California Publications in American Archaeology and Ethnology,* Vol. 38. Berkeley: University of California Press.

1941 Culture Element Distributions: XV, Salt, Dogs, Tobacco. *Anthropological Records,* Vol. 6, pp. 1-20. Berkeley: University of California Press.

1954 The Nature of Land-Holding Groups in Aboriginal California. *University of California Archaeological Reports,* No. 56, pp. 19-58. Berkeley: University of California Press.

Kroeber, A. L., and S. A. Barrett
1960 Fishing Among the Indians of Northwestern California. *Anthropological Records,* Vol. 21, No. 1. Berkeley: University of California Press.

Kroeber, A. L., and E. W. Gifford
1949 World Renewal: A Cult System of Native Northwest California. *Anthropological Records,* Vol. 13, No. 1, pp. 1-154. Berkeley: University of California Press.

Kunkel, Peter H.
1962 *Yokuts and Pomo Political Institutions: A Comparative Analysis.* Ph. D. dissertation, University of California, Los Angeles.

1974 The Pomo Kin-Group and the Political Unit in Aboriginal California. *Journal of California Anthropology,* Vol. 1, No. 1. Riverside: Malki Press.

Lantis, M.
1960 *Eskimo Childhood and Interpersonal Relations.* Seattle.

Latta, F. F.
    1929   *Uncle Jeff's Story.* Tulare.
    1949   *Handbook of Yokuts Indians.* Bakersfield: Kern County
           Museum.
Lawton, Harry W.
    1968   *The Dying God of the Cahuilla: Ethnohistoric Evidence
           of a Colorado River-derived Agricultural Complex in
           Southern California.* Graduate Seminar Paper in English
           275A, The Oral Epic. University of California, Riverside.
Lawton, Harry W., and Lowell John Bean
    1968   A Preliminary Reconstruction of Aboriginal Agricultural
           Technology Among the Cahuilla. *The Indian Historian,*
           Vol. 1, No. 5, pp. 18-24, 29.
La Pérous, Jean F. G. de
    1968   *A Voyage Round the World Performed in the Years
           1785, 1786, 1787, and 1788 by the Boussole and Astrolobe.*
           Vol. 1. New York: Da Capo Press.
LeConte, John L.
    1855   Account of Some Volcanic Springs in the Desert of the
           Colorado, in Southern California. *The American Journal
           of Science and Arts,* Vol. 19, pp. 1-6.
Lee, Dorothy
    1938   Conceptual Implications of an Indian Language. *Philoso-
           phy of Science,* Vol. 5, pp. 89-102.
    1944   Linguistic Reflection of Wintu Thought. *International
           Journal of American Linguistics,* Vol. 10, pp. 181-7.
    1951   Notes on the Conception of the Self Among the Wintu
           Indians. *Journal of Abnormal and Social Psychology,* Vol.
           45, pp. 538-43.
Lee, Milicent
    1937   *Indians of the Oaks.* Boston: Ginn & Co.
Lee, Richard B., and Irven DeVore (editors)
    1968   *Man the Hunter.* Chicago: Aldine.
Leis, P.E.
    1963   Washo Witchcraft: A Test of the Frustration-Aggression
           Hypothesis. In *The Washo Indians of California and
           Nevada,* W. L. d'Azevedo (editor), pp. 57-68. Salt Lake
           City.
Levine, Linda
    1968   Appendix VI: Midden Analysis of LAn-229. *UCLA*

Archaeological Survey Annual Report, 1968, Vol. 10, pp. 154-61. Los Angeles: University of California Press.

Lewis, Henry T.
1972   The Role of Fire in the Domestication of Plants and Animals in Southwest Asia: A Hypothesis. *Man*, No. 7, pp. 195-222.
1973   *Patterns of Burning in California: Ecology and Ethnohistory*. Ballena Press Anthropological Papers 1. Ramona: Ballena Press.

Linton, Ralph
1936   *The Study of Man*. New York: Appleton, Century, Crofts.
1945   *The Cultural Background of Personality*. New York.

Loeb, Edwin M.
1926   Pomo Folkways. *University of California Publications in American Archaeology and Ethnology*, Vol. 29, pp. 149-405. Berkeley: University of California Press.
1932   The Western Kuksu Cult. *University of California Publications in American Archaeology and Ethnology*, Vol. 33, pp. 1-137. Berkeley: University of California Press.
1933   The Eastern Kuksu Cult. *University of California Publications in American Archaeology and Ethnology*, Vol.33, pp. 139-232. Berkeley: University of California Press.

Loud, Llewellyn
1918   Ethnography and Archaeology of the Wiyot Territory. *University of California Publications in American Archaeology and Ethnology*, Vol. 14, pp. 221-436. Berkeley: University of California Press.

Lowie, R. H.
1924   Notes on Shoshonean Ethnography. *Anthropological Papers, American Museum of Natural History*, Vol. 20, Part 3. New York.
1934   Relationship Terms. *Encyclopaedia Britannica*, 14th edition.
1939   Ethnographic Notes on the Washo. *University of California Publications in American Archaeology and Ethnology*, Vol. 36, pp. 301-52. Berkeley: University of California Press.

Luomala, Katherine
1963   Flexibility in Sib Affiliation Among the Diegueño. *Ethnology*, Vol. 2, No. 3, pp. 282-301. Pittsburgh:

University of Pittsburgh Press.

n.d.   Unpublished manuscript on the Diegueño Indians.

McKern, William C.

1922   Functional Families of the Patwin. *University of California Publications in American Archaeology and Ethnology,* Vol. 13, pp. 235-58. Berkeley: University of California Press.

McKusick, Marshall B.

1959   Introduction to Anacapa Island Archaeology. *UCLA Archaeological Survey Annual Report, 1958-1959,* pp. 71-104. Los Angeles: University of California Press.

McMillan, James Harold

1956   *The Aboriginal Human Ecology of the Mountain Meadows Area in Southwestern Lassen County, California.* MS. Thesis, Sacramento State College.

Meighan, Clement W.

1959   California Cultures and the Concept of an Archaic State. *American Antiquity,* Vol. 24, pp. 289-305. Salt Lake City: University of Utah Press.

Meighan, Clement, and S. Rootenberg

1957   A Prehistoric Miner's Camp on Catalina Island. *Masterkey,* Vol. 31, pp. 176-84. Los Angeles.

Merriam, A., and W. L. d'Azevedo

1957   Washo Peyote Songs. *American Anthropologist,* Vol. 59, pp. 615-41. Menasha: American Anthropological Association.

Mooney, J.

1896   The Ghost Dance Religion and the Sioux Outbreaks of 1890. *Fourteenth Annual Report, Bureau of American Ethnology,* Part II. Washington, D.C.

Murdock, George P.

1949   *Social Structure.* New York: Macmillan.

1960   Social Structure in Southeast Asia. *Viking Fund Publications in Anthropology,* No. 29.

1965   Tenino Shamanism. *Ethnology,* Vol. 4, pp. 165-71.

1967   *Ethnographic Atlas.* Pittsburgh: University of Pittsburgh.

Murphy, J. M.

1964   Psychotherapeutic Aspects of Shamanism on St. Lawrence Island. In *Magic, Faith, and Healing,* A. Kiev (editor), pp. 53-83. New York.

Nadel. S. F.
    1946   A Study of Shamanism in the Nuba Mountains. *Journal of the Royal Anthropological Institute,* Vol. 76, pp. 25-37. London.
Nash, Manning
    1966   *Primitive and Peasant Economic Systems.* Scranton, Pa.
Nomland, G. A.
    1935   Sinkyone Notes. *University of California Publications in American Archaeology and Ethnology,* Vol. 36, pp. 149-78. Berkeley: University of California Press.
    1938   Bear River Ethnography. *Anthropological Records,* Vol. 2, pp. 91-124. Berkeley: University of California Press.
Odum, Eugene P.
    1975   *Ecology.* New York: Holt, Rinehart & Winston.
Olson, Ronald L.
    1930   Chumash Prehistory. *University of California Publications in American Archaeology and Ethnology,* Vol. 28, pp. 1-21. Berkeley: University of California Press.
O'Neal, Lila M.
    1932   Yurok-Karok Basket Weavers. *University of California Publications in American Archaeology and Ethnology,* Vol. 32, pp. 1-184. Berkeley: University of California Press.
Opler, M. E.
    1938   Dirty Boy: A Jicarilla Tale of Raid and War. *American Anthropological Association Memoir,* No. 52. Menasha: American Anthropological Association.
    1945   Themes as Dynamic Forces in Culture. *American Journal of Sociology,* Vol. 51, pp. 198 ff.
    1946   An Application of the Theory of Themes. *Journal of the Washington Academy of Sciences,* Vol. 36, pp. 137-66.
Opler, M. K.
    1959   Dream Analysis in Ute Indian Therapy. In *Culture and Mental Health,* M. K. Opler (editor), pp. 97-118.
    1961   On Devereux's Discussion of Ute Shamanism. *American Anthropologist,* Vol. 63, pp. 1091-3. Menasha: American Anthropological Association.
Ord, E. O. C.
    1850   Lt. E. O. C. Ord's First Report to General Riley. Executive Document No. 47, 31st Congress, *Senate,* 1st Session,

pp. 119-27.

Orr, Phil C.
   1968   *Prehistory of Santa Rosa Island.* Santa Barbara: Santa
          Barbara Museum of Natural History.

Park, W.
   1936   *Shamanism in Western North America.* Evanston.

Parson, Elsie C.
   1940   Taos Tales. *Memoirs, American Folklore Society,* No. 34.

Patch, R. W.
   1951   Irrigation in East Central California. *American Antiquity,*
          Vol. 17, No. 1, pp. 50-2. Washington, D.C.: Society for
          American Archaeology.

Patencio, Francisco
   1943   *Stories and Legends of the Palm Springs Indians.* Los
          Angeles: Times-Mirror Co.

Piddocke, Stuart
   1969   The Potlatch System of the Southern Kwakiutl, A New
          Perspective. In *Environment and Cultural Behavior,*
          Andrew P. Vayda (editor), pp. 130-56. Garden City, N.Y.:
          Natural History Press.

Piette, Maximin (editor)
   1946   An Unpublished Diary of Fray Juan Crespi, O. F. M.
          (1770). *The Americas,* Vol. 3, No. 1, pp. 102-14.
          Washington: Academy of American Franciscan History.

Pospisil, Leopold
   1963   *The Kapauku Papuans of West New Guinea.* New York:
          Holt, Rinehart and Winston.

Pourade, Richard F.
   1960   *The History of San Diego: The Explorers.* Vol. 1. San
          Diego: The Union-Tribune Publishing Company.

Powers, Stephen
   1877   Tribes of California. *Contributions to North American
          Ethnology,* Vol. III. Washington, D.C.: U.S. Government
          Printing Office.

Priestley, Herbert I. (translator)
   1937   *Pedro Fages, A Historical, Political and Natural
          Description of California.* Berkeley: University of
          California Press.

Radin, P.
   1937   *Primitive Religion.* New York.

Rappaport, R. A.
  1968   *Pigs for the Ancestors: Ritual in the Ecology of a New Guinea People.* New Haven: Yale University Press.

Ray, Verne F.
  1963   *Primitive Pragmatists.* Seattle: University of Washington Press.

Reid, Hugo
  1926   *The Indians of Los Angeles County.* Privately printed.

Riddell, Francis
  1966   Comments on Ecology and Culture Change. In *The Current Status of Anthropological Research in the Great Basin: 1964*, Warren L. d'Azevedo, Wilbur A. Davis, Don D. Fowler, and Wayne Scuttles (editors). Reno: Desert Research Institute.

Rogers, David Banks
  1929   *Prehistoric Man of the Santa Barbara Coast.* Santa Barbara: Santa Barbara Museum of Natural History.
  1937   A Reconnaissance of the Manzana State Game Refuge, Santa Barbara County, California. *American Antiquity*, Vol. 2, No. 2, pp. 184-6. Washington, D.C.: Society for American Archaeology.

Rostlund, Erhard
  1952   Freshwater Fish and Fishing in Native North America. *University of California Publications in Geography*, Vol. 9. Berkeley.

Sahlins, Marshall
  1968   Notes on the Original Affluent Society. In *Man the Hunter*, R. B. Lee and I. Devore (editors), pp. 85-9. Chicago: Aldine.
  1972   *Stone Age Economics.* Chicago: Aldine.

Sauer, Carl
  1936   American Agricultural Origins. In *Essays in American Anthropology*, Robert H. Lowie (editor). Berkeley: University of California Press.

Schaeffer, V. B.
  1958   *Seals, Sea-Lions, and Walruses.* Palo Alto: Stanford University Press.

Schumacher, Paul
  1879   The Method of Manufacture of Soapstone Pots. *U.S. Geological Surveys West of the Hundredth Meridian*, Vol. 7,

pp. 117-21. Washington, D.C.: Government Printing
Office.

Schwartz, Theodore
  1963 Systems of Areal Integration: Some Considerations Based
         on the Admiralty Islands of Northern Melanesia. *Anthro-
         pological Forum*, Vol. 1, No. 1, pp. 56-97. Nedlands:
         University of Western Australia Press.

Service, Elman R.
  1962 *Primitive Social Organization: An Evolutionary
         Perspective*. New York: Random House.
  1966 *The Hunters*. Englewood Cliffs: Prentice Hall.

Shimkin, Demitri B., and Russell M. Reid
  1970 Socio-cultural Persistence Among Shoshoneans of the
         Carson River Basin (Nevada). In *Languages and Cultures
         of Western North America*, Earl H. Swanson, Jr. (editor).

Shipek, Florence C.
  1971 Prepared Direct Testimony of Florence C. Shipek,
         Anthropologist. Exhibit B-50. *Federal Power Commission
         Project No. 176*, San Diego County, California.

Simpson, Lesley B. (translator and editor)
  1939 *California in 1792: The Expedition of Longinos Martinez*.
         San Marino, Calif.: Huntington Library.

Siskin, E.
  1941 *The Impact of the Peyote Cult Upon Shamanism Among
         the Washo Indians*. Unpublished Ph.D. dissertation, Yale
         University.

Smith, Donald E., and Frederick J. Teggart (editors)
  1909 Diary of Gaspar de Portolá During the California
         Expedition of 1769-1770. *Publications of the Academy of
         Pacific Coast History*, Vol. 1, No. 3, pp. 31-89.

Smith, J. Russell
  1929 *Tree Crops, A Permanent Agriculture*. New York:
         Harcourt Brace.

Sparkman, Philip Stedman
  1908 The Culture of the Luiseño Indians. *University of Cali-
         fornia Publications in American Archaeology and
         Ethnology*, Vol. 8, pp. 197-234. Berkeley: University of
         California Press. (Reprinted in 1972 by Ballena Press.)

Spencer, R., and J. Jennings
  1965 *The Native Americans*. New York.

Spier, Leslie
    1923   Southern Diegueño Customs. *University of California Publications in American Archaeology and Ethnology,* Vol. 20, pp. 297-358. Berkeley: University of California Press.

Spinden, H. J.
    1917   The Origin and Distribution of Agriculture in America. *Proceedings of the 19th International Congress of Americanists,* 1915, pp. 269-76.

Steward, Julian H.
    1929   Irrigation Without Agriculture. *Papers of the Michigan Academy of Science, Arts, and Letters,* Vol. 22, pp. 149-56.
    1933   Ethnography of the Owens Valley Paiute. *University of California Publications in American Archaeology and Ethnology,* Vol. 33, pp. 223-350. Berkeley: University of California Press.
    1936   The Economic and Social Basis of Primitive Bands. In *Essays in Anthropology Presented to A. L. Kroeber,* R. H. Lowie (editor), pp. 331-50. Berkeley: University of California Press.
    1938   Basin-Plateau Aboriginal Sociopolitical Groups. *Bulletins of the Bureau of American Ethnology,* No. 120. Washington, D.C.
    1941   Culture Element Distributions: XIII, Nevada Shoshone. *Anthropological Records,* Vol. 4, No. 2, pp. 209-59. Berkeley: University of California Press.
    1955   *Theory of Culture Change: The Methodology of Multilinear Evolution.* Urbana: University of Illinois Press.

Stewart, Omer C.
    1941   Culture Element Distributions: XIV, Northern Paiute. *Anthropological Records,* Vol. 4, pp. 361-446. Berkeley: University of California Press.
    1943   Notes on Pomo Ethnogeography. *University of California Publications in American Archaeology and Ethnology,* Vol. 40, pp. 29-62. Berkeley: University of California Press.

Stickney, Fenner S., Dwight F. Barnes, and Perez Simpson
    1950   Date Palm Insects in the United States. *United States*

Department of Agriculture Circular, No. 846.

Stratton, R. B.
  n.d.   *The Captivity of the Oatman Girls*. San Francisco.

Strong, William D.
  1929   Aboriginal Society in Southern California. *University of
         California Publications in American Archaeology and
         Ethnology*, Vol. 26, pp. 1-358. Berkeley: University of
         California Press. (Reprinted by Malki Museum Press,
         Banning, California, 1972.)
  1935   Archaeological Explorations in the Country of the Eastern
         Chumash. *Exploration and Fieldwork of the Smithsonian
         Institution in 1934*, pp. 69-72. Washington, D.C.

Struever, Stuart
  1971   Comments on Archaeological Data Requirements and
         Research Strategy. *American Antiquity*, Vol. 36, No. 1,
         pp. 9-19. Washington, D.C.: Society for American
         Archaeology.

Suttles, Wayne
  1968a Coping with Abundance: Subsistence on the Northwest
         Coast. In *Man the Hunter*, Richard B. Lee and Irven
         DeVore (editors), pp. 56-68. Chicago: Aldine.
  1968b Variation in Habitat and Culture on the Northwest Coast.
         In *Man in Adaptation; the Cultural Present*, Yehudi Cohen
         (editor), pp. 93-106.

Swartz, B. K.
  1960   Blade Manufacture in Southern California. *American
         Antiquity*, Vol. 25, pp. 405-7. Washington, D.C.: Society
         for American Archaeology.

Tac, Pablo
  1952   Indian Life and Customs at Mission San Luis Rey, Minna
         and Gordon Hewes (editors and translators). *The
         Americas, A Quarterly Review of Inter-American Cultural
         History*.

Thompson, Laura
  1945   Logico-Aesthetic Integration in Hopi Culture. *American
         Anthropologist*, Vol. 47, pp. 540-53. Menasha: American
         Anthropological Association.

Tibesar, Antonine (editor)
  1955   *Writings of Junipero Serra*. Vol. 1. Washington: Academy
         of American Franciscan History.

Toffelmier, G., and K. Luomala
  1936 Dreams and Dream Interpretation of the Diegueño Indians of Southern California. *Psychoanalytic Quarterly*, Vol. 5, pp. 195-225.

Treganza, Adan E.
  1947 Possibilities of an Aboriginal Practice of Agriculture Among the Southern Diegueño. *American Antiquity*, Vol. 12, pp. 169-73. Washington, D.C.: Society for American Archaeology.

True, D. L.
  1957 Fired Clay Figurines from San Diego County, California. *American Antiquity*, Vol. 22, pp. 296-391. Washington, D.C.: Society for American Archaeology.

Underhill, Ruth M.
  1965 *Red Man's Religion: Beliefs and Practices of the Indians North of Mexico.* Chicago: University of Chicago Press.

Valory, Dale
  1970 *Yurok Doctors and Devils: A Study in Identity, Anxiety and Deviance.* Ph.D. dissertation, University of California, Berkeley.

Vayda, Andrew P.
  1967 Pomo Trade Feasts. In *Tribal and Peasant Economies*, George Dalton (editor), pp. 495-500. Garden City, N.Y.: Natural History Press.
  1969 Expansion and Warfare Among Swidden Agriculturists. In *Environment and Cultural Behavior*, Andrew Vayda (editor), pp. 202-20. Garden City, N.Y.: Natural History Press.

Veatch, John A.
  1858 Notes of a Visit to the "Mud Volcanoes" in the Colorado Desert in the Month of July, 1857. *The American Journal of Science and Arts*, Vol. 26, pp. 288-95.

Voegelin, E. W.
  1938 Tübatulabal Ethnography. *Anthropological Records*, Vol. 2, No. 1. Berkeley: University of California Press.
  1942 Culture Element Distribution: XX, Northeast California. *Anthropological Records*, Vol. 7, pp. 1-251. Berkeley: University of California Press.

Voget, F.
  1950 A Shoshone Innovator. *American Anthropologist*, Vol. 52,

pp. 53-63. Menasha: American Anthropological
Association.

Vogl, Richard J.
  1968   Fire Adaptations of Some Southern California Plants.
         *Proceedings, California Tall Timbers Fire Ecology Con-
         ference*, November 9-10, 1967. Tallahassee: Tall Timbers
         Research Station.

Wagner, Henry R.
  1929   Spanish Voyages to the Northwest Coast of America in the
         Sixteenth Century. *California Historical Society Special
         Publications*, No. 4. San Francisco.

Wallace, William J.
  1957   The Clay Figurine from Death Valley National Monument,
         California. *Masterkey*, Vol. 31, No. 4, pp. 131-4. Los
         Angeles.

Washington, F. B.
  1906   Customs of the Indians of Western Tehama County,
         Journal of American Folklore, Vol. 19.

Waterman, T. T.
  1920   Yurok Geography. *University of California Publications in
         American Archaeology and Ethnology*, Vol. 16, pp.
         177-314. Berkeley: University of California Press.
  1925   Village Sites in Tolowa and Neighboring Areas of North-
         west California. *American Anthropologist*, Vol. 27, pp.
         528-43. Menasha: American Anthropological Association.

Waterman, T. T. and A. L. Kroeber
  1938   The Kepel Fish Dam. *University of California Publications
         in American Archaeology and Ethnology*, Vol. 35, pp.
         49-80. Berkeley: University of California Press.

Watson, James D.
  1970   Society as Organized Flow: The Tairora Case. *South-
         western Journal of Anthropology*, Vol. 26, No. 2, pp.
         107-24. Albuquerque: University of New Mexico Press.

Weatherwax, Paul
  1954   *Indian Corn in Old America*. New York: Macmillan
         Company.

White, Raymond C.
  1957   The Luiseño "theory of knowledge." *American Anthro-
         pologist*, Vol. 59, pp. 1-19. Menasha: American
         Anthropological Association.

1963 Luiseño Social Organization. *University of California Publications in American Archaeology and Ethnology*, Vol. 48, pp. 1-194. Berkeley: University of California Press.

White, Theodore
1953 Aboriginal Utilization of Food Animals. *American Antiquity*, Vol. 18, pp. 396-8. Washington, D.C.: Society for American Archaeology.

Whiting, B.
1950 Paiute Sorcery. *Viking Fund Publications in Anthropology*, No. 15, pp. 1-110.

Wilke, Philip J., Robert Bettinger, Thomas F. King, and James O'Connell
1972 Harvest Selection and Domestication in Seed Plants. *American Antiquity*, Vol. 46, pp. 203-9. Washington, D.C.: Society for American Archaeology.

Wilke, Philip J., and Douglas Fain
1972 *An Archaeological Cucurbit from Coachella Valley, California.* Archaeological Research Unit, Department of Anthropology, University of California, Riverside. 3 pp. (Mimeo.)

Willey, G. R., and P. Phillips
1955 Method and Theory in American Archaeology II: Historical-Developmental Interpretation. *American Anthropologist*, Vol. 57, pp. 723-819. Menasha: American Anthropological Association.

Willoughby, Nona Christensen
1963 Division of Labor Among the Indians of California. *University of California Archaeological Survey Report*, No. 60. Berkeley: University of California Press.

Wissler, Clark
1911 The Psychological Aspects of the Culture Environment Relation. *American Anthropologist*, Vol. 14, pp. 217-25. Menasha: American Anthropological Association.

Wolf, Carl B.
1945 *California Wild Tree Crops.* Anaheim: Rancho Santa Ana Botanic Garden of the Native Plants of California.

Woodward, Arthur
1934a An Early Account of the Chumash. *Masterkey*, Vol. 8, No. 4, pp. 118-9. Los Angeles.
1934b Notes on the Indians of San Diego County from the Manu-

scripts of Judge Benjamin Hayes. *Masterkey*, Vol. 8, pp. 140-50. Los Angeles.

Yates, L. G.
  1900 Archaeology of California. In *Prehistoric Implements: a Reference Book*, Warren K. Moorhead (editor), pp. 230-52. Cincinnati: Robert Clarke Co.
  1957 Fragments of the History of a Lost Tribe. *University of California Archaeological Survey Report*, No. 38, pp. 36-9. Berkeley: University of California Press.

Yengoyan, Aram A.
  1968 Demographic and Ecological Influences on Aboriginal Australian Marriage Sections. In *Man the Hunter*, Richard B. Lee and Irven DeVore (editors), pp. 185-99. Chicago: Aldine.

Ziegler, Alan C.
  1968 Quasi-Agriculture in North-Central California and its Effect on Aboriginal Social Structure. *Kroeber Anthropological Society Papers*, Vol. 38, pp. 52-67.

Zohary, D.
  1969 The Progenitors of Wheat and Barley in Relation to Domestication and Agricultural Dispersal in the Old World. In *The Domestication and Exploitation of Plants and Animals*, P. J. Ucko and G. W. Dimbleby (editors). Chicago.

Sources

Bean and Lawton — "Some Explanations for the Rise of Cultural Complexity in Native California with Comments on Proto-Agriculture and Agriculture." From *Patterns of Indian Burning in California: Ecology and Ethnohistory* by Henry Lewis. Ballena Press, 1973.

Gould — "Ecology and Adaptive Response Among the Tolowa Indians of Northwestern California." From *Journal of California Anthropology*, Vol. 2, No. 2, pp. 148-70, 1975.

Gayton — "Culture-Environment Integration: External References in Yokuts Life." From *Southwestern Journal of Anthropology*, Vol. 2, pp. 252-67, 1946.

Bean — "Social Organization in Native California." From *?Antap: California Indian Political and Economic Organization* by Lowell J. Bean and Thomas F. King (eds.). Ballena Press, 1974.

Goldschmidt — "Social Organization and Status Differentiation Among the Nomlaki." From "Nomlaki Ethnography," *University of California Publications in American Archaeology and Ethnology,* Vol. 42, pp. 303-436, 1951.

Gayton — "Yokuts-Mono Chiefs and Shamons." From *University of California Publications in American Archaeology and Ethnology*, Vol. 24, pp. 361-420, 1930.

Blackburn — "Ceremonial Integration and Social Interaction in Aboriginal California." From *?Antap: California Indian Political and Economic Organization* by Lowell J. Bean and Thomas F. King (eds.). Ballena Press, 1974.

Luomala — "Flexibility in Sib Affiliation Among the Diegueño." From *Ethnology*, Vol. 2, No. 3, pp. 282-301, 1963.

Kunkel — "The Pomo Kin Group and the Political Unit in Aboriginal California." From *Journal of California Anthropology*, Vol. 1, No. 1, pp. 6-18, 1974.

King — "Chumash Inter-Village Economic Exchange." From *Indian Historian*, Vol. 4, No. 1, pp. 30-43, 1971.

Aginsky — "The Socio-Psychological Significance of Death Among the Pomo Indians." From *American Imago*, Vol. 1, pp. 1-11, 1940.

Devereux — "Mohave Soul Concepts." From *American Anthropologist*, Vol. 39, pp. 417-22, 1937.

Garth — "Emphasis on Industriousness Among the Atsugewi." From *American Anthropologist*, Vol. 47, pp. 554-66, 1945.

White — "Religion and its Role Among the Luiseño." From "Luiseño Social Organization," *University of California Publications in American Archaeology and Ethnology,* Vol. 48, pp. 1-194, 1963.

Handelman — "The Development of a Washo Shaman." From *Ethnology*, Vol. 6, pp. 444-64, 1967.

Bean — "Power and its Applications in Native California." From *Journal of California Anthropology*, Vol. 2, No. 1, pp. 25-33, 1975.